Appalachian Images in
Folk and Popular Culture

American Material Culture and Folklife

Simon J. Bronner, Series Editor

Professor of Folklore and American Studies
The Pennsylvania State University at Harrisburg

Other Titles in This Series

Appalachian Images in Folk and Popular Culture

Edited by
W. K. McNeil

With a Foreword by
Loyal Jones

1888-89
AMERICAN
FOLKLORE
SOCIETY
CENTENNIAL
1988-89

U·M·I Research Press

Ann Arbor / London

Copyright © 1989
William Kinneth McNeil

Produced and distributed by
UMI Research Press
an imprint of
University Microfilms Inc.
Ann Arbor, Michigan 48106

Library of Congress Cataloging in Publication Data

**Appalachian images in folk and popular culture / edited
by W. K. McNeil.**
p. cm.—(American material culture and folklife)
Includes index.
ISBN 0-8357-1972-3 (alk. paper)
1. Appalachian Region, Southern—Social life and customs.
2. Appalachian Region, Southern—Popular culture—History—20th
century. 3. Handicraft—Appalachian Region, Southern. I. McNeil,
W. K. II. Series.
F217.A65A656   1989
974—dc20   89-34601
                                                                CIP

British Library CIP data is available.

58726

To the memory of Rufus and Evelyn Davis McNeil,
Appalachian mountaineers

Contents

Part III: Change Comes to the Appalachian Mountaineer

Part IV: Rethinking Usages: The Age of Functional Studies

Foreword

The self-proclaimed "experts" on Appalachia, and there have been many, are usually frauds or are deceived by the appearances on which they happen to focus at the moment. One truth is that this region (land and people) is complex and varied. The army of observer-writers who have commented on it usually had a narrow focus and have found support for whatever favorite notion each one carried. Thus, there is a mass of confusing and contradictory writings about the place and people. John C. Campbell introduced his superb *The Southern Highlander and His Homeland* (1921) with these words:

> Let us now come to the Highlands—a land of promise, a land of romance, and a land about which, perhaps, more things are known that are not true than any other part of our country.

Campbell and his wife, Olive Dame Campbell, who finished this book after his death, were among the first "outsiders" to see the problems in Appalachian scholarship. They saw that the local color writers, the sensationalist newswriters, the industrialists and even the missionaries had hopelessly distorted the picture of the mountain people for their own purposes. Emma Bell Miles had even earlier noted this problem in her *Spirit of the Mountains* (1905). Later writers such as Henry Shapiro and David Whisnant have written at length on the same problem. One might assume that the record has been straightened up by now and that there is a reliable set of writings to give one a balanced picture of Appalachia. Unfortunately, this is not so. There are many good books and articles that deal with one aspect or another of life in the region but no one book or series of books on which one might rely for the whole truth. Books and articles keep appearing that are shaped by narrow interest, popular ideology, prejudice, or else, and sometimes worse, by romantic nonsense. And the old stereotypes are constantly being recycled. For example, Dianne McWhorter, reviewing Pinckney Benedict's book of West Virginia short stories *Town Smokes* in *The New York Times Book Review,* had this to say about Benedict's setting and characters:

> [H]is turf is the dismal sludge underneath the strokes of Al Capp's Dogpatch. Amid the familiar moonshine stills, dog pits and junked cars of every double-wide trailer are creatures who have reached adulthood too broken to bond with anything more demanding than a bottle of beer. . . . The preferred form of communication is murder.
>
> On the cusp of two vital American cultures—the northerly one devoted to the making of money, the other the making of myth—the border has little of either. The marginal middle class of Mr. Benedict's regional compatriots has sacrificed the one quality that southern lives and literature have had in excess: meaning. (July 12, 1987, pp. 13–14)

In the September 27, 1987, issue of the same publication (p. 54), Rodger Cunningham, author of *Apples on the Flood: The Southern Mountain Experience,* responded to this review and concluded with this:

> The sad thing is that while "two vital American cultures" join hands over the presumably moribund form of "moonshine America" whenever something like this comes along to confirm their interlocking prejudices, the "national" literary world remains nearly unaware of the burgeoning of writing within the region in the past generation. There is an enormous amount of first-rate poetry and fiction by native Appalachians of all backgrounds which fits neither century-old convention—pastoral idyll or degrading stereotype—but seldom is it reviewed in "national" publications unless . . . it lends itself to misunderstanding in stereotypical terms. If *The Book Review* can still deal in this sort of thing today, what can we expect from anyone else?

Indeed! However, it is a good sign that both mainline and regional presses are turning out an impressive number of books on Appalachia. Those wishing to learn what is authentic about the region have perhaps more grist for their mill than time. Therefore, it is helpful to have volumes such as this one with an editor as sage as W. K. McNeil to point out some of the pitfalls in reading material that is laced with stereotypes and romantic notions as well as with valuable observations and insights.

McNeil's purpose here is to collect the best of articles that shed light on the folklife of the Appalachian people. His introductory notes preceding each article help the reader to focus on what is most valuable and to be wary of claims that have proven questionable in the light of more recent scholarship. McNeil's own scholarship, undergirding his status as an Appalachian native, is well known throughout the region. An academic folklorist, his interest goes beyond just folk songs and tales to the sayings and doings of the Appalachians and to all of the things they make or use in their daily lives.

McNeil's study points out a number of erroneous beliefs: that Appalachia is a monolithic place with the same kind of people from one end to the other, or that Appalachia means poverty, or that it is like no other part of the country, or that all Appalachians speak Elizabethan English, or that all are Scotch-Irish (or have been dominated by them), or that all worship in the same way. McNeil's research successfully demonstrates that the region is varied, with different "classes" of people that don't all do the same things in the same ways.

This is a valuable book for understanding the folklife of Appalachia. It contains many instructive articles from the past as well as several from more recent scholars, evidence of an ongoing fascination with the region. McNeil's excellent introductory essay shows his knowledge of the literature of the region, even that which is relatively unknown. This book should fill a void in folk studies classes, which are presently forced to glean course material from various articles and books that may or may not deal primarily with folklife. McNeil's collection corrects many of the long-held misconceptions about the region and sets the stage for the serious research that remains to be done.

LOYAL JONES
BEREA, KENTUCKY

Acknowledgments

This book, like any other, is the result of a collaboration between the editor and several other people who contributed time, knowledge, and advice in an altruistic manner. It is impossible to repay them adequately for their help but mention here, at least, is an indication that their efforts are greatly appreciated. Those who willingly came to my aid include Rebecca Brooks, Michael Dabrishus, Ellen Garrison, Ellen Hackney, Loyal Jones, Charlene Kaufmann, Eric Olson, Gerald F. Roberts, and James Stimpert. Last, but certainly not least, I must acknowledge numerous debts to Simon J. Bronner. He is editor of this series and is also one of America's outstanding folklore scholars but, more importantly, he is a valued friend who has helped refine my thinking on Appalachia and on folklore.

Introduction

This book is about the traditional culture of the Appalachian Mountains, more specifically the southern part of that chain of mountains extending 1,300 miles from Vermont to northern Alabama.[1] Depending on how and where one draws the boundaries the southern Appalachians consist of as few as 190 counties in seven states or as many as 230 counties in nine states.[2] For present purposes the larger region is used, meaning that, as defined here, the southern Appalachians consist of portions of Maryland, Virginia, Kentucky, North Carolina, South Carolina, Tennessee, Georgia, and Alabama, and all of West Virginia. Within this section of over 100,000 square miles there are three subsidiary regions, the Allegheny-Cumberland region, the Blue Ridge, and the Great Appalachian Valley. The Allegheny-Cumberland region extends through part of West Virginia, Kentucky, Tennessee, and Alabama; the Blue Ridge lies in Maryland, Virginia, North Carolina, and Georgia; the Great Appalachian Valley is spread over part of Maryland, Virginia, Tennessee, Georgia, and Alabama. Yet, despite being a mountain region containing the highest peaks east of the Rockies, very little of the southern Appalachian area is truly mountainous. The loftiest summits are in the Blue Ridge and in parts of eastern and southeastern West Virginia. These higher elevations are also the most sparsely populated parts of the region, most residents of Appalachia living in the valleys or hill lands.

For over four centuries people have known of the southern Appalachians. In 1540, Spanish explorer Hernando de Soto became lost in the southern Blue Ridge, reportedly naming the mountains for the Apalachee Indians who hindered his approach into the area. In his "New and Improved Description of the Lands of the World" (1569) cartographer Gerardus Mercator located fairly accurately a mountain area that he called "Apalechen." By 1650 English traders were regularly traveling through the mountains and by 1750 the various Appalachian ridges were being accurately situated on maps. In the late eighteenth century a number of famous travelers, such as William Bartram, were extolling the natural beauty of the mountains.

These publications were merely the first of what has been a continuing activity, writing down impressions of the Appalachian South.

It was well over a century after the establishment of the first English colonies along the Atlantic seaboard before white men began to settle the Appalachians. For many years the mountains were considered a barrier to westward settlement but, beginning around the middle of the eighteenth century, some whites living in Pennsylvania moved into the Appalachians through a break in the Blue Ridge. A road was built through the Great Appalachian Valley and then through Cumberland Gap opening up the lands west of Appalachia to settlement by whites. While many moved west, some settlers, particularly those in the section of the Great Valley in Virginia, stayed in Appalachia. At the time of the first United States census in 1790 there were less than 200,000 people living in Southern Appalachia, slightly more than half in Virginia. By 1800 the population had leaped by 118,000 people and continued to grow by an average of 160,000 every decade for the next half century. So, by 1850 the region achieved a population of over 1,000,000, the bulk of its residents coming from the piedmont sections of North and South Carolina, eastern and western Pennsylvania.

The earliest settlement in Southern Appalachia was in the valley regions; the more mountainous sections did not begin to be settled until about 1820. This process was speeded up when the Cherokee Indians were forcibly removed from their homes in northern Georgia in 1836, and gold was discovered in the same general area about the same time. Even then, the population of the more mountainous sections proceeded at a slower pace than that in other parts of Appalachia. Although there has been much dispute about the character and origin of the first whites settling the region, all such statements are ultimately speculation.[3] Suffice it to say that there is no evidence to suggest that those settling the mountains were appreciably different from the rest of the nation's population in the late eighteenth and early nineteenth century. Furthermore, there are no reliable data that prove to what ethnic group the settlers belonged. Similarly, there is no justification for any of the numerous claims that a pure Scotch-Irish or Anglo-Saxon population resides in Appalachia today.

Whatever their origins, character, or personal traits, the mountaineers living in the southern part of Appalachia have for two centuries been perceived as living in isolation. Like all popularly held conceptions this one has an element of truth. No one can honestly deny that throughout much of the history of white settlement in Appalachia the mountains have made travel through the area relatively difficult. Moreover, many of the people have lived in sparsely populated communities remote from large towns. But, isolation is relative, and at no time have these people been totally cut off from the outside world and have thus been isolated only in comparison with some more urban region. Yet, whether the isolation is real or only perceived, it is indisputably one of the major "facts" popularly held about Appalachia. Until approximately the time of the Civil War this feature did not seem to distinguish the region from other remote, unexplored, and undeveloped American locales. Then, Appalachia came to be viewed in a different light. Now, it became a place that was not just isolated but also unique, having its own peculiar people. This realization did not come about overnight, having been suggested as far back as 1824 by novelist George Tucker who included the mountaineer M'Culloch in the cast of *The Valley of the Shenandoah*. Although Tucker did not press the claim, he seemed to be hinting that mountaineers constituted a distinct group.[4]

Once Appalachia's traditional culture was "discovered" it received considerable attention in magazine articles published throughout the late nineteenth century, but it was not until the twentieth century that any books were devoted to the topic. The first of these volumes was written by a tubercular native of Evansville, Indiana, Emma Bell Miles (1879–1919), who, except for two years spent studying art in St. Louis, lived all but her first eleven years in the Tennessee mountains.[5] An intellectual, artist, and writer, Miles was a darling of the Chattanooga economic and social elite who purchased her paintings and murals which they proudly displayed in their homes. These same people also pitied Miles who they felt made a bad choice in marrying George Frank Miles, a mountain man from nearby Walden's Ridge. Her husband was hardly the stupid, insensitive mountaineer of stereotype, for he and Emma spent long afternoons on walks through the woods and one of their favorite pastimes was reading Thoreau's *Walden* aloud to each other. Nevertheless, the marriage was a troubled one and there is little doubt that Miles suffered a "painful ambivalence" toward both the mountain culture and that of the outside world.[6] Her sense of biculturalism was one of the factors motivating Emma to write *The Spirit of the Mountains* (1905).

The ten chapters of Miles's book touch on such matters as home life, schooling, relations between men and women, relations between neighbors, folk narrative, religious beliefs, music, dialect, rhymes, and proverbs. In short, except for a relative lack of attention to material culture, essentially the topics that a folklife specialist would cover. Moreover, Miles reported the material in context, that is she included items of folklore and the social situations in which they were used. This approach was not common in 1905 even among folklorists, indeed it is only in the past three decades that it has become important in those circles. Miles, who made no claim to being anything other than an interested and knowledgeable observer, without any model to guide her recognized the value of including such information. She was far-thinking in other regards, notably in her attention to the style in which songs were performed and even in questioning why they were performed in certain ways. Miles offered no answer to the latter query but in an era when few collections of Appalachian folklore existed, and those which did were almost uniformly unanalytical, it is significant that she asked the question at all. In 1905 it was innovative, even avant-garde.

The Spirit of the Mountains also differs from most previous and subsequent examinations of mountain lore in that the author's tone is not condescending. Where ethnocentric commentators would lead their readers to believe mountaineers were ignorant Miles injects a tone of relativism. If the students at the King's Creek School are lacking in some types of knowledge it is compensated for by their store of valuable ancient lore. Therefore, if "the young minds wander afield . . . what matter? Perhaps they learn at such times something not to be found between the covers of Webster."[7] She is also quick to dispense with "that widespread popular idea . . . that no class of people in America is more lawless than the mountaineers!"[8] Neither does she find mountaineers dirty, degenerate, ignorant savages although she admits that there are such people in the mountains. She quickly adds that "I have lived in many different localities in the Kentucky and Tennessee mountains and have never seen it yet."[9] Based on extended observation, Miles concluded that many of the negative traits typically assigned to mountaineers were no more frequently encountered in the mountains than elsewhere.

Perhaps because of her own marital situation and her interest in women's suffrage, Miles gives extended consideration to relationships between men and women in the mountains. She laments the rift that "is set between the sexes at babyhood" and "that is never closed even by the daily interdependence of a poor man's partnership with his wife."[10] For her the sad part of this situation is that even married couples "know so pathetically little of each other's lives."[11] Basically the division results in women providing much of the strength and endurance of mountain culture. Older women, in particular, occupy a place of special importance. The range of their experience is extensive and they are held in awe. They are "repositories of tribal lore—tradition and song, medical and religious learning. They are the nurses, the teachers of practical arts, the priestesses, and their wisdom commands the respect of all."[12]

Admirable though it is *The Spirit of the Mountains* is not a flawless performance. Although not condescending Miles's prose often leans toward the romantic and rhapsodic. Some of her statements about music are inaccurate or misleading, and in her remarks about dialect she refers to "corruptions" of "pure Saxon words." Even so, Miles's slender volume is a noteworthy achievement that is all the more remarkable because it appeared long before most of the substantive work in Appalachian folklore began.

Since the first book dealing with the total culture of Appalachia was written by a woman it is perhaps fitting that the second such volume was produced by a man. Like Emma Bell Miles, Horace Sowers Kephart (1862–1931) was not a native of the region. Born in East Salem, Pennsylvania he spent the first forty-two years of his life in the northeast and in St. Louis. Then, in 1904, he gave up his position as a professional librarian and moved to the Great Smoky Mountains where he spent the remainder of his life. During this period Kephart produced the two books by which he is remembered, *Camping and Woodcraft* (1906) and *Our Southern Highlanders* (1913). Kephart also was very active in the movement that culminated in the establishment of the Great Smoky Mountains National Park and was instrumental in plotting the route the Appalachian Trail followed through the Smokies.

Our Southern Highlanders has been consistently praised from the time of its initial publication to the present. In its most recent reprinting, in 1976, it was hailed as "the finest regional study yet written by an American."[13] Such an evaluation is overly zealous, but Kephart's volume certainly has its virtues. Like Miles before him, Kephart relies heavily on anecdotal presentations which have the added benefit of giving the context as well as the lore. Kephart doesn't just talk about moonshining and mountain legal concepts, he also provides anecdotes from his own experience that illustrate the points he makes. Moreover, he injects a note of relativism into his narrative, commenting that many of the features, both negative and positive, of mountain society are found in far-flung parts of the world. Although he believes that "no white race is nearer a state of nature than these highlanders" he also affirms that they are not "shallow-minded."[14] Kephart's remarks are often perceptive, revealing that he was a careful observer. For example, he notes that one of the problems with novels that contain dialect is that the "characters speak it too consistently." In reality "the dialect varies a good deal from place to place, and even in the same neighborhood, we rarely hear all families speaking it alike."[15]

Although *Our Southern Highlanders* is generally sympathetic Kephart does not shrink from showing the "dark side" of mountain life. He discusses in some detail homicides, particularly those resulting from feuds but also points out that even among the worst elements in the mountains there exist "certain sterling qualities of manliness that our nation can ill afford to waste."[16] Inbreeding resulting in a high percentage of "defectives" Kephart finds relatively common and the unsanitary conditions of mountain life are "so gross that I can barely hint at them."[17] Yet, each negative feature is justified or at least shown to have some logical explanation. Thus, "half-wits" and other unfortunates are not confined to institutions as they would be in lowland society for two reasons: in the mountains "there are few, if any, public refuges for this class." Equally important, though, is the power of home ties which, as long as it is bearable to have them around, enables mountain unfortunates to "go at large and reproduce their kind."[18]

Throughout *Our Southern Highlanders* the words of Emma Bell Miles are quoted admiringly and that is fitting, for Kephart's work bears great similarity to *The Spirit of the Mountains.* Both volumes were written by outsiders who, at the time of publication, had spent less than two decades in the mountains. Both were sympathetic works that tended to romanticize but yet were not condescending. The two authors found both good and bad traits among mountaineers but took the attitude that the negative features were not appreciably more common in Appalachia than elsewhere in American society. To a certain extent both writers were bicultural and cognizant that future development must be along lines not alien to the nature of mountaineers. Kephart, in particular, considered the staunch individualism that was a charming feature of mountain life also a barrier to the mountaineers' incorporation into American life.

In at least one respect, *The Spirit of the Mountains* and *Our Southern Highlanders* are dissimilar. Whereas Miles places greatest emphasis on the life of women in mountain society Kephart gives greater attention to men and their occupations. Moonshining, hunting, feuding, and other activities, most of which are glossed over by Miles, fill large portions of Kephart's book. He does not, of course, ignore women but doesn't provide the same detail about their lives that Miles gives. The differing emphases could reflect nothing more than the different sexes of the two authors: they may have found it easier to gather information about the occupations and pastimes of their respective sexes. Certainly there is no difference in Miles's and Kephart's assessments of the lot of women. Where Miles laments that at "twenty the mountain woman is old in all that makes a woman old—toil, sorrow, childbearing, loneliness and pitiful want"[19] Kephart says that the "mountain farmer's wife is not only a household drudge, but a field-hand as well."[20]

The third book dealing with the traditional culture of Appalachia is not only a pioneering work in folklore and anthropology but is also a reasonably accurate history of the region before the era of industrialization. It is also a memoir of a churchman and educator whose ideas about Appalachia's future "were to dominate America's conception of the region for two decades after his death."[21] This man was John Charles Campbell (1867–1919) and his book *The Southern Highlander and His Homeland* (1921), which was published posthumously. Although issued nearly seventy years ago Campbell's volume is still among the best works ever written on Appalachia. It is, as Richard Drake notes, "the most complete conceptualization of the Appalachian area" published prior to World War II.[22] Like

Figure 1-1.   John C. Campbell (1867–1919)
(Southern Appalachian Archives, Berea College)

Kephart and Miles, Campbell was not born in the region but spent the last years of his life in Appalachia. A native of La Porte, Indiana he first came to the mountains in 1895 when he was appointed principal of an academy in northern Alabama. Later he served as principal of a school in Tennessee, president of Piedmont College, Demorest, Georgia, and from 1908 until his death as director of the Southern Highland Division of the Russell Sage Foundation.

Campbell's statement of mountain attitudes and values is, like those of Miles and Kephart, sympathetic and relativistic. In common with the two earlier authors, Campbell is not condescending in his approach and attempts to be objective while at the same time giving an accurate picture of the region. Thus, he does not just paint a glowing picture but discusses the beneficial features of schools, churches, and religious rivalry alongside such less desirable occurrences as feuds. He even notes that denominational competition and jealousy have sometimes contributed to mountain problems, an admission that must have been difficult for a dedicated churchman like Campbell. Like Miles and Kephart, Campbell tries to reveal a logical explanation behind certain undesirable aspects of mountain life. For example, he remarks that feuds occur in many parts of the mountains, usually being kept alive, if not originated, by miscarriages of law and justice. When an offender is turned loose "to run at large among the near relatives of him whom he had slain" it inclines people to "take the law into their own hands" and kill. This action sets a vicious cycle in motion, hence the feuds.[23]

While Campbell found many mountain attitudes admirable and some undesirable he placed a few on both the plus and minus side of the ledger. This was true of the much vaunted attributes of self-reliance and individualism, traits that were survivals from earlier times. "Remote from ordered law and commerce, the Highlander learned by hard necessity to rely upon himself." This circumstance led to a situation where "each household in its hollow lived its own life. The man was the provider and the protector. He actually was the law, not only in the management of affairs within the home, but in the relation of the home to the world without." Ultimately, the force of circumstances led "him to depend upon his own action until he came to consider independent action not only a prerogative, but a duty."[24] While the independence thus established was an admirable symbol of the courage and resourcefulness of the pioneer it was also an anachronism in a new age "that calls for cooperative service and community spirit." In this new era individualism was "evidence of a people strange and peculiar and somewhat dangerous withal."[25]

In two major ways Campbell differed from most previous writers on mountain life. Of great significance is his understanding that, despite the then common assumption, there was no homogeneous culture in Appalachia. There were instead many cultures, a fact that "makes it difficult to define the Southern Highlander."[26] This definitional problem may be one of the major reasons that Campbell was unable to finish his book. It is much more difficult to put together a manuscript that has to show the complexity of cultures than it is to present one that discusses one uniform culture found throughout a region. Campbell's belief that the real clue to lifting the Highlanders out of their isolation and poverty was by working through their folk tradition was less radical. Miles, Kephart, and others hinted at this earlier, but in their writings it was merely a suggestion. Campbell went further and offered a plan by which his ideas might be implemented. Basically his idea was to transplant the folk school concept that originated in Denmark in the 1840s to Appalachia. He felt that such schools "might be adapted readily to meet the changing and varied needs of this land."[27] His concept never caught on, but the John C. Campbell Folk School in Brasstown, North Carolina, more or less along the lines envisioned by Campbell, was established in 1926.

In the years since *The Southern Highlander and His Homeland* appeared there have been a large number of studies of Appalachian folklife, mostly written by outsiders lacking Campbell's intimacy with mountain culture. First among these later writers was James Watt Raine (1869–1949), a native of England who spent thirty-three years as head of the English department at Berea College, Berea, Kentucky. In *The Land of Saddle-bags* (1924) and *Saddlebag Folk* (1942) Raine provided two sympathetic, anecdotal books in which the people were viewed as having little sense of history but were nonetheless always guided and molded by tradition. He did have some comprehension of the people as shown by his descriptions of regional customs, speech, and his presentation of folk attitudes. His books, however, also contain some mistakes as, for example, in his statement that the relatively recent instrument, the mountain dulcimer, is Elizabethan and his implication that a uniform culture exists throughout Appalachia. Both books contain several good black-and-white photographs and the two volumes are still useful as long as one keeps in mind Raine's essentially romantic outlook.

In the 1930s a large number of "community studies" appeared, the first in book form being Mandel Sherman and Thomas R. Henry's *Hollow Folk* (1933), which dealt with a Virginia Blue Ridge community. Their account of Colvin Hollow is typical of the genre in that an isolated community, whose extreme isolation makes it not typical of Appalachia, was the object of study. These studies gave the impression that no one in Appalachia lived in towns and, as some people define it, "true mountaineers" do not. Perhaps the most famous of the "community studies" was Muriel Early Sheppard's

Cabins in the Laurel (1935), which substituted a section of western North Carolina for Sherman and Henry's Virginia hollow. In several respects, though, the two books are interchangeable, only the location differs. Other works of this type have continued down to the present, although several of the most recent writers have divested themselves of the romantic trappings of Sheppard.[28]

Charles Morrow Wilson's *Backwoods America* (1935) appeared one year before *Cabins in the Laurel* and may have paved the road for Sheppard's book.[29] Both were issued by the same publisher and with their selective examples spelling out the "Elizabethan" nature of Appalachia were similar in content, although Wilson's book was not a "community study." By the 1930s arguments such as those espoused by Sheppard, Wilson, and others were old and not entirely convincing. Far more original and valuable was Allen Eaton's *Handicrafts of the Southern Highlands* (1937), still the best book on Appalachian crafts. Eaton (1878–1962), a native of Oregon, was trained as a sociologist and spent most of his working career in the employ of the Russell Sage Foundation. Originally in the Surveys and Exhibits Division he later became director of the Foundation's Department of Arts and Social Work. Eaton's ideal was to gather and record material and also put it to use in educational and constructive programs that would benefit society. One means by which he sought to achieve that goal in Appalachia was by stimulating craft production and marketing. With this motivation he collected the data used in his book.

Handicrafts of the Southern Highlands has its limitations but it is nonetheless a valuable work. It is the earliest attempt at an inclusive study of a single aspect of Appalachian folklife. What is more, it is a book that is very readable and thus useful for popular audiences as well as more specialized ones. Much information about Appalachian crafts not otherwise available is contained in the book and considerable detail about tools, materials, construction, design, form, and pattern of crafts as well as the working vocabulary of craftsmen is supplied. Also included is information about the degree of support—both economically and culturally—for individual crafts throughout the region. Eaton also gives a sense of the community in which the craftsman exists, a topic that many crafts books fail to consider. Even more importantly, Eaton does not fall victim to the geriatric syndrome as have many other collectors of folk materials. He was dealing with living, rather than memory, culture and thus included not only the old, the dying, the surviving, but the new, which he considered merely a continuation of the old. Likewise, he did not confine his attention to elderly craftsmen, although they were his main informants. Eaton's broadmindedness in these matters enabled him to give a more accurate picture of Appalachian crafts than those writers who dealt only with survivals or the avant-garde.

Some of the drawbacks of *Handicrafts of the Southern Highlands* are those that have marred other books about Appalachian folklore and others are in part due to the author's goals. Certainly, by 1937 the generally romantic manner in which mountaineers and their crafts are presented was old hat. As Rayna Green notes the "book often reads like a travelogue in which the narrator describes things seen at the side of a road at sunset."[30] Eaton did view the Highlanders in a romantic light but he probably also saw this as the most effective way in which to depict them. After all, one of his stated goals was "to acquaint those outside the region with this great reservoir of handwork ... and to encourage a wider use of these products."[31] Then, what better way to talk about mountaineers and their crafts than the manner in which most Americans probably already viewed them. Eaton's overemphasis on the "rewards" and the therapeutic and recreational aspects of handicrafts is also understandable because he was concerned with showing how crafts could be helpful to the Highland people. Because Eaton's aims were not those of folklorists he did not engage in analysis and because of his refusal to include anything that might reinforce negative stereotypes he provides a picture of mountain life that borders on the antiseptic. Ultimately, though, *Handicrafts of the Southern Highlands* is best considered as a special plea that is also a useful description of Appalachian crafts.

Since World War II there have been many books dealing with Appalachian folklife but few broadly inclusive works on the order of John C. Campbell's or Allen Eaton's. If one restricts the list to volumes regarded by their authors as folklore studies then the number of broadly inclusive books is small indeed. Often folklore is merely included as one of the topics covered in publications that are primarily sociological or historical. For example, one of the most ballyhooed studies of Appalachia, Thomas R. Ford's *The Southern Appalachian Region: A Survey* (1962) includes two chapters, of the total twenty-one, on folklore topics, although aspects of folklife are referred to and early students of the region's folk traditions are frequently mentioned in most of the other nineteen chapters. Jack Weller's *Yesterday's People* (1965) contains several allusions to folk culture, the term being used in a fuzzy, reckless, and ultimately, meaningless way. In Weller's hands folk culture refers to anything he finds distinctive about Appalachia that contrasts with the presumed pattern of life among the professional upper middle class; his book seems nothing more than an ethnocentric account of Appalachian culture produced by an outsider. As Allen Batteau notes, *"Yesterday's People* offers a better guide to the preconceptions of the American middle class than to the social life of the Appalachian mountain people."[32]

The best known works on Appalachian folklife are the nine Foxfire books, the first of which appeared in 1972. Although they have been highly praised and have now become a national phenomenon the various Foxfire volumes are more important as an educational experiment than as folklore works. Eliot Wigginton, a teacher at the Rabun Gap-Nacoochee School in northern Georgia, found his students bored with his classes. So, he hit upon the then novel idea of sending them out into the countryside where they interviewed their families, neighbors, and older friends about traditional ways of life. The information thus recorded was written up in papers subsequently published in *The Foxfire Magazine* which the class put out collectively. Selections from this magazine were compiled to form *The Foxfire Book.* Wigginton's Foxfire project soon became a national sensation; the book and its eight successors were sold in supermarkets and other places where folklore books rarely appeared and Wigginton received a grant of $196,000 from IDEAS (Institutional Development and Economic Affairs Service) to collect and publish folklore. Soon, similar projects arose in other areas but none achieved quite the success of Foxfire, although the Bittersweet project in Lebanon, Missouri did publish two books and kept a magazine in operation for ten years.[33]

Despite the acclaim Foxfire received the contribution of the books to folklore studies is small, although not, as some have claimed, nonexistent. The main virtue is that the books and the magazine do call positive attention to Appalachian folk culture but, unfortunately, in ways that are often misleading. Widespread traditions are often presented as though they were unique to Appalachia, and even more regrettably, the articles tend to perpetuate romantic stereotypes of Appalachia. Admittedly, this feature probably aided sales because the books and magazine present mountain culture as the general public wants to see it portrayed. With their overemphasis on survivals and old-fashioned ways, the Foxfire publications are largely exercises in nostalgia rather than folklore scholarship.

Laurel Shackelford and Bill Weinberg's *Our Appalachia* (1977) is, its title notwithstanding, primarily concerned with eastern Kentucky. Of the forty-seven "narrators" quoted, thirty-five are from Kentucky, seven from Virginia, and five from North Carolina, although several of the twelve from Virginia and North Carolina are natives of Kentucky. The interviews are taken from tape recordings deposited at the Appalachian Oral History Project based at Alice Lloyd College, Pippa Passes, Kentucky. *Our Appalachia* does have some strengths beyond the obvious one of including the actual words and opinions of mountaineers discussing their region. Various age groups are represented, although the majority of the informants are past middle age. Unlike most previous works on Appalachia, which focus on the supposed racial purity of mountaineers, Shackelford and Weinberg's texts come from blacks, and people of non-English European ethnic backgrounds, as well as those with ancestries more popularly associated with Appalachia. *Our Appalachia* also includes interviews with people of varying economic levels and the editors wisely note that there is no "typical mountaineer."

One of the most influential recent works on Appalachia is Henry D. Shapiro's *Appalachia on Our Mind: The Southern Mountains and Moun-taineers in the American Consciousness, 1870–1920* (1978). Shapiro's concern is not Appalachian folklife, indeed it is not even Appalachia, but, rather, "the idea of Appalachia" as manifested in the roughly fifty years after the Civil War and what that idea reveals about "the nature and meaning of American civilization."[34] He does, however, include two chapters dealing with folklore, one on the crafts revival and one on folksongs. Some of Shapiro's comments indicate a naïveté about folklore scholarship and his conclusions are debatable, but his remarks are essential reading even if only as examples of a non-folklorist's views on the study and use of Appalachian folklore.

Of the relatively few books on Appalachian folk culture written by an insider one of the most enjoyable is Verna Mae Slone's *What My Heart Wants to Tell* (1979). Slone produced this slender volume partly to counter books such as *Stay on Stranger,* a history of the Caney Creek Community Center in eastern Kentucky near her home, which she considers a grossly inaccurate work, but it was also written so that her grandchildren could know more about their family history. In twenty-six chatty chapters Slone covers such topics as quilting, plant lore, nicknaming, wood lore, moonshin-ing, funeral and burial practices, clothing, crops, morals, and attitudes on various subjects. Interestingly, Slone subscribes to the idea that mountain-eers speak a language that is heavily laced with Shakespearean English, a concept that most folklorists reject. She does, however, go to some lengths to prove incorrect some views commonly held about mountaineers. For example, when told that twenty-five percent of the children born in her region die in infancy she puts the statistics to the test by counting all the infant births and deaths in each hollow and branch of Caney Creek, coming up with a figure that is far below the supposedly accurate twenty-five percent. Brimming with opinions and interesting anecdotes, *What My Heart Wants to Tell* is a pleasant, entertaining introduction to the life story of one Appalachian family.

Two other books deserve mention here, the most important from a folklore viewpoint being David Whisnant's *All That Is Native and Fine: The Politics of Culture in an American Region* (1983). Focusing on the Hind-man Settlement School in eastern Kentucky, the work of Olive Dame Campbell throughout the mountains, and the White Top Folk Festival on the Virginia-North Carolina border, Whisnant provides a perceptive exami-nation of cultural intervention in Appalachia. Specifically he seeks to determine "the role of formal institutions and forceful individuals in defining and shaping perspectives, values, tastes, and agendas for cultural change."[35] In his three case studies Whisnant brings forth persuasive evidence that many of those who sought to aid the mountaineer understood his culture only dimly. Too often, cultural intervenors, such as the settlement school administrators, presented an unrealistic picture of mountain life whose falseness was not lessened by the altruistic motives of its promoters. Ultimately, the failure to comprehend mountain culture and, in some cases, racial and cultural bigotry doomed the efforts of settlement schools, craft cooperatives, folk festivals, and other institutions of noble intent. Whisnant tells a compelling story, producing one of the few works that extensively examines the ways in which Appalachian folklore has been used.

Among the various books touching on Appalachian folklife there are few that deal in any substantive way with non-white traditions. One can hardly claim that William H. Turner and Edward J. Cabbell's *Blacks in Appalachia* (1985), though estimable in several regards, does much to correct the shortcoming of earlier volumes. Seemingly the twenty-one essays arranged in eight categories that cover the early history of blacks in the region, studies of black communities, relations between blacks and whites, blacks in coal mining, and political issues, would contain much of interest for folklife specialists but, while there is some relevant material, there is much less than might be expected. Of greatest value from a folklore standpoint is a brief section of personal anecdotal accounts of black life and a resource guide listing cultural organizations, service organizations, films, filmstrips, records, various presentations of the John Henry legend, and theses and dissertations. Surprisingly the book reveals very little about some aspects of modern Appalachian black folklife, such as the black church and religious practices. In fact, almost no feature of black life in Appalachia receives much attention except coal mining, and contradictory information is presented on that topic. For example, most of the essayists find that the racist nature of the mining towns created interracial strife but in "Class over Caste: Interracial Solidarity in the Company Town" David A. Corbin suggests that the opposite situation prevailed in West Virginia.

This survey by no means covers every volume published to date on the subject of Appalachian folklife. It does, however, discuss some of the best known and most important works in this specialized area and also touches on the major themes and approaches adopted by the various authors. Major attention has been given to those books that dealt with, or purported to treat, all of Appalachia. Obviously there have been many more articles than books dealing with the traditional culture of Appalachia but usually the books have proven more influential. This is not surprising since in most cases the books have been more accessible to a wide audience than the journals in which the articles appeared. Nevertheless, the two publication forms do share some common ground.

Both books and articles have combined to fix in the popular mind an image of Appalachia as a unique region with its own distinctive traditions. Essays on the subject began about the time of the Civil War and books specifically addressing the matter first appeared in the early twentieth century. If one takes into account novels and short stories about Appalachia then the date can be set back at least twenty years when Mary Noailles Murfree and others began producing their fictional accounts of mountain life. It is significant that many of the numerous publications concerned with Appalachian folklife were not regarded by their authors as folklore studies at all, but rather as sociological works dealing with the "problem" of Appalachia and how to treat its various ills. This is especially true of the "community studies" but applies to most of the other publications on Appalachian folklife that appeared prior to the 1960s. Most also dealt exclusively with the WASP population of the mountains. In recent years this situation has changed only slightly; for all practical purposes work on the various non-Anglo-Saxon cultural groups in Appalachia is nonexistent. Apparently, most writers on the region have followed the advice given in the Latin proverb "via trita, via tuta" (the beaten path is the safe path). Also, until very recent times most authors writing on Appalachia have depicted mountaineers in a romantic way that, although having the virtue of being positive has the disadvantage of being unrealistic. This romanticizing, of course, continues today but now there are many more publications than in the past that do not take this approach.

In one very important respect articles, at least those written before World War II, differed from books about Appalachia: the articles give much greater attention to eastern Kentucky than to other sections of Appalachia. Certainly, from the very first there were essays on other areas of the mountains, but the vast majority of the publications that appeared in magazines or journals dealt with the Kentucky section of Appalachia. Reasons for this heavy emphasis are many but a few stand out: first, many of the people writing essays, such as William Goodell Frost, James Lane Allen, and John Fox, were from Kentucky, or at the time of publication were working in the state; second, eastern Kentucky, for many people, represented the quintessence of Appalachia; third, many of the more colorful and more widely discussed aspects of mountain life, such as feuding, were erroneously associated solely with Kentucky; fourth, many of the major organizations and institutions encouraging study of Appalachia, such as Berea College, were headquartered in Kentucky.

The present volume is composed of material that initially appeared in magazines or journals. Most of the essays have never appeared in book form, the single exception being James Lane Allen's "Through Cumberland Gap on Horseback," which was first reprinted in his 1892 volume *The Blue-Grass Region of Kentucky and Other Kentucky Articles.* Entries have been chosen that deal with Appalachia's folklife. In other words, this book deals with the total traditional culture with greater emphasis placed on material culture than on other aspects of Appalachian folklore. For various reasons articles solely concerned with music, such as Emma Bell Miles's "Some Real American Music," and those that have recently been reprinted, such as George E. Vincent's "A Retarded Frontier," are omitted.[36] In past volumes music has been perhaps overemphasized at the cost of focus on material culture. By relying solely on magazine and periodical publications one is dealing with articles that are generally inaccessible and, at the same time, providing a good account of the image of Appalachian folk culture given to readers of periodical literature during the thirteen decades since this mountain region was recognized as a unique area with its own distinctive traditions.

There are twenty-one essays presented here in chronological order according to the date of original publication. These articles, which appeared from 1860 to 1987, represent four eras of thinking about Appalachian folklife, each characterized by a specific viewpoint. During the years 1860 to 1899 Appalachia was being "discovered" by various observers. Although as early as 1864 Superintendent of the Census Joseph C. G. Kennedy defined the area stretching "from Pennsylvania, through Virginia, Eastern Tennessee, &c., to Northern Alabama" as one of the seven "natural divisions" of the country it was not until the late 1890s that anyone suggested that the southern mountains constituted a region in the modern sense of an area defined by its location, characteristics, and culture.[37] William Goodell Frost, the person credited with making the suggestion, also coined the phrase "contemporary ancestors" by which mountaineers often were described in the years after 1899, that term eventually being replaced by "yesterday's people" which also came from a very popular publication. Yet, long before Frost's essay appeared, Appalachian residents were considered by many writers to be "strange and peculiar" and somehow ever-attached to the past. For example, Louise Coffin Jones, in a popular *Lippincott's Magazine* article of 1883, found the "tanned, athletic mountaineer" to be "a figure suggestive of the Homeric age."[38] Such descriptions were used to posit the esthetic distance between observer and observed, but Frost's achievement was that he encapsulated that esthetic distance in a convenient catch phrase that not only described the difference of the mountaineers but explained the reasons for it as well. Somehow these people had been arrested in time and thus were really from a world different from modern America.

After the appearance of Frost's seminal essay, many publications were issued in which Appalachia was viewed not only as a distinctive region but also as an area made up of people who were, in most cultural respects, Elizabethan. Although such works continue to the present day the greatest number appeared during the years 1900 to 1930. Following that era came the period 1930–50 in which much attention was devoted to change in mountain life. Many of these essays talked about how the "contemporary ancestors" were forsaking their "Elizabethan" ways and adopting those of modern civilization. This had been a relatively frequent theme since 1916 when B. H. Shockle of the Indiana State Teacher's College, Terre Haute, published "Changing Conditions in the Kentucky Mountains," but it became even more common from 1930 to 1950.[39] That era was followed by what is dubbed here the age of functional studies where the great concern of many authors was not only to describe aspects of folklore but also to consider the ways in which they functioned in Appalachian society. That the four broad periods given here are not perfect is seen in the appearance of works in this last era, 1950 to the present, that take the viewpoints most prominent in the three earlier eras.

All the articles reprinted here are selected either because they are historically significant, influential, or representative of a particular viewpoint or methodology. No claim is made that this is the definitive anthology of essays about Appalachian folklife; the major assertion made is that this book contains some valuable essays from the voluminous literature on Appalachian folklife. Hopefully, publication of these articles will give readers some understanding of the varied ways in which numerous observers sought to comprehend Appalachian traditional culture. Like most writers dealing with such matters they sought to reduce a reality that was very complex into simplicity, but they also demonstrated that the subject was indeed worthy of study.

Notes

1. In this introduction unless specifically stated otherwise the word "Appalachia" refers to southern Appalachia.

2. For varying views on where the boundaries of southern Appalachia are see John C. Campbell, *The Southern Highlander and His Homeland* (Lexington: The University Press of Kentucky, 1969; reprint of a work originally issued in 1921), pp. 10–18; Rupert B. Vance, "The Region: A New Survey" in Thomas R. Ford, ed., *The Southern Appalachian Region: A Survey* (Lexington: University of Kentucky Press, 1967; reprint of a work originally issued in 1962), p. 3; Jack E. Weller, *Yesterday's People: Life in Contemporary Appalachia* (Lexington: University of Kentucky Press, 1966), p. 9; and W. D. Weatherford and Earl D. C. Brewer, *Life and Religion in Southern Appalachia* (New York: Friendship Press Inc., 1962).

3. For two extreme views of Appalachian mountaineers, their character and origin see Jean Thomas, *Ballad Makin' in the Mountains of Kentucky* (New York: Oak Publications, Inc., 1964; reprint of a work originally issued in 1939) and Harry M. Caudill, *Night Comes to the Cumberlands: A Biography of a Depressed Area* (Boston: Little, Brown and Company, 1963). Thomas takes an essentially romantic view, speaking of mountaineers descended from Queen Elizabeth I, while Caudill takes the opposite view, arguing that the mountaineers are descended from shiftless, lazy, unskilled, and illiterate runaway indentured servants and outlaws and that they degenerated into wild and cruel denizens of the hills.

4. See Cratis D. Williams, "The Shaping of the Fictional Legend of the Southern Mountaineer" in *Appalachian Journal* 3 (1976): 103.

5. For biographical information on Miles see Kay Baker Gaston, *Emma Bell Miles* (Signal Mountain, Tennessee: Walden's Ridge Historical Association, 1985) and David E. Whisnant's introduction to Emma Bell Miles, *The Spirit of the Mountains* (Knoxville: The University of Tennessee Press, 1975), xv-xxxv. See, in particular, Gaston, p. 3, and Whisnant, xvii.

6. Whisnant, "Introduction," xxi.

7. Miles, p. 5.

8. Ibid., p. 74.

9. Ibid., pp. 75–76.

10. Ibid., p. 69.

11. Ibid., p. 70.

12. Ibid., p. 37.

13. George Ellison, "Introduction" to Horace Kephart, *Our Southern Highlanders* (Knoxville: The University of Tennessee Press, 1976; reprint of a work originally issued in 1913 and revised in 1922), xlvi.

14. Kephart, p. 278.

15. Ibid., p. 353.

16. Ibid., p. 465.

17. Ibid., p. 304.

18. Ibid., pp. 296–97.

19. *The Spirit of the Mountains,* p. 64.

20. Kephart, p. 331.

21. This statement is made by Henry D. Shapiro in his "Introduction" to the 1969 reprint of Campbell, xxx.

22. Richard Drake, "Appalachian America: The Emergence of a Concept, 1895–1964." *Mountain Life and Work* 40 (1965): 7.

23. Campbell, p. 111.

24. Ibid., p. 93.

25. Ibid., p. 94.

26. Ibid., p. 19.

27. Ibid., p. 297.

28. Other "community studies" in addition to Sherman and Henry's and Sheppard's include Marion Pearsall, *Little Smoky Ridge: The Natural History of a Southern Appalachian Neighborhood* (1959); Elmora Messer Matthews, *Neighbor and Kin: Life in a Tennessee Ridge Community* (1965); John B. Stephenson, *Shiloh: A Mountain Community* (1968); Rena Gazaway, *The Longest Mile* (1969); John Fetterman, *Stinking Creek* (1970); F. Carlene Bryant, *We're All Kin: A Cultural Study of a Mountain Neighborhood* (1981); and Durwood Dunn, *Cades Cove: The Life and Death of a Southern Appalachian Community, 1818–1937* (Knoxville: The University of Tennessee Press, 1988).

29. Although Charles Alan Watkins says this is not the case in "Merchandising the Mountaineer: Photography, the Great Depression, and *Cabins in the Laurel," Appalachian Journal* 12 (1985): 217. He does say that photographs for both books were supplied by Bayard Wootten, and inaccurately states that Wilson's book was set in the Ozarks. Actually, *Backwoods America* deals with both Appalachia and the Ozarks.

30. "Introduction" to Allen H. Eaton, *Handicrafts of the Southern Highlands* (New York: Dover Publications, Inc., 1973; reprint of a work originally issued in 1937): xv.

31. Ibid., p. 34.

32. Allen Batteau, "Appalachia and the Concept of Culture: A Theory of Shared Misunderstandings." *Appalachian Journal* 7 (1979–80): 11.

33. *Bittersweet* magazine was published from 1973 to 1983; the two books, *Bittersweet Country* (1978) and *Bittersweet Earth* (1985), were both edited by Ellen Gray Massey, the project's advisor.

34. Henry D. Shapiro, *Appalachia on Our Mind: The Southern Mountains and Mountaineers in the American Consciousness, 1870–1920* (Chapel Hill: The University of North Carolina Press, 1978), p. 14.

35. David E. Whisnant, *All That Is Native and Fine: The Politics of Culture in an American Region* (Chapel Hill: The University of North Carolina Press, 1983), p. 15.

36. Vincent's essay is reprinted in Simon J. Bronner, *Folklife Studies from the Gilded Age: Object, Rite, and Custom in Victorian America* (Ann Arbor, Michigan: UMI Research Press, 1987), pp. 105–17. Miles's article appears as a chapter in her book *The Spirit of the Mountains.*

37. Quoted in Fulmer Mood, "The Origin, Evolution, and Application of the Sectional Concept, 1750–1900" in Merrill Jensen, *Regionalism in America* (Westport, Connecticut: Greenwood Press, 1975; reprint of a work originally issued in 1965), p. 74.

38. Louise Coffin Jones, "In the Highlands of North Carolina." *Lippincott's Magazine* 32 (1883): 378.

39. The article originally appeared in *Scientific Monthly* 3 (1916): 105–31, and was condensed and uncredited in *Geographical Review* 3 (1917): 146–47.

I

A Strange Land and a Peculiar People

1

A Week in the Great Smoky Mountains

R., of Tennessee

Who R. of Tennessee was and his reasons for choosing anonymity remain mysteries. There is no doubt, however, about the reasons for his journey into the Smokies. He, and his doctor, subscribed to a then relatively new medical theory that fresh, or "pure," air and exercise were ideal for one suffering from respiratory ailments. Thus, in November, 1859 R. set off alone on a trip along the Little Pigeon River in eastern Tennessee and western North Carolina, essentially the same area now traversed by Interstate Highway 40. His account of this journey is firmly in the tradition of travel writing but is useful for present purposes because of the considerable attention R. pays to describing natives, their customs, life style, and their food. Although the introductory remarks indicate that R. viewed the mountaineers as people different from the "civilized" folk he normally associated with, they are still discussed in sympathetic terms. They are "bold and hardy men," the women are genial, economical, and hospitable even though they may also be "coarse, rough, and strong-minded." Sometimes the knowledge these people acquired through intuition or practical experience is impressive. Thus R. compares one man favorably to François Huber, the eighteenth-century Swiss master of apiary science. Moreover, in light of comments made by some later observers of mountain life it is interesting that R. finds that, despite living in an isolated region under "rough" conditions, the natives are not completely out of touch with the outside world, they simply prefer their way of life to that available elsewhere.

R.'s article refers to or describes a variety of matters that are interesting to folklorists, cultural historians, and anthropologists. These include the clothing and dress of the "rude rustics," the infair or infare (a type of post-wedding rite of passage usually involving a dinner and other activities that are often prankish), corn-huskings, bear-gut ribbons, robbing of bee gums, singing, protracted meetings, and several anecdotes. Most of these probably attracted his attention because he thought they would be unusual or exotic for his readers, but that doesn't apply in each case. Note, for example, his mention of corn-huskings, a traditional neighborly activity of many rural areas that received frequent discussion in nineteenth-century travel literature. There is no

Reprinted from *The Southern Literary Messenger* 31 (August 1860): 117–31.

reason to doubt the accuracy of R.'s comments regarding these subjects but on another matter one of his "facts" is wrong. Quonacatoose, now generally known as Clingman's Dome after Thomas L. Clingman (1812–1897), a member of the party that first measured the mountain in 1858, has an altitude of 6,642 feet and is the highest point in the Smokies but is not the highest spot east of the Rocky Mountains. That honor is claimed by Mount Mitchell, in nearby Yancey County, which has an altitude of 6,684 feet. R.'s mistake is understandable because in 1860 the claim was in dispute.

For more recent discussions of the Smokies see Laura Thornborough, *The Great Smoky Mountains* (New York: Thomas Y. Crowell Co., 1937); Roderick Peattie, *The Great Smokies and the Blue Ridge* (New York: Vanguard Press, 1945); and Michael Frome, *Strangers in High Places: The Story of the Great Smoky Mountains* (New York: Doubleday & Company, Inc., 1966).

* * *

"All you need now," said my physician, "is some vigorous out-door exercise in a cold, bracing climate. What say you, Mr. R., to a jaunt of a few weeks into Minnesota? St. Pauls would be just the place for you—dry, cold, sunny and no wind."

"No doubt, Doctor, you are quite right," said I, "but then St. Pauls is so devilish far off! Why not say the Smoky Mountains? They are so much nearer home, and as some of their peaks are nearly seven thousand feet high, I imagine a poor fellow could manage to keep quite cool enough on the top of them. Zounds, Doctor, seven thousand feet up in the air in November! Why the very thought of it makes my teeth chatter sitting here by a good fire."

"The Smoky Mountains," said he, "you will find very rough, and you will have to walk a great deal if you ascend them. But so much the better. I would have mentioned them instead of St. Pauls, had I not thought you would have demurred to the roughness of the accommodations to which you will necessarily be subjected among the cabins of the mountaineers."

"Why, my dear sir," I exclaimed, "do you take me for a milksop! I have been in the mountains often. I have slept, sir, upon the top of Black Mountain, with nothing over me save a blanket, the balsam trees and the stars."

"Oh, very well," said my Doctor with a smile—"but take care you do not go to the Smoky Mountains only to stay by the fire of some hunter. Remember, my only prescription for you is—cold, dry, fresh *air* and plenty of it, and vigorous out-door *exercise,* stopping short of fatigue."

So, reader, instead of giving me quack nostrums, my physician ordered me to take for hemmorhage of the lungs, simply—*air* and *exercise!* It rejoices one to find that besides Dr. Hall of N.Y., there is one other man in the healing profession who believes in God and nature.

Having tried in vain to get any one to accompany me to the mountains, which lie between Tennessee and North Carolina, called the Great Smoky, I determined to go alone. Upon Thursday, 3rd of November, 1859, I left Knoxville, the capital of East Tennessee, upon horse-back, taking with me two blankets, an over-coat, in one pocket of which there was a pint flask of the best brandy, a pair of saddlebags, in one side of which I had stuffed two or three pairs of socks and as many shirts, and a copy of Dr. Draper's Physiology, and in the other side, to make the balance even, a quart bottle of the same article with which the pint flask was filled. Of course I did not mean to use the quart of brandy, for then the saddlebags would have lost their balance and fallen off.

My intended route was first to Sevierville, and then up the Little Pigeon River—at the head of which stream the mountains attain an elevation of 6700 feet. Mt. Washington, in New Hampshire, is 6226—so the Great Smoky Mountains are 544 feet higher than the highest point of the White Mountains, and thus *Quonacatoosa*, as the highest peak of the Smoky is called, is by far the loftiest elevation east of the Rocky Mountains, *Quonacatoosa* would I climb—that was my determination:

> For I longed, like another Belus, to mount
>   up, yea, to heaven,
> Nor sought I rest, until my feet had spurned
>   the crest of earth.

Bless my soul, if I have not been betrayed into quoting from master M. Farquhar Tupper! If the Lord will forgive me for this once, I promise most solemnly never again to be guilty of a like offence—never.

Well, then, having been mounted sometime, what hinders us, reader, from starting—you and I? Nothing—so plunging my spurs into the sides of *Billy Button* we are off. Then "might have been a solitary traveller slowly wending his way" to the banks of Holston River; arrived at which, he found the boat was on the further shore and no boatman in sight. Nice fix for a man just getting about after a hemmorhage—hollering so as to be heard by a man half a mile off and in a house. But there is no help for it—so here goes—Halloo! No answer—a little louder if you please—Halloo! Why I never shouted louder or clearer in my life!

"*Helloo* yourself!" echoes a man running out the house on the other side—"do you want the boat?"

Of course I do. A cool question that and a provoking. I wonder if the fellow ever knew any one to stand on the bank and bawl, to the splitting of his throat, merely for the love of hollering?

Giving the wheel of his buoy boat a turn, over the water it sped like an arrow.

"A *buoy Boat*—turned a *wheel!* why what is a buoy boat, pray, and how can turning a wheel take it over a river?"

You do not mean to say, gentle reader, that you do not know what a buoy boat is?

"Most certainly, sir, I do—for I never heard of such a thing in my life before."

Well, then, I will explain it. A buoy boat is used in streams with very rapid currents, and it saves immense labour, as it is so constructed that it is carried across the river simply by the downward pressure of the flowing water. I am not aware that such boats are used anywhere else in the Union except in the mountains of Tennessee and Pennsylvania; but they are often met with in Europe, especially on the Po and the Rhine. To a boat made like the ordinary ferry boat, a long rope, or better, a chain, is attached; the other end of the rope or chain is carried several hundred yards up the river and made fast to the top of a tree. If there be an island convenient, the rope is made fast to a tree on it, but if not, to the most convenient tree on the bank. The rope, or chain, is kept elevated out of the water by small, light boats, placed at suitable intervals for that purpose. These are called buoys—hence the ferry is said to be crossed by a *buoy boat.* The rope, or chain, instead of being made fast to the boat's side, is passed over a pulley fixed at one end of the boat, and having been wound round a large wheel in the middle of the boat, it is taken over another pulley at the far end and then is made fast to the rope, or chain, again some forty or fifty feet up the river. The reader who has a turn for mechanics, will see that the boatman, by revolving the wheel, can give the upper side of his boat what inclination to the stream he pleases. There is also a large, wide plank attached to the upper and outside of the boat, but so fixed that the boatman, by a lever, can lower or elevate it at pleasure. By experience he learns how best to adjust his wheel and plant at different points, so as to get the full benefit of the current against the boat. The boat being powerfully pressed upon by the current, and tied to a tree above so that it cannot go down stream, of necessity moves in the arc of a circle, and thus a child's strength is sufficient to make it ply from side to side of a large river. It is a beautiful sight to see such a boat and its accompanying buoys—it swims as easily and gracefully as a swan and her brood of cygnets.

There is nothing note-worthy between Knoxville and Sevierville, except the battle-ground on Boyd's Creek. Here, in 1782, the bold pioneers, who had annihilated Ferguson's force upon King's Mountain, on their return to their mountain homes, came upon a host of savages about to take advantage of their absence to tomahawk and scalp their defenceless wives and children. Under the leadership of the gallant Colonel Sevier, the Indians were most signally defeated. In honour of this bold and accomplished man, the county of Sevier is named, and also the county seat Sevierville.

Were you aware, reader, that in 1784, just after the close of the Revolutionary War, the people inhabiting what is now East Tennessee declared themselves independent of North Carolina, to which State they belonged, and formed a separate and independent commonwealth, calling it *"Franklin,"* in honor of Benjamin Franklin? Colonel John Sevier was chosen Governor of Franklin, and acted as such until 1788, when North Carolina agreeing that at a proper time she would consent to a separation, the State of Franklin ceased to exist by the voluntary failure of the people to elect any more officers. But so strong a hold had John Sevier upon the popular heart of the bold mountaineers of Franklin, that after the State of Tennessee was admitted into the Union in 1796, they elected him Governor of the new State six several times—and then sent him to Congress—an instance of the constancy of popular favour almost without a parallel.

Some of the legislation of the State of Franklin has been the subject of no little mirth to the descendants of these bold and hardy men. And as illustrating the then state of society, I would cite the following act in regard to the payment of the State tax.

"Be it enacted, That it shall and may be lawful for the aforesaid land tax and all free polls to be paid in the following manner: good *flax linen,* ten hundred at 3 shillings and 6 pence per yard; nine hundred at 3 shillings—eight hundred 2 shillings and 9 pence, seven hundred 2 shillings and 6 pence, six hundred 2 shillings; *tow linen* 1 shilling and 9 pence; *linsey* 3 shillings, and woolen and cotton linsey 3 shillings and 6 pence per yard; good clean *beaver skins* 6 shillings; cased *otter skins* 6 shillings; uncased ditto 5 shillings; *raccoon* and *fox skins* 1 shilling and 3 pence; *woolen cloth* at 10 shillings per yard; *bacon,* well cured, 6 pence per lb.; good clean *tallow* 6 pence per lb.; good clean *beeswax* 1 shilling per lb.; good distilled *rye whiskey* at 2 shillings and 6 pence per gallon; good peach or apple *brandy* at three shillings per gallon, (Maine Law nonsense did not exist then, reader,) good country made *sugar* 1 shilling per lb.; *deer skins,* the pattern six shillings; good neat and well managed *tobacco,* fit to be prized, that may pass inspection, 15 shillings the hundred, and so on in proportion for a greater or less quantity!"

In quoting this act of the Franklin Legislature, I have no disposition to sneer at the bold men who so largely contributed to the achievement of our independence. Let *dilettanteism* sneer if it will, but the very list itself shows that the people were already independent of the Mother Country in all material respects, and that they were able to manufacture for themselves, even at that early day, everything they needed. Indeed, 1776 is too late a date for the Declaration of American Independence; philosophically and truly it was made one hundred and fifty years earlier at Plymouth and Jamestown.

Well, here we are for the night, at Sevierville, right under the Smoky Mountains. Somewhat different are things now to what they were in 1784. Sevierville is quite a neat village—has several substantial brick stores, a large and not inelegant brick court house, and last, but to the traveller not least, a comfortable tavern. My landlady's daughter, I should judge, must be quite the village belle; that she is very pretty is beyond question. From many little niceties of the female toilet, I imagine the village beauty surrendered her own room to me for the night. On the table lay the last ten numbers of Harper's Magazine, and a pile of the back numbers of "The Waverly Magazine," published at Boston. I confess till then I did not know there was a Waverly Monthly—but that only argues myself unknown. But who would have expected to find Harper at the foot of the Great Smoky? Truly, the "Little Giant," of Illinois, knew through what medium to best address the million. There lay the September number, containing all the plausible sophistications of the Senator.

Friday, November 4th. After a good night's rest and a good cup of coffee, I start again for the mountains. My road leads just up the bank of the west fork of the Little Pigeon. A more beautiful stream than the Pigeon it is scarcely possible to imagine. For the first ten miles the road is good, the farms very fine, the farm-houses good, and the cultivation of the land above the ordinary tillage of East Tennessee. It surprised me to see negroes gathering cotton almost upon every farm—and very good cotton, too, it appeared to be. The women, everywhere along the road, were making molasses out of sorghum, or Chinese sugar cane. To the rapidity of spread of the cultivation of this cane there is no parallel, except the mania that prevailed, a few years since, in regard to *morus multicaulis.* Now one sees nothing of the mulberry. Sorghum will be quite as short-lived, I imagine. Nothing, indeed, derived from China seems to be able to keep a permanent foothold in this country, except rice and broomcorn.

Just above Sevierville there appears to have formerly been a large Indian town. There are there two large mounds, and the ground for several acres around is covered with pieces of pottery. I was told that these mounds have never yet been opened. I passed by a vein of most beautiful Breccia marble near Sevierville, and I also noticed a quarry of slate which one day must become valuable for covering houses.

About ten miles from Sevierville, the road becomes nothing more than a rough path, and the river a large mountain torrent, plunging madly from rock to rock. The mountains close in upon the river, and tower above you for hundreds and thousands of feet on either side. The fords become really dangerous, and as the path crosses the river very frequently, it is quite annoying to have to plunge in so often, not knowing at what moment your horse may slip from the rough boulders and break one of your limbs. To avoid going over the river so often, the mountaineers have cut paths along the precipitous sides of the mountain; but the danger of your horse falling from them, makes the crossing the fords, bad as they are, preferable. The ford about thirteen miles from Sevierville is the worst one by far. The immense outjutting rocks, with which it is filled, look like the snaggled teeth of some great earth-giant which has there opened its mouth to swallow the river entire. Headlong the river plunges "into the jaws of death, into the mouth of hell." There is no help for it, so in Billy Button and I go—but about midway, losing his foothold, headlong into the foaming waters we went. But Billy is a noble fellow, and quickly recovered himself and made for the bank, with no damage done, save a few scratches to himself and a ducking to me. While Billy was shaking himself dry, I emptied part of the contents of my flask down my throat. I had frequently heard that if one gets thoroughly wet, there is no danger of taking cold, so as I was wet on the outside, nothing remained to make it a *thorough* soaking but to moisten the *inside* likewise.

Note.—Some foolish people are in the habit of mixing water with their liquor. Now my experience in this matter satisfies me that the best way, by far, is to take them separate—the water outwardly on the face, hands or person, and the cognac down the throat, *straight.* Try it so, reader, next time you get a ducking.

I never was treated with more distinguished honour in my life than to-day. Losing my way, I rode up to where a group of urchins were playing near a cabin, arrayed in the simplest of costumes—*videlicet,* a tow-shirt. I called to a little fellow of ten or twelve summers to come and tell me the way to Mr. Huskey's. It seems the little chap was the fortunate owner of his first pair of Sunday breeches, and that for the pleasure and grandeur of donning them now and then, had them lying near him on a log. So when called to him he very gravely took up his much-prized nether integuments and calmly put them on slowly and with dignity, buttoning them entirely up to the last button-hole flap and all, for half the grandeur of the breeches lay in the *flap,* you observe. Fully dressed, he then came forward and gave the desired information with great clearness and politeness. That boy is certainly Beau Brummel in *embryo.* Had I smoked, I would have given him a cigar—then he would have been a MAN *instanter*!

I had been advised by my friend Gen'l C. to get Jack Bradley to go with me as a guide, and was told that Jack lived some two miles this side of Mr. Huskey's, where the General advised me to make my headquarters. Near nightfall I came to a cabin with three large letters rudely painted on the door—A. J. B. Rightly concluding that A. J. B. could signify nothing but *Andrew Jackson Bradley,* I rode up to the door and said to a bold, hardy looking mountaineer, dressed in hunting-shirt and coon-skin cap:

"How are you, Jack?"

"Well, stranger," he replied, "you have the advantage of me."

The almost universal way the country people have of intimating they do not know who you are.

Giving Jack my name, and telling him my cousin, General C., had told me to get him to go with me to the Alum Cave and to the top of Quonaca-toosa, Jack's face brightened, and he exclaimed:

"The Gineral, you say, told you to git me. Why, God bless him, how is the Gineral? Of course I will go with you, if you are kin to the Gineral. But I can't go to-morrow—I must git in my corn, you see; but on Sunday I will go with you, if you say so."

And so we arranged it. Finding that Gen'l C.'s name was a tower of strength in that quarter among the people, whose sons had been to Mexico with him, I determined to use it freely. Now C. is not exactly a cousin of mine—he only married my cousin—but that is tantamount to the same thing.

Coming at last to a large double cabin, with all sorts of skins nailed up on its sides, I rightly concluded that I was at Mr. Huskey's—the greatest hunter of all that region. Hallooing, I was answered by the fierce outcry of "both mongrel, whelp and hound and cur of low degree," which brought to the door a tall, fine looking man of between fifty and sixty years of age, and a large woman, who would weigh say 250 pounds, looking fat, fair and fifty. The pretty faces of two mountain lasses peered out of the doorway. Ordering his dogs off, the old hunter called out to me:

"Light, stranger, light!"

"Judging from the skins on the sides of your house, and the bee-gums all round your yard," said I, "I suppose I am at Mr. Huskey's."

"Yes, Mister," he answered, "that's my house."

"And I suppose," said I, offering my hand to the large woman, "that this is Aunt Dolly."

"Yes, Mister," answered she, pleasantly, "that is what they call the *little* that's left of me."

"Well, then, my name is R.," said I, "and I am a cousin of General C., who told me to come here to stay, as it is the best house in the mountains, he says."

"Well, Mister, you will find our house mighty rough," said the old man, "but you may look at my old woman there to see if we starve up here in the mountains."

"Why didn't you fetch the Gineral along with you?" exclaimed Aunt Dolly. "The last time the Gineral was here eh brought his little son with him. I mind I was powerful sick then, and I do believe, Mister, I should 'a' died but for some truck the Gineral gave me, God bless him!"

So as cousin of the General who had performed so miraculous a cure of the old lady, I was on good, not to say intimate, terms with the whole family almost immediately.

Here, then, at last we are, reader, on the side of the Great Smoky, and at the foot of Quonacatoosa.

A nicer supper I never ate than old Mrs. Huskey and her rosy daughters prepared for me—good coffee, good bread, both corn and wheat, fresh, nice butter, rich milk, nicely cooked chicken and venison, and last though not least, the most delicious honey in the honey-comb. Truly, old man, you may well say you do not starve at the foot of Quonacatoosa. That I did ample justice to Aunt Dolly's cookery you may dare swear. And now, at any early hour, a nice bed having been fixed for me by the careful hands of the prettiest of Aunt Dolly's two pretty daughters, I was soon taking more ease in mine inn, rapt in the elysium of entire unconsciousness, too tired and too sleepy to be disturbed by a single dream.

SATURDAY, Nov. 5th.—I slept at the rate of ten knots an hour, until old Mr. Huskey came and shook me, telling me breakfast was ready. Hastily donning my clothes, I rushed out to the shed where the eating at Mr. H.'s is done, feeling no little pride in the fact that I was up before sunrise.

"Good morning," said I. "There is nothing, Aunt Dolly, after all, for health like being in the country and getting up early."

"I hope you do not call this early, Mister," exclaimed the old woman.

"Why, is it not before sunrise?" said I.

"Yes," she replied, "the sun is just coming up over the Smoky Mountains—but I wish you would step into the house and look at the clock, Mister."

I did so, and will you believe me, reader, when I tell you it was nearly nine!

Being in a gorge of the mountains, and in the shadow of the Great Smoky, the sun is not visible at Mr. H.'s until nearly nine, and it disappears a little after three in the afternoon! What a glorious place for long-spent naps in the morning is Mr. H.'s, and you still have the satisfaction of rising before sun up a thing impossible to accomplish, however found in less favoured localities.

My landlady I find to be quite a character. She tells me she is the mother of seventeen children—nine boys and eight girls. The youngest boy and the two youngest girls still live at home—the others have all married off, and live about in the neighboring coves. Her youngest child, Susan, is a fine looking girl of sixteen or seventeen. The next, Caroline, if drest a la mode, would be called pretty anywhere. The old lady continually reminded me of *Mrs. Poyser* in *Adam Bede,* which I had just been reading,—coarse, rough, strong-minded, sarcastic, and genial withal.

Mrs. Huskey's passions seem to be cleanliness, comfort, and economy—not bad qualities in a housewife. The sugar she uses is maple-sugar of her own make, but so thoroughly clean and white that it has lost the distinctive taste of tree-sugar. She told me that her "old man," as she called her husband, once, when she was sick, had bought some "store sugar;" "but, Mister, when I got well," said she, "I clarified some of it, and you can't think what a power of nastiness I got out of it. I have never used any sugar made by them nasty niggers sence."

The *chef d'oeuvre* of Mrs. Huskey's housewifery is a strong cup of "good *yaller* coffee," as she styles it. I doubt whether a better article can be found on this side of Constantinople than is made by this fat old woman of the Smoky Mountains! She had just sent $20 to Baltimore by one of the merchants of Sevierville, she told me, for the best Java coffee there. One cup, reader, of the coffee she will prepare next spring will be worth a trip across the Atlantic ocean to taste.

After breakfast, as I sat reading in *Dr. Draper's Physiology,* Aunt Dolly caught my eye resting on something which looked very peculiar to me, tacked to the bed-curtains of her bed. Getting up, she waddled across the room, loosed one of them, and brought it to me, exclaiming: "I bet, Mister, you can't tell what that is?"

I was always addressed by the mountaineers as "Mister," never by my name. The article handed to me was some twenty or thirty feet long, three or four inches wide, and looked like the most delicate tissue-paper. The color of the one handed me was red, though there were others tacked to the curtains of different colors, some red, some yellow, &c. I was completely puzzled. "I give it up, Aunt Dolly," said I. "Pray what in the world is it?"

"Smell it," said Aunt Dolly, laconically.

Accordingly I applied it to my proboscis, hoping to get some information in that direction.

"Does it smell any, Mister?" asked Aunt Dolly triumphantly.

"Not a particle; it has no smell whatever that I can perceive," said I.

"See if you can break it," said Mrs. Huskey.

"I do not like to tear it," said I.

"Never mind, Mister, it's strong enough for a plough-line," said Mrs. H.

So I twisted it round my hands, and after tugging at it awhile with all my might, succeeded in breaking off a small piece from one end.

"You have got a powerful grip in your hands, Mister," said Mrs. H. admiringly.

"Well do tell me what it is, Aunt Dolly, for I have not the least idea," said I.

Mrs. Huskey's answer was very short, very characteristic, but very satisfactory: "*Bear*-gut, Mister, *bear*-gut!"

"Well, I never saw anything handsomer," said I.

"Are you married, Mister?" asked Aunt Dolly, graciously.

"No, Madam," said I; "it is my misfortune or my crime never to have been married."

"Well I am sorry," said Mrs. H., "for I was going to send one of these to your wife as a present. They are so pretty—for *ribbons!*" she added, in explanation.

The piece of "Smoky Mountain ribbon" which I had broken off I put carefully away in my pocket-book, and will take great pleasure in showing it to you at any time. You may call at my office.

Now, reader, you may think the foregoing scene exaggerated, but I assure you it occurred literally just as I have detailed it. But let not the city belle toss her head in derision of "Smoky Mountain ribbon," while she retains as necessary adjuncts of her own fastidious toilet—"bear's oil," "castor," "civet," and "musk,"—especially the three last.

To practice for the morrow's climbing, I concluded to walk down and see my guide, Jack Bradley. I found him in the midst of a large heap of Indian corn, which, with the assistance of some of his neighbours, he was busily husking, preparatory to storing away for the winter. Corn-huskings have been so frequently described, that I suppose every one is familiar with these meetings, where, with fun and frolic, neighbours assist each other to garner up the year's supply of corn. Having lent a helping hand for a while, I concluded to walk on down to a Baptist *"protracted* meeting" then going on some two miles further down the mountain—promising Jack, however, to be back in time for his late dinner. Arrived at the church, I found a large gathering of mountain people, drest in every variety of costume—some in hunting shirts—some in roundabouts, and others in their shirt-sleeves. The garments worn by men and women seemed all to be of homespun, manufactured by the fair hands of the mountain women themselves. I saw scarcely any calico, and of course crinoline has never penetrated these coves of the mountains. Eugenia's sway extends not so far. When I got to the "meeting house," a very inflammable sort of person was beating the drum ecclesiastic to a very brimstonish sort of tune, and from the way he held on, I should say it was *long measure.* After he was through, another minister arose to "exhort" and to "call up mourners." Quite a number of both sexes went up to be prayed for, and the same scenes were gone through with, with which every reader is familiar who has been to a "camp-meeting." But more earnestness and apparent devotion I have seldom seen manifested than was shown by these rude rustics of the mountain. The Deity nowhere, that I can find, has said—"give me fine churches only—gorgeously decorated—let worshipers come before me only in purple and fine linen, linsey woolsey I cannot bear with—let the pews in my house all be cushioned with the most slumberous and drowsy materials—let all the books used in my service be gilt edged, and as for music, my taste is decidedly operatic, and my ministers, let them regard an error of pronunciation or grammar, as equally heinous with the infraction of any or all the precepts of the Decalogue." I have been able to find none of all this, but I do find it written, "son give me thy *heart.*" Which injunction, I dare say, is *nearly* as well obeyed in the Smoky Mountains as in 5th Avenue!

Jack Bradley's dinner, after my seven miles walk, I enjoyed very much; all that can be said of it, however, is that there was plenty of meat and bread and any quantity of good humour and appetite among the guests to give it a relish. Renewing my engagement with Jack, for our trip to the "Alum Cave" on the morrow, I set out again for Mr. Huskey's where I arrived just in time to catch Mrs. H., in all the glory of robbing one of her fifty odd bee gums. The great equanimity with which the old lady let swarms of bees crawl all over her, was something not dreamt of in my philosophy before. She worked away as though they were so many house flies, buzzing around her, and when they clustered too thick around the edges of her cap, she brushed them off with a delicacy and gentleness which showed she was thoroughly imbued with the spirit of Uncle Toby. "Go poor devil, I would not hurt a hair of thy head." At last one indignant worker, feeling he could not longer stand by and see the entire industry of his nation swept away in a moment, without at least some show of resistance, pounced upon Aunt Dolly's nose, and most audaciously stung the old woman just upon the end of it. Surely thought I, the old soul will now lose her patience and temper. I was mistaken—for with the utmost *sang froid* she called out, "Susan, go and fetch me my bottle of Radway's; Ready Relief," and applying a few drops of that celebrated preparation to her proboscis, she continued her work of robbery as though nothing had occurred. And for the benefit of Dr. Radway, I will add, that so far as I could see, the nasal organ of Mrs. Husky, after the affliction, seemed to be wholly unaffected by the bee-sting. Upon my expressing some astonishment at the coolness with which she stood bee-stings, she exclaimed—"Well, mister, I reckon I am not so delicate and finiky as your Knoxville gals. I hear a parcel of them come up to Greenbriar Cove this summer, to attend them Springs, and whenever a gnat bit one of them, they would call out for a nigger to bring them their smelling bottles to keep them from fainting. Now, mister, is them the kind of gals you have about Knoxville!" I was obliged to own that it might be possible, we had some so very delicate as she described.

I had quite a long and very interesting conversation with old Mr. Huskey, about bees and their habits. The extent and variety of his knowledge in regard to them, would have done no descredit to a Huber. He seemed to have also made wasps, yellow jackets, hornets and bumble bees his study. The old lady sat working away with her honey, and listening the while at our talk. At last she broke out with, "Well, mister, you seem to have a good deal of book larning about bees—now I want to know what them book makers say is the business of the drones?"

"Why, madam," I replied, "they are, if I may so express myself, the husbands of the queen."

"Hoot a toot," exclaimed Aunt Dolly, "to hear a lawyer talk such nonsense!"

She had somehow ascertained that I was a disciple of Blackstone.

"Well, madam," said I meekly, "I profess, you know, only to tell you what I have read. But what then do you say drones do?"

"Why, mister, my old man there knows more about bees, in one day, than them book men of yourn in all their lives. Husbands of the queen indeed! Now you may go and look through all them gums, and I will give you a silver dollar for every drone you can find in them—but there aint none there. Now, mister, the queen she goes to laying in February and lays on into spring. So you see it's all nonsense what your book men say about the drones being the queen's husbands—cause when she is laying, there aint none of them in the hive," said Aunt D. clinchingly.

"Well, Aunt Dolly," I replied—"you must be right and Huber and all the rest of them wrong. But really now, what is your idea on the subject—what are drones for?"

"Why for nothing else, mister," she exclaimed triumphantly, "but to make music during the summer, while the workers are making honey, to keep them in a good humour, and for company like!" Having given utterance to this new theory of hers, she continued: "The old queen always goes with the young bees when they swarm, and my old man has seen the same queen swarm four or five times. How do you suppose, mister, he knowed it was the same queen?"

"Well, I suppose, he must have clipt her wings," I replied, "for had he cut her head off there would have been an end of her."

"You have hit it mister," said she, "and I do declare I believe a body might larn a lawyer something, if he would only use his own eyes and sense, and not be forever gwine to his books to ax them everything!"

"Madam, I feel very much flattered," said I, "by what you say."

What magnificent honey, in the comb, we had for supper! You may talk of strawberries and cream, mashed peaches and cream, and other such delicacies, but pure fresh honey in the honey-comb surely is the daintiest eating that the great God of nature ever yet let mortal taste!

And what glorious fires, too, they have in the country, where the price of wood is nothing! What immense chimney-places they have! I am not exaggerating, to say that the one at Mr. Huskey's would hold fully half a cord. Night coming on so soon there, bed time was a great way off after supper. So while the old woman and her pretty daughter sat sewing round the fire, the old hunter would recount over to me all his hunting adventures. It seems he has killed some twenty-five or thirty panthers in his time, and bears and deer innumerable. He shot a large panther a few weeks before I was there, and I saw its skin upon the side of his house. From time to time the girls would bring in their aprons full of Irish and sweet potatoes, which, roasted in the ashes, ate very finely I assure you. To-night, while the old fellow was telling me how a panther had once, in the night, run one of his sheep over a precipice, at the foot of which he found it lying dead next morning, and that from appearances he thought the panther had also plunged over the precipice and crawled off wounded:—old Aunt Dolly exclaimed—

"Well, old man, why do you spile that story in that way? why don't you say you found the *painter* lying dead beside the sheep!"

"Because, old woman, that would not be true," mildly replied the husband.

"Pshaw! don't be so particular—other hunters are not so. Take my advice then, and the next time you tell that story, have the painter beside the sheep dead too."

"Mammy, is it true," said Susan, the youngest and the pet, looking up from her potato-roasting, "that when you come home with daddy to this cabin, you had nothing to eat at the *infair* but roasted taters?"

"You get out now—none of your sass," said the old woman with assumed dignity of manner; "There warn't no infair at all; but it is true child, that the first time I eat in this cabin, we had nothing to cook but taters. But if you marry that fellow that was following you from meeting last Sunday, my opinion is, you won have even taters to eat."

At which home thrust the pretty Susan hung her head abashed and dropt the subject.

Sunday, 6th Nov.—Jack Bradley made his appearance this morning before breakfast, and of course before sunrise, ready to start to the Alum Cave with me. Jack carried his gun and a blanket, a hand axe and a sack filled with provisions—for you see we intended to stay all night and next day in the mountains. After breakfast, having added some more bread and meat from Mrs. Huskey's supply, we set out on foot;—I carrying two blankets and my saddle-bags emptied of everything except the quart bottle which was *not* empty. The saddle-bags I needed to bring away specimens from the Cave. Why the bottle was left in it I cannot well tell, unless it was because of Jack's remark, "the rattle-snakes is sometimes powerful bad in the Smoky." But as the times Jack alluded to must have been in July and August, and as all such reptiles were then snug in their winter quarters, that could not have been the reason. After all I suppose we simply *forgot* to take it out— that must have been it.

It is useless to attempt to describe the wild and romantic scenery through which we passed. We went the whole day through laurel thickets, with no path to guide us, passed over rapid mountain torrents by springing from rock to rock, many times at places I should never have thought of attempting, had not Jack gone before, climbed up steep mountain sides by pulling ourselves along by the bushes overhead, and at about two o'clock, arrived at Alum Cave, thoroughly and utterly exhausted by our toilsome climbing and walk of seven miles. The last half mile was nearly perpendicular. I do not believe I could possibly have held out to climb one hundred yards more. Bathed in perspiration, and my heart beating as though it would jump out of my mouth, I threw myself on the ground in the entrance of Alum Cave. As I lay there panting, Jack took one of the blankets and threw it over me, reminding me that it was very cold up there, and that I would certainly make myself sick if I cooled off too rapidly. I thanked him for his considerate kindness.

"But, Jack, is it possible to get any water up here?" said I, "for I feel almost dying from thirst."

"Give me your cup off of your flask," said the kind fellow, "and I will go where the water generally drops out of the sides of the Cave."

Jack soon returned however, saying that it had been so dry all fall, that there was no water there—the cave was as dry as a powder horn. Reader, did you ever find out, by personal experience, what an amount of suffering there is in extreme thirst? I was just about to trespass so far on Jack's good nature and kindness, as to ask him to return down the mountain to the last water we had crossed, when I spied a large onion lying beside me, left there doubtless by some hunter. Seizing upon it, I devoured half of it, and gave the other half to Jack. Now whether such would be the ordinary effect of an onion, I cannot say, but almost immediately all thirst was gone, and my strength returned. Jack also professed to find great benefit from the piece he ate. The passion of Southern and tropical people for onions, may probably depend upon their tendency to allay thirst. You remember that we are told in the Pentateuch, that the Children of Israel, in marching over the deserts of Arabia, cried for the *garlic* and *onions* of Egypt.

Well, here we are at Alum Cave! Some five or six thousand feet up in the air. A wilder, grander spot I never saw before. It is not strictly a cave, it is what they call in mountains "a *rock-house*,"—that is, a precipice so far projecting over its base, as to shelter the space beneath from rain and snow. At Alum Cave the projection is so great that it may well be called a cave. On the brow of the overhanging cliff above there are quite a number of eagle's nests. They live there all the time, Jack told me. I saw several careering about, and heard others screaming among the rocks above. I was reminded of Macaulay's lines in *Horatius:* "Like an eagle's nest hangs on the crest / Of purple Appenine!" I hope they may never be disturbed or driven away—'twould almost be treason to our flag to do so.

At the lower edge or end of the cave is what is called the "Devil's Leap." This is a cliff which, though not quite perpendicular, must be one thousand feet to the bottom. The very thought of taking such a leap almost makes one's hair stand on end. At the upper edge of the cave, the precipice closes quite down to the side of the mountain below, so that progress in that direction is impossible. Just to the west of the cave rises another rugged mountain peak, whose sides are so steep that no one has yet been able to climb to the top of it. This precipice seems within a stone's throw of the mouth of the cave, but as my friend J. C. R. was not along, I cannot say whether one could throw so far or not. Had R. gone with me as he promised, his passion for stone-throwing would certainly have led him to test the matter. Through the sides of this beetling cliff are great holes. They look from where I stood as large as a hogshead, and give the cliff a very peculiar and grand appearance.

The cave is called *Alum,* because the water exuding from the side of the cave is strongly impregnated with alum. At the lower edge of the cave there are immense beds of almost pure alum. I got several large blocks of it loose with Jack's axe, and brought them home with me; they are very beautiful.

At the upper part of this extraordinary cave are large beds of sulphate of magnesia, or Epsom salts. Beautiful pieces of this, too, I brought off with me.

The reader who wishes to refer to a scientific account of this cave, can do so by turning to pages 118 and 119 of Professor Stafford's "Geological

Reconnoisance of Tennessee." By the way, I see by a note of the Professor at that place, that Jack Bradley accompanied him to the cave, and he thanks Jack for his kindness to him. Jack, however, is ignorant that the Professor has thus spoken of him. He told me of the Professor's visit, and seemed to think his passion for knocking off bits of rock and looking at them, indicated that the gentleman was slightly demented—which impression I fear I only partially succeeded in removing from Jack's untutored mind.

The peaks just above the Alum Cave, are called by the hunters *"Bull's Head."* Their altitudes have recently been taken, and one of them has been found to be 6670 feet high. This one has been called Mt. Le Conte, in honour of Professor Le Conte of South Carolina. The other peak is 6559 feet high, and has been called Mt. Safford, for the State Geologist of Tennessee. Mt. Washington, it will be recollected, is 6226 feet high—so the peak in the side of which Alum Cave is, is 444 feet higher than Mt. Washington. Another peak near the Alum Cave has been named Mt. Guyot, in honour of Professor Guyot of New Jersey. It is 6734 feet high.

Having wandered about for an hour or two in the cave, I left, with regret, just before sun-down, to find some water at which to camp for the night. We had intended to stop in the cave, but could not do without water till morning. We found water in about half a mile, and making up a large log-heap fire, we cooked our evening meal—that is, we cooked our meat by frying it stuck on the end of a stick. Reader, nothing can be so delicious as a piece of middling and corn bread after climbing all day in the mountains. I said something about honey awhile back, but not having eaten it under such circumstances, I cannot say whether it would be equal to the middling or not. I am disposed to doubt it, however. We have some fresh pig along, but Jack and I both determined in favour of the middling—though roast pig is not to be sneezed at. It is Lamb, I believe, who says roast pig is a Chinese discovery. A fire having burned down a Chinaman's hut, among the ruins was a pig roasted alive—or rather, *dead.* The Chinaman touching it to ascertain what it was, burnt his fingers, and naturally sticking them in his mouth to cool, made the discovery that roast pig is the sweetest of meat. Lamb says, to this day whenever a man in China wishes to eat roast pig, he places one in his house and burns it over the pig's head—that being the way his ancestors did, and John Chinaman never never innovates.

Supper over, we wrapped our blankets around us, and threw ourselves on the ground before the fire to sleep.

"How clear and beautiful the stars look to night," said I.

"Yes," answered Jack, "but how cold and distant!"

After gazing at them a moment, I turned to pour out to Jack the thoughts his words had called up, and—will you believe it?—he was snoring! Sound asleep in half a minute! astonishing facility that some people have of courting the embraces of "tired nature's sweet restorer—balmy sleep." How I envy them the gift. Good night!

Monday, Nov. 7th.—Up early and mending our fire, we discussed our frugal meal. I felt not the slightest soreness from walking, nor inconvenience from sleeping on the ground in the open air. To-day we mean to go to the top of Quonacatoosa, the highest peak of the Smoky, and to get back to Mr. Huskey's by night—a distance, in all, of sixteen miles. So off we started. After going about three or four miles, we crossed the path by which we would return to Mr. H.'s, and there we left all of our baggage, taking with us nothing but a piece of bread and meat for our dinner.

When within two miles of the top of the gap through which the path leading to North Carolina goes, we came upon five most beautiful falls, or cascades, made by the head waters of the Pigeon, tumbling over the cliffs. Jack informing me they had no name, I determined to christen them, telling Jack their names, so that he might inform future visitors, which he most religiously promised to do. The first one come to near the the Two Mile Tree from the top of the gap, I called *"Elise Cascade,"* in honour of Miss E. R. of South Carolina; the second, about one hundred yards above the first, I called the *"Maria Louisa Falls,"* in honour of a young lady of Mississippi; the third, some two or three hundred yards above, I named the *"Ella Falls,"* in honour of Miss E. B. of Tennessee; the fourth *"Mary's Cascade,"* for Miss M. B. S. of Kentucky, and the fifth the *"Laura Falls,"* for a young lady in Tennessee. It would be difficult to decide which is the most beautiful of these charming cascades. Just by the "Ella Falls" is an overhanging rock, under which a young man from South Carolina, of the name of Psatter lost his life by freezing to death. He endeavoured to cross the mountains against the urgent remonstrance of the people at Mr. Huskey's, who told him a snow storm was coming on. The storm came, and to protect himself from it, crawled under that rock. A week after, he was found sitting there dead, with both his eyes pecked out by the birds. The hunters dug a grave for him where they found him, and there buried him—*requiescat in pace.*

Having reached the gap, we turned to the right or west to get to the top of Quonacatoosa. We climbed along the crest of the mountains on the dividing line between Tennessee and North Carolina. We came at last to a spot which Jack told me was the highest point. I insisted he must be mistaken—that we ought to go further west. I found, in a day or two, that I was right, and again returned by myself, going some six miles from the gap before I got to the top of Quonacatoosa. But more of that anon.

Jack and I got back to Mr. Huskey's about dark, having made our sixteen miles—pretty good walking for one who had a large hemorrhage a few weeks before, was it not? Aunt Dolly soon had us some of her "good yaller coffee." Needed no rocking to sleep to-night.

Tuesday, Nov. 8th.—Hearing something unusual at my door this morning, I jumped out of bed, and peeping through the cracks of the clap-board door, I saw Aunt Dolly standing there swinging a cow-bell to and fro quite earnestly. Is the old soul poking fun at me? thought I. No, that can't be it, for she looks quite serious. Ah, I have it! Aunt Dolly has heard of breakfast bells and gongs—and knowing I am from town, she has concluded to ring a bell too. Having only a sheep and a cow bell, she had to choose between them. I felt complimented that she selected the larger one. Hastily donning my toggery, laughing the while at the breakfast bell of Aunt Dolly, I appeared before her soon as I could get my face straight.

"Well, Mister," she exclaimed, as soon as I took my seat at the table, "I let you sleep, thinking you was tired, till past ten; but I was afraid your coffee would spoil, so I rung you up to breakfast."

"Thank you, Aunt Dolly for doing so. I have slept quite long enough," said I.

I was anxious to hear Aunt D.'s ideas in regard to *crinoline,* and so, drew her out this morning. I assure you her views were very refreshing on that topic—rich, rare and racy. But as Eugenie has abolished the style, and discretion is the better part of valour, I believe I must forego the pleasure of letting Mrs. H. enlighten the world on this most vexed question.

Learning I am within twenty-five or thirty miles of Quallatown, where some fifteen hundred Cherokee Indians reside, I determined to ride over there to-morrow.

Walked down to see Jack and back, and read Draper. By the way this is one of the best books Messrs. Harpers have ever published. I am surprised it is not introduced into every college and high school in the land as a text book.

Wishing to shave this morning after breakfast, I asked Aunt Dolly to favour me with some hot water. In trying it she said, "Well, suppose you try some of the soap I made for my old man;—he thinks it shaves mighty well, and makes powerful fine lather."

Of course I acceded to the polite request, and finding the soap very good, said as much.

"Well, Mister," said Aunt D., "I'll bet you can't tell what that soap is made out of?"

Remembering the *"ribbon"* I gave it up at once.

"Well, it is made out of *painter* grease! Some years since my old man killed a powerful fat painter, and I thought it was a pity to throw it away; and as he was not fit to eat, I concluded to make soap of him. He made sich powerful nice soap that my old man has made me keep some of it ever since for him to shave with.

I wonder how many people in this world ever used panther soap? Of course I begged a piece of it from Aunt Dolly, and brought it home with me.

As we sat down to supper Mr. H.'s son came running in, saying, "Daddy, there's fire in the mountains! and it's coming down this way." To the mountaineer the cry of "fire in the mountains" is more fearful than was, "the Philistines be upon thee," in the days of yore. In a few minutes, sometimes, his house and all are swept away by the tempest of fire let loose upon him by the carelessness of some hunter. The only remedy is to "fire against it," as it is termed; that is, to set fire to the woods all around the premises sought to be protected;—thus fighting fire with fire. If this is done in time, all is safe; but when the wind is high the "fire in the mountains" flies with race-horse speed, rushing upon the humble cabin before any notice has been taken of its approach. Incontinently we all turned out at Mr. H.'s—I to assist the pretty Caroline; and by working like Trojans, were soon able to fire around H.'s sixty or seventy acres of cleared land. But, what a sublime sight a fire in the mountains is! The whirlwind of flame leaps to the highest tree tops, stripping them of every leaf in a moment. Here and there, all through the forest, stand dead trees, rendered thoroughly combustible by the summer's sun. Around these the fire seems to flap its wings with wild and savage joy, leaving them for days and nights after as burning pillars to mark the line of its victorious march.

Wednesday, Nov. 9th.—Started alone to Quallatown on horse-back some thirty miles distant. Sometimes I rode, sometimes I had to climb, on foot, leading my horse after me. I passed by my five cascades, and touched my flask to my lips in honour of each young lady as I passed by her cascade. Now, whether I drank any of the brandy in the flask, further this deponent saith not—to tell that, might injure his character with the aforesaid young ladies, and no one is bound, you know, to criminate himself. How profound is the silence of the vast uninhabited mountains! For fifteen miles there is not a single cabin or sign of life. I saw nothing but one pheasant and one snow bird. For fifteen miles I seemed to be riding through some vast grave-yard—so solemn and gloomy did everything appear. The fire of the night before had filled the atmosphere with a dense cloud of smoke, adding a sombre hue to everything. The wind wailed and sighed through the pine trees. Poor Psalter! what a lonesome time you have lying there all alone, amid the interminable forest of Quonacatoosa!

After getting into North Carolina the path is much better. It leads down the headwaters of the Oconalufta, a most beautiful stream with a beautiful Indian name. The hunters abbreviate the word, calling it the Lufta River.

"Dark as winter is the flow of Lufta rolling rapidly!" The first cabin you come to is that of Mr. Robert Collins, who is more thoroughly acquainted with the mountains than any one in that region. He has, with the assistance of the Indians, cut a path to the top of Quonacatoosa, and from him I learned that I had not gone to the top of Mt. Q. by several miles. From Mr. Collins' to Quallatown the road is pretty good, and the farms on either side of Lufta very beautiful.

Having inquired the road to Qualla, I was told to keep to the plainest road down the Oconalufta—and that a white man by the name of Encloe lived at the Indian town, with whom I could stay. Thinking this sufficient I rode on, making no further inquiries. Presently I saw nothing but Indian huts on either side of my road—the squaws making molasses out of the ubiquitous Sorghum. Thinking I should soon be at Qualla I rode on. As night-fall approached, I met at every step droves of Indians returning from gathering chesnuts, hunting, &c. They were all kinds and sizes—old men and maidens, young men and boys; some with game, some with fish, some with guns, some with bows and arrows, and some with *"blow-guns"*—that is, long pieces of cane bored out, through which an arrow is propelled by the mouth. None of them seemed to know English, and my stock of Cherokee was quite limited, consisting in one phrase, "O-see-u!" which means, "how do you do?" To each group, as I passed, I said "O-see-u," and they all echoed very politely, *O-see-u!* It was now getting dusk rapidly, and every face I saw was quite as dusky. I thought I would enquire if I was in the right road, but I got nothing in response but unintelligible Indian gutturals, so I rode on thinking of Lover's story of, "Lind me the loan of a gridiron." At last it became no laughing matter—I knew I must be out of my road, or before that I should have been at Qualla. I was just about to conclude that I should have to stay at some wigwam, and make the Indian understand I wished something to eat, by putting my finger in my mouth, and doing the same for my horse, when I saw an old squaw in a cabbage patch that I thought I had once seen in Tennessee selling baskets. Calling the old crone I was rejoiced to find that she answered me in broken English. I found I was going up the Soco, and that the road I was in led through nothing but Indian huts for ten or fifteen miles—that I would have to go back and take the other road at the first fork. Arrived at which place I found three paths met there, all equally plain. How to proceed I knew not. Just then, out of the bushes stepped a tall, graceful, handsome Indian girl, well clad, and by far the prettiest one I had seen. She seemed some seventeen or eighteen years old, and had the look of a lady. Accompanying her was a bright faced boy of ten or twelve, with all the bearing of a gentleman's son. The girl, I learned the next day, was the daughter of *Sawnooka,* the head Chief, and the boy his nephew. The young princess had a very pretty Indian name, which I forget, but it is almost as pretty in English. Her name, translated into English, is "The Evening Cloud." She answered "O-see-u" with such a soft and beautiful accent that I felt certain I could make her understand me. So, pointing along one road and then another, I said intermediately, "Qualla?" My beauty, with the sweetest little smile imaginable, and the most musical of tones, said, "Qualla!" and pointed across the creek. "How far is it?" said I, holding up my fingers one at a time. She seemed to catch my meaning immediately, for she answered—"Qualla!" and held up one of her fingers, meaning it was one mile, I supposed. Instinctively I raised my cap and thanked her. She did not understand my words, but seemed to catch my meaning from my manner. Inclining her head in response, "The Evening Cloud" floated gracefully off. I have half a suspicion that I was about half in love with her, on first sight, and that with a woman's quickness she knew it. The "Evening Cloud" had directed me right; in about a mile I came to Quallatown, and found Mr. Encloe's.

Here then, I am, reader, at Quallatown, in Jackson county, N.C., surrounded by some fifteen hundred Indians. At supper Mr. Encloe and I sat down to table with several Indians, and two of Mr. E.'s negroes waited on us. The ends of the earth seemed to have met around that table—Europe, America and Africa, were all there!—the children of Japhet, of Shem, and of Ham. That Scripture occurred to me, as I sat eating—"God shall enlarge Japhet, and he shall dwell in the tents of Shem, and Canaan shall be his servant!"

I found the Indians call the highest point of the Smoky Mountains *"Quonacatoosa."* As the name is very beautiful, and as it is always in better taste to retain the Indian names when we can, I insist that it shall not be called either Mt. *Clingman* or Mt. *Buckly,* as each of these gentlemen seem to wish but that it shall be still known by the euphonious name of *Quonacatoosa.* It is 6,770 feet high, and is the highest spot East of the Rocky Mountains.

Reader, perhaps in some future number I may give you "Quallatown and the ascent of Quonacatoosa." For the present, good night!

2

A Strange Land and a Peculiar People

Will Wallace Harney

Will Wallace Harney (1831–1912) was a frequent contributor to popular magazines, such as *Lippincott's* in which the present essay originally appeared, during the immediate post–Civil War years when the North was "discovering" the South. Towards the end of his life several of Harney's stories, sketches, and poems were published under the title *The Spirit of the South* (1909). Not a particularly skillful writer who inclines towards overblown prose, Harney's claims to fame are twofold. He was one of the pioneers in recognizing the literary potentialities of Florida and also among the first to discuss Appalachia as a distinctive region rather than merely an undeveloped area like all other undeveloped areas. A comparison of Harney's essay with that of R. of Tennessee's is instructive. Whereas the latter refers to the mountaineers as "rude rustics" Harney calls them "strange and peculiar."

Harney's title suggests something of a sensational nature but there is nothing of the sort in his article. He does, however, convey a sense of adventure and of the exotic in this anecdotal discussion. His 1869 journey takes him to a place abounding in "geological and botanical curiosities" among a people having "marked peculiarities of the anatomical frame." Mingled in with Harney's Civil War stories are brief comments on planting by signs, water-witching, and speech, all of which are cited as "peculiar to the mountains." Some of the folk speech examples are valuable for they have not otherwise been reported. This seems to be the case with the dialect word, "I-uns," apparently the first person of the English "we-uns" and "you-uns." Harney's information, however, is sometimes inaccurate as, for example, his assertion that "critter," meaning an animal, "is peculiar to the mountains." But, Harney's significance is not so much in the material he reports but in his characterization of Appalachia as a place in, but not of, America. This claim has been repeated countless times since, even down to the present day.

For information on Harney see Henry D. Shapiro, *Appalachia on Our Mind: The Southern Mountains and Mountaineers in the American Consciousness* (Chapel Hill: University of North Carolina Press, 1978), 3–4, 267–68.

Reprinted from *Lippincott's Magazine* 12 (October 1873): 429–38.

* * *

A NODULE of amygdaloid, a coarse pebble enveloped in a whitish semi-crystalline paste, lies on the table before me. I know that a blow of the hammer will reveal the beauties of its crystal interior, but I do not crush it. It is more to me as it is—more than a letter plucked from the stone pages of time. Coarse and plain, it is an index to a chapter of life. In the occupations of a busy existence we forget how much we owe to the sweet emotional nature which, by mere chance association, retains the dearer part of the past fixed in memory, just as the graceful volutes of a fossil shell are preserved in the coarse matrix of a stony paste. In this way the nodule connects itself with my emotional life, and recalls the incidents of this sketch.

We were journeying over the mountains in the autumn of 1869. Our camp was pitched in a valley of the ascending ridges of the Cumberland range, on the south-east border of Kentucky. At this point the interior valley forms the letter J, the road following the bend, and ascending at the foot of the perpendicular.

It is nearly an hour since sunset, but the twilight still lingers in softened radiance, mellowing the mountain-scenery. The camp-wagons are drawn up on a low pebbly shelf at the foot of the hills, and the kindled fire has set a great carbuncle in the standing pool. A spring branch oozes out of the rocky turf, and flows down to meet a shallow river fretting over shoals. The road we have followed hangs like a rope-ladder from the top of the hills, sagging down in the irregularities till it reaches the river-bed, where it flies apart in strands of sand. The twilight leans upon the opposite ridge, painting its undulations in inconceivably delicate shades of subdued color. Although the night is coming on, the clear-obscure of that dusk, like a limpid pool, reveals all beneath. A road ascending the southern hill cuts through a loamy crust a yellow line, which creeps upward, winding in and out, till nothing is seen of it but a break in the trees set clear against the sky. No art of engineer wrought these graceful bends: it is a wild mountain-pass, followed by the unwieldy buffalo in search of pasturage. Beyond, the mountain rises again precipitously, a ragged tree clinging here and there to the craggy shelves. Around and through the foliage, like a ribbon, the road winds to the top. A blue vapor covers it and the hills melting softly in the distance. At the base of the hills a little river winds and bends to the west through a low fertile bottom, the stem of the J, which is perhaps a mile in width. It turns again, its course marked by a growth of low water-oaks and beeches, following the irregular fold in the hills which has been described.

Leaning against the bluffs hard by the camp is a low white cottage, with its paddock and pinfold, and the cattle are coming up, with bells toning irregularly as they feed and loiter on the way. The supper-horn sends forth a hoarse but mellow fugue in swells and cadences from the farm-house. Over all this sweet rural scene of mountain, valley, river and farm, and over the picturesque camp, with stock, tent and wagons, now brightened by the grace of a young girl, the twilight lingers like love over a home. As I listen and look a soft voice from the carriage at my side says, "Is the ground damp? May I get out?"

I turn to my little prisoner, and as the mingled lights cross her features I see that her wide, dark-gray eyes are swimming in tears. "Why, what is it?" I ask.

"Nothing: everything is so sweet and tranquil. I was wondering if our new home would be like this—not the hills and valleys, you know, but so quiet and homelike."

So homelike! With that vague yearning, we, like so many Southerners of the period, were wagoning from old homesteads, a thousand miles of travel, to a resting-place.

"It will be like home if you are there," I think as I assist her to alight— the burden daily growing lighter in my arms, and heavier on my heart—but I say nothing.

Pretty soon she is at her usual relaxation, looking for shells, ivy berries and roots of wild vines to adorn that never attainable home. The kindly, generous twilight, so unlike the swift shrift of the Florida levels, still lingers; and presently, amid bits of syenite, volcanic tuff and scoria, she has found this nodule of amygdaloid. It differs from the fossil shells and alluvial pebbles she is used to find, and she is curious about it.

I tell the story of the watershed of the Ohio as well as I can—how it was the delta of a great river, fed by the surfage of a continent lying south-eastwardly in the Atlantic; of the luxuriant vegetation that sprang up as in the cypress-swamps of her old home in Louisiana, passing, layer by layer, into peat, to be baked and pressed into bituminous coal, that slops over the flared edges of the basin in Pennsylvania, like sugar in the kettles, and is then burnt to anthracite. I promise her that in some dawn on the culminating peak, when the hills below loom up, their tops just visible like islands in a sea of dusk, I will show her a natural photograph of that old-world delta, with the fog breaking on the lower cliffs like the surf of a ghostly sea. She listens as to a fairy tale, and then I tell her of the stellar crystals concealed in the rough crust of the amygdaloid. She puts it away, and says I shall break it for her when we get home. We have traveled a long way, by different paths, since then, but it has never been broken—never will be broken now.

In addition to the geological and botanical curiosities the mountains afford, my companion had been moved alternately to tears and smiles by the scenes and people we met—their quaint speech and patient poverty. We passed eleven deserted homesteads in one day. Sometimes a lean cur yelped forlorn welcome: at one a poor cow lowed at the broken paddock and dairy. We passed a poor man with five little children—the eldest ten or twelve, the youngest four or five—their little stock on a small donkey, footing their way over the hills across Tennessee into Georgia. It was so pitiful to see the poor little babes-in-the-wood on that forlorn journey; and yet they were so brave, and the poor fellow cheered them and praised them, as well he might. Another miserable picture was at the white cottage near our camp. The lawn showed evidences of an old taste in rare flowers and vines, now choked with weeds. I knocked, and a slovenly negress opened the door and revealed the sordid interior—an unspread bed; a foul table, sickly with the smell of half-eaten food and unwashed dishes; the central figure a poor, helpless old man sitting on a stool. I asked the negress for her master: she answered rudely that she had no master, and would have slammed the door in my face. Why tell the story of a life surrounded by taste and womanly adornments, followed by a childless, wifeless old age? The poor, wizened old creature was rotting in life on that low stool among his former dependents, their support and scorn. The Emancipation Proclamation did not reach him. But one power could break his bonds and restore the fallen son and the buried wife—the great liberator, Death.

The natives of this region are characterized by marked peculiarities of the anatomical frame. The elongation of the bones, the contour of the facial angle, the relative proportion or disproportion of the extremities, the loose muscular attachment of the ligatures, and the harsh features were exemplified in the notable instance of the late President Lincoln. A like individuality appears in their idiom. It lacks the Doric breadth of the Virginian of the other slope, and is equally removed from the soft vowels and liquid intonation of the southern plain. It has verbal and phraseological peculiarities of its own. Bantering a Tennessee wife on her choice, she replied with a toss and a sparkle, "I-uns couldn't get shet of un less'n I-uns married un." "Have you'uns seed any stray shoats?" asked a passer: "I-uns's uses about here." "Critter" means an animal—"cretur," a fellow-creature. "Long sweet'nin'" and "short sweet'nin'" are respectively syrup and sugar. The use of the indefinite substantive pronoun *un* (the French *on*), modified by the personals, used demonstratively, and of "done" and "gwine" as auxiliaries, is peculiar to the mountains, as well on the Wabash and Alleghany, I am told, as in Tennessee. The practice of dipping—by which is meant not baptism, but chewing snuff—prevails to a like extent.

In farming they believe in the influence of the moon on all vegetation, and in pork-butchering and curing the same luminary is consulted. Leguminous plants must be set out in the light of the moon—tuberous, including potatoes, in the dark of that satellite. It is supposed to *govern* the weather by its dip, not *indicate* it by its appearance. The cup or crescent atilt is a wet moon—i.e., the month will be rainy. A change of the moon forebodes a change of the weather, and no meteorological statistics can shake their confidence in the superstition. They, of course, believe in the water-wizard and his forked wand; and their faith is extended to the discovery of mineral veins. While writing this I see the statement in a public journal that Richard Flannery of Cumberland county (Kentucky) uses an oval ball, of some material known only to himself, which he suspends between the forks of a short switch. As he walks, holding this extended, the indicator announces the metal by arbitrary vibrations. As his investigations are said to be attended with success, possibly the oval ball is highly magnetized, or contains a lodestone whose delicate suspension is affected by the current magnetism, metallic veins being usually a magnetic centre. Any mass of soft iron in the position of the dipping-needle is sensibly magnetic, and a solution of continuity is thus indicated by the vibrations of the delicately poised instrument. Flaws in iron are detected with absolute certainty by this method. More probably, however, the whole procedure is pure, unadulterated humbug. In all such cases the failures are unrecorded, while the successes are noted, wondered at and published. By shooting arrows all day, even a blind man may hit the mark sometimes.

During this journey it was a habit with me to relate to my invalid companion any fact or incident of the day's travel. She came to expect this, and would add incidents and observations of her own. In this way I was led to compile the following little narrative of feminine constancy and courage during the late war.

It begins with two boys and a girl, generically divided into brother and sister and their companion, living on the divide-range of mountains between Kentucky and Tennessee. The people raised hogs, which were fattened on the mast of the range, while a few weeks' feeding on corn and slops in the fall gave the meat the desired firmness and flavor. They cultivated a few acres of corn, tobacco and potatoes, and had a kitchen-garden for "short sass" and "long sass"—leguminous and tuberous plants. Apples are called "sour sass." The chief local currency was red-fox scalps, for which the State of Kentucky paid a reward: the people did not think of raising such vermin for the peltry, as the shrewder speculator of a New England State did. They sold venison and bear-meat at five cents a pound to the lame trader at Jimtown, who wagoned it as far as Columbia, Kentucky, and sold it for seventy-five cents. They went to the log church in the woods on Sundays, and believed that Christ was God in the flesh, with other old doctrines now rapidly becoming heretical in the enlightened churches of the east. Living contentedly in this simple way, neither rich nor poor, the

lads grew up, nutting, fishing, hunting together, and the companion naturally looked forward to the day when he would sell enough peltry and meat
to buy a huge watch like a silver biscuit, such as the schoolmaster wore,
make a clearing and cabin in the wild hills, and buy his one suit of store
clothes, in which to wed the pretty sister of his friend.

Then came the war. Although it divided the two friends, the old kindness kept their difference from flaming forth in the vendetta fashion peculiar to the region. It was a great deal that these two young fellows did not
believe that military morality required them to shoot each other on sight.
Yet, on reconsideration, I will not be so sure of their opinion on this point.
Perhaps they thought that, morally and patriotically, they ought to do this,
and were conscious of weakness and failure of duty in omitting to do it.
Perhaps the old goodwill survived for the girl's sake; and if so, I do not think
the Union was the worse preserved on that account.

The young lover went into the ranks of Wolford's regiments of loyal
mountaineers, and rose—slowly at first, more rapidly as his square sense
and upright character became known.

The girl, in her retirement, heard of her lover's advancement with
pride and fear. She distrusted her worth, and found the hard menial duties
of life more irksome than before. Not that she shrank from labor, but she
feared its unfitting her for the refinement required by her lover's new social
position. She had few examples to teach her the small proprieties of small
minds, but a native delicacy helped her more than she was conscious of.
She read her Bible a great deal, and used to wonder if Mary and "the other
Mary" were ladies. She thought Peter was probably an East Tennesseean,
or like one, for when he denied his Lord they said he did not talk like the
others. It seemed hard that to say "we-uns" and "you-uns," as she habitually
did, though she tried not, and to use the simple phrases of her childhood,
should be thought coarse or wrong. Such matters were puzzles to her which
she could not solve. She got an old thumbed Butler's *Grammar* and tried
hard to correct the vocables of her truant tongue. I am afraid she made
poor progress. She had a way of defying that intolerable tyrant, the nomina-
tive singular, and put all her verbs in the plural, under an impression, not
without example, that it was elegant language. She had enough hard work
to do, poor girl! to have been quit of these mental troubles. Her brother
was away, her parents were old, and all the irksome duties of farm-house
and garden fell upon her. She had to hunt the wild shoats on the range, and
to herd them; to drive up the cows, and milk them; to churn and make the
butter and cheese. She tapped the sugar trees and watched the kettles, and
made the maple syrup and sugar; she tended the poultry, ploughed and
hoed the corn field and garden; besides doing the house-work. Her old
parents could help but little, for the "rheumatiz," which attacks age in the

mountains, had cramped and knotted their limbs, and they were fit for nothing except in fine dry weather. Surely, life was hard with her, without her anxieties about her lover's constancy and her own defects. Letter-writing was a labor not to be thought of. She tried it, and got as far as "I am quite well, and I hope these few lines will find you the same," and there stopped. She ascribed the difficulty to her own mental and clerical defects, but I think it lay quite as much in the nature of the relation. How was she to express confidence when she distrusted? how express distrust when her maidenly promptings told her it was an indelicate solicitation? She could say Brindle had gone dry and the blind mare had foaled, or that crops were good; but what was that to say when her heart was thirsting and drying up? She blotted the paper and her eyes and her hands, but she could not write a line. She was a sensible girl, and gave it up, leaving her love to grow its own growth. The tree had been planted in good ground, and watered: it must grow of itself.

By and by military operations brought her lover into the old neighborhood. I cannot say he put on no affectations with his new rank, that he did not air his shoulder-straps a taste too much; but the manly nature was too loyal to sin from mere vanity. He seemed natural, easy, pleased with her, and urged a speedy wedding.

We may guess how the Lassie—we must give her a name, and that will do—worshiped her King Cophetua in shoulder-straps. Had he not stooped from his well-won, honorable height, the serene azure of his blue uniform, to sue for her? In all the humility of her pure loving heart she poured out her thankfulness to the Giver of all good for this supreme blessing of his love.

In the midst of this peace and content her brother appeared with a flag of truce. He was hailed as a prosperous prodigal, for he too was a lad of metal, but he brought one with him that made poor Lassie start and tremble. It was a lady, young and beautiful, clad in deep mourning. Although sad and retiring, there was that dangerous charm about her which men are lured by, and which women dread—a subtle influence of look and gesture and tone that sets the pulses mad. She was going for the remains of her husband, and told a pathetic story, but only too well. She used always the same language, cried at the same places, and seemed altogether too perfect in her part for it to be entirely natural. So, at least, Lassie thought, even while reproaching herself for being hard on a sister in affliction. Yet she could not escape the bitterness of the thought that the widow, Mrs. G——, was "a real lady"—that ideal rival she had been so long dreading in her lover's absence; and now that he had come, the rival had also come.

Her brother dropped a hint or two about the lady: Mrs. G—— had the "shads," "vodles" of bank-stock and niggers, and she paid well for small service. If King Cophetua could get leave to escort her to head-quarters, Mr. G—— would foot the bills and do the handsome thing. It was hard such a woman should have to go on such a sad business alone.

What could his sister say? She had herself put off the wedding a month: she wanted to get her ample store of butter, eggs and poultry to the trader at Jimtown, or, better still, to the brigade head-quarters at Bean's Station. With her own earnings she could then buy such simple muslins for her wedding-dress as became her and would not shame her lover. She wished she had married him, as he had urged, in her old calico gown. If he had asked her now, if he had pressed a little, she would have yielded; but he did not. He seemed to accept the proprieties and woman's will as unalterable. In fact, he did follow Mr. G——'s motions with only too lively an admiration. Perhaps he did not know himself what his feelings were—what this new fever in his pulses meant. Besides the calm, holy connubial love there is a wild animal passion that tears through moral creeds and laws. Once, Lassie saw her brother give him a half-angry stare, that passed into a laugh of cool scorn. "Take care of Mrs. G——," he said to King Cophetua. "You will get bit there if you don't look out."

How the sister would have pressed that warning had she dared! Innocent as her lover might be, she believed that Mr. G—— saw the growing passion and encouraged it. But there was nothing to take hold of. There was nothing bold, forward or inviting in her manner. If a lady has long lashes, must she never droop them lest she be charged with coquetry? May not a flush spring as naturally from shy reserve as from immodesty?

Lassie's lover did take charge of this dangerous siren to escort her to the headquarters at Louisville. But just before starting he came to Lassie with a certain eagerness, as one who is going into battle might, and assured her, again and again, of his faith. Did he do this to assure her or himself? I think the last.

How weary the month was! She occupied herself as well as she could with her sales and purchases, making a very good trade. The brigade had been at Bean's Station long enough to eat up all the delicacies to be found there, so that the little maid, who was a sharp marketer, got fabulous prices. She made up her simple wedding furniture, gave her mother a new gown and underwear, and pleased her old father with a handsome jean suit, the labor of her own nimble fingers. All that belonged to her would appear well on that day, as became them and her.

At any other time she would have followed up that thrifty market at Bean's Station. She would have huckstered around the neighborhood, and made a little income while it lasted; but now she had no heart for it. Her lover's leave was out, yet his regimental associates knew nothing about him.

A week after the day set for her marriage her brother came again with the flag of truce. He too was vexed—not so much at Cophetua's absence as at not meeting the widow, whom he had been sent to escort to the Confederate lines. But he treated his sister's jealous suspicions with a dash of scorn: "There was nothing of that kind, but if Cophetua would fool with a loaded gun, he must expect to be hurt. If ever there was a hair-trigger, it was Mrs. G——."

"Who is she?" asked his sister eagerly. "Tell me: you say there is something strange, dangerous about her, and I can see it. Who is she?"

"Humph!" said her brother. "She is a lady, and that is enough. If she is dangerous, keep out of her way."

This only deepened the mystery. But she had no time to think. Her brother left in the morning. In the afternoon the colonel of her lover's regiment came to see her with a very grave face. The young man had been arrested for dealing with the enemy, harboring spies and furnishing information of the disposition and number of the Federal forces. "If we could get at the true story of his connection with that woman," said the colonel, "I am satisfied he has only been indiscreet, not treacherous. He is one of my best, most trusted officers, and his arrest is a blot on the regiment. If he will tell anybody, he will tell you. Can you go to Louisville at once?"

Yes, at once. The traveling-dress, made up for so different an occasion, was donned, and under escort she went, by a hundred miles of horseback ride, to the nearest railway station. There was no tarrying by the way: the colonel's influence provided relays. On the evening of the third day she was with her lover.

It was as the colonel had supposed: the woman had got her lover in her toils, and he had been imprudent. He had every reason for believing that her story of her husband's remains was false. She was a dealer in contraband goods: this much he knew. Other officers, of higher rank, knew as much and corresponded with her. If they chose to wink at it, was he, a subordinate, to interfere? She had trusted him, depended on him, and he had a feeling that it would be disloyal to her confidence to betray her, to pry into what she concealed, and expose what his superiors seemed to know. But after she was gone the story leaked out: she was not only a smuggler, but a very dangerous spy. Some one must be the scapegoat, and who so fit as the poor, friendless Tennesseean who had escorted her to head-quarters and acted for her in personal matters?

That was his story, but what a poor story to tell to a court-martial! What was she to do? Poor, simple child of the woods! what did she know of the wheels within wheels, and the rings of political influence by which a superior authority was to be invoked? She knew nothing of these things, and there was no one to tell her. She thought of but one plan: her brother could find that woman. She would seek her out—she would appeal to her.

We need not follow her on that return journey and her visit to the Confederate camp. Fortunately, the Confederates were nearer than she supposed. She came upon their pickets, and was taken into the commanding officer's presence. Her brother was sent for, and when he came, she told him she was looking for his friend, Mrs. G——.

"Looking for her!" said her brother. "Why, that is what we moved out this way for! She is in camp now. We brought her and her luggage in last night."

She eagerly entreated to be taken to her, and was carried to a pavilion, or marquee, a little apart from the officers' quarters. Mrs. G—— came in richly but simply dressed, attended by a portly, handsome, but rather dull-looking officer.

"Why, Lassie!" said Mrs. G—— in surprise. "So you have come to see me? Here are the remains of my poor dear," she added with a little laugh, presenting the gentleman. "Do you think he is worth all the trouble I took to get him?"

"Ha! much pleased! Devilish proper girl!" said the man with a stupid blush, justifying the stolidity of his good looks.

"But where is your *preux chevalier,* Captain Cophetua? I declare, I almost fell in love with him myself. Frank here is quite jealous."

"Oh, Mrs. G——," broke out the poor girl, "you have killed him! They are going to try him and hang him for helping you to spy."

"Nonsense!" said the lady with a little start. "The poor fellow did nothing but what, as a gentleman, he was compelled to do. But how can I help you?"

"Save him," said Lassie. "You have your wealth, your wit, your husband: I have but him!" and she sank down in tears.

"Stupid," said the lady, turning sharply on her husband, "tell me what to do? Don't you see we must not let them hang the poor fellow?"

"Of course not," said the big man dryly. "Just countermand the order of execution. No doubt the Yankees will obey: I would."

"Of course you would: a precious life you would lead if you did not," said his wife, who evidently commanded that squad. "Never mind: there is more sense in what you said than I expected of you.—Jane," to the smart maid who attended on her, "pen, ink, paper and my portfolio."

Opening the last, she took out a bundle of letters, and, running them rapidly over as a gambler does his cards, she selected one. "This," she said to Lassie, "is a note from General ———. It is written without the slightest suspicion of my character as a spy; but you will see it involves him far more dangerously than your friend. He cannot well explain it away. Keep the letter. I will write to him that you have it to deliver over in return for his kind assistance in effecting the release of your friend. Don't fear: I ask him to do nothing he ought not to do without asking, and you give him a letter that would be misconstrued if it fell into other hands."

Armed with these instructions and the letters, Lassie returned home, passed on to Louisville, and delivered her message. The general promptly interfered thanking her for calling his attention to the matter. His influence, and a more exact understanding of the means and appliances of the artful widow in obtaining information, effected her lover's acquittal and restoration to his former position.

"I owe her my life and good name," said the tall Tennesseean, taking Baby No. 2 from her arms. "I-uns ain't wuth such a gal."

"No," say I drily. "What did you take him for?" to her. Then I get the answer before quoted. But my companion, with a truer perception, went quietly up and kissed her Tennessee sister, a little to the surprise of both, I think, but they seemed touched by the silent little tribute more than by any words.

I have spoken of the character of the hostilities in that "debatable land." War is a bad thing always, but when it gets into a simple neighborhood, and teaches the right and duty of killing one's friends and relatives, it becomes demoniac. Down about Knoxville they practiced a better method. There it was the old game of "Beggar your Neighbor," and they denounced and "confiscated" each other industriously. Up in the poor hills they could only kill and burn, and rob the stable and smoke-house. We were shown the scene of one of these neighborhood vengeances. It is a low house at the side of a ravine, down whose steep slope the beech forest steps persistently erect, as if distrusting gravitation. Thirty Confederates had gathered in that house at a country-side frolic, and the fiddle sang deep in the night. The mountain girls are very pretty, having dark, opalescent eyes, with a touch of gold in them at a side glance, slight, rather too fragile figures, and the singular purity of complexion peculiar to high lands.

The moon went down, and the music of the dance, the shuffle of feet on the puncheon floor, died away into that deep murmurous chant, the hymn of Nature in the forest. The falling water, sleeping in the dam or toiling all day at the mill, gurgles like the tinkling of castanets. Every vine and little leaf is a harp-string; every tiny blade of grass flutes its singly inaudible treble; the rustling leaves, chirping cricket, piping batrachian, the tuneful hum of insects that sleep by day and wake by night, mingle and flow in the general harmony of sound. The reeds and weeds and trunks of trees, like the great and lesser pipes of an organ, thunder a low bass. The melancholy hoot of the owl and the mellow complaint of the whippoorwill join in the solemn diapason of the forest, filling the solitudes with grand, stately marches. There are no sounds of Nature or art so true in harmony as this ceaseless murmur of the American woods. So accordant is it with the solemn majesty of form and color that the observer fails to separate and distinguish it as an isolated part in the grand order of Nature. He has felt an indescribable awe in the presence of serene night and unbounded shadow, but to divide and distinguish its constituent causes were as vain as in the contour and color of a single tree to note the varied influence of rock, soil and river.

Over the little farm-house in the ravine in the fall of 1863 there fell with the sinking moon these solemn dirges of the great dark woods. The stars brightened their crowns till *Via Lactea* shone a highway of silver dust or as the shadow of that primeval river rolling across the blue champaign of heaven. The depths of repose that follow the enjoyment of the young irrigated their limbs, filling the sensuous nerves and arteries with a delicious narcotism—a deep, quiet, healthful sleep, lulled by the chant of the serene mother-forest.

Hush! A light step, like a blown leaf: the loose wooden latch rises at the touch of a familiar hand; familiar feet, that have trodden every inch of that poor log floor, lead the way; and then all at once, like a bundle of Chinese crackers, intermingled with shrieks and groans and deep, vehement curses, the rapid reports of pistols fill the chambers. The beds, the floors, the walls, the doors are splashed with blood, and the chambers are cumbered with dead and dying men in dreadful agony. Happy those who passed quietly from the sweet sleep of Nature to the deeper sleep of death! Of thirty young men in the flush of youth, not one escaped. Six Federal scouts had threaded their way since sunset from the Federal lines to do this horrible work. Oh, Captain Jack, swart warrior of the Modocs! must we hang you for defending your lava-bed home in your own treacherous native way, when we, to preserve an arbitrary political relation, murder sleeping men in their beds?

Let me close with an incident of that great game of war in which the watershed of the Ohio was the gambler's last stake.

The Confederacy was a failure in '62, held together by external pressure of hostile armies. It converted civil office into bomb-proofs for the unworthy by exempting State and Federal officials; it discouraged agriculture by levying on the corn and bacon of the small farmers, while the cotton and sugar of the rich planter were jealously protected; it discouraged enlistment by exempting from military service every man who owned twenty negroes, one hundred head of cattle, five hundred sheep—in brief, all who could afford to serve; it discouraged trade by monopolies and tariffs. But for the ubiquitous Jew it would have died in 1862–63, as a man dies from stagnation of the blood. It was the rich man's war and the poor man's fight.

This suicidal polity had its effect. Cut off from all markets, the farmer planted only for family use. At the close of the war the people of Georgia,

Alabama and the Carolinas had to be fed by the government. The farmers in 1864 refused to feed the Southern army. Seventy thousand men deserted east of the Mississippi between October 1, 1864, and February 3, 1865. They were not recalled: the government could not feed them. The Confederacy was starved out by its own people—rather by its own hideous misgovernment, for the people were loyal to the cause.

One fact was apparent as early as 1863: the South would not feed the armies—the North must. That plan, so far as the Atlantic coast States were involved, was foiled at Gettysburg. The only resource left was in the West, the watershed of the Ohio, which Sherman was wrenching out of General Johnston's fingers. In a military point of view, the great Confederate strategist was right: he was conducting the campaign on the principle Lee so admirably adopted in Virginia. But President Davis had more than a military question to solve. If he could not seize the granaries of the watershed, the Confederacy would die of inanition.

That was what caused the change of commanders in Georgia, and the desperate invasion that blew to pieces at Nashville; and it introduces a little scouting incident upon which the event of that campaign may have partially turned. General Hood was in camp at Jonesborough: Forrest and Wheeler were detached to destroy Sherman's single thread of supplies. Prisoners pretended to have been on half rations, and the sanguine opinion at headquarters was that Sherman was on the grand retreat. That able strategist had disappeared, enveloping himself in impenetrable vidette swarms of cavalry. He had pocketed one hundred thousand men in the Georgia hills, and no one could find them; at least, General Hood could not.

But others were not sanguine about Sherman's falling back. General Jackson selected a major, a trusted scout, with twenty-five men, with instructions to find Sherman. Again and again the scout and his little band tried to pierce that impenetrable cloud, and could not. Then he tried another plan. He snapped up a Federal squad, clothed a select part of his little band in their uniform, and sent the others back with the prisoners. Then he plunged boldly into the cloud, a squad of Federals, bummers, pioneers. Does the reader reflect upon the fine fibre of the material requisite for such an exploit? It is not strength, courage or tactical cunning that is most wanted, but that most difficult art, to be able to put off your own nature and put on another's—to play a part, not as the actor, who struts his hour in tinsel and mouths his speeches as no mortal man ever walked or talked in real life, but as one who stakes his life upon a word, an accent; requiring subtlety of analytic sense and quickness of thought. Polyglot as was the speech of the Federal forces, suspicion, started by that test, would run rapidly to results. Then there was the danger of collision with the regiment whose uniform they had assumed. Swift, constant motion was required.

They swept to the head of the column, and, to be brief, the first Federal pontoon thrown across the Chattahoochee was laid with the assistance of these spies. The leader threw himself on the bank and counted the regiments by their insignia as they passed, until he saw the linen duster and the glittering staff of the great commander himself as they clattered over the bridge. Then to Campbellton, hard by, where their horses were rendezvoused, and whip and spur to Jonesborough.

A council of war was sitting when the scout arrived. He was hurried into it presence, and told his story with laconic, military precision. Sherman's whole force was across the Chattahoochee and marching on Jonesborough, twenty miles away.

"I have sure information to the contrary," said the commanding general, singularly deceived by a strong conviction, enforced by scouts who depended on rumor for authority. "It is some feint to cover the general movement."

"I counted the flags, guidons, regimental insignia—such force of cavalry, artillery, infantry," giving the numbers. "I saw and recognized General Sherman," said the scout briefly.

His report was not, even then, credited, but, as a precaution, a brigade of cavalry, with his battalion in the van, was sent out to beat up the enemy. A short distance beyond Flint River they struck the Federal line, which attacked at once, without feeling—a sure indication of strength. The battalion was hurled back on the brigade, the brigade rushed across Flint River, and back into the infantry line, now throwing up tardy entrenchments at Jonesborough. The rest is historical. It was but one of the rash throws of the dice for that great stake, the watershed of the Ohio, and helps to show the principles of military action by which it was lost.

3

Through Cumberland Gap on Horseback

James Lane Allen

Novelist and short-story writer James Lane Allen (1849–1925) had his first major success in 1891 with the publication of his first book, *Flute and Violin, and Other Kentucky Tales and Romances.* For the next twelve years he enjoyed great popularity both at home and abroad; his fame began to decline after the publication of *The Mettle of the Pasture* (1903) although he never fell completely out of favor with readers and critics. Today, he is best remembered for his novel *The Choir Invisible* (1897), fiction based on historical facts, and for works such as *The Blue Grass Region of Kentucky and Other Kentucky Articles* (1892), a selection of essays previously published in a variety of magazines. He is generally regarded as the writer most responsible for making Kentucky's Bluegrass Region well known to his countrymen and Europeans.

Allen spent the years 1872–84 as a teacher but in 1885 decided to change careers. For some time he had been practicing the art of writing and, after leaving the schoolroom behind, went to New York seeking advice on how to further himself in his newly chosen profession. There, he was told to find "a definite field" and explore it for literary materials, the suggestion being made that he might concentrate on the region around his hometown of Lexington. Acting on this recommendation, Allen set out to establish Kentucky as his "definite field." Beginning in 1886 Allen published a series of articles on the state, the first on the bluegrass region and the second, the essay reprinted here. His concern was to seek out local color, record it in a descriptive sketch that could then be utilized in a short story. This method of guaranteeing the "realism" of his fiction was not unique to Allen, it had been the *modus operandi* of several earlier writers, the most notable being Mary Noailles Murfree who wrote under the name Charles Egbert Craddock.

"Through Cumberland Gap on Horseback" is notable for several reasons. Allen's theme of "two Kentuckys" is, of course, not original but it is more clearly stated here than in most previous writings. His characterization of the mountaineers and their culture as arrested early English civilization would be reiterated by many later authors, and his assertion that they were people "utterly exempt from all the obligations and

Reprinted from *Harper's Magazine* 73 (June 1886): 50–66. Later reprinted in *The Blue-Grass Region of Kentucky and Other Kentucky Articles* (New York: Harper and Brothers, 1892), 217–46.

other phenomena of time" and lacking a "sense of accumulation" is merely his own version of sentiments expressed by several other writers. But, Allen's recognition that the existence of a "second Kentucky" was problematic and required solution was innovative. Although Allen agreed that the mountaineer's culture was relatively homogeneous, he differed from several later writers in noting that their folk traditions "vary widely in different localities." Allen's quest for local color largely focused on folklore and material culture. Thus, he describes housing, dress, place-names, food, and various rites of passage. His comments on some funeral practices are among the earliest published remarks on an aspect of folklife that is generally overlooked.

For information on Allen see John Wilson Townsend, *James Lane Allen, a Personal Note* (Louisville: Courier-Journal Job Printing Company, 1928); Grant Knight, *James Lane Allen and the Genteel Tradition* (Chapel Hill: University of North Carolina Press, 1935). Allen published a second Kentucky mountain sketch, "Mountain Passes of the Cumberland" (1890), that consisted mainly of a description of the economic development of Appalachia. That essay also appeared in *Harper's* and, like "Through Cumberland Gap on Horseback," was reprinted in *The Blue-Grass Region of Kentucky.*

* * *

I

Fresh fields lay before us. We had left the rich, rolling plains of the blue-grass region in central Kentucky, and had set our faces toward the great Appalachian uplift on the southeastern border of the State. There Cumberland Gap, that high-swung gateway through the mountain, abides as a landmark of what Nature can do when she wishes to give an opportunity to the human race in its migrations and discoveries, without surrendering control of its liberty and its fate. Such way-side pleasures of hap and scenery as might befall us while journeying thither were ours to enjoy; but the especial quest was more knowledge of that peculiar and deeply interesting people, the Kentucky mountaineers. It can never be too clearly understood by those who are wont to speak of "the Kentuckians" that this State has within its boundaries two entirely distinct elements of population—elements distinct in England before they came hither, distinct during more than a century of residence here, and distinct now in all that goes to constitute a separate community—occupations, manners and customs, dress, views of life, civilization. It is but a short distance from the blue-grass country to the eastern mountains: but in traversing it you detach yourself from all that you have ever experienced, and take up the history of English-speaking men and women at the point it had reached a hundred or a hundred and fifty years ago.

Leaving Lexington, then, which is in the midst of the blue-grass plateau, we were come to Burnside, a station on the Cincinnati Southern Railway

some ninety miles away, where begin the navigable waters of the Cumberland River, and the foot-hills of the Cumberland Mountains.

Burnside is not merely a station, but a sub-mountainous watering-place.
The water is mostly in the bed of the river. We had come thither to get
horses and saddle-bags, but to no purpose. The hotel was a sort of transition
between the civilization we had left behind and the primitive society we
were to enter. On the veranda were some distinctly modern and conventional red chairs; but a green and yellow gourd vine, carefully trained across
so as to shut out the distant landscape, was a novel bit of local color. Under
the fine beeches in the yard was swung a hammock, but it was made of
boards braced between ropes, and was covered with a weather-stained
piece of tarpaulin. There were electric bells in the house that did not seem
to electrify anybody particularly, and near the front entrance three barrels
of Irish potatoes, with the tops off, spoke for themselves in the absence of
the bill of fare. After supper, the cook, a tall, blue-eyed white fellow, walked
into my room without much explanation, and carried away his guitar, showing that he had been wont to set his sighs to music in that quarter of the
premises. Of a truth he was right, for the moon hung in that part of the
heavens and no doubt ogled him into many a midnight frenzy. Sitting under
a beechtree in the morning, I had watched a child from some distant city,
dressed in white, and wearing a blue ribbon around her goldenish hair,
amuse herself by rolling old barrels (potato barrels probably, and she may
have had a motive) down the hill-side and seeing them dashed to pieces
on the railway track below. By-and-by some of the staves of one fell in, the
child tumbled in also, and they all rolled over together. Upon the whole, it
was an odd overtopping of two worlds, and a promise of entertaining things
to come. When the railway was first opened through this region a young
man established a fruit store at one of the stations, and as part of his stock
laid in a bunch of bananas. One day a native mountaineer entered. Arrangements generally struck him with surprise, but everything else was soon
forgotten in an adhesive contemplation of the mighty aggregation of fruit.
Finally he turned away with this note: "Blame me if them ain't the darnedest
beans I ever seen!"

The scenery around Burnside is very beautiful, and the climate salubri-
ous. In the valleys was formerly a fine growth of walnut, but the principal
timbers now are oak, ash, and sycamore, with some yellow pine. I heard of
a wonderful walnut-tree formerly standing, by hiring vehicles to go and see
which the owner of a livery-stable made three hundred and fifty dollars. Six
hundred were offered for it on the spot; but the possessor, never having
read of the fatal auriferous goose, reasoned that it would bring him a fortune
if cut into many pieces, and so ruined it, and sold it at a great loss. The hills
are filled with the mountain limestone—that Kentucky oolite of which the

new Cotton Exchange in New York is built. Here was Burnside's depot of supplies during the war, and here passed the great road—made in part a corduroy road at his order—from Somerset, Kentucky, to Jacksborough, over which countless stores were taken from central Kentucky and regions further north into Tennessee. Supplies were brought up the river in small steam-boats or through in wagons, and when the road grew impassable, pack-mules were used. Sad sights there were to be seen in those sad, sad days: the carcasses of animals at short intervals from here to Knoxville, and now and then a mule sunk up to his body in mire, and abandoned, with his pack on, to die. Here were batteries planted and rifle-pits dug, the vestiges of which yet remain: but where the forest timbers were then cut down a vigorous new growth has long been reclaiming the earth to native wildness, and altogether the aspect of the place is peaceful and serene. Doves were flying in and out of the cornfields on the hill-sides: there were green stretches in the valleys where cattle were grazing: and these, together with a single limestone road that wound upward over a distant ridge, recalled the richer scenes of the blue-grass lands.

Assured that we would find horses and saddle-bags at Cumberland Falls, we left Burnside, and were soon set down at a station some fifteen miles further along, where a hack was to convey us to another of those mountain watering-places that are being opened up in various parts of eastern Kentucky for the enjoyment of a people that has never cared to frequent in large numbers the Atlantic seaboard.

Capps was the driver of the hack—a good-looking mulatto, wearing a faded calico shirt and a straw hat of most uncertain shape and variable colors.

Capps stopped frequently on the road: once to halloo from the lofty ridge along which we were riding, down into a valley, to inquire of a mountain woman, sitting in her door with a baby in her arms, whether she had any "millions"; and again at a way-side grocery to get a bushel of meal from a man who seemed to be dividing his time pretty equally between retailing meal and building himself a new house. Here we asked for a drink of water, and got it—hot from a jug, there being no spring near. Capps knew a hawk from a handsaw when it came to talking about "moonshine" whiskey, and entered with some zest into a technical discrimination between its effects and those of "old Bourbon" on the head after imbibing incontinently. His knowledge seemed based on experience, and we waived a discussion.

Meantime the darkness was falling, and the scenery along the road grew wilder and grander. A terrific storm had swept over these heights, and the great trees lay uptorn and prostrate in every direction, or reeled and fell against each other like drunken giants—a scene of fearful elemental violence. On the summits one sees the tan-bark oak; lower down, the white oak; and lower yet, fine specimens of yellow poplar; while from the valleys to the crests is a dense and varied undergrowth, save where the ground has been burnt over, year after year, to kill it out and improve the grazing. Twenty miles to the southeast we had seen through the pale-tinted air the waving line of Sellico Mountains, in Tennessee. Away to the north lay the Beaver Creek and the lower Cumberland, while in front of us rose the craggy, scowling face of Anvil Rock, commanding a view of Kentucky, Tennessee, and Virginia. The utter silence and heart-oppressing repose of primeval nature was around us. The stark white and gray trunks of the immemorial forest dead linked us to an inviolable past. The air seemed to blow upon us from over regions illimitable and unexplored, and to be fraught with unutterable suggestions. The full-moon swung itself aloft over the sharp touchings of the green with spectral pallor; and the evening-star stood lustrous on the western horizon in depths of blue as cold as a sky of Landseer, except where brushed by tremulous shadows of rose on the verge of the sunlit world. A bat wheeled upward in fantastic curves out of his undiscovered glade. And the soft tinkle of a single cow-bell far below marked the invisible spot of some lonely human habitation. By-and-by we lost sight of the heavens altogether, so dense and interlaced the forest. The descent of the hack appeared to be into a steep abyss of gloom; then all at once we broke from the edge of the woods into a flood of moonlight: at our feet were the whirling, foaming rapids of the river: in our ears was the near roar of the cataract, where the bow-crowned mist rose and floated upward and away in long trailing shapes of ethereal lightness.

The Cumberland River runs and throws itself over the rocks here with a fall of seventy feet, or a perpendicular descent of sixty-two, making a mimic but most beautiful Niagara. Just below, Eagle Falls drops over its precipice in a lawny cascade. The roar of the cataract, under favorable conditions, may be heard up and down stream a distance of ten or twelve miles. You will not find in mountainous Kentucky a more picturesque spot. The hotel stands near the very verge of the waters; and the mountains, rising one above another around, shut it in with infinite security from all the world.

While here, we had occasion to extend our acquaintance with native types. Two young men came to the hotel, bringing a bag of small, hard peaches to sell. Slim, slab-sided, stomachless, and serene, mild and melancholy, they might have been lotus-eaters, only the suggestion of poetry was wanting, and they had probably never tasted any satisfying plant whatsoever. Their unutterable content came not from opiates, but from their souls. If they could sell their peaches, they would be happy; if not, they would be happy. What they could not sell, they could as well eat; and since no bargain was made on this occasion, they took chairs on the hotel veranda, opened the bag, and fell to. One of us tried to catch the mental attitude of the Benjamin of his tribe, while the other studied his bodily pose.

"Is that a good 'coon dog?"
"A mighty good 'coon dog. I hain't never seed him whipped by a varmint yet."
"Are there many 'coons in this country?"
"Several 'coons."
"Is this a good year for 'coons?"
"A mighty good year for 'coons. The woods is full o' varmints."
"Do 'coons eat corn?"
"'Coons is bad as hogs on corn, when they git tuk to it."
"Are there many wild turkeys in this country?"
"Several wild turkeys."
"Have you ever caught many 'coons?"
"I've cotched high as five 'coons out o' one tree."
"Are there many foxes in this country?"
"Several foxes."
"What's the best way to cook a 'coon?"
"Ketch him and parbile him, and then put him in cold water and soak him, and then put him in and bake him."
"Are there many hounds in this country?"
"Several hounds."

Here, among other discoveries, was a linguistic one—the use of "several" in the sense of a great many, probably an innumerable multitude, as in the case of the 'coons.

They hung around the hotel for hours, as beings utterly exempt from all the obligations and other phenomena of time.

"Why should we only toil, the roof and crown of things?"

True to promise, the guide bespoken the evening before had made all arrangements for our ride of some eighteen miles—was it not forty?—to Williamsburg, and in the afternoon made his appearance with three horses. Of these three horses one was a mule, with a strong leaning toward his father's family. Of the three saddles one was a side-saddle, and another was an army saddle with refugee stirrups. The three brutes wore among them some seven shoes. My own mincing jade had none on. Her name may have been Helen of Troy (all horses are named in Kentucky), so anciently must her great beauty have disappeared. She partook with me of the terror which her own movements inspired, and if there ever was a well-defined case, outside of literature, in which the man should have carried the beast, this was the one. While on her back I occasionally apologized for the injustice by handing her some sour apples, which she appeared never to have tasted before, just as it was told me she had never known the luxury of wearing shoes. It is often true that the owner of a horse in this region is too poor or too mean to have it shod.

Our route from Cumberland Falls lay through what is called "Little Texas," in Whitley County—a wilderness some twenty miles square. I say route, because there was not always a road; but for the guide, there would not always have been a direction. Rough as the country appears to one riding through it on horseback, it is truly called "flat woods country," and viewed from Sellico Mountains, whence the local elevations are of no account, it looks like one vast sweep of sloping, densely wooded land. Here one may see noble specimens of yellow poplar in the deeper soil at the head of the ravines; pin oak and gum and willow, and the rarely beautiful wild-cucumber. Along the streams in the lowlands blooms the wild calacanthus, filling the air with fragrance, and here in season the wild camellia throws open its white and purple splendors. There are few traces of human presence in this great wilderness, except along the road that one comes to by-and-by; and it seems easy to believe that Williamsburg had a population of one hundred and thirty-nine in 1870, having increased fourteen souls in ten years. Since then, indeed, railway connection has caused it to double its population many times—once within the past two years.

There is iron in Whitley County so pure as to require some poorer ore to be mixed with it to smelt it successfully, while other requires only limestone to flux it; but we did not come upon "Swift's Silver Mine." From the Tennessee line south to the Ohio line north one may pass through counties that claim the location of "Swift's Silver Mine"—that El Dorado spot of eastern Kentucky, where, a hundred and twenty-five years ago, one John Swift said he made silver in large quantities, burying some thirty thousand dollars and crowns in a large creek: fifteen thousand dollars a little way off, near some trees, which were duly marked: a prize of six thousand dollars close by the fork of a white oak: and three thousand dollars in the rocks of a rock house: all which, in the light of these notes, it is allowed any one who will to hunt for.

It was not until we had passed out of "Little Texas" and reached Williamsburg, had gone thence to Barbourville, the county seat of the adjoining county of Knox, and thence again into Bell County, that we stopped between Flat Lick and Cumberland Ford, on the old Wilderness road from Kentucky through Cumberland Gap. Around us were the mountains—around us the mountaineers whom we wished to meet intimately face to face.

II

Straight, slim, angular, white bodies: average or even unusual stature, without great muscular robustness: features regular and colorless, unanimated but intelligent in the men sometimes fierce, and in the women often sad: among the latter occasional beauty of a pure Greek type; a manner shy and deferential, but kind and fearless: eyes with a slow, long look of mild inquiry, or of general listlessness, or of unconscious and unaccountable melancholy: the key of life a low minor strain, losing itself in reverie; voices monotonous in intonation; movements uninformed by nervousness—these are characteristics of the Kentucky mountaineers. Living to-day as their forefathers lived before them a hundred years ago; hearing little of the world, caring nothing for it; responding feebly to the influences of civilization near the highways of travel in and around the towns, and latterly along the lines of railway communication, but sure to live here, if uninvaded and unaroused, in the same condition for a hundred or more years to come; utterly lacking the spirit of development from within; utterly devoid of any sympathy with that boundless and ungovernable activity which is carrying the Saxon race in America from one state to another, whether better or worse. The origin of these people, the relation they sustain to the different population of the central region—in fine, an account of them from the date of their settling in these mountains to the present time, when, as it seems, they are on the point of losing their isolation, and with it their distinctiveness—would imprison phases of life and character valuable alike to the special history of this country and to the general history of the human mind. The land in these mountains is all claimed, but it is probably not all covered by actual patent. As evidence, a company has been formed to speculate in lands not secured by title. The old careless way of marking off boundaries by going from tree to tree, by partly surveying and partly guessing, explains the present uncertainty. Many own land by right of occupancy, there being no other claim. The great body of the people live on and cultivate little patches which they either own, or hold free, or pay rent for with a third of the crop. These not infrequently get together and trade farms as they would horses, no deed being executed. There is among them a mobile element—squatters—who make a hill-side clearing and live on it as long as it remains productive, when they move elsewhere. This accounts for the presence throughout the country of abandoned cabins, around which a dense new forest growth is springing up. Leaving out of consideration the few instances of substantial prosperity, the most of the people are abjectly poor, and they appear to have no sense of accumulation. The main crops raised on the patch are corn and potatoes. By the scant gardens will be seen little patches of cotton, sorghum, and tobacco; flax also, though less than formerly. Many make insufficient preparation for winter, laying up no meat, but buying a piece of bacon now and then, and paying for it by working. In some regions the great problem of life is to raise two dollars and a half during the year for county taxes. Being pauper counties, they are exempt from State taxation. Jury fees are highly esteemed and much sought after. The manufacture of illicit mountain whiskey—"moonshine"—was formerly, as it is now, a considerable source of revenue to them; and a desperate self-destructive sub-source of revenue from the same business has been the betrayal of its hidden places. There is nothing harder or more dangerous to find now in the mountains than a secret still.

Formerly, also, digging "sang," as they call ginseng was a general occupation. For this, of course, China was a great market. It has nearly all been dug out now except in the wildest parts of the country, where entire families may still be seen "out sangin'." They took it into the towns in bags, selling it at a dollar and ten cents—perhaps a dollar and a half—a pound. This was mainly the labor of the women and the children, who went to work barefooted, amid briers and chestnut burrs, copperheads and rattlesnakes. Indeed, the women prefer to go barefooted, finding shoes a trouble and constraint. It was a sad day for the people when the "sang" grew scarce. A few years ago one of the counties was nearly depopulated in consequence of a great exodus into Arkansas, whence had come the news that there "sang" was plentiful. Not long since, too, during a season of scarcity in corn, a local store-keeper told the people of a county to go out and gather all the mandrake or "May-apple" root they could find. At first only the women and children went to work, the men holding back with ridicule. By-and-by they also took part, and that year some fifteen tons were gathered, at three cents a pound, and the whole county thus got its seed-corn. Wild ginger was another root formerly much dug; also to less extent "golden-seal" and "bloodroot." The sale of feathers from a few precarious geese helps to eke out subsistence. Their methods of agriculture—if methods they may be styled—are of the most primitive sort. Ploughing is commonly done with a "bull-tongue," an implement hardly more than a sharpened stick with a metal rim; this is often drawn by an ox, or a half-yoke. But one may see women ploughing with two oxen. Traces are made of hickory or papaw, as also are bed-cords. Ropes are made of lynn bark. In some counties there is not so much as a fanning-mill, grain being winnowed by pouring it from basket to basket, after having been threshed with a flail, which is a hickory withe some seven feet long. Their threshing-floor is a clean place on the ground, and they take up grain, gravel, and some dirt together, not knowing or not caring for the use of a sieve. The grain is ground at their homes in a hand tub-mill, or one made by setting the nether millstone in a bee-gum, or by cutting a hole in a puncheon-log and sinking the stone into it. There are, however, other kinds of mills: the primitive little water-mill which may be considered almost characteristic of this region; in a few places improved water-mills, and small steam-mills. It is the country of mills, farmhouses being furnished with one about as frequently as with coffee-pots or spinning wheels. A simpler way of preparing corn for bread than by even the hand-mill is used in the late summer and early autumn, while the grain is too hard for eating as roasting-ears, and too soft to be ground in a mill. On a board is tacked a piece of tin through which holes have been punched from the under side, and over this tin the ears are rubbed, producing a coarse meal, of which "gritted bread" is made. Much pleasure and doubtless much health do they get from their "gritted bread," which is withal a sweet and wholesome bit for a hungry man. Where civilization has touched on the highways and the few improved mills have been erected, one may see women going to mill with their scant sacks of grain, riding on a jack, a jennet, or a bridled ox. But this is not so bad as in North Carolina, where, Europa-like, they ride on bulls.

Aside from such occupations as have been herein pointed out, the men have nothing to do—a little work in the spring, and nine months' rest. They love to meet at the country groceries and cross-roads, to shoot matches for beef, turkeys, or liquor, and to gamble. There is with them a sort of annual succession of amusements. In its season they have the rage for pitching horseshoes, the richer ones using dollar pieces. In consequence of their abundant leisure, the loneliness of the mountains, which draws them thus together, their bravery and physical vigor, quarrels among them are frequent, and feuds are deadly. Personal enmities soon serve to array entire families in an attitude of implacable hostility, and in the course of time relatives and friends take sides, and a war of extermination ensues. The special origins of these are various: blood heated and temper lost under the influence of "moonshine"; reporting on the places and manufacturers of this; local politics; the survival of resentments engendered during the civil war—these, together with all causes that lie in the passions of the human heart and spring from the constitution of all human society, often make the remote and insulated life of these people turbulent, reckless, and distressing. But while thus bitter and cruel toward each other, they present to strangers the aspect of a polite, kind, unoffending, and most hospitable race. They will divide with you shelter and warmth and food, however scant, and will put themselves to trouble for your convenience with an unreckoning, earnest friendliness and good nature that is touching to the last degree. No sham, no pretence; a true friend, or an open enemy. Of late they have had much occasion to regard new-comers with distrust, which, once aroused, is difficult to dispel, and now they will wish to know you and your business before treating you with that warmth which they are only too glad to show.

The women appear to do most of the work. From the few sheep, running wild, which the farm may own, they take the wool, which is carded, reeled, spun, and woven into fabrics by their own hands and on their rudest implements. One or two spinning-wheels will be found in every house. Cotton from their little patches, too, they clear by using a primitive hand cotton-gin. Flax, much spun formerly, is now less used. It is surprising to see from what appliances they will bring forth exquisite fabrics; all the garments for personal wear, bedclothes, and the like. When they can afford it they make carpets.

They have, as a rule, luxuriant hair. In some counties one is struck by the purity of the Saxon type, and their faces in early life are often very handsome. But one hears that in certain localities they are prone to lose their teeth, and that after the age of thirty-five it is a rare thing to see a woman whose front teeth are not partly or wholly wanting. The reason of this is not apparent. They appear passionately fond of dress, and array themselves in gay colors and in jewelry (pinchbeck), if so be that their worldly estate justifies the extravagance. Oftener, if young, they have a modest shy air, as if conscious that their garb is not even decorous. Whether married or unmarried, they show much natural diffidence. It is told that in remoter districts of the mountains they are not allowed to sit at the table with the male members of the household, but serve them as in ancient societies. Commonly, too, in going to church, the men ride and carry the children, while the women walk. Dancing in some regions is hardly known, but in others is a favorite amusement, and in its movements men and women show the utmost grace. The mountain preachers oppose it as a sin.

Marriages take place early, and they are a most fecund race. I asked them time and again to fix upon the average number of children to a family, and they gave as the result seven. In case of parental opposition to wedlock, the lovers run off. There is among the people a low standard of morality in their domestic relations, the delicate privacies of home life having little appreciation where so many persons, without regard to age or sex, are crowded together within very limited quarters.

The dwellings—often mere cabins with a single room—are built of rough-hewn logs, chinked or daubed, though not always so. Often there is a puncheon floor and no chamber roof. One of these mountaineers, called into court to testify as to the household goods of a defendant neighbor, gave in as the inventory, a string of pumpkins, a skillet without a handle, and "a wild Bill." "A wild Bill" is a bed made by boring auger-holes into a log, driving sticks into these, and overlaying them with hickory bark and sedgegrass—a favorite couch. The low chimneys, made usually of laths daubed, are so low that the saying, inelegant though true, is current, that you may sit by the fire inside and spit out over the top. The cracks in the walls give ingress and egress to a child or a dog. Even cellars are little known, their potatoes sometimes being kept during winter in a hole dug under the hearth-stone. More frequently a trap-door is made through the plank flooring in the middle of the room, and in a hole beneath are put potatoes, and, in case of some wealth, jellies and preserves. Despite the wretchedness of their habitations and all the rigors of a mountain climate, they do not suffer with cold, and one may see them out in snow knee-deep clad in low brogans, and nothing heavier than a jeans coat and hunting shirt.

The customary beverage is coffee, bitter and black, not having been roasted but burnt. All drink it from the youngest up. Another beverage is "mountain tea," which is made from the sweet-scented golden-rod and from winter-green—the New England checkerberry. These decoctions they mollify with home-made sorghum molasses, which they call "long sweetening," or with sugar, which by contrast is known as "short sweetening." Of home government there is little or none, boys especially setting aside at will parental authority; but a sort of traditional sense of duty and decorum restrains them by its silent power, and moulds them into respect. Children while quite young are often plump to roundness, but soon grow thin and white and meager like the parents. There is little desire for knowledge or education. The mountain schools have sometimes less than half a dozen pupils during the few months they are in session. A gentleman who wanted a coal bank opened engaged for the work a man passing along the road. Some days later he learned that his workman was a school-teacher, who, in consideration of the seventy-five cents a day, had dismissed his academy.

Many, allured by rumors from the West, have migrated thither, but nearly all come back, from love of the mountains, from indisposition to cope with the rush and vigor and enterprise of frontier life. Theirs, they say, is a good lazy man's home.

Their customs respecting the dead are interesting. When a husband dies his funeral sermon is not preached, but the death of the wife is awaited, and *vice versa.* Then a preacher is sent for, friend and neighbor called in, and the respect is paid both together. Often two or three preachers are summoned, and each delivers a sermon. More peculiar is the custom of having the services for one person repeated; so that the dead get their funerals preached several times months and years after their burial. I heard of the unspeakably pitiful story of two sisters who had their mother's funeral preached once every summer as long as they lived. You may engage the women in mournful conversation respecting the dead, but hardly the men. In strange contrast with this regard for ceremonial observances is their neglect of the graves of their beloved, which they do not seem at all to visit when once closed, or to decorate with those symbols of affection which are the common indications of bereavement.

Nothing that I have ever seen in this world is so lonely, so touching in its neglect and wild irreparable solitude, as one of these mountain grave-yards. On some knoll under a clump of trees, or along some hill-side where dense oak-trees make a mid-day gloom, you walk amid the unknown, un-distinguishable dead. Which was father and which mother, where are lover and stricken sweetheart, whether this is the dust of laughing babe or croon-ing grandam, you will never know; no foot-stones, no head-stones; some-times a few rough rails laid around as you would make a little pen for swine. In places, however, one sees a picket-fence put up, or a sort of shed built over.

Traditions and folk-lore among them are evanescent, and vary widely in different localities. It appears that in part they are sprung from the early hunters who came into the mountains when game was abundant, sport unfailing, living cheap. Among them now are still-hunters, who know the haunts of bear and deer, needing no dogs. They even now prefer wild meat—even "possum" and "'coon" and ground-hog—to any other. In Bell County I spent the day in the house of an aged woman—eighty years old, in fact—who was a lingering representative of a nearly extinct type. She had never been out of the neighborhood of her birth, knew the mountains like a garden, had whipped men in a single-handed encounter, brought down many a deer and wild turkey with her own rifle, and now, infirm, had but to sit in her cabin door and send her trained dogs into the depths of the forests to discover the wished-for game: a fiercer woman I never looked on.

III

Our course now lay direct toward Cumberland Gap, some twenty miles southward. Our road ran along the bank of the Cumberland River to the ford, the immemorial crossing-place of early travel—and a beautiful spot—thence to Pineville, situated in that narrow opening in Pine Mountain where the river cuts it, and thence through the valley of Yellow Creek to the wonderful pass. The scenery in all this region is one succession of densely wooded mountains, blue-tinted air, small cultivated tracts in the fertile valleys, and the lovely watercourses.

Along the first part of our route the river slips crystal clear over its rocky bed, and beneath the lone green pendent branches of the trees that crowd the banks. At the famous ford it was only two or three feet deep at the time of our crossing. This is a historic point. Here was one of the oldest settlements in the country; here the Federal army destroyed the houses and fences during the civil war: and here Zollikoffer came to protect the Ken-tucky gate that opens into East Tennessee. At Pineville, just beyond, we did not remain long. For some reasons not clearly understood by travellers a dead line had been drawn through the midst of the town, and not knowing on which side we were entitled to stand, we hastened on to a place where we might occupy neutral ground. The situation is strikingly picturesque: the mountain looks as if cleft sheer and fallen apart, the peaks on each side rising almost perpendicularly, with massive overhanging crests wooded to the summits, but showing gray rifts of the inexhaustible limestone. The river when lowest is here at an elevation of nine hundred and sixty feet, and the peaks leap to the height of twenty-two hundred. Here in the future will most probably pass a railroad, and be a populous town, for here is the only opening through Pine Mountain from "the brakes" of Sandy to the Tennessee line, and tributary to the watercourses that center here are some five hundred thousand acres of timber land.

The ride from Pineville to the Gap, fourteen miles southward, is one of the most beautiful that may be taken. Yellow Creek becomes in local pronunciation "Yaller Crick." One cannot be long in eastern Kentucky without being struck by the number and character of the names given to the watercourses, which were the natural avenues of migratory travel. Few of the mountains have names. What a history is shut up in these names! Cutshin Creek, where some pioneer, they say, damaged those useful members; but more probably where grows a low greenbrier which cuts the aforesaid parts and riddles the pantaloons. These pioneers had humor. They named one creek "Troublesome," for reasons apparent to him who goes there: another, "No Worse Creek," on equally good grounds: another, "Defeated Creek": and a great many, "Lost Creek." In one part of the country it is possible for one to enter "Hell fur Sartain," and get out at "Kingdom Come." Near by, strange to say, there are two liquid impersonations of Satan, "Upper Devil" and "Lower Devil." One day we went to a mountain meeting which was held in "a school-house and church-house" on "Stinking Creek." One might suppose they would have worshipped in a more fragrant locality; but the stream is very beautiful, and not malodorous. It received its name from its former canebrakes and deer licks, which made game abundant. Great numbers were killed for choice bits of venison and hides. Then there are "Ten-mile Creek" and "Sixteen-mile Creek," meaning to clinch the distance by name; and what is philologically interesting, one finds numerous *"Trace* Forks" originally *"Trail* Forks."

Bell County and the Yellow Creek Valley serve to illustrate the incalculable mineral and timber resources of eastern Kentucky. Our road at times cut through forests of magnificent timbers—oak (black and white), walnut (black and white), poplar, maple, and chestnut, beech, lynn, gum, dogwood, and elm. Here are some of the finest coal fields in the known world, the one on Clear Creek being fourteen feet thick. Here are exceedingly pure canned coals and cooking coals. At no other point in the Mississippi Valley are iron ores suitable for steel-making purposes so close to fuel so cheap. With an eastern coal-field of ten thousand square miles, with an area equally large covered with a virgin growth of the finest economic timbers, with water-courses feasible and convenient, it cannot be long before all eastern Kentucky will be opened up to the great industries of the modern world. Enterprise has already turned hither, and the distinctiveness of the mountaineer race has already begun to disappear. The two futures before them are, to be swept out of these mountains by the in-rushing spirit of contending industries, or to be aroused, civilized, and developed.

Long before you come in sight of the great Gap, the idea of it dominates the mind. At length, while yet some miles away, it looms up, sixteen hundred and seventy-five feet in elevation, some half a mile across from crest to crest, the pinnacle on the left towering to the height of twenty-five hundred.

It was late in the afternoon when our tired horses began the long, winding, rocky climb from the valley to the brow of the pass. As we stood in the passway, amid the deepening shadows of the twilight and the solemn repose of the mighty landscape, the Gap seemed to be crowded with two invisible and countless pageants of human life, the one passing in, the other passing out; and the air grew thick with ghostly utterances—primeval sounds, undistinguishable and strange, of creatures nameless and never seen by man; the wild rush and whoops of retreating and pursuing tribes; the slow steps of watchful pioneers; the wail of dying children and the songs of homeless women; the muffled tread of routed and broken armies—all the sounds of surprise and delight, victory and defeat, hunger and pain and weariness and despair, that the human heart can utter. Here passed the first of all the white race who led the way into the valley of the Cumberland; here passed that small band of fearless men who gave the Gap its name; here passed the "Long Hunters"; here rushed the armies of the civil war; here has passed the wave of westerly emigration, whose force has spent itself only on the Pacific slopes; and here in the long future must flow backward and forward wealth beyond the dreams of avarice. Beneath the shadows of the pinnacle—the limit of our journey reached—we slept that night in the Poor Valley of Tennessee.

4

The Moonshiner of Fact

Francis Lynde

One aspect of Appalachian and southern mountain life that has appealed to the outside world is that of moonshining, the illegal production of whiskey. As the author of the following essay indicates, the conception exists that all mountaineers are moonshiners. Indeed, he even subscribed to the viewpoint himself "and so was once moved to add his mite to the unrealities of mountain literature." Probably the earliest published references to Appalachian moonshining are two brief notes by Alfred Haddon Guernsey in *Harper's Weekly* (1867). Since that time a relatively large body of literature on the topic has been issued. A few of these publications include an unsigned article "The Moonshine Man: A Peep into His Haunts and Hiding Places," *Harper's Weekly* 21 (October 21, 1877): 820–22; George Wesley Atkinson, *After the Moonshiners, By One of the Raiders; A Book of Thrilling Yet Truthful Narratives* (Wheeling, West Virginia: Frew and Campbell, Steam Book and Job Printers, 1881); Leonidas Hubbard, Jr., "The Moonshiner at Home," *Atlantic Monthly* 90 (August 1902): 234–41; Charles S. Pendleton, "Illicit Whiskey Making," *Tennessee Folklore Society Bulletin* 12 (March 1946): 1–16; Loyal Durrand, Jr., "'Mountain Moonshining' in East Tennessee," *Geographical Review* 46 (April 1956): 168–81; Cratis D. Williams, "Moonshining in the Mountains," *North Carolina Folklore* 15 (May 1967): 11–17; Esther Kellner, *Moonshine; Its History and Folklore* (Indianapolis: Bobbs-Merrill, 1971); Jess Carr, *The Second Oldest Profession: An Informal History of Moonshining in America* (Englewood Cliffs, New Jersey: Prentice-Hall, 1972); and Joseph Earl Dabney, *Mountain Spirits: A Chronicle of Corn Whiskey from King James' Ulster Plantation to America's Appalachians and the Moonshine Life* (Lakemont, Georgia: Copple House Books, Inc., 1974); Dabney, *Mountain Spirits II: The Continuing Chronicle of Moonshine Life and Corn Whiskey, Wines, Ciders & Beers in America's Appalachians* (Lakemont, Georgia: Copple House Books, Inc., 1980).

Francis Lynde (1856–1930) was a native of New York who spent the last thirty-nine years of his life on a farm near Chattanooga, Tennessee. For approximately twenty

Reprinted from *Lippincott's Magazine* 57 (January 1896): 66–76.

years Lynde was employed by various railroad companies, eventually holding executive positions with several Western roads. While working in New Orleans for the Union
Pacific he made the acquaintance of Maurice Thompson, a novelist later to achieve
fame for *Alice of Old Vincennes* (1900), who encouraged Lynde to become a writer.
His first article was rejected but the incipient author set himself the task of learning how
to write successful fiction. By 1893 Lynde was able to give up his railroad position and
devote all of his time to literary work. His first novel, *A Question of Courage,* appeared
in 1894 and for the next thirty-six years he produced about one novel a year, many of
them based upon his railroad experiences. Lynde also wrote a lengthy number of
magazine articles, at least two of which dealt with moonshining. As the essay reprinted
here indicates, Lynde desired that his own writings be factually accurate.

Although Lynde was very prolific and a literary figure of secondary importance in
his own day there is no lengthy study of his life and career. A list of his publications,
along with a brief biographical sketch, appears in the 1930–31 edition of *Who's Who
in America.*

*   *   *

Some three years ago, my friend Pencraft made a flying trip through Dixie.
He was writing a novel at the time, in which one of the characters was a
Southern colonel, and, having never been south of the Potomac, he concluded to take a week in which to familiarize himself with the type. We
met on the platform of the railway station at Cartersville, Georgia; and while
we were waiting for the train, Pencraft complained rather bitterly of the
scarcity of types in the South.

"So far as I can see, you have no types," said he. "I've been down here
five days now, and I've covered the ground pretty thoroughly from Virginia
to Louisiana. In all that time I haven't met Colonel Carter, or the Major, or
the Joel Chandler Harris darky, or the Miss Murfree mountaineer."

It was certainly exasperating, considering the time spent, and, wishing
to be helpful, I looked about among the groups on the platform for something typical enough to assuage Pencraft's disappointment. There was a
family of country-people standing near us, and, suggesting the possibility
of literary material therein, I stood aside while Pencraft made his notes.
When completed, they read something like this:

"Southern types:—family Georgians. Father tall, stoop-shouldered—
fifty or more—cotton shirt, brown jeans, discouraged slouch hat—stands
with hands in pockets and stares hard at nothing. Mother—same type—
sallow complexion, faded brown eyes, thin hair (no particular color), general aspect of dejection accented by snuff-stick in mouth. Elder daughter
with unwashed baby—younger edition of old woman—has lateral curvature
of spine from carrying child on left arm—stands silently, like the others, as
if in rapt contemplation. (*Mem.*—Find out if Southern ruralist has subcon-

scious esoteric leanings.) Son—awkward youth of voice-changing age—belongs to the ruminants, and is slowly surrounding himself with circle of tobacco-juice—is greatly abashed when sister gives him baby to hold while she ties ribbon on younger daughter's hair. Younger daughter—magnificent type country beauty—black hair and eyes—tinted brunette skin—black eyebrows, nearly straight—nose slightly aquiline and large enough to harmonize with firm mouth and chin. Is decked out with much care—evidently going on journey, which others have come to speed. Train arrives—silent leave-taking in which no one speaks. Black-eyed beauty kisses whole family, beginning with stoop-shouldered father. Awkward youth much disconcerted—fights when his turn comes, but is handicapped by baby. Beauty's eyes snap—her face lights up with aroused determination—is evidently not accustomed to refusals—grapples with unwilling lout—kisses him twice very forcibly—then darts up the steps into the car."

Pencraft read the sketch aloud when we had taken our seats in the Pullman, and asked for a classification of his subjects. I answered that the people were most probably Georgia mountaineers.

"Mountaineers? Not moonshiners?"

"Why, certainly. All mountaineers are moonshiners. Didn't you know that?"

"Great Scott! and you never so much as hinted at the possibility! You're no man's friend. Never mind though: I can make a story out of nothing more than that girl's face."

He did it; and, so far as the character of the young woman was concerned, it was doubtless a true picture. Beyond the heroine, however, verisimilitude handed the pen to literary tradition. The old man became a buccaneer whose regard for human life was a minus quantity; the boy was transformed into a promising young cutthroat to whom all strangers were "revenuers" and such to be "killed up" without compunction. And for the minor characters there was a "Jake Manders," an "Anderson" or two, and a young mountaineer whose name I forget,—all as ferocious desperadoes as one would seek to avoid in a day's journey. They were the moonshiners of fiction; and, regarded as artistic conceptions of the necessary accessories to the development of a dramatic and somewhat painful plot, they left nothing to be desired.

The following year Pencraft made himself a holiday, and spent it tramping in the mountains of East Tennessee. When he came out, I took occasion to ask if he had been gathering material for more moonshiner stories. He appeared to be somewhat disquieted at the question, and would have avoided it. When that was no longer possible, he burst out with some warmth:

"See here: what did you let me make a bally fool of myself for? You knew there were no such people as I put into that story, and yet you let me go on and write myself down an idiot along with the rest of them. Why couldn't you give me a hint?"

I said something about not wishing to interfere with the literary unities.

"Unities be hanged! I went into the mountains at Morristown with a Winchester, a revolver, and a guide, determined to sell my life at a fancy price. On the third day I sent the whole armament back to town and went on empty-handed and alone. I might have sent my money back, too, for all the use I had for it. These people are poor and ignorant and simple and primitive,—anything you like along that line,—but they're as hospitable as the Arabs, as honest as they are simple, and as harmless as unspoiled country-folk are anywhere."

"Then you didn't meet any moonshiners?"

"Didn't I? I've eaten with them, drunk with them, slept in their cabins, stood watch with them—in short, I've been a moonshiner myself for the past month. And now do you know what's going to happen? I do the 'new books' for *The Literary Junia,* and the first fellow who comes out with a fairy-tale about these people will get himself slated."

"How about 'The Moonshiner's revenge,' by Pelton Pencraft?"

"Oh, Lord! I forgot that asinine thing. Well, I suppose that shuts me off. I can't commit hari-kari. It would be playing Samson, wouldn't it?—and I can't afford to bury myself in the ruins. Just the same, old man, I'll owe you a grudge as long as I live; you've stood by and watched me miss the chance of a lifetime."

Among those who know him best, Pencraft has the name of being an enthusiast and an extremist; none the less, in the matter of the moonshiners he told the simple truth. He erred, however, in believing his experience with the mountaineers to be singular; it was merely that of every one who has gone among them in any character whatsoever save that of informer, spy, or "revenuer."

Not to draw too heavily upon the account of hearsay, a leaf from my own notebook will serve to illustrate further the difference between the moonshiner of the novelists and the dramatists and the illicit distiller of fact. I had been whipping the streams for reluctant trout all day up and down the gorges of the great mountain which the fathers belittled by calling it Walden's Ridge, when I stumbled unexpectedly upon a mountaineer who had doubtless been watching my progress up the rocky ravine. He was armed with the traditional rifle; his position commanded the path; and the gorge was wild enough and isolated enough to form the stage-setting for any scene of violence, however lurid and blood-curdling. According to all precedent, I should have been arrested, tried by summary process, and—if

not rescued by some mountain Pocahontas—flung from the brow of a precipice, to become food for the unkindly buzzards. For the sake of the unities
in literature, it is to be regretted that nothing of the kind occurred. The
man nodded, gave and received the inevitable "howdy," and would have
gone about his business without further speech if I had not inquired the
way to a cabin whose owner was my friend's friend.

"Ol' Jeff Ande'son's?—hit's a good two hour an' more f'om the head o'
this yer gulch. Was ye 'lowin' to put up over-night 'long 'ith Jeff?"

I admitted it, emphasizing the past tense; whereupon the man who—
speaking after the manner of the craft—should have shot me down without
ceremony, or led me captive to my undoing, invited me to pass the night
under his roof. The invitation was accepted willingly enough; and, inasmuch
as the man's personality and mode of life were typical, they may be taken
as the part which represents the whole.

The cabin, one degree more primitive than the "two pens and a passage" of the valley farmer, stood at the entrance to a shallow cove at the
head of the ravine. Logs and split shingles were the materials used in its
construction, and these but sparingly, since there were but a single room
and a loft,—the latter reached by a ladder from the outside. Small as it was,
however, the cabin sheltered three generations. There was the old grandfather in the chimney-nook, a veteran of the Mexican War, and there were
the mountaineer and his wife, with a gamut of children running up from the
toddler under foot to the eighteen-year-old daughter, whose uninherited
beauty and heroic disloyalty to kith and kin have furnished the groundwork
for many a moving tale of the story-tellers.

If the cabin and its indwellers were typically primitive, the welcome
was in perfect keeping. When the dogs had been pacified by sundry kicks
and a well-aimed blow or two from the rifle-butt, I was bidden enter.

"Come awn, come right in, stranger—ef ye kin git in for the dirt an' the
chillern. We ain't nowise fixed for comp'ny, but they's allens a welcome,
sich as hit air."

In the cramped interior, which at once served the various purposes of
kitchen, dining-room, parlor, and dormitory, the wife and daughter were
preparing the evening meal in front of the wide open fireplace; but room,
and the most comfortable split-bottomed chair in the cabin, were quickly
forthcoming for the guest. In the waiting interval, the grandfather, in whom
age had thawed the ice of mountain reticence, beguiled the time with
stories of the pioneers; but the others were silent, and one who knew them
not might have doubted the sincerity of his welcome.

In a little while the housewife raked the sweet potatoes from the ashes
and drew the corn-pones out of the hearth oven; but not even the supper,
which was a bountiful one for a mountaineer's cabin, served to breach the

barrier of reticence. After the first invitation, "Make ye an arm, stranger, make ye an arm an' reach—ye're full welcome," the silence which is golden came again and brooded over the table; but afterwards, when we gathered about the fire to smoke, the spell was broken by degrees. Being a hunter and fisherman from necessity, my host was naturally curious to know why one should turn his back upon the comforts of the town to tramp un-counted miles through the mountains with a fly-rod; and in the cross-fire of question and answer he was led by littles to speak more freely of the things concerning himself and his kind.

"Yes, I reckon you-uns'd 'low hit was a toler'ble pore sort of a way to git along. Times I 'low that-a-way myself, but hit thess nacherly look like there hain't nothin' else for we-uns to do. Times I 'low hit'd be better to th'ow hit all up an' go somewhars else—Texas, 'r the like. Ever be'n to Texas?"

I answered, and then diplomatically steered him away from the divagation.

"No, thar's toler'ble little that we-uns kin do to raise money. Times hit seem like we-uns cayn't make enough to pay the taxes. The lan's mighty pore on these yer mountings, an' what little craps we-uns do git cayn't be hauled nowhars whar they'll sell."

At this point in the conversation I ventured to suggest that some of the mountaineers knew how to transmute their corn into something which was at once portable and salable. My host eyed me in silence for a while speaking again when his native shrewdness assured him that he was not entertaining an enemy unawares.

"'Stillin' hit, I reckon ye mean. Yes, but thar's a heap o' resk about that thar. The revenuers air purty toler'ble thick, an' a 'stiller nev' knows what minute's a-gwine to be the nex'. I nev' could onderstand why the gover'*ment*'s so mighty partic'lar 'bout that thar. Bes' we-uns kin do, thar cayn't be enough liquor 'stilled in the mountings to hurt nobody; more'n all that, we-uns fit for the gover'*ment* in war-times, an' hit thess nacherly look like hit ortn't to be hard on we-uns atter that thar'."

I agreed with him honestly, and then tried to show that the net of the revenue law, though set to capture the big fish, must of necessity take in both great and small; that the underlying principle of equal rights would not admit of exceptions.

"I reckon ye're right; but hit do seem like the gover'*ment* mought raise hits taxes 'thout starvin' we-uns plum out'n the country. I ric'lect a man on this yer ve'y mounting that nev' did 'stil nare bushel o' corn 'ceppin' to raise the money to pay his'n taxes; an' yit they-all tuk him an' sent him to the pen'tenshry, an' the woman an' chillern might' nigh starve' 'fore ever he come back."

Admitting the premises, the argument was unanswerable; and presently my host went out, and I saw him no more. The reason for his absence suggested itself at once, and the inference became a conclusion when the daughter gave me a candle and left me at the foot of the ladder which led to my bed in the loft. It was a moonlight night, and the small cornfield filling the cove behind the cabin made a yellow blur on the landscape. Here was a farmer who appeared to keep no animals, and whose holding was miles from any market and practically inaccessible for wheeled vehicles. Why should the man raise corn under such conditions? There was only one answer to that question, and it received its confirmation in the morning when my host kept his bed during breakfast.

"Andy he's sort o' porely this mornin', an' I 'lowed he'd better not git up," said the wife, in explanation; but he seemed to be sleeping soundly enough, so far as one might judge from appearances, and I went my way silently incredulous, regretting a little that I had been so near to a secret still without having been permitted to share the vigil of its owner.

I have quoted the mountaineer at some length, both because it is interesting to get the moonshiner's point of view in his own speech and because he sets forth in so many words the reasons for his existence. Whiskey-making is no new thing to him. His forefathers, the pioneers, who cleared the way before the advancing army of agriculturists in the early settlement of the region west of Virginia and the Carolinas, were distillers before they were law-breakers. Aside from wood-craft, it was their single art, handed down from father to son from the days when their ancestors made poteen in the Irish hills or usquebaugh in the Scottish Highlands.

When the Excise Act of 1891 made their industry illegal, the mountaineers were already a people separate and apart, insulated by their manners, customs, and encompassments from their more prosperous neighbors in the fertile valleys. Hence they were enabled to ignore the law, and for more than half a century they were practically unmolested in the exercise of what came to be considered an inalienable right. The moral effect upon the people of this long period of immunity can scarcely be estimated. To the mountaineer, turning his corn into whiskey seems as natural and right as changing his apples into cider does to the Northern owner of orchards. From his restricted point of view, the tax on the manufacture of spirituous liquors is a thing accursed,—an unjust measure directed against his inherent right to do what he will with his own. For this cause it is next to impossible to convince him that an infraction of the revenue laws is a thing intrinsically wrong; he is not sufficiently in touch with modern civilization or the body politic to realize his moral obligations as a citizen.

Moreover, aside from his convictions in the matter, his temptations to become a law-breaker are very considerable. In addition to the fact that he cannot market his crop in its natural state,—a condition which puts him at once in the very forefront of the battle in the struggle for existence,—he is usually remote from towns and so unable to procure even the small alcoholic basis needed for the simple remedies which he compounds from the roots and herbs of his native forests. A trifling need, one may say, yet sickness is a mighty lever; and since the penalties imposed by law extend to the *carrier* of untaxed liquor, many a mountaineer has been led into wrong-doing by motives which were quite the reverse of criminal.

To cite an example. In a certain townless district of the Great Smoky Mountains, an old man once trudged many miles through the darkness of a stormy night to buy a quart of whiskey at a secret still. His wife was sick, and the liquor was needed for medicinal purposes; therefore, in the sight of his neighbors, at least, the man had just cause for setting aside his scruples, if he had any. He obtained the whiskey, but on his return home was apprehended with the telltale bottle in his possession. He thought his case a hard one at best; but when he was brought into court and there learned that the law made his punishment three times heavier than that of the men who distilled the liquor, it is safe to presume that his loyalty as a citizen suffered a shock from which it never fully recovered. One thing is certain; when the judge, in view of the extenuating circumstances, exercised his prerogative and suspended judgment, the old man went back to the mountains with a story which was calculated to make his district a difficult one for the officers; and so it remains to this day.

Notwithstanding such prosecutions, however, and the consequent ill feeling stirred up by them, the moonshiners and their sympathizers generally offer little more than a passive resistance to the raids of the revenue officers. And this is the more remarkable when one remembers that the mountaineers come of fighting stock, and that personal wrongs among them are usually redressed without the aid of judge or jury. A closer study of the mountain character—and one which the novelist seems not to have made— explains the apparent contradiction, and also reveals much that is praiseworthy. As a people the mountaineers are simple and primitive; but, while they have taken on none of the gloss of civilization, they are singularly free from its vices. Theft is uncommon, immorality is rare, and truthfulness is the rule rather than the exception. Their poverty is great, but their hospitality is unbounded. Their enmity is apt to be lasting, but their loyalty to kinsmen and friends is invincible. The latter-day economist may call them thriftless and improvident, but they take privations as a matter of course and ask aid of no man. In the steeple-chase of modern progress they have been left far behind; lacking the means to encourage the schoolmaster, they have gradually lost the inclination; the world around them has moved forward, but they have stood still.

Out of such material is made the illicit distiller of fact. He is neither a bandit nor a highwayman, a disturber of the peace nor, in respect to formularies other than the revenue statutes, a law-breaker. Least of all, perhaps, is he a desperado. Within a month of this present writing, a traveler on one of the Tennessee railways entered the smoking-car of the train. In the rear sat an officer in charge of a "covey" of moonshiners flushed by him on the mountain the night before. There were twelve in the party; they had yielded without resistance to one man; and—most singular circumstance of all, in the South—the deputy had not found it necessary to put them in irons.

At their trial the members of this party will doubtless plead guilty to a man, though a little hard swearing would probably clear half of them; they will beg for mercy or for light sentences; and those of them who promise amendment will most likely never be again brought in on the same charge, for the mountaineer is prone to keep his promises, amendatory or otherwise.

A venerable judge, in whom judicial severity is tempered by a generous admixture of loving-kindness and mercy, and whose humane decisions have made his name a word to conjure with among the dwellers in the waste places, tells a story which emphasizes the promise-keeping trait in the mountain character. A hardened sinner of the stills, whose first and second offences were already recorded against him, was once again brought to book by the vigilance of the revenue-men. As an old offender, who had neither promised nor repented, it was like to go hard with him; and he begged earnestly, not for liberty, but for a commutation of his sentence which would send him to jail instead of the penitentiary, promising that so long as the judge remained upon the bench he would neither make nor meddle with illicit whiskey. He won his case, and was sent to jail for a term of eleven months. This was in summer. Six months later, when the first snows began to powder the bleak summits of Chilhowee, the judge received a letter from the convict. It was a simple-hearted petition for a "furlough" of ten days, pathetic and eloquent in its primitive English and quaint misspelling. Would the good judge let him off for just ten days? Winter was coming on, and the wife and children were alone in the cabin on the mountain, with no one to make provision for their wants. He would not overstay the time, and he would "certain shore" come back and surrender himself.

His petition was granted, and, true to his word, the mountaineer returned on the tenth day and gave himself up to the sheriff. He served the remainder of his sentence, and after his release kept his pledge so long as the judge remained on the bench. I would the story ended here, but the truth is pitiless. When the conditions of his promise no longer bound him, the mountaineer went back to his old trade; and only a few days since, his still was raided and he was shot and killed.

Mountain whiskey, known in its habitat as "moonshine," "wild-cat," "corn," "old corn," or "pine-top," is a colorless liquid, raw and fiery to the civilized palate, with a faint smoky aroma which is its only quality in common with the usquebaugh of the Scottish Highlands. Its makers know none of the arts of adulteration, hence it is pure and free from drugs. As a beverage, it is unique; and as an intoxicant, for the outlander at least, it is a profound success. Singularly enough, though the mountaineers themselves drink it freely, over-indulgence among them is rare, and, in a region where whiskey is rather more plentiful than the necessaries of life, there are but few drunkards.

Commenting upon its combative properties, an old resident of one of the valley towns said to me, "It's a blame' ugly drunk; I reckon ther' ain't no more fightin'er liquor this side o' the Mexican aguardenty. Now, ther' was the time when Jim Hallabee got hisself killed up in that ther' argy*ment* long with Jud Byars. They'd both been fillin' up on pine-top, an' Jud he——" I had to listen to his pointless narrative of battle, murder, and sudden death, but the reader shall be spared.

The moonshiner's distillery is a very primitive affair. Occasionally it is housed in a cave, or in a crevice of the cliff; oftener it is found in a little ravine, in a laurel-screened hollow on the plateau, or in the depths of the forest. Failing the shelter afforded by a cave, the apparatus is covered by no roof other than the sky, and shut in by no walls save those builded by the trees or the undergrowth. The "copper" is set in a furnace built of stones and plastered with clay; a stream of water from the nearest brook serves for a condensing bath for the worm; and these, with a tub to catch the drippings, complete the plant.

Notwithstanding the fact that the still is often the common property of an entire neighborhood, its capacity is usually very small,—so small, indeed, that were the law to take cognizance of quantity the moonshiner would be the most inconsequent of offenders. Stories are not lacking to tell of apple-brandy stills made out of a teapot; and in at least one authenticated case the legend has a basis of fact. An old mountaineer was arrested and taken three hundred miles from his home on Sand Mountain to answer for an alleged infraction of the revenue laws. The still was produced in court; it was a common tin teapot, with a series of wooden tubes for a worm. The judge dismissed the case, sent the old man home, and gave a free rendering of the law of common sense to the over-zealous constabulary.

In operating a secret still, every man interested bears an equal share. Sentries are posted day and night, and a surprise by the officers is an infrequent occurrence. A resort to violence in its defense is the exception, since the most ignorant of the mountaineers knows that a single officer has the authority and resources of the government at his back. Strangers, however, whose business is unknown are sometimes intimidated, though this, too, is the exception. Oftener the wayfarer who happens to stumble upon a still is invited to make himself useful by cutting a stick of wood, or by feeding the fire,—services which are supposed to make him *particeps criminis* in the illegal industry.

In disposing of his product the moonshiner is compelled to resort to various artifices to escape detection. Formerly he used to bring his whiskey to town on "first Mondays," or other court-days, dispensing it from a spigoted cask in his wagon to all comers and in quantities to suit, much as the Northern farmer vends his cider. Later, when an increase in the number of deputy collectors made this plan impracticable, it became the custom to sell the liquor through some friendly valley farmer. When this, in turn, grew dangerous, the mountaineer retreated to his stronghold and let it be noised about that his customers must seek him. In some localities a distiller bolder than his companions would hold nightly appointments with thirsty humanity on some lonely cliff; and a modification of this plan was adopted by a band of moonshiners operating on the plateau of the Cumberlands above a small mining town on the railway. Shortly after dark on pleasant summer evenings the townsfolk would hear the mellow notes of a wooden horn echoing over the valley, and a light would be seen swinging on the crest of an inaccessible cliff which rises abruptly behind the village. It was the signal of the moonshiners; and whosoever would climb to the base of the crag would find a cord dangling below the light, with a buckskin wallet and a hook at its lower end. Putting his money in the wallet and hanging his jug on the hook, the bibulous one had only to wait until the line could be drawn up and lowered again.

After a time this plan too became hazardous, and at present much more circuitous methods are employed. A hollow tree or a stump in the forest on the mountain is designated by common consent. In this the purchaser deposits his money and a receptacle for the liquor and goes his way in peace for an hour or more. When he returns,—if he has been acting, meanwhile, in good faith,—the money has been taken and the jug filled; by whom, the buyer least of all men is able to say. Here and there, in the remoter districts, a friendly "fence" is yet to be found in the neighborhood of a secret still, but in this case the liquor is sold only to those who are known to be tried men and true; a stranger will bargain in vain, though he urge in extenuation all the ills to which the flesh is heir.

Those are the ordinary methods of sale adopted when the market for his product is normally active; but in time of need the moonshiner who has the courage of his convictions will not hesitate to take greater risks. Now and then he will venture into town with a few filled jugs concealed under a load of corn, garden-produce, or split stove-wood, taking his chances on disposing of the liquor as opportunity may offer. Again, he will sling a small jug to a stout belt, provide himself with a tin cup and a funnel, and, with his portable saloon hidden under a great-coat, will hang upon the edges of a crowd at an open-air political meeting or other gathering, filling bottles or selling by the drink. Under such circumstances he takes his liberty in his hand. If detected, he will usually fight before he is taken; and, knowing little of the ethics of civilized warfare, he is very likely to make the struggle a battle royal, as many a less primitive person might under similar conditions.

There are also occasions when he will even resist the officers in his native mountains; and, admitting his premises, it is a wonder that he does not always do so. From the mountaineer's point of view, the moonshiner's occupation is not only blameless, but it is pursued under exigencies and harassments that must appear grievous and oppressive. It is only with the greatest difficulty that he can procure and assemble the various parts of his distilling apparatus; and when it is in working order he must hide it in the loneliest place he can find, remote from even the scanty comforts of the mountaineer's cabin. After that, he must guard it with unremitting vigilance, watching it day and night, and living the life of a hunted outlaw between-times; and all this when he is only doing what he firmly believes he has a perfect right to do. Then comes the catastrophe. A band of armed deputies swoops down upon his secluded retreat; if he surrender, he has to stand quietly by and witness the destruction of his property, and the comforting assurance that the jail or the penitentiary will presently make a longer or shorter gap in his freedom. The alternative is resistance, and occasionally he accepts it, though rarely with the enthusiastic ardor ascribed to him by the novelist or the newspaper space-writer. A precipitate retreat, a running fight through the forest punctuated by a few dropping shots from squirrel rifles and Winchesters, and the morning papers announce in leaded head-lines,—

FIERCE BATTLE WITH THE WILDCATTERS!
MOONSHINE JAKE'S SECRET STILL
RAIDED BY THE DEPUTIES!
A DESPERATE STRUGGLE, IN WHICH THE
FATAL WINCHESTER GETS IN ITS
DEADLY WORK!

After which startling introduction one goes on to the details given in the small type of the despatch with quickened pulse and apprehensive interest sharp-set, only to find that the reporter has most unaccountably omitted a list of the dead and wounded or any further mention thereof.

Such battles there are now and then, but their infrequency is the best possible proof of the mountaineer's good sense and peaceable inclinations; and their bloodlessness becomes evident when it is remembered that in a single judicial district in Tennessee there are at present over two hundred moonshiners awaiting trial, all of whom were taken without loss of life, and most of whom surrendered without resistance of any sort.

This, then, is the moonshiner of fact, defined in general terms and without prejudice to the assumption that here and there in the thinly peopled and slightly policed mountain region one may occasionally stumble upon bands of desperadoes who are also illicit distillers. Such bands there are, but they are generally made up of escaped criminals who have taken to moonshining as an occupation at once less dangerous and more remunerative than highway-robbery or petty larceny. The outlaws from whom they are recruited are not always mountaineers,—save by adoption,—and it is but just to add that they are held in equal disrepute by the men of the plateaus and the farmers of the valleys.

From my study window one may look out upon a forest-clad mountain whose summit lifts the sky-line of the western horizon, and whose gray cliffs are near enough to reflect the rays of the morning sun. Somewhere in one of its many gorges is said to be the haunt of a noted outlaw and his clansmen, among whom there are escaped criminals of every degree of turpitude. One is a murderer, two more are horse-thieves, others are convicts from the State chain-gangs. They are said to be moonshiners; and, as they commit no open depredations, the inference is plausible. But on no account should the simple-hearted mountaineer, who raises corn that he cannot sell and distils it because he thinks he has an inherent right so to do, be made to answer for their sins in addition to his own. He has nothing in common with them save the occupation in which they are, in a certain sense, his competitors. In the gang in question, so far as may be ascertained, the people of the plateaus have no representatives; and I shall have written in vain if the fact be not clearly established that the sheriff could raise a posse for its capture or dispersal quite as readily on the mountain as in the valley.

To the raids of the deputy collectors these escaped criminals often oppose the most desperate resistance, not because they are distillers, but because many of them are wanted for far more serious crimes; and in his reports of such conflicts the war-correspondent may perhaps be excused for mistaking a consequence for a cause. None the less, it is an injustice to the moonshiner *per se,* of whom his very judges say that he is but an ignorant countryman, obstinately honest, perversely truthful, unlettered but shrewd, and, withal, never a criminal in the dictionary definition of the word.

And, finally, a word to the fellow-craftsmen of the guild of letters, from one who, like Pencraft, lacked prescience and so was once moved to add his mite to the unrealities of mountain literature. Hang not, I pray you, the wickedness of your mountaineer villain upon the peg of illicit distilling. Make him a desperado incarnadine *and* a moonshiner, if you please, but not the former because of the latter. Moreover, what is written is written, but let nothing herein set forth be taken as an admission that the sunny Southland, urban or rural, mountain or valley, is deficient in sound, flawless timber for the making of fictional evil-doers, gentle or simple. The while the rising tide of civilization laves but the foot of the mountain; so long as the personal quarrel is fought out between man and man; and what time the ready weapon anticipates the Anglo-Saxon fist,—the folk-lore of the South will honor the draft of the story-teller even though it be filled out to four figures and written in red ink.

II

Our Contemporary Ancestors

Figure 5-1.   William Goodell Frost (1854–1938)
(Southern Appalachian Archives, Berea College)

5

Our Contemporary Ancestors
in the Southern Mountains

William Goodell Frost

This essay is probably the best known of all those included in this anthology, and perhaps the most famous ever written about Appalachia. Its phrases were repeated both by the author and others who wrote about the people living in the "mountainous backyards of nine states." This popularity is probably due to several factors, the most noteworthy being that it encapsulated many of the widely held ideas previously expressed about Appalachia, offered a succinct explanation of the reasons Appalachia existed as a distinct and unique American region, while at the same time advancing a lucid argument legitimizing the concept of Appalachian coherence and homogeneity. That the author also named the region Appalachian America likely gave his article additional appeal.

William Goodell Frost (1854–1938), teacher, scholar, and executive, who for twenty-eight years, 1892–1920, was president of Berea College, was largely responsible for the orientation of this Kentucky school towards the southern Appalachian region. At the time he assumed presidency of the small liberal arts school, it was in danger of extinction. Although founded in 1855 by anti-slavery southerners sympathetic to integrated education, admission of Negro students on the same terms as whites offended many southerners and the white student population declined until by the early 1890s it was virtually nonexistent. Frost suggested bringing in more white students form the North as a means of recovering white students from the mountains. This plan proved successful, for when Frost retired in 1920 there was a total of 2780 students compared to 351 in 1892. Moreover, since the 1890s Berea has been nationally recognized for its educational efforts directed towards southern Appalachian youth.

Frost had been active in religious work before coming to Berea so it is not surprising that he thinks of Appalachia in theological terms, labeling it "one of God's grand divisions." Much of his essay sounds a familiar theme as, for example, when

Reprinted from *Atlantic Monthly* 83 (March 1899): 311.

he likens mountaineers to biblical patriarchs and Homeric heroes. He argues for the purity of the racial group, offering surnames as proof of the Anglo-Saxon heritage of mountaineers. These "racially pure" people are childlike, distinctive from other Americans by their lesser intelligence and relatively fewer passions. Their use of pioneer forms such as log cabins, spinning, colorful place names, music "in a weird minor key," and a "literature of the illiterate" are all paraded as evidence of the "Rip Van Winkle sleep" of Appalachian mountaineers. In 1899 these arguments carried great weight but are less persuasive to-day. That a distinct racial group that remained racially pure for generations settled the Appalachian region is doubtful. It is impossible to ascertain the origins of the first settlers because the evidence needed to make such determinations doesn't exist. The use of surnames is of little help because many people changed their names over the years. Moreover, despite what Frost and many other writers have said, Appalachia is not, and probably never has been, culturally coherent and homogeneous.

Frost saw that the existence of "contemporary ancestors" posed a problem for America. Considering his background it is not surprising that he found the solution to lie in education. In his view, mountaineers should become intelligent but not sophisticated and become able to help themselves; the latter is essentially the goal of Berea College. For information on Frost see his *For the Mountains: An Autobiography* (New York: Fleming H. Revell Company, 1937) and Elisabeth S. Peck, *Berea's First 125 Years 1855–1980* (Lexington: The University Press of Kentucky, 1982), pp. 47–48, 68–74.

* * *

At the close of the Revolutionary War there were about two and one half million people in the American colonies. To-day there are in the Southern mountains approximately the same number of people—Americans for four and five generations—who are living to all intents and purposes in the conditions of the colonial times! These people form an element unaccounted for by the census, unreckoned with in all our inventories of national resources. And their remoteness is by no means measured by the mere distance in miles. It is a longer journey from northern Ohio to eastern Kentucky than from America to Europe; for one day's ride brings us into the eighteenth century. Naturally, then, these eighteenth-century neighbors and fellow countrymen of ours are in need of a friendly interpreter; for modern life has little patience with those who are "behind the times." We hear of the "mountain whites" (they scorn that appellation as we would scorn the term "Northern whites") as illiterates, moonshiners, homicides, and even yet the mountaineers are scarcely distinguished in our thought from the "poor white trash." When we see them from the car window, with curious eyes, as we are whirled toward our Southern hotel, their virtues are not blazoned on their sorry clothing, nor suggested by their grave and awkward demeanor. They are an anachronism, and it will require a scientific spirit and some historic sense to enable us to appreciate their situation and their character.

The case of the mountain whites illustrates in a most impressive manner the importance of intercommunication as a means of progress. To a marvelous degree the Northern frontiersman was kept in touch with the thought centres of the East. He ascended the lordly Hudson, and that was his highway to the seaboard. The Hudson was too short, and De Witt Clinton lengthened it with the Erie Canal, so that all the lake region was hitched to civilization. Thus the waterways maintained communication until the railways appeared, and the pioneer shared in large degree the progress of the metropolis.

Now, the ancestors of our mountain friends "went West" under the same mighty impulse which peopled western New York and Ohio. But they unconsciously stepped aside from the great avenues of commerce and of thought. This is the excuse for their Rip Van Winkle sleep. They have been beleaguered by nature. The vastness of the mountain region which has enveloped this portion of our fellow countrymen has been concealed by the fact that it was parceled out among so many different commonwealths. The mountainous back yards of nine states abut upon the lofty ridges which separate the Virginias, bound Kentucky on the east, divide Tennessee from North Carolina, and end in Georgia and Alabama. There are some two hundred mountain counties, covering a territory much larger than New England. This is one of God's grand divisions, and in default of any other name we shall call it Appalachian America. It has no coast line like Scotland, no inland lakes or navigable rivers like Switzerland. The surface varies greatly in elevation and geologic structure, but as a place for human habitation the entire region has one characteristic—the lack of natural means of communication. Its highways are the beds of streams; commerce and intercourse are conditioned by horseflesh and saddlebags.

In this vast inland and upland realm may be found a contemporary survival of that pioneer life which has been such a striking feature in American history. Beginning with the survivals in matters external, we are at once introduced to the first type of American architecture,—the log cabin. The blind or windowless one-room cabin is replaced in the broader valleys by the double log cabin,—two cabins side by side, with a roofed space between serving for dining-room most of the year; in county towns even a second story with balcony is sometimes developed. In the Carolinas "stick chimneys" prevail, but in Tennessee and Kentucky substantial stone chimneys are the rule, aesthetically placed upon the outside of the wall. The great characteristic in the log-cabin stage of life is the absence of "conveniences." For a camping party this is very interesting, though sometimes embarrassing. To the mountain people, as to our pioneer ancestors, it is a

Figure 5-2.   A Mountain Cabin, about 1900
(Southern Appalachian Archives, Berea College)

matter of course. The writer recalls an early experience when enjoying the hospitality of a mountain home. His feminine companion thought of a possible return of hospitalities, wondering whether her hostess ever came to Berea, fifteen miles away, for shopping.

"When you cannot get what you need at this little store down by the creek, where do you go?"

The mountain woman answered with a frank smile, "I go without."

And it appeared that she had never been to any town or city in her life! It is brought home to a visitor in this region that the number of things which people can go without is very great. We expected to find our sylvan hosts without electric lights, but it did strike us as barbarous for them to burn kerosene lamps without chimneys. Still, it is a delicate matter to carry a lamp chimney safely over twenty miles of mountain road, on horseback. Possibly if we lived where they do we should live somewhat as they do!

One of our college women, in a "university extension" tour, desired to starch her waist, and asked her wondering hostess for a little wheat flour.

"Oh'yes," was the reply, "we've got some wheat flour." And then followed the search. No storeroom, flour bin, or even flour barrel or flour bag appeared. The woman's eyes were cast among the rafters whence depended numerous bags and bunches.

"Oh yes, we've got some wheat flour." And at last it came forth from a cleft between the logs, a scant pint of flour "wrapped up in a napkin." The dreariness of this destitution is greatly relieved by what are to us the novel resources of sylvan life. If these primitive folk cannot step to the telephone and by a supernatural fiat "order" whatever may be desired, they can step into the forest and find or fashion some rude substitute. (Though in truth the handmade product is not a substitute, but an archetype.) Is the lamp chimney lacking? The mountain potteries are still making flambeaux, lamps of almost classic pattern in which grease is burned with a floating wick. Is the sawmill remote? In the high mountains where streams are small and mills impracticable the whipsaw is brought into use, and two men will get out three or four hundred feet of boards from the logs in a day. Handmills for grinding can still be constructed by well-brought-up mountain men, and in some places they have not yet lost the tradition of the fashioning of the old English crossbow! And who does not have a feeling akin to reverence in the presence of a hand loom? When a mountain maid speaks of her "wheel" she does not refer to a bicycle, but to the spinning-wheel of our ancestors, her use of which here in our mountains calls to mind the sudden and entire disappearance of cloth-making from the list of household industries. Not a single member of the Sorosis could card, spin, dye, or weave. Their mothers, for the most part, had forgotten these arts, yet their grandmothers, and their foremothers for a hundred generations, have been spin-

Figure 5-3. At about the time of this photograph (around 1900), this spinning wheel had been in use for 80 years. (*Southern Appalachian Archives, Berea College*)

Figure 5-4.   Woman Spinning, Bear Knob, Kentucky, 1898
(Southern Appalachian Archives, Berea College)

ners. Spinning, in fact, has helped to form the character of our race, and it is pleasant to find that here in Appalachian America it is still contributing to the health and grace and skill of womankind.

Along with these Saxon arts we shall find startling survivals of Saxon speech. The rude dialect of the mountains is far less a degradation than a survival. The Saxon pronoun "hit" holds its place almost universally. Strong past tenses, "holp" for helped, "drug" for dragged, and the like, are heard constantly; and the syllabic plural is retained in words in -st and others. The greeting as we ride up to a cabin is "Howdy, strangers. 'Light and hitch yer beasties." Quite a vocabulary of Chaucer's words which have been dropped by polite lips, but which linger in these solitudes, has been made out by some of our students. "Pack" for carry, "gorm" for muss, "feisty" for full of life, impertinent, are examples.

The lumber industry—driving and rafting logs—is still in these mountains the chief means of contact with the outside world. The trades are the primitive ones of the blacksmith, miller, and cobbler. The "upright farms" yield principally corn. String beans are on the table almost the year round. There are small patches of flax, cotton, and tobacco for home consumption. Some lands are held two or three dollars higher per acre—a double price—because of the coal which will some time be of incalculable value.

Two other pioneer reminders are large families and a scarcity of money. Barter is carried on at every store, where the tall gaunt figure and immobile face, so well described by Miss Murfree and proverbially characteristic of Americans in the pioneer stage of development, still predominate at every counter.

A little sympathy and patience are necessary if we would recognize these marks of our contemporary ancestors through the exterior which is, at first sight, somewhat rude and repellent. The characteristics thus far noted are only on the surface; it will require still more insight and imagination to really know the heart of a mountain man. As in external matters the great characteristic is "going with things," so in the realm of ideas we are first impressed by the immense blank spaces. Can you divest your mind of those wonderful ideas which have been born since the Revolution, and have expanded and filled the modern world—evolution and the rest? Appalachian America may be useful as furnishing a fixed point which enables us to measure the progress of the moving world! And yet to set down the mountain people with the scornful verdict "behind the times" would be almost brutal. There is a reason for their belated condition, and they have large claims upon our interest and our consideration.

Subtract the ideas which have been born since the Revolution, and we come back to some very distinct and interesting notions. To begin with, we have the Revolutionary patriotism. Mr. Henry Cabot Lodge has recently told anew the story of the battle of King's Mountain, in which the back-woodsmen of Appalachian America annihilated a British army. Cedar kegs used as canteens, and other accoutrements which saw service in that enterprise, may still be found in mountain cabins. As Appalachian America has received no foreign immigration, it now contains a larger proportion of "Sons" and "Daughters" of the Revolution than any other part of our country.

The feeling of toleration and justification of slavery, with all the subtleties of state rights and "South against North," which grew up after the Revolution did not penetrate the mountains. The result was that when the civil war came there was a great surprise for both the North and the South. Appalachian America clave to the old flag. It was this old-fashioned loyalty which held Kentucky in the Union, made West Virginia "secede from secession," and performed prodigies of valor in east Tennessee, and even in the western Carolinas. The writer was describing this loyalty to a woman's club in a border city when a fine old Southern lady, with entire good nature but much spirit, exclaimed, "Ah, sir, if those mountain folks had been educated they would have gone with their states!" Probably she was right.

The political ideas of the mountains are, of course, those of the Southern rather than those of the Northern colonies, born of the county system of Virginia, and lacking the training of the New England town meeting. Two results are noticeable: a greater individuality and hesitancy in coöperation, and a tendency not to combine for a principle or a policy, but to follow a leader in the old feudal way. Here is the psychological explanation of "the use of money at the polls" in some mountain counties. To a portion of the people the issues of national or state politics seem remote, and the election appeals to them as a personal encounter between Judge Goodlet, we will say, and Judge Britteredge. A part of these voters are attached by family or other traditional ties to one of these chieftains, and a part to the other. The adherents of Judge Goodlet could on no account be induced to vote for his opponent; that would strike them as altogether out of character. But in voting for Judge Goodlet they feel that they are doing him a favor, and they expect a dollar on election day as a kind of feudal largess. The receiving of such a gift does not involve the moral degradation of a "bribe," although it would be possible only where political consciousness is still in a rudimentary state. Yet the unlettered voter sometimes grasps a political issue with real argumentative ability. Kentucky and West Virginia were carried for "sound money" two years ago because the mountain men responded to the appeal, "Ef yeou lend a neighbor a bag o' flour yeou don't want ter be paid back in meal."

If the mountaineer's patriotism is old-fashioned, his literary sustenance, if such it may be called, is simply archaic. His music is in a weird minor key, and like that of Chaucer's Prioress, "entuned in hire nose full swetely." The hymns which are lined out and sung in unison in very slow time are usually quite doleful. The banjo, as well as most secular music, is commonly accounted wicked. Yet not a few old English ballads, familiar in Percy's Reliques, have been handed down from mother to daughter, with interesting variants like those of the Homeric lays. For example, the mountain minstrel represents the hero of Barbara Allen as coming not "out of the west countree," but (for all the world!) out of the Western States! And besides these transmissions there is a certain mass of stock phrases, anecdotes always related in the same words, standing illustrations, and the like, which are of the nature of literature, and might be called the literature of the illiterate. As an instance of this we recently jotted down the following apothegm of a mountain preacher. "Yeou cayn't help a-havin' bad thoughts come inter yer heads, but yeou hain't no necessity fer ter set 'em a cheer." The saying was repeated in a gathering of ministers in the East, and an aged man who was born in England said that he had heard the same thing from an unlearned country preacher when he was a boy. Doubtless that saying has been passed from mouth to mouth for generations. With these literary treasures may be mentioned the examples of slow Saxon wit exhibited in the names of places in the moutains. The post-office department has pruned away many expressive names like "Hell-fer-sartin" and "Stand-around" (why not as classic as Tarrytown?), but has spared many imaginative and picturesque designations, as Fair Play, Wide-Awake, Cutshin, Quality Valley, Saddler, Amity, Troublesome, Stamping Ground, and Nonesuch.

In examining social life, and its variations in the mountains, we discover a new kind of isolation, a higher potency of loneliness. The people are not only isolated from the great centres and thoroughfares of the world, but also isolated from one another. The families who live along one valley form a community by themselves, and the children grow up with almost no examples or analogies of life outside these petty bounds. As we need a fresh air fund for the little ones of the city, we need a fresh idea fund for these sons and daughters of solitude. The very words by which a stranger is directed are suggestive of this isolation of each locality. In place of the street and number of a city, or the "range" and "section" of the west, we are directed by the watercourses. We are told to follow the middle fork of the Kentucky River, go up such a creek, and turn off on such a branch. The mountain world is mapped out by "forks," "creeks," and "branches." This double isolation produces many marked variations in social conditions. It may happen, for example, that one or two leading families on the "branch"—the pillars of the narrow society—die out, or move out, and the social state, left unsupported, collapses. The tales of awful degradation in the mountains may be true. But such tales are not to be taken as representative. The very next valley may be filled with homes where home-spun linen table-cloths, and texts and hymns handed down by tradition, witness to a self-respect and character that are unmistakable.

We have only to read our Old Testament to be reminded that mere illiteracy is not fatal to character. The patriarchs were illiterate, and there are people in the mountains who remind us of them,—men and women who with deep though narrow experiences have reflected upon the problems of life, and subjected themselves to its disciplines, until they have gained the poise and power of true philosophers. This is something different from that repose of manner, quite common in the South, which comes from the mere absence of all haste, and makes the veriest roustabout somewhat akin to the representatives of our most distinguished leisure class.

The ancestry of the mountain folk is for the most part creditable. As has been indicated already it is almost wholly Revolutionary and British. In Kentucky a majority of the families may be traced back to rural England, both by distinct English traits and by the common English names like Chrisman, Baker, Allen, and Hazelwood. In other parts of the mountains the Scotch-Irish strain predominates, with corresponding names, including all the Macs. The impression has been made that some of the early settlers in the Southern colonies were "convicts," but it must be remembered that many of them were only convicted of having belonged to Cromwell's army, or of persisting in attending religious meetings conducted by "dissenters." But, whatever their origin, the "leading families" of the mountains are clearly sharers in the gracious influences which formed the English and Scottish people, and when a mountain lad registers by the name of Campbell or Harrison we have learned to expect that he will not prove unworthy of his clan.

A word deserves to be said of the native refinement of many of the mountain women. The staid combination of a black sunbonnet and a cob pipe is not unusual, and the shrill voice that betokens desperation in life's struggles may be heard. There is an utter frankness in questioning a stranger. "Who might you-all be? Where are ye aimin' ter go? What brung ye up this air way off branch? Where do ye live at? Where's yer old man? [This to a lady engaged in extension work!] How old be ye?" Yet there is withal a real kindliness and a certain shy modesty, and often a passionate eagerness to note points of superiority which may be imitated. As a rule, the proprieties of life are observed to a surprising degree; and a mountain woman certainly proves her descent form Eve when she appears at a meeting on the hottest summer's day wearing woolen mitts as her tribute to conventionality! Love of home and kindred is nowhere more marked than among these simple dwellers in the hills. The mountaineer has fewer passions than we, but his passions are more irresistible. When all the living branches of a family are in one county, perhaps in one valley, and a girl has never slept beneath more than a single roof, she deserves the name of heroine for starting off to a distant school, and may be pardoned for some homesickness after she is there.

The reverse side of family affection is the blood feud, which still survives in full vigor. Thoroughly to trace the origin, motives, and code of the bold feud in the mountains would require an article by itself. As an institution it has its roots deep in Old World traditions. Yet it seems to have been decadent when the confusions of the civil war gave it a new life. It is made possible by the simple fact that the people of this region have not yet grasped the decidedly modern notion of the sacredness of life. Mountain homicides are not committed for purposes of robbery. They are almost universally performed in the spirit of an Homeric chieftain, and the motive is some "point of honor."

Among the social virtues of the mountaineer hospitality has a high place. This virtue is to be found in solitary places the world over. Its two blending motives are compassion for a stranger, and curiosity to learn whatever news he may bring; and both motives are creditable. While we cannot here trace all the social codes of mountain life, it is important to note that there are social codes and moral standards which are most strictly observed. Herein the "mountain white" shows his genus. It is his social standards and his independent spirit that prove his worth, or at least his promise. He is not a degraded being, although, to tell the truth, he has not yet been graded up! The "poor whites" were degraded by actual competition with slave labor. The "mountain whites" had little contact with slavery, and retained that independent spirit which everywhere belongs to the owners of land. Mr. John Fox, Jr., is responsible for the statement that when a man was sent with a sum of money to relieve distress in a plague-stricken district in the mountains of Kentucky, he could find none who would confess their need, and rode for days without being able to execute his commission. The mountaineer is not a suppliant for old clothes. When Mr. Fox gave a reading from his Cumberland tales in Berea, the mountain boys were ready to mob him. They had no comprehension of the nature of fiction. Mr. Fox's stories were either true or false. If they were true, then he was "no gentleman" for telling all the family affairs of people who had entertained him with their best. If they were not true, then, of course, they were libelous upon the mountain people! Such an attitude may remind us of the general condemnation of fiction by the "unco' gude" a generation ago.

This proof of the narrowness of their horizon may prepare us to understand their religion. Here they have distinctly degenerated; they have lost the great Protestant idea that a minister must be an educated man. Ignorance makes men positive, and the barriers of orthodoxy have been raised to a very commanding height. The same positiveness leads to a multitude of sects, and is reinforced by the feudal spirit for following a partisan leader. Theological thought turns upon such points as the validity of baptism not performed in running water, and the origin of Melchizedek. Naturally, and happily, such discussions do not greatly affect practical life. With some tenets, however, the case is different. The mountains seem the natural home of fatalism. It is in helplessness that they cry out beside the bedside of their dear one, "If he's to die, he's to die." And this "hardshell" predestinarian teaching does not hesitate to condemn missions and Sunday-schools as an unwarrantable interference with the decrees of the Almighty. The habit of literal interpretation has raised up many champions of the doctrine of a flat earth. "Dew yeou perpose to take Joshuar inter yeour leetle school, and larn him the shape of the yearth? Don't the Bible tell us that the yearth's got eends, an' foundations, an' corners? And that the sun runs from one eend on hit ter the other? Let God be true and every man a liar!" With all this ranting, however, there are some noble men among the mountain preachers. Occasionally we have real eloquence, and in rare instances even some liberality. An example of the latter occurred recently when, after a long discourse in which the natural obstacles in the narrow way were quite lost sight of while the preacher brought the opening down to a mere crack by the piling in of ritualistic and doctrinal tests, at the close the good man, with a glance at one of our extension lecturers who was present, exclaimed, "I hain't a-sayin' that God cayn't let in a truly repentant sinner that don't come up ter this yere standard. The Lord air powerful good, an' if he neow and then lets in a sinner as has plumb repented, even if he don't come up to this yere standard, I hain't a-goin' ter object. There may be some in other churches as don't know no better, and the Lord may, now an' then, take pity on some on 'em. But, brethering, mine's the reg'lar way."

Though the points of resemblance between these lonely people of the hills and our forefathers on the bleak new England shore are numerous and striking, there are one or two points of contrast which place them very far apart. Judged by modern standards, the early settlers in the New World were rude of speech, and stinted in all material resources. More than this, they were but babes in all scientific conceptions, and strangers to many of the ideas with which every modern child is familiar. They were crude, poor, narrow, *but they were at the head of the procession.* They shared the best thought of their time, and were consciously in motion. They were inspired by the great task of nation building. The mountain folk, on the contrary, the best of them, are consciously stranded. They are behind relatively as well as absolutely, and their pride is all the more vehement because conscious of an insecure foundation. Shy, sensitive, undemonstrative, the mountain man and woman are pathetically belated. The generations of scorn from the surrounding lowlands have almost convinced them, inwardly, that "what is, must be," and they are but feebly struggling with destiny.

Such people are so far out of touch with modern life that they surprise and disappoint some who, without intimate acquaintance, try to give them assistance. Few teachers can really begin simply enough, and condescend to teach the things which "we always knew." I recall a breezy mountain top, and a young hunter—a Doryphorus rather than an Apollo—whose woodcraft had won my admiration. Delicately I touched upon the question of education.

"Can you write numbers?"

The answer came slow and guarded.

"Reckon I can write some numbers."

Then on a piece of bark I drew the nine digits. He read them all. Next came the combination of figures, and I included the date 1897.

"I don't guess I can tell that thar."

I explained it. And then a new test occurred to me.

"Do you know what 1897 means?"

"Hit's the year, haint't hit?"

"But why is this year called 1897? It is 1897 years since what?"

"I never heard tell."

Another instance came to light through the distribution of reading matter. When I was young in the mountains I distributed a barrel of copies of the New York Independent, and had great satisfaction in observing the eagerness with which they were taken. A little later I discovered that these simple folk could not comprehend the high themes discussed in that excellent periodical, and that their eagerness was only to secure paper for the walls of their cabins! Yet in many places a mere scrap of printed paper will be cherished. More than once one of our extension lecturers has been intercepted in attempting to throw into the fire the paper which had been wrapped around some toilet article.

"Don't burn thet thar, stranger, hit mought have some news on hit."

So, too, it is pitiful to see how helpless these people are in estimating the things of the outside world. "Furriners" have impressed them with the wonders of train and telegraph, and they have no standard from which to decide where credulity should stop. The story is quite credible of the mountaineer in Georgia who inquired why the folks of the county town were not more "tore up" over the Spanish war. "It hav been giv out in our settlement," said he, "thet them Spanish has flyin' squadroons, and we 'low thet if one of them things should 'light in our parts they would be as hard on us as the rebs."

But the mountain folk should inspire more than an antiquarian interest. They are part and parcel of the nation, and their place in it and their future are topics of general concern. When we consider the separate elements of our population the mountaineer must not be overlooked. He certainly belongs to the category of the "native born." But his characteristics are the exact complement of those which we now consider American. Lacking the intelligence which is the leading trait of latter-day Americans, he has the unjaded nerves which the typical modern lacks. And while in more elegant circles American families have ceased to be prolific, the mountain American is still rearing vigorous children in numbers that would satisfy the patriarchs. The possible value of such a population is sufficiently evident.

The few representatives of this obscure people who have made their way to regions of greater opportunity have shown no mean native endowment. Lincoln himself is an example. His great career hinged upon the fact that his mother had six books: he was "that much" ahead of contemporary mountain lads, and it gave him his initiative. The principal building of Berea College is named after this greatest American, and we expect to find other similar outcroppings from the same strata. The latent ability of these people often shows itself in other lines, and is sometimes accidentally discovered; as in the case of a totally unlettered man who was aroused by the incoming of the Chesapeake and Ohio Railway, and took and executed large contracts, managing cuts, fills, tunnels, and bridges, and handling armies of workmen, without the aid of either pen or pencil. Another fact to be considered in appraising this mountain population is its central location in the heart of the South. When once enlightened this highland stock may reinforce the whole circle of Southern States.

How the mountains are to be enlightened, however, is a double problem; first as to the means, and secondly as to the method. The first question is one of philanthropy, and the second question is one of pedagogics. There could not be a clearer call for the intervention of intelligent, patriotic assistance. We are sometimes remonstrated with for breaking in upon this Arcadian simplicity, and we have had our own misgivings. But it must be remembered that ruthless change is knocking at the door of every mountain cabin. The jackals of civilization have already abused the confidence of many a highland home. The lumber, coal, and mineral wealth of the mountains is to be possessed, and the unprincipled vanguard of commercialism can easily debauch a simple people. The question is whether the mountain people can be enlightened and guided so that they can have a part in the development of their own country, or whether they must give place to foreigners and melt away like so many Indians.

The means for extending this saving aid must be furnished by the patriotic people of the nation. It cannot be left to the states concerned; for these are all poor Southern states, inexperienced in popular education. Appalachian America is a ward of the nation, such a ward as we have never had before. The mountain man is not to be compared with the negro, except in the basal fact of need. Nor can he be compared with the Western pioneer, for the Western frontier had always a certain proportion of educated leaders, and it was closely knit by family and commercial ties with the older and richer parts of the land. But Appalachian America is a frontier without any related back tier, and must be dealt with accordingly.

The question of the method by which these contemporary ancestors of ours are to be put in step with the world is an educational one. I wish only to bring forward two suggestions. In the first place, the aim should be to make them intelligent without making them sophisticated. As a matter both of taste and of common sense, we should not try to make them conform to the regulation type of Americans; they should be encouraged to retain all that is characteristic and wholesome in their present life. Let us not set them agog to rush into the competition of cities, but show them how to get the blessings of culture where they are. Let them not be taught to despise the log cabin, but to adorn it. So, too, the whole aim of our aid should be to make them able to help themselves. Industrial education, instruction in the care of their forests, rotation of crops, and similar elementary matters will make them sharers in the gifts of science. Normal instruction will help them to get some benefit from the newly organized and very inadequate public schools. Publications adapted to their present needs, and university extension lectures upon such elementary themes as hygiene, United States history, and settling quarrels without bloodshed, are in order.

The native capacity of the mountain people is well established, and their response to well-directed efforts has been surprisingly ready. On more than one occasion they have adjourned court to listen to an extension lecture. Mountain boys will walk a hundred miles, over an unknown road, in quest of an education whose significance they can but dimly comprehend. Why may we not expect to see *our* people as worthy and intelligent as those of Drumtochty? Suppose that Drumtochty had had only a bridle path to connect it with the world, so that its farmers and shepherds could reach the market town only twice a year instead of twice a week; suppose there had been no university on the far horizon to beckon its aspiring lads; and then suppose that Drumsheuch and the "meenister" had been illiterate men, jealous of all "high-heeled notions" from the outside world. Who would have known whether there was ever a scholar born in Drumtochty or not?

6

Romance and Tragedy of
Kentucky Feuds

Josiah Stoddard Johnston

While some writers, such as Frost, sought to explain the peculiarities of Appalachian life as survivals, or arrested cultural development, other explanations were offered. In this article, which was widely cited at the turn of the century, Josiah Stoddard Johnston (1833–1913) offers an environmental determinist argument. He provides no explanation to back up his assertion, he merely states that it "is too self-evident to need argument." Johnston parts company with Frost in other ways. Although subscribing to the idea of cultural homogeneity he doesn't think mountaineers are all descended from the most desirable ancestors. Unlike Frost, who specifically denied that the early settlers included convicts, Johnston states that criminals were indeed among the first arrivals in the mountains, although he adds that these immigrants were no better or worse than those in other parts of the country. Johnston also dismisses the opinion that the mountaineers are "of a different stock" than the rest of America, their obvious differences are merely a result of their environment. But, even though his argument differs, Johnston speaks of Appalachian mountaineers in the same terms as Frost. Thus, he refers to the "Rip Van Winkle sleep," the Anglo-Saxon heritage, and the survival of cultural attitudes. For this "problem" Johnston offers a simple solution—the coming of railroads, which he notes have in only a few years brought about vast improvements.

In treating the mountain feuds Johnston touched on an aspect of culture that in stereotype, along with moonshining, typifies Appalachian life. Unlike several others commenting on the subject who blame the feuds on tensions resulting from Civil War days, the lack of good law enforcement, or similar reason, Johnston attributes the feuds to Scottish cultural traits. His list of feuds underscores the fact that the incidence of interfamily violence was hardly the everyday occurrence it is sometimes thought to be. For further information on feuding see S. S. MacClintock, "The Kentucky Mountains and Their Feuds," *American Journal of Sociology* 7 (July, September 1901): 1–28,

Reprinted from *Cosmopolitan* 27 (September 1899): 551–58.

171–87; O. O. Howard, "The Feuds in the Cumberland Mountains," *Independent* 56 (April 7, 1904): 783–88; Charles G. Mutzenberg, *Kentucky's Famous Feuds and Tragedies: Authentic Histories of the World Renowned Vendettas of the Dark and Bloody Ground* (New York: R. F. Fenno, 1917); Virgil Carrington Jones, *The Hatfields and the McCoys* (Chapel Hill: University of North Carolina Press, 1948); Otis K. Rice, *The Hatfields and the McCoys* (Lexington: The University Press of Kentucky, 1982); William Lynwood Montell, *Killings: Folk Justice in the Upper South* (Lexington: The University Press of Kentucky, 1986); and Altina L. Waller, *Feud: Hatfields, McCoys, and Social Change in Appalachia, 1860–1900* (Chapel Hill: University of North Carolina Press, 1988).

* * *

Kentucky has so long suffered in reputation from the feuds which have from time to time existed within its borders, that it is only fair to show that they are confined to but one portion of the state, under conditions peculiar to that section. Justice requires that the great body of its people, who are as peaceful as those of any part of the Union, should not suffer from the enlightened censure of the world for acts in which they have no part, and which they condemn as thoroughly as the most rigorous advocates of law and order.

An eminent scientist has said that if one would tell him the geological structure of a country, he would tell its topography; vice versa, if one would describe the slope or undulations of a country, he would tell the character of its geological formation. In fact, he went farther, and said that with either of the two premises he would not only make good his assertion, but give the nature of the soil, its growth of timber, and the characteristics of its people, the scale of their social and intellectual development. This was simply one form of affirming a great law of nature, that man is largely a creature of environment, and that the most important factor in his development and progress lies in the physical character of the country which he inhabits, and its adaptability for promoting his elevation in the scale of moral and intellectual, as well as physical, progress.

That the environment, which includes difference in soil and topography, has an important influence in fixing the status and shaping the lives of men, is too self-evident to need argument. Members of the same family, reared under the same roof, soon assume different characteristics, habits of thought and action, by a change of locality; those living in a city showing a marked difference in this respect from those leading a rustic life, while those living on fertile lands in thickly settled neighborhoods differ widely from those who live on rougher, poorer soil, where the population is more sparse, and the facilities for education and the cultivation of the social graces of society are less favorable. This is a fair illustration of the difference noted in Kentucky between the mountain population and that of the more favored sections of the state; and it is said without implying disparagement to the former, as regards the native capacity or moral worth. It is not that they are of a different stock, since they are quite the same, for in its natural elements there is no state in which the population is more homogeneous as to birth and innate traits of character. Their stock is essentially English, in which is included a large percentage of Scotch-Irish blood, and with less infusion of Continental blood than is to be found in any other aggregation of people of like number in America.

The mountains of Kentucky, or that region commonly so designated, comprise about ten thousand square miles, being with slight exception conterminous in boundary with the Eastern coal-field. The greater portion of this section is still thickly timbered, and threaded with many streams, which constitute the headwaters of most of the rivers of the state. Few within the territory are navigable, but most of them are available for rafting timber at periods of high tide. The soil is not sterile, most of it being adapted for cultivation, with some rich land in the valleys and coves; but lack of transportation for the products of agriculture and mines has retarded the development of a region possessing great possibilities for the future.

To comprehend the condition of the population, it must be borne in mind that prior to the civil war there was not a mile of railroad within this whole boundary, and that while it was the first portion of the state to receive the footprint of the pioneer it has been the last to feel the awakening touch of modern development. The physical difficulties to be overcome, and the great expense of railroad construction, coupled with the fact that the coal from Pennsylvania and West Virginia can be delivered to the centers of population, and distributed cheaper, owing to water transportation, than native coal from this field, explain this apparent want of enterprise in Kentucky. That it is not real, is shown by the railroad facilities in other parts of the state, there being no less than ten roads which stretch across the state from north to south, and railroad construction is costly in the most favored portions. Thus the sturdy stock which settled in these mountains have been victims of a condition over which they had no control, and have had to await long the relief which could come only from the outside, to break their isolation and unlock the stores of wealth which lie latent among them.

By the law of emigration which leads the seekers of new homes to select a country of features similar to that in which they were reared, the ancestors of these pioneers had, in coming to America, early left the tidewater region and settled in the highlands of the southern colonies, even as they had lived in those of England and Scotland. The same law led them, when they passed westward through Cumberland gap, to select for their new homes the mountainous portion of Kentucky. Some, in seeking a cause for the present difference between the people of the mountains, and those of other more favored regions of the state, have claimed that the former were the descendants of the petty convicts and indentured servants who were sent from Great Britain in colonial days. and sold for a term of years. But this is error. There was an element of this kind in Virginia and North Carolina, but in the tide of emigration westward there was no such line of segregation. Some of them did doubtless stop in that region, and may have been degenerates from the start, furnishing in modern times in their descendants the criminal class, and the men who murder from ambush or for pay, but the great body of mountain settlers were as good as the average of immigrants, with many of education and wealth who brought their slaves with them. The immigration to the interior was, on the other hand, not exclusively of the first families of Virginia, as these optimists would have us believe, but included its full proportion of this inferior class, from which grew full crops of criminals, overseers and negro traders. The mountain people have had enough to bear in the way of internal feuds, privation and repression, without having this slur on their lineage. They were of the same blood with the great body of immigrants, and their deterioration, actual or apparent, is the result of their environment.

They were a thrifty people when they came here, and any one who goes among them will see abundant evidences of it. They brought the loom and the spinning-wheel. Even now there may be found in the homes of their descendants, beyond the reach of modern fashion, pieces of furniture, handsome in their day, brought with great labor over the mountains. Homemade fabrics still form much of the material of their dress and domestic economy. The visitor to one of these hospitable, if humble, homes, will sleep between linen sheets, and eat from a linen table-cloth of attractive pattern, woven on the loom which sits in the shed-room of many homes, as in colonial days; and in such homes hospitality to the stranger is hearty and without price. Even in the most humble the inmates will share the last dish of meal with one (in some remote localities privation comes at times, and the food for main reliance may consist of pounded corn, or meal made by grating hard corn in the ear).

The trouble is that, while the tide of emigration has swept on to the Pacific, and the blessings of an advanced civilization have brightened the homes of the descendants of others who started west with them, but pushed on to the richer cane and blue-grass lands, these were caught in an eddy, and have stood still or retrograded. Their unhappy fate is not from want of capacity, but of opportunity. The same class of men who went on wrested our fair lands from the Indians and progressed rapidly in everything. They were in touch with the world. They started newspapers in the woods, founded schools and colleges, penetrated the Spanish markets down the Mississippi for their products, and then raised such a protest against the efforts of the Dons to condemn them to a pastoral life that the Federal government enforced their doctrine of free navigation of the great river. There were abundant energy, enterprise and grit in Kentucky among this same kind of men who wore buckskin or homespun before what is called Yankee energy was known west of the Hudson. They held the western line of battle in the Revolution against the British and their savage allies, and one of them, with a handful of men, wrested from the foe the territory north of the Ohio, with an area greater than France, and four times that of New England. They built the first railroad in the West and one of the first in America, bringing the locomotive from England across the Alleghany mountains; gridironed the state with turnpikes; and all while the mountains, by force of their isolation, were wrapped in a Rip Van Winkle sleep and covered with a Lethean gloom. The waves of progress and civilization have washed all around the confines of this unfortunate region, this vast Sargasso, a dead sea surrounded by an ocean of life.

In physical energy they are not lacking, being capable of enduring much fatigue in hunting or labor; great walkers, who can keep pace all day with a horse, barefoot, like a Scotch gillie. I have seen them in the dead of winter, when they would come down on rafts to the capital of the state from the foot of the Cumberland range, thinly clad in homespun jeans, without overcoats, and exposed, on the swollen river, without shelter to the bitter cold. I sighed to think that such splendid material for a state's greatness should have no better avenue for its latent power. Simple, direct and uncomplaining, when their journey was complete they started afoot for their mountain homes with a pittance for their labor, and unable to take back, for want of transportation, any of the comforts or luxuries of civilization. And thus they illustrate the wastefulness of that system of commerce which drains a country of its raw material without enabling it to receive in exchange the products of its customers.

But the condition which I have described as existing in the mountains a quarter of a century ago has vastly improved since that time. Help has come to these marooned people. The Chesapeake and Ohio railroad in the northern tier of counties, and the Louisville and Nashville system in the southern, with the Kentucky Eastern piercing the center, have worked wonders along their routes, as is evidenced by thrifty towns, with churches, institutions for higher education, mills, furnaces and mines, which may now be seen where formerly all was stagnant.

Some have charged that the feuds originated in the civil war; others conjecture that they took their rise between the patriots and Tories in the war of the Revolution. Both are wrong. They have every earmark of the

Scotch feuds among the clans, and none more than in the savage custom of waylaying and killing from ambush. In truth, it is war, and war is to kill. There is no fair combat between individuals except the duel, and that is rightfully prohibited by law. If death ensues from an attack without warning, it is assassination; if with premeditation, under any circumstances except self-defense, it is murder.

The scheme of the civil compact vests the war-making power solely in the state and recognizes the right of none, either singly or in combination, to take life in redress of personal grievance. The feud and its methods, therefore, constitute one of the gravest violations of law, and should subject those who engage in them to penalties next only to treason, which is waging war against the state and giving aid and comfort to the enemy.

The exciting causes of these feuds are manifold, and frequently of a trifling nature. In a region where the local agencies of the law are weak or indisposed to act, resort to violence requires little provocation. Altercations between friends suddenly angered or drinking, disputes over business settlements, or family discords—of which the son-in-law is credited with many—may all lead to an outbreak the end of which may not be foretold.

Perhaps the best explanation of the feud is to be found in "The Kentuckians," by John Fox, Jr., who made the Kentucky mountaineers a practical study by residing among them for the purpose. In a scene which he presents between the Governor's daughter and a young mountaineer sent to the penitentiary for taking part in one of these disturbances of the peace, she asks the youth why his people fight that way.

"Well," replies the boy, "suppose some sorry feller was to shoot your brother or your daddy, an' the high sheriff was afeerd o' him an' wouldn't arrest him. What would you do? You know mighty well. You'd jest go git yo' gun an' let him have it. Then mebbe his brother would layway you; an' all yo' folks 'ud git mad an' take hit up; an' things 'ud git frolicsome ginerally."

The delinquency of the sheriff here noted is the prime cause of the trouble, whether from fear or, as is too often the case, from sympathy with one of the factions. The same may apply to the other county officers—judge, clerk, jailer and magistrates; if not partisans of the stronger faction, they may be overawed into inaction. But it may be asked, why does the Governor permit such practices without sending troops to preserve the peace? Under the law, when, upon proper request from the civil authorities, he sends troops to a county, they must go as a posse to the local officers; and while frequent instances have occurred in which their presence has been salutary, where the officers are partisans troops would only prove in effect a reinforcement to the side favored by the official to whom they would report. In the absence of some intervening power—either the law, public opinion or the intercession of mutual friends of influence—the solution rests in the conquest, or approach to extinction, of one faction by the other. This has sometimes occurred, the defeated party moving, in the vernacular, "higher up the creek," "roosting lower," or migrating beyond the state.

The Turner-Sizemore feud, in Knott county, in the central mountain region, began in 1875, and before it ended spread over parts of the adjoining counties of Floyd and Letcher. Its specific origin is unknown, the first outbreak of bad feeling, probably long festering, having taken place at a Christmas dinner given by "Old Jeff Turner" on Beaver creek, to which a number of his friends were invited. The festivities, which had been hilarious, closed with a fight in which Turner, the hospitable host, and Bug Sizemore were killed, and eight or ten others badly wounded. Then ensued a long and bloody war, in which the two factions were arrayed under the names of the principals in the tragedy. In the several years in which hostilities were kept up twenty or thirty were killed, the inaccessibility of the country and the wide-spread field of operations preventing the intervention of troops. The most noted figure in the feud was a man called "Old Talt Hall," in contradistinction from his son of the same name, who was almost as notorious. He took part with the Sizemores, and long after the local dissensions ceased, by death on each side and the efforts of the law, the Halls continued their career of crime in several other counties of Kentucky, and when driven thence became outlaws in West Virginia and eastern Tennessee. Both were finally brought to justice, the last having been hanged in Tennessee a few years ago.

The Strong-Amis (generally spelled and pronounced Amy) feud, of Breathitt county, was led by Capt. Bill Strong, who commanded a Federal company in the civil war, on one side, and John Amy on the other. Although originating not long after the war, it was personal and not political. Both parties were numerically strong and several pitched battles were fought, all efforts of the local authorities to command the peace being ineffectual.

In 1874 a company of State Guards was sent to them in midwinter, marching over roads so bad for nearly a hundred miles that it required oxen to haul the artillery. Peace reigned for a time, but in 1877 the feud broke out with renewed violence, and in the winter following the Governor sent two well-drilled companies of the State Guard for the arrest of the offenders and their protection during trial. As special judge he sent Judge W. L. Jackson, of the Louisville circuit, an ex-Confederate brigadier-general of cavalry and a judicial officer noted for his breadth and firmness. As commonwealth's attorney he sent W. R. Kinney, an ex-Federal major, also of Louisville, a lawyer of reputation and courage. The moral effect of such a demonstration was quite as potent as any other, for while a number of the indicted were sent to the penitentiary, the presence of the troops and the influence of such able officers of the law entirely overawed the spirit of lawlessness, and brought about a permanent reconciliation between the factions. Captain Strong resumed his peaceful vocation as a farmer, while Jerry Little, a conspicuous leader on the other side, was convicted, but later pardoned, joined the Methodist church, and after having passed safely through the dangers of the feud was crushed to death while logging in the mountains. The newspapers did not fail to work the usual parodies on Goldsmith's lines appropriate to his name pending his trial. As already stated, a railroad now penetrates the county, and a new life is infused in everything.

The Rowan county feud, which in its day created much notoriety, being specially conspicuous for the thoroughness with which it was quelled by the arm of the law, had its origin in an election quarrel between two members of the Martin and Toliver families in 1884. After the quarrel, Craig Toliver, a young man of great physical strength and a dangerous character, became the leader of a faction bearing his name, and waged a deadly warfare against the Martins, who suffered for the lack of a leader of similar capacity. The Youngs, a family of influence, sided with the Tolivers, and the Logans with the Martins. To strengthen his power, Craig Toliver became a candidate for marshal of the town of Morehead, the county-seat, and by intimidation at the polls secured a majority of the votes polled.

The feud progressed with the ordinary incidents, but I do not purpose to weary the reader with its details, the point of interest being in the wind-up, the more tragical the more interesting. Troops were in time sent, and a compromise was effected by which it was arranged that Toliver should expatriate himself in Missouri for one year and Cook Humphries, the sheriff, who was a Martin leader, for the same period in Texas. But, like all compromises with crime, it availed little. Several months before the expiration of the period fixed, Toliver returned, and resuming the functions of the office, renewed his atrocities with increased violence.

Finally two young Logans were assassinated by one of Toliver's posses, and the people were aroused. The Governor, Proctor Knott, was on the eve of sending troops to the county to insure Toliver's arrest, when Boone Logan, a cousin of the two young men who had been murdered, proposed that if authorized he would arrest Toliver without the aid of troops. The Governor assented to his proposition, and warrants having been quietly issued and placed in Logan's hands, he secretly organized a posse of seventy-five men, led by himself and the sheriff, and suddenly surrounded the town. Everybody gave in except Toliver and a few of his immediate associates, who barricaded themselves in the railway-station and proposed to stand a siege. They all perished from the Winchester rifles in the hands of

Boone Logan and his men, who avenged the law and their friends at the same time. The names of the dead were Craig Toliver, Jay Toliver, Bud Toliver and Hiram Cook. It was the 22d day of June, 1887, a day noted in the calendar of that county, as it ended the feud and introduced a new era of peace and prosperity.

The feud which next excited attention, and tended to keep alive the idea that every nook and corner of Kentucky was infested with murderous ruffians—through stirring head-lines of newspapers, many of which had in the same issue in obscure corners in nonpareil type notices of more murders and other crimes in their own bailiwicks than occur in an ordinary feud of several years' duration—was in Bell county, in the extreme southeastern corner of the state.

In the valley of Yellow creek, which flows north into the Cumberland, where now stands the town of Middlesboro, founded in 1888 by English capitalists, there dwelt prior to that date a primitive mountain people, among whom were some notoriously bad men. The locality was then a hundred miles from a railroad in Kentucky, though somewhat nearer to one in Tennessee. The turbulent in his beautiful valley were known as the "Yellow Creekers," among whom were two factions led by Alvis Turner and "Gen" Sowders, which developed a feud known in the hyphenated category as the Turner-Sowders feud. It was similar to all other feuds in waylayings, shooting from the "brush" and all the concomitants. Alvis Turner and many of his name and clan met violent death, as did many of their opponents, but "Gen" Sowders came out in the ascendant, and with the awakening caused by the building of the railroad made a good citizen.

The event was rendered picturesque by the prominence given in the papers to Andy Johnson, who had six or eight nicks in his notch-stick. When the boom came, he settled down in Pineville, where lots sold at public outcry for one hundred dollars per front foot, and became a speculator and officer of the peace, living long enough to see lots sink to their normal level, and finally dying, as was to have been expected, with his boots on. Now over the valley of Yellow creek hovers the smoke of many tall chimney-stacks, while it is adorned with a beautiful city, which has picturesque views surpassed by none, and socially is one of the most attractive towns in the state. The building of the railroads gave occupation to the men who, quitting the "brush," follow peaceful vocations, and in the orderly divertissements of the lively young city work off their accumulated nervousness without further inconvenience than is inseparable from undue excess in a well-governed municipality with a firm police judge.

The county of Harlan—named for Silas Harlan, the pioneer ancestor of Mr. Justice Harlan of the United States Supreme Court—lies north of Bell county, just spoken of, on the headwaters of the Cumberland river. It is the most mountainous region in the state, having within its limits Black mountain, four thousand feet high, the greatest elevation in the Cumberland branch of the Appalachian chain. The population is similar to that in other counties, except more primitive in its wilder portions, having in its dialect old English words long obsolete in America.

A famous one, known as the Turner-Howard feud—note how English are all the names I have given—broke out in 1886 between the sons of George B. Turner, the leading native attorney of Mt. Pleasant, the county-seat, and Wilson Howard, who became the leader of his faction. The fathers in the two families remained friends. The usual killing went on by spurts, Howard's tactics being to hold a fortified camp at his home on Martin's fork, fifteen miles above Mt. Pleasant, while the Turners made the latter place their headquarters, and generally stood on the defensive, declining to bushwhack, while shooting from ambush was Howard's strong card.

The result was that three of the Turner boys were killed without ever seeing their slayers, and that Howard would have doubtless wiped out the whole faction and dominated the county, but for one fortunate circumstance, gruesome as it may sound. He had, before undertaking to clean out Harlan, murdered a man in Missouri, and in the midst of his successful career as a waylayer it became known that a large reward had been offered in Missouri for his capture. This stimulated extra efforts on the part of local peace-officers, and by the aid of the state troops his gang was broken up, he becoming a fugitive, his brother being sent to the penitentiary for life; and peace was restored to Harlan. He eluded arrest for a number of years, but was finally captured and hanged at Lebanon, Missouri. Unclouded peace has reigned in Harlan since. In fact, even during the feud there was little danger to those not engaged on one side or the other, as while it was pending Governor Buckner and Mr. Charles Dudley Warner rode through the county on horseback from "eend to eend," the latter giving in one of the monthlies an interesting account of this trip.

I pass over several feuds which have not in their history any special attraction, and come to the latest, which is now on. I refer to the Baker-Howard feud, in Clay county, which has some features and presents some threatening aspects which render it of more than ordinary interest. Clay county also lies toward the south-eastern part of Kentucky, on the waters of the south fork of the Kentucky river; its county-seat, Manchester, named for the English manufacturing town as an earnest of the hopes and expectations of its founders, being twenty-four miles east of London, the nearest railroad station, over a difficult mountain road. The county was formed in 1806, and named for Gen. Green Clay, the father of Gen. Cassius M. Clay. It is nearly half as large as the state of Rhode Island, with twelve thousand inhabitants. In natural resources, fertility of soil, and wealth and intelligence of its principal citizens, it has long ranked as first among the mountain counties. In fact, it was noted more than a hundred years ago for the salt-wells on Goose creek, near the county-seat, which then and for many years furnished the principal supply of salt for a wide territory extending beyond the state, the streams of the county providing transportation to the Ohio and a market. Its manufacture is still an industry, but on a reduced scale.

In 1844 a noted killing took place there, Dr. Abner Baker, the leading physician, having killed Daniel Bates, who had married his sister and was separated from her. It caused much bad feeling between several prominent families who had before been intimate friends. Dr. Baker was indicted, and after a noted trial, a report of which was published in book form, was convicted and hanged.

Among the wealthy salt-makers were Daniel Garrard and Hugh White, both men of strong character and friends. The former was the son of James Garrard, second Governor of Kentucky, who had settled in Clay county in 1805, and served many years in the state Senate and House. Hugh White was equally prominent, and has many descendants of distinction living and dead, some of them of national reputation, among them John White, who was member of Congress five consecutive terms and Speaker of the Twenty-seventh Congress, and John D. White, his nephew, who represented the same district 1881–85. The Garrards defended and the Whites prosecuted Baker, and while the present feud has no relation to that difficulty, the older people and those who know the history of the tragedy referred to note with an uneasy significance the fact that in the present trouble the Whites and Garrards, still prominent and numerous, have opposite sympathies.

Gen. Theophilus T. Garrard, son of Daniel Garrard, who pleaded ineffectually with the Governor to pardon his friend, Doctor Baker, has been the passive friend and bondsman of the Bakers of to-day, while the Whites, who, it is said, have held or controlled the offices of the county for fifty years, have lost one of their family in this feud at the hands of Tom Baker, the principal of his faction, and are active sympathizers with the opposite or Howard faction. General Garrard, like his father, has served as state senator and representative, and was a distinguished Federal general of cavalry in the civil war. He was born in sight of his present residence in 1812, and lives in a large double brick house, with tall ceilings and hand-carved mantels, built by his father seventy-five years ago. At the age of eighty-seven he still conducts the business of a salt manufacturer.

The origin of the Baker-Howard feud was in a difficulty arising between two partners in business. Tom Baker, who, with a family of ten children, lived on Crain creek, twelve miles from Manchester, followed logging in connection with a farm. A. B. Howard engaged him to cut some timber from his land on shares. They fell out under circumstances too tedious to detail, with the usual preliminary first words, then threats, then Winchesters. In the first ambush party, the Baker faction got one of the Howard boys and Burt Stores, and wounded the senior Howard; then another Howard son sent a Winchester ball through the elder Baker; then Tom Baker shot to death William L. White, brother of the sheriff, who he alleged had instigated the murder of his brother; then Gilbert Garrard, son of General Garrard, a merchant, was fired on from ambush while riding with his wife to a Sunday-school mission under unfounded suspicion that he was more actively in sympathy with Baker than he ought to be. He removed to Pineville to avoid further complications. His father, being advised of probable intentions to molest him, had two men to guard his premises at night, a nephew of Tom Baker and a negro man, and both these were shot from the "brush" shortly after the last two incidents. This was the situation a year ago.

Now, Tom Baker did not relish the idea of giving himself up to the sheriff, Beverly T. White, brother of the man he had killed and kinsman to the clerk, jailer and judge. So he took to the hills until troops were sent to the county, when he surrendered himself to them. He was then tried in the Knox Circuit Court on change of venue, and sentenced to the penitentiary for life. His attorneys took the case up to the Court of Appeals for error and secured a reversal of the verdict of the lower court, which entailed a new trial, pending which he was released on bail, and went to his farm on Crain creek. In June the time for his second trial approached, and again the Governor sent a company of the State Guard with a Gatling gun to give confidence. On their arrival they pitched tent in the court-house yard, with the Gatling gun in good position for action, and sent a squad to Crain creek for Tom Baker. They found him at home and took him back to Manchester. His wife feared the worst, whether she stayed at home unprotected or went with him, but she chose the latter, and took with her all the children, nine of whom were boys, two of these being old enough to handle a Winchester and being also wanted by the law.

For reasons not clear, Tom Baker was placed in a guard-tent instead of a house with brick walls. The officer in charge thought he would be safe with guards about the tent, but in a fatal moment he stepped incautiously to the door of the tent, when the crack of a Winchester rang out in the morning air, and he fell dead from a bullet shot from the unoccupied residence of the sheriff, a hundred yards or so distant at the foot of the wooded mountain, whither the assassin made his escape.

In the bustle of calling the camp to arms and training the Gatling gun, the lamentations of the devoted wife, who received the falling form of the murdered man, mingled with vows to rear all her boys with an oath to avenge their father's death—with which she charged the Whites, saying they had done it in retaliation for their brother's murder.

Next day the troops retreated safely to Barbourville, taking the Baker family and the Gatling gun, and by a bold piece of strategy thwarted an alleged scheme of the Howard-White faction to ambush and capture the Gatling gun. They also safely returned to Frankfort without casualty of any kind on the trip. Peace now reigned in Warsaw, Manchester resumed its wonted quiet; but yet another act in this tragedy of blood remained. On the 17th of July, while four of the Philpot subfaction of the Baker side were peaceably on their way to their logging-camp, carrying their Winchesters, they were met by a deputy sheriff, who served a warrant on one of the party and proposed to release him upon his signing a bond. He was in the act of signing the paper when four men of the Morris subfaction on the Howard-White side appeared in the road and proceeded to do business with their Winchesters. The man in the act of signing the bond was first killed by the firing, which soon became general. When the neighbors arrived on the scene, they found three men lying dead in the road, with three mortally, and two others seriously, wounded, the honors being evenly divided.

This is the state of the case up to date a week after the killing, and no arrests have been made or troops sent. I know it is a difficult problem, in the present state of the law regulating the sending of troops, and I would not imply censure of the Governor for his inaction. But surely something should be done, in the way of either force or arbitration, to put a stop to this lamentable state of affairs. At this very moment the United States has an army in the Philippines trying to effect a peace in which our people have little else than a sentimental interest. And at The Hague we have commissioners for the purpose of preventing or humanizing wars between the parties participating in the congress. Yet here at home a war is raging as savage as that in Luzon and no hand or voice is lifted to stay its bloody work. There is a provision in the Constitution providing for the intervention of the Federal government in certain cases when the state is impotent to quell disturbances. Yet there seems no indication of sending troops here. On the contrary, at London, almost within the sound of a Gatling gun in Clay county, there is a recruiting station for raising troops for the new regiments intended for service in the Philippines. Send a company, a regiment, a brigade, a division corps, or an army if necessary, but send something or somebody, if only to make terms, for the defenseless and innocent people, with those who have the law of Kentucky by the throat.

7

The Southern Mountaineer

John Fox, Jr.

John Fox, Jr. (1862–1919), is the only late nineteenth-/early twentieth-century writer of Appalachian novels whose work still enjoys a wide readership. His popularity today rests primarily on his novels *The Little Shepherd of Kingdom Come* (1903) and *The Trail of the Lonesome Pine* (1908). In these, and his other works of fiction, Fox presents his views on southern mountaineers and their background. In his early publications, such as *A Cumberland Vendetta* (1895), he indicates willingness to accept the idea that their heritage is varied and may include some poor white ancestry. Later works, such as *The Heart of the Hills* (1913), reveal an altered viewpoint in which mountaineers are thought to be derived from one basic stock with considerable gradations in quality brought about by numerous social forces that have resulted in varied economic status. Fox also displayed his ideas in a series of articles in popular magazines, one of them being the piece reprinted here. In this two-part essay Fox emphasizes that environment, not personal characteristics, "keeps the Southern mountaineer to the backwoods civilization of the revolution."

Fox studied at Transylvania University under James Lane Allen who initially aroused his interest in writing. Eventually, like his mentor, Fox came to know mountaineers firsthand by making trips into the region. He soon came to know them much better than Allen, or any other novelist of his day, and became intrigued by the differences between the world he came from and that of the mountain people. Indeed, the conflict between the two cultures is a recurring theme in his fiction; all of his novels, except *A Cumberland Vendetta* (1895), include a lowlander who is representative of civilization and thus stands in marked contrast to the arrested culture of the mountaineers. For Fox, and many other Appalachian observers at the time, these differences were not desirable and needed to be eliminated. Yet, because they were the result of environmental factors over which the people had little control, Fox was optimistic that they could be dissolved. Like J. Stoddard Johnston, he maintained that given the opportunity to enter civilization the mountaineer would gladly do so.

Reprinted from *Scribner's Magazine* 29 (April–May 1901): 387–99, 556–70.

The anecdotal essay reprinted here, with its accounts of funerals, folk speech, singing, and meetings with moonshiners, indicates that Fox knew mountaineers on intimate terms. He was better acquainted with Kentucky hillfolk than those in other sections of Appalachia, but because he believes in the cultural homogeneity of the mountaineers he regards eastern Kentuckians as quintessentially Appalachian. It is, at least, a moot point that "any trait common to the Southern mountaineer" is "intensified in the mountaineer of Kentucky." Some of his other "facts" are also debatable. For example, the wandering minstrel was more common than Fox leads the reader to believe. For information on Fox, see William Cabell Moore, *John Fox, Jr.: 1862–1919. An Address Delivered October 21, 1957, at the Club of Colonial Dames, Washington, D.C.* (Lexington: University of Kentucky Library, 1957); Cratis D. Williams, "The Primitive Stereotype in Conflict with Outside Influences," *Appalachian Journal* 3 (Spring, 1976): 211–22; and Donald Askins, "John Fox, Jr. a Re-appraisal; or, With Friends like That, Who Needs Enemies?" in Helen Matthews Lewis, Linda Johnson and Donald Askins, *Colonialism in Modern America: The Appalachian Case* (Boone, North Carolina: The Appalachian Consortium Press, 1978), pp. 251–57.

* * *

It was only a little while ago that the materialists declared that humanity was the product of heredity and environment; that history lies not *near* but *in* Nature; and that, in consequence, man must take his head from the clouds and study himself with his feet where they belong, to the earth. Since then, mountains have taken on a new importance for the part they have played in the destiny of the race, for the reason that mountains have dammed the streams of humanity, have let them settle in the valleys and spread out over plains; or have sent them on long detours around. When some unusual pressure has forced a current through some mountain-pass, the hills have cut it off from the main stream and have held it so stagnant, that, to change the figure, mountains may be said to have kept the records of human history somewhat as fossils hold the history of the earth.

Arcadia held primitive the primitive inhabitants of Greece, who fled to its rough hills after the Dorian invasion. The Pyrenees kept unconquered and strikingly unchanged the Basques—sole remnants perhaps in western Europe of the aborigines who were swept away by the tides of Aryan immigration; just as the Rocky Mountains protect the American Indian in primitive barbarism and not wholly subdued to-day and the Cumberland range keeps the Southern mountaineer to the backwoods civilization of the revolution. The reason is plain. The mountain dweller lives apart from the world. The present is the past when it reaches him; and though past, is yet too far in the future to have any bearing on his established order of things. There is, in consequence, no incentive whatever for him to change. An arrest of development follows; so that once imprisoned, a civilization, with its dress, speech, religion, customs, ideas, may be caught like the shapes of lower life in stone, and may tell the human story of a century as the rocks tell the story of an age. For centuries the Highlander has had plaid and kilt; the peasant of Norway and the mountaineer of the German and Austrian Alps each a habit of his own; and every Swiss canton a distinctive dress. Mountains preserve the Gaelic tongue in which the scholar may yet read the refuge of Celt from Saxon, and in turn Saxon from the Norman-French, just as they keep alive remnants like the Rhaeto-Roman, the Basque and a number of Caucasian dialects. The Carpathians protected Christianity against the Moors, and in Java, the Brahman faith took refuge on the sides of the Volcano Gunung Lawa and there outlived the ban of Buddha.

So, in the log cabin of the Southern mountaineer, in his household furnishings, in his homespun, his linsey and, occasionally, in his hunting shirt, his coon-skin cap and moccasins one may summon up the garb and life of the pioneer; in his religion, his politics, his moral code, his folk songs and his superstitions one may bridge the waters back to the old country, and through his speech one may even touch the remote past of Chaucer. For to-day he is a distinct remnant of Colonial times—a distinct relic of an Anglo-Saxon past.

It is odd to think that he was not discovered until the outbreak of the Civil War, although he was nearly a century old then, and it is really startling to realize that when one speaks of the Southern mountaineers, he speaks of nearly three millions of people who live in eight Southern States—Virginia and Alabama and the Southern States between—and occupy a region equal in area to the combined areas of Ohio and Pennsylvania, as big, say, as the German Empire and richer, perhaps, in timber and mineral deposits than any other region of similar extent in the world. This region was and is an unknown land. It has been aptly called "Appalachian America," and the work of discovery is yet going on. The American mountaineer was discovered, I say, at the beginning of the war, when the Confederate leaders were counting on the presumption that Mason and Dixon's Line was the dividing line between the North and South, and formed therefore the plan of marching an army from Wheeling, in West Virginia, to some point on the lakes, and thus dissevering the North at one blow. The plan seemed so feasible that it is said to have materially aided the sale of Confederate bonds in England, but when Captain Garnett, a West Point graduate, started to carry it out, he got no farther than Harper's Ferry. When he struck the mountains, he struck enemies who shot at his men from ambush, cut down bridges before him, carried the news of his march to the Federals, and Garnett himself fell with a bullet from a mountaineer's squirrel rifle at Harper's Ferry. Then the South began to realize what a long, lean powerful arm of the Union it was that the Southern mountaineer stretched through its very vitals; for that arm helped hold Kentucky in the Union by giving preponderance to the Union sympathizers in the Blue-grass; it kept the East Tennesseans loyal to the man; it made West Virginia, as the phrase goes, "secede from secession"; it drew out a horde of one hundred thousand volunteers, when Lincoln called for troops, depleting Jackson County, Ky., for instance of every male under sixty years of age, and over fifteen, and it raised a hostile barrier between the armies of the coast and the armies of the Mississippi. The North has never realized, perhaps, what is owes for its victory to this non-slaveholding Southern mountaineer.

The war over, he went back to his cove and his cabin, and but for the wealth of his hills and the pen of one Southern woman, the world would have forgotten him again. Charles Egbert Craddock put him in the outer world of fiction, and in recent years railroads have been linking him with the outer world of fact. Religious and educational agencies have begun work on him; he has increased in political importance, and a few months ago he went down heavily armed with pistol and Winchester—a thousand strong—to assert his political rights in the State capital of Kentucky. It was probably one of these mountaineers who killed William Goebel, and he no doubt thought himself as much justified as any other assassin who ever slew the man he thought a tyrant. Being a Unionist, because of the Revolution, a Republican, because of the Civil War, and having his antagonism aroused against the Blue-grass people, who, he believes, are trying to rob him of his liberties, he is now the political factor with which the Anti-Goebel Democrats—in all ways the best element in the State—have imperiled the Democratic Party in Kentucky. Sooner or later, there will be an awakening in the mountainous parts of the other seven States; already the coal and iron of these regions are making many a Southern ear listen to the plea of protection; and some day the National Democratic party will, like the Confederacy, find a subtle and powerful foe in the Southern mountaineer and in the riches of his hills.

In the march of civilization westward, the Southern mountaineer has been left in an isolation almost beyond belief. He was shut off by mountains that have blocked and still block the commerce of a century, and there for a century he has stayed. He has had no navigable rivers, no lakes, no coasts, few wagon-roads, and often no roads at all except the beds of streams. He has lived in the cabin in which his grandfather was born, and in life, habit and thought he has been merely his grandfather born over again. The first generation after the Revolution had no schools and no churches. Both are rare and primitive to-day. To this day, few Southern mountaineers can read and write and cipher; few, indeed, can do more. They saw little of the newspapers and were changeless in politics as in everything else. They cared little for what was going on in the outside world, and indeed they heard nothing that did not shake the nation. To the average mountaineer the earth was still flat and had four corners. It was the sun that girdled the earth, just as it did when Joshua told it to stand still, and precisely for that reason. The stories of votes yet being cast for Andrew Jackson are but little exaggerated. An old Tennessee mountaineer once told me about the discovery of America by Columbus. He could read his Bible, with marvelous interpretations of the same. He was the patriarch of his district, the philosopher. He had acquired the habit of delivering the facts of modern progress to his fellows, and it never occurred to him that a man of my youth might be acquainted with that rather well-known bit of history. I listened gravely, and he went on, by and by, to speak of the Mexican War as we would speak of the fighting in China; and when we got down to so recent and burning an issue as the late civil struggle, he dropped his voice to a whisper and hitched his chair across the fireplace and close to mine.

"Some folks had other idees," he said, "but hit's my pussonal opinion that *niggahs was the cause o' the war.*"

When I left his cabin, he followed me out to the fence.

"Stranger," he said, "I'd ruther you wouldn' say nothin' about whut I been tellin' ye." He had been a lone rebel in sympathy and he feared violence at this late day, for expressing his opinion too freely. This old man was a "citizen"; I was a "furriner" from the "settlements"—that is, the Blue-grass. Columbus was one of the "outlandish," a term that carried not only his idea of the parts hailed from but his personal opinion of Columbus. Living thus, his interest centred in himself, his family, his distant neighbor, his grist mill, his country store, his county town; unaffected by other human influences; having no incentive to change, no wish for it, and remaining therefore unchanged, except where civilization during the last decade, has pressed in upon him the Southern mountaineer is thus practically the pioneer of the Revolution, the living ancestor of the Modern West.

The national weapons of the pioneer—the axe and the rifle—are the Southern mountaineer's weapons to-day. He has still the same fight with Nature. His cabin was, and is yet in many places, the cabin of the backwoodsman—of one room usually—sometimes two, connected by a covered porch, and built of unhewn logs with a puncheon floor, clapboards for shingles and wooden pin and augur-hole for nails. The crevices between the logs were filled with mud and stones when filled at all, and there were holes in the roof for the wind and the rain. Sometimes there was a window with a batten wooden shutter, sometimes no window at all. Over the door, across a pair of buck antlers, lay the long, heavy, home-made rifle of the backwoodsman, sometimes even with a flint lock. One can yet find a crane swinging in a big stone fireplace, the spinning-wheel and the loom in actual use; sometimes the hominy block that the pioneers borrowed from the

Indians, and a hand-mill for grinding corn like the one, perhaps, from which one woman was taken and another left in biblical days. Until a decade and a half ago they had little money, and the medium of exchange was barter. They drink metheglin still, as well as moonshine. They marry early, and only last summer I saw a fifteen-year-old girl riding behind her father, to a log church to be married. After the service, her pillion was shifted to her young husband's horse, as was the pioneer custom, and she rode away behind him to her new home. There are still log-rollings, house-raisings, house-warmings, corn-shuckings and quiltings. Sports are still the same—as they have been for a hundred years—wrestling, racing, jumping, and lifting barrels. Brutally savage fights are still common in which the combatants strike, kick, bite, and gouge until one is ready to cry "enough." Even the backwoods bully, loud, coarse, profane, bantering—a dandy who wore long hair and embroidered his hunting shirt with porcupine-quills—is not quite dead. I saw one not long since, but he wore store clothes, a gorgeous red tie, a dazzling brass scarf-pin—in the bosom of his shirt. His hair was sandy, but his mustache was blackened jet. He had the air and smirk of a lady-killer, and in the butt of the huge pistol buckled around him, was a large black bow—the badge of death and destruction to his enemies. Funerals are most simple. Sometimes the coffin is slung to poles and carried by four men. While the begum has given place to hickory bark when a cradle is wanted, baskets and even fox-horns are still made of that material.

Not only many remnants like these are left in the life of the mountaineer, but, occasionally, far up some creek it was possible, as late as fifteen years ago, to come upon a ruddy, smooth-faced, big-framed old fellow, keen-eyed, taciturn, avoiding the main-travelled roads; a great hunter, calling his old squirrel rifle by some pet feminine name—who, with a coon-skin cap, the scalp in front, and a fringed hunting-shirt and moccasins, completed the perfect image of the pioneer as the books and tradition have handed him down to us.

It is easy to go on back across the water to the Old Country. One finds still among the mountaineers the pioneer's belief in signs, omens, and the practice of witch-craft; for whatever traits the pioneer brought over the sea, the Southern mountaineer has to-day. The rough-and-tumble fight of the Scotch and the English square stand-up and knock-down boxing-match were the mountaineer's ways of settling minor disputes—one or the other, according to agreement—until the war introduced musket and pistol. The imprint of Calvinism on his religious nature is yet plain, in spite of the sway of Methodism for nearly a century. He is the only man in the world whom the Catholic Church has made little or no effort to proselyte. Dislike of Episcopalianism is still strong among people who do not know or pretend not to know what the word means.

"Any Episcopalians around here?" asked a clergyman at a mountain cabin. "I don' know," said the old woman. "Jim's got the skins of a lot o' varmints up in the loft. Mebbe you can find one up thar."

The Unionism of the mountaineer in the late war is in great part an inheritance from the intense Americanism of the back-woodsman, just as that Americanism came from the spirit of the Covenanters. His music is thus a trans-Atlantic remnant. In Harlan County, Ky., a mountain girl leaned her chair against the wall of her cabin, put her large bare feet on one of the rungs and sang me an English ballad three hundred years old, and almost as long as it was ancient. She said she knew many others. In Perry County, where there are in the French-Eversole feud, McIntyres, McIntoshes, McKnights, Combs, probably McCombs and Fitzpatricks, Scotch ballads are said to be sung with Scotch accent, and an occasional copy of Burns is to be found. I have even run across the modern survival of the wandering minstrel—two blind fiddlers who were about the mountains making up "ballets" to celebrate the deeds of leaders in Kentucky feuds. One of the verses ran:

> The death of these two men
> Caused great trouble in our land,
> Caused men to say the bitter word,
> And take the parting hand.

Nearly all songs and dance tunes are written in the so-called old Scotch scale, and like negro music, they drop frequently into the relative minor; so that if there be any truth in the theory that negro music is merely the adaptation of Scotch and Irish folk-songs and folk-dance, and folk-dances with the added stamp of the negro's peculiar temperament, then the music adapted is to be heard in the mountains to-day as the negro heard it long ago.

In his speech, the mountaineer touches a very remote past. Strictly speaking, he has no dialect. The mountaineer simply keeps in use old words and meanings that the valley people have ceased to use; but nowhere is this usage so sustained and consistent as to form a dialect. To writers of mountain stories, the temptation seems quite irresistible to use more peculiar words in one story than can be gathered from the people in a month. Still, unusual words are abundant. There are perhaps two hundred words, meanings, and pronunciations that in the mountaineer's speech go back unchanged to Chaucer. Some of the words are: afeard, afore, axe, holp, crope, clomb, peert, beest (horse), cryke, eet (ate), farwel, fer (far), fool (foolish—"them fool-women"), heepe, hit (it), I is, lepte, pore (poor), right (very), slyk, study (think), souple (supple), up (verb), "he up and done it," usen, yer for year, yond, instid, yit, etc. There are others which have English dialect authority: blather, doated, antic, dreen, brash, faze (now modern slang), fernent, ferninst, master, size, etc. Many of these words, of course, the upper classes use throughout the South. These the young white master got from his negro playmates, who took them from the lips of the poor whites. The double negative, always used by the old English who seem to have resisted it no more than did the Greeks, is invariable with the mountaineer. With him a triple negative is common. A mountaineer had been shot. His friends came in to see him and kept urging him to revenge. A woman wanted them to stop.

"Hit jes' raises the ambition in him and *don't* do *no* good *nohow.*"

The "dialect" is not wholly deterioration then. What we are often apt to regard as ignorance in the mountaineer is simply our own disuse. Unfortunately, the speech is a mixture of so many old English dialects that it is of little use in tracing the origin of the people who use it.

Such has been the outward protective effect of mountains on the Southern mountaineer. As a human type he is of unusual interest.

No mountain people are ever rich. Environment keeps mountaineers poor. The strength that comes from numbers and wealth is always wanting. Agriculture is the sole stand-by and agriculture distributes population because arable soil is confined to bottom-lands and valleys. Farming on a mountain-side is not only arduous and unremunerative—it is sometimes dangerous. There is a well-authenticated case of a Kentucky mountaineer who fell out of his own corn-field and broke his neck. Still, though fairly well-to-do in the valleys, the Southern mountaineer can be pathetically poor. A young preacher stopped at a cabin in Georgia to stay all night. His hostess, as a mark of unusual distinction, killed a chicken and dressed it in a pan. She rinsed the pan and made up her dough in it. She rinsed it again and went out and used it for a milk-pail. She came in, rinsed it again, and went to the spring and brought it back full of water. She filled up the glasses on the table and gave him the pan with the rest of the water in which to wash his hands. The woman was not a slattern; it was the only utensil she had.

This poverty of natural resources makes the mountaineer's fight for life a hard one. At the same time it gives him vigor, hardihood, and endurance of body; it saves him from the comforts and dainties that weaken; and it makes him a formidable competitor, when it forces him to come down into the plains as it often does. For this poverty was at the bottom of the marauding instinct of the Pict and Scot, just as it is at the bottom of the migrating instinct that sends the Southern mountaineers west in spite of a love for home that is a proverb with the Swiss, and is hardly less strong in the Southern mountaineer to-day. Invariably the Western wanderer comes home again. Time and again an effort was made to end a feud in the Kentucky mountains by sending the leaders away. They always came back. The last but one of the Turners in the Howard-Turner feud was urged by his friends to leave the mountains. The Howard leader was "waitin' in the lorrel" for him, as the mountaineers characterize waiting in ambush—a thing the Turner scorned to do. His answer was that he would rather stay where he was a year and die than live to old age away from home. In less than a year he was waylaid and killed.

It is this poverty of arable land that further isolates the mountaineer in his loneliness. For he must live apart not only from the world but from his neighbor. The result is an enforced self-reliance, and through that the gradual growth of an individualism that has been "the strength, the weakness; the personal charm, the political stumbling-block; the ethical significance and the historical insignificance of the mountaineer the world over." It is this isolation, this individualism that makes unity of action difficult, public sentiment weak, and takes from the law the righting of private wrongs. It is this individualism that has been a rich mine for the writer of fiction. In the Southern mountaineer, its most marked elements are religious feeling, hospitality, and pride. So far these last two traits have been lightly touched upon, for the reason that they appear only by contrast with a higher civilization that has begun to reach them only in the last few years.

The latch-string hangs outside every cabin-door if the men-folks are at home, but you must shout "hello" always outside the fence.

"We 'uns is pore," you will be told, "but y'u're welcome ef y'u kin put up with what we have."

After a stay of a week at a mountain cabin a young "furriner" asked what his bill was. The old mountaineer waved his hand "Nothin'," he said, "'cept come agin!"

A belated traveller asked to stay all night at a cabin. The mountaineer answered that his wife was sick and they were sorter out o' fixins' to eat, but he reckoned he mought step over to a neighbor's an borrer some. He did step over and he was gone three hours. He brought back a little bag of meal, and they had corn-bread and potatoes for supper and for breakfast, cooked by the mountaineer. The stranger asked how far away his next neighbor lived. "A leetle the rise o' six miles I reckon," was the answer.

"Which way?"

"Oh, jes' over the mountain thar."

He had stepped six miles over the mountain and back for that little bag of meal, and he would allow his guest to pay nothing next morning.

I have slept with nine others in a single room. The host gave up his bed to two of our party, and he and his wife slept with the rest of us on the floor. He gave us supper, kept us all night, sent us away next morning with a parting draught of moonshine apple-jack, of his own brewing by the way, and would suffer no one to pay a cent for his entertainment. That man was a desperado, an outlaw, a moonshiner, and was running from the sheriff at that very time.

Two outlaw sons were supposed to be killed by officers. I offered aid to the father to have them decently clothed and buried, but the old man, who was as bad as his sons, declined it with some dignity. They had enough left for that; and if not, why he had.

A woman whose husband was dead, who was sick to death herself, whose four children was almost starved, said, when she heard the "fur-riners" were talking about sending her to the poor-house, that she "would go out on her crutches and hoe corn fust" (and she did), and that "people who talked about sending her to the po'-house had better save their breath to make prayers with."

It is a fact—in the Kentucky mountains at least—that the poor-houses are usually empty, and that it is considered a disgrace to a whole clan if one of its members is an inmate. It is the exception when a family is low and lazy enough to take a revenue from the State for an idiot child. I saw a boy once, astride a steer which he had bridled with a rope, barefooted, with his yellow hair sticking from his crownless hat—and in blubbering ecstasy over the fact that he was no longer under the humiliation of accepting $75 a year from the State. He had proven his sanity by his answer to one question.

"Do you work in the field," asked the commissioner.

"Well, ef I didn't," was the answer, "thar wouldn't be no work done."

I have always feared, however, that there was another reason for his happiness than balm to his suffering pride. Relieved of the ban of idiocy, he had gained a privilege—unspeakably dear in the mountains—the privilege of matrimony.

Like all mountain races, the Southern mountaineers are deeply religious. In some communities religion is about the only form of recreation they have. They are for the most part Methodists and Baptists—sometimes, Ironsides feet-washing Baptists. They will walk, or ride, when possible, eight or ten miles, and sit all day in a close, windowless log-cabin on the flat side of a slab supported by pegs, listening to the high-wrought emotional and, at times, unintelligible ranting of a mountain preacher, while the young men sit outside whittling with their Barlows and huge jack-knives, and swapping horses and guns.

"If anybody wants to extribute anything to the export of the gospels hit will be gradually received." A possible remark of this sort will gauge the intelligence of the pastor. The cosmopolitanism of the congregation can be guessed from the fact that certain elders, filling a vacancy in their pulpit, once decided to "take that ar man Spurgeon if they could git him to come." It is hardly necessary to add that the "extribution to the export of the gospels" is very, very gradually received.

Naturally, their religion is sternly orthodox and most literal. The infidel is unknown, and no mountaineer is so bad as not to have a full share of religion deep down, though, as in his more civilized brother, it is not always apparent until death is at hand. In the famous Howard and Turner war, the last but one of the Turner brothers was shot by a Howard while he was drinking at a spring. He leaped to his feet, and fell in a little creek where, from behind a sycamore-root, he emptied his Winchester at his enemy, and between the cracks of his gun he could be heard, half a mile away, praying aloud.

The custom of holding funeral services for the dead annually, for several years after death, is common. I heard the fourth annual funeral sermon of a dead feud leader preached a few summers ago, and it was consoling to hear that even he had all the virtues that so few men seem to have in life, and so few to lack when dead. But in spite of the universality of religious feeling and a surprising knowledge of the Bible, it is possible to find an ignorance that is almost incredible. The mountain evangelist, George O. Barnes, it is said, once stopped at a mountain cabin and told the story of the crucifixion as few other men can. When he was quite through, an old woman who had listened in absorbed silence asked:

"Stranger, you say that that happened a long while ago?"

"Yes," said Mr. Barnes; "almost two thousand years ago."

"And they treated him that way when he'd come down fer nothin' on earth but to save 'em?"

"Yes."

The old woman was crying softly, and she put out her hand and laid it on his knee.

"Well, stranger," she said, "let's hope that hit ain't so."

She did not want to believe that humanity was capable of such ingratitude. While ignorance of this kind is rare, and while we may find men who know the Bible from "kiver to kiver," it is not impossible to find children of shrewd native intelligence who have not heard of Christ and the Bible.

Now, whatever interest the Southern mountaineer has as a remnant of pioneer days, as a relic of an Anglo-Saxon past, and as a peculiar type that seems to be the invariable result of a mountain environment—the Kentucky mountaineer shares in a marked degree. Moreover he has an interest peculiarly his own; for I believe him to be as sharply distinct from his fellows, as the blue-grass Kentuckian is said to be from his.

The Kentucky mountaineers are practically valley people. There are the three forks of the Cumberland, the three forks of the Kentucky, and the tributaries of Big Sandy—all with rich river-bottoms. It was natural that these lands should attract a better class of people than the average mountaineer. They did. There were many slave-holders among them—a fact that has never been mentioned, as far as I know, by anybody who has written about the mountaineer. The houses along these rivers are, as a rule, weather-boarded, and one will often find interior decorations, startling in color and puzzling in design, painted all over porch, wall, and ceiling. The people are better fed, better clothed, less lank in figure, more intelligent. They wear less homespun, and their speech, while as archaic as elsewhere, is, I believe, purer. You rarely hear "you uns" and "we uns," and similar untraceable confusions in the Kentucky mountains, except along the border of Tennessee. Moreover, the mountaineers who came over from West Virginia and from the southwestern corner of old Virginia were undoubtedly the daring, the hardy, and the strong, for no other kind would have climbed gloomy Black Mountain and the Cumberland Range to fight against beast and savage for their homes.

However, in spite of the general superiority that these facts give him, the Kentucky mountaineer has been more isolated than the mountaineer of any other State. There are regions more remote and more sparsely settled, but nowhere in the Southern mountains has so large a body of mountaineers been shut off so completely from the outside world. As a result he illustrates Mr. Theodore Roosevelt's fine observation that life away from civilization simply emphasizes the natural qualities, good and bad, of the individual. The effect of this truth seems perceptible in that any trait common to the Southern mountaineer seems to be intensified in the mountaineer of Kentucky. He is more clannish, prouder, more hospitable, fiercer, more loyal as a friend, more bitter as an enemy, and in simple meanness—when he is mean, mind you—he can out-Herod his race with great ease.

To illustrate his clannishness: Three mountaineers with a grievance went up to some mines to drive the book-keeper away. A fourth man joined them and stood with drawn pistol during the controversy at the mines, because his wife was a first cousin by marriage of one of the three who had the grievance. In Republican counties, county officers are often Democratic—blood is a stronger tie even than politics.

As to his hospitality: A younger brother of mine was taking dinner with an old mountaineer. There was nothing on the table but some bread and a few potatoes.

"Take out, stranger," he said, heartily. "Have a 'tater—take two of 'em—take nigh all of 'em!"

A mountaineer who had come into possession of a small saw-mill, was building a new house. As he had plenty of lumber a friend of mine asked why he did not build a bigger house. It was big enough, he said. He had two rooms—"one fer the family, an' t'other fer company." As his family numbered fifteen, the scale on which he expected to entertain can be imagined.

The funeral sermon of a mountaineer, who had been dead two years, was preached in Turkey Foot at the base of Mount Scratchum in Jackson County. Three branches run together like a turkey's foot at that point. The mountain is called Scratchum because it is hard to climb. "A funeral sermon," said the old preacher, "can be the last one you hear, or the fust one that's preached over ye atter death. Maybe I'm a-preachin' my own funeral sermon now." If he was, he did himself justice, for he preached three solid hours. The audience was invited to stay to dinner. Forty of them accepted—there were just forty there—and dinner was served from two o'clock until six. The forty were pressed to stay all night. Twenty-three did stay, seventeen in one room. Such is the hospitality of the Kentucky mountaineer.

As to his pride, that is almost beyond belief. I always hesitate to tell this story, for the reason that I can hardly believe it myself. There was a plague in the mountains of eastern Kentucky, West Virginia, and the southwest corner of old Virginia in 1885. A cattle convention of St. Louis made up a relief fund, and sent it for distribution to General Jubal Early of Virginia. General Early sent it to a lawyer of Abingdon, Va., who persuaded D. F. Campbell, another lawyer now living in that town, to take the money into the mountains. Campbell left several hundred dollars in Virginia, and being told that the West Virginians could take care of themselves went with the balance, about $1,000, into Kentucky, where the plague was at its worst. He found the suffering great—nine dead, in one instance, under a single roof. He spent one month going from house to house in the counties of Letcher, Perry, and Pike, carrying the money in his saddle-bags and riding unarmed. Every man, woman, and child in the three counties knew he had the money and knew his mission. He left $5 at a country store, and he got one woman to persuade another woman whose husband and three children were just dead, and who had indignantly refused his personal offer of assistance, to accept $10. The rest of the money he distributed without trouble on his own side of the mountain.

While in Kentucky he found trouble in getting enough to eat for himself and his horse. Often he had only bread and onions; and yet he was permitted to pay but for one meal for either, and that was under protest at a regular boarding-house in a mountain-town. Over the three counties, he got the same answer.

"You are a stranger. We are not beggars, and we can take care of ourselves."

"They are a curious people over there," said Campbell, who is a born Virginian. "No effort was made to rob me, though a man who was known as 'the only thief in Perry County,' a man whom I know to have been trusted with large sums by his leader in a local war, sent me a joking threat. The people were not suspicious of me because I was a stranger. They concealed cases of suffering from me. It was pride that made them refuse the money—nothing else. They are the most loyal friends you ever saw. They will do anything for you, if they like you. They will get up and go anywhere for you day or night, rain or snow. If they haven't a horse, they'll walk. If they haven't shoes, they'll go barefooted. They will combine against you in a trade, and take every advantage they can. A man will keep you at his house to beat you out of a dollar, and when you leave your board-bill is nothing."

This testimony is from a Virginian, and it is a particular pleasure for a representative of one of the second-class families of Virginia who, as the first families say, all emigrated to Kentucky, to prove, by the word of a Virginian, that we have some advantage in at least one section of the State.

Indeed no matter what may be said of the mountaineer in general, the Kentucky mountaineer seems to go the fact one better. Elsewhere, families are large—"children and heepe," says Chaucer. In Jackson County, a mountaineer died not long ago, not at an extreme old age, who left two hundred and seven descendants. He had fifteen children and several of his children had fifteen. There was but one pair of twins among them—both girls—and they were called Louisa and Louïsa. There is in the same county a woman forty-seven years of age, with a granddaughter who has been married fifteen months. Only a break in the family tradition prevented her from being a great-grandmother at forty seven.

It may be that the Kentucky mountaineer is more tempted to an earlier marriage than is the mountaineer elsewhere, for an artist who rode with me through the Kentucky mountains said that not only were the men finer looking, but that the women were far handsomer than elsewhere in the southern Alleghanies. While I am not able to say this, I can say that in the Kentucky mountains the pretty mountain girl is not always, as some people are inclined to believe, pure fiction. Pretty girls are, however, rare; for usually the women are stoop-shouldered and large waisted from working in the fields and lifting heavy weights; for the same reason their hands are large and so are their feet, for they generally go barefoot. But usually they have modest faces and sad, modest eyes, and in the rich river-bottoms, where the mountain farmers have tenants and do not send their daughters to the fields—the girls are apt to be erect and agile, small of hand and foot and usually they have a wild shyness that is very attractive. I recall one girl in crimson homespun, with very big dark eyes, slipping like a flame through the dark room, behind me, when I was on the porch; or gliding out of the one door, if I chanced to enter the other, which I did at every opportunity. A friend who was with me saw her dancing in the dust at twilight, next day, when she was driving the cows home. He helped her to milk and got to know her quite well, I believe. I know that, a year later, when she had worn away her shyness and most of her charm, at school in her county seat, she asked me about him, with embarrassing frankness, and a look crept into her eyes that told an old tale. Pretty girls there are in abundance, but I have seen only one very beautiful mountain girl. One's standard can be affected by a long stay in the mountains, and I should have distrusted mine had it not been for the artist who was with me, fresh from civilization. We saw her, as we were riding up the Cumberland, and we silently and simultaneously drew rein and asked if we could get buttermilk. We could and we swung from our horses. The girl was sitting behind a little cabin with a baby in her lap, and her loveliness was startling. She was slender; her hair was gold-brown; her hands were small and, for a wonder, beautifully shaped. Her teeth, for a wonder, too, were very white and even. Her features were delicately perfect: her mouth shaped as Cupid's bow never was and never would be, said the artist, who christened her eyes after Trilby's— "twin gray stars"—to which the eyebrows and the long lashes gave an indescribable softness. But I felt more the brooding pathos that lay in them, that came from generations of lonely mothers before her, waiting in lonely cabins for the men to come home—back to those wild pioneer days, when they watched with an ever-present fear that they might not come at all.

It was late and we tried to get to stay all night, for the artist wanted to sketch her. He was afraid to ask her permission on so short an acquaintance, for she would not have understood, and he would have frightened her. Her mother gave us buttermilk and we furtively studied her, but we could not stay all night: there were no men-folks at home and no "roughness" for our horses, and we rode regretfully away.

Now, while the good of the mountaineer is emphasized in the mountaineer of Kentucky, the evil is equally marked. The Kentucky mountaineer may be the best of all—he *can* be likewise the worst of all.

A mountaineer was under indictment for moonshining in a little mountain town that has been under the refining influence of a railroad for several years. Unable to give bond, he was ordered to jail by the judge. When the sheriff rose, a huge mountaineer rose, too, in the rear of the court-room and whipped out a big revolver. "You come with me," he said, and the prisoner came, while judge, jury, and sheriff watched him march out. The big fellow took the prisoner through the town and a few yards up a creek. "You go on home," he said. Then the rescuer went calmly back to his house in town, and nothing further has been said or done to this day. The mountaineer was a United States deputy marshal, but the prisoner was his friend.

This marshal was one of the most picturesque figures in the mountains. When sober he was kind-hearted, good tempered, and gentle; and always he was fearless and cool. Once, while firing at two assailants who were shooting at him, he stopped long enough to blow his nose deliberately, and then calmly went on shooting again. He had a companion at arms who, singularly enough, came from the North, and occasionally these two would amuse themselves. When properly exhilarated, one would put a horse-collar on the other, and hitch him to an open buggy. He would fill the buggy with pistols, climb in, and drive around the court-house—each man firing off a pistol with each hand and yelling himself hoarse. Then they would execute an Indian war-dance in the court-house square—firing their pistols alternately into the ground and into the air. The town looked on silently and with great respect, and the two were most exemplary until next time.

A superintendent of some mines near a mountain town went to the mayor one Sunday morning to get permission to do some work that had to be done in the town limits that day. He found the august official in his own jail. Exhilaration!

It was at these mines that three natives of the town went up to drive two young men into the bushes. Being met with some firmness and the muzzle of a Winchester, they went back for reinforcements. One of the three was a member of a famous fighting clan, and he gave it out that he was going for his friends to make the "furriners" leave the country. The young men appealed to the town for protection for themselves and property. There was not an officer to answer. The sheriff was in another part of the county and the constable had just resigned. The young men got Winchester repeating shotguns and waited for a week for their assailants who failed to come; but had they been besieged, there would not have been a soul to give them assistance, except perhaps the marshal and his New England friend.

In this same county a man hired an assassin to kill his rival. The assassin crept to the window of the house where the girl lived, and seeing a man sitting by the fire, shot through the window and killed him. It was the wrong man. Assassinations from ambush have not been uncommon in every feud, though, in almost every feud, there has been one faction that refused to fight except in the open. I have even heard of a snare being set for a woman, who though repeatedly warned, persisted in carrying news from one side to the other. A musket was loaded with slugs and placed so that the discharge would sweep the path that it was believed she would take. A string was tied to the trigger and stretched across the foot road and a mountaineer waited under a bluff to whistle so that she would stop, when she struck the string. That night the woman happened to take another path. This, however, is the sole instance I have ever known.

Elsewhere the Southern mountaineer holds human life as cheap; elsewhere he is ready to let death settle a personal dispute; elsewhere he is more ignorant and has as little regard for law; elsewhere he was divided against himself by the war and was left in subsequent conditions just as lawless; elsewhere he has similar clannishness of feeling, and elsewhere is an occasional feud which is confined to family and close kindred. But nowhere is the feud so common, so old, so persistent, so deadly, as in the Kentucky mountains. Nowhere else is there such organization, such division of enmity to the limit of kinship.

About thirty-five years ago two boys were playing marbles in the road along the Cumberland River—down in the Kentucky mountains. One had a patch on the seat of his trousers. The other boy made fun of it, and the boy with the patch went home and told his father. Thirty years of local war was the result. The factions fought on after they had forgotten why they had fought at all. While organized warfare is now over, an occasional fight yet comes over the patch on those trousers and a man or two is killed. A county, as big as Rhode Island, is still bitterly divided on the subject. In a race for the legislature not long ago, the feud was the sole issue. And, without knowing it, perhaps, a mountaineer carried that patch like a flag to victory, and sat under it at the capital—making laws for the rest of the State.

That is the feud that has stained the highland border of the State with blood and, abroad, has engulfed the reputation of the lowland bluegrass, where there are, of course, no feuds—a fact that sometimes seems to require emphasis, I am sorry to say. Almost every mountain county has, or has had, its feud. On one side is a leader whose authority is rarely questioned. Each leader has his band of retainers. Always he arms them; usually he feeds them; sometimes he houses and clothes them, and sometimes, even, he hires them. In one local war, I remember, four dollars per day were the wages of the fighting man, and the leader on one occasion, while besieging his enemies—in the county court-house—tried to purchase a cannon, and from no other place than the State arsenal, and from no other personage than the governor himself.

It is the feud that most sharply differentiates the Kentucky mountaineer from his fellows, and it is extreme isolation that makes possible in this age such a relic of medieval barbarism. For the feud means, of course, ignorance, shiftlessness, incredible lawlessness, a frightful estimate of the value of human life; the horrible custom of ambush, a class of cowardly assassins who can be hired to do murder for a gun, a mule, or a gallon of moonshine.

Now these are the blackest shadows in the only picture of Kentucky mountain life that has reached the light of print through the press. There is another side and it is only fair to show it.

The feud is an inheritance. There were feuds before the war, even on the edge of the bluegrass; there were fierce family fights in the backwoods before and during the Revolution—when the war between Whig and Tory served as a pretext for satisfying personal animosities already existing, and it is not a wild fancy that the Kentucky mountain feud takes root in Scotland. For while it is hardly possible that the enmities of the Revolution were transmitted to the civil war, it is quite sure that whatever race instinct, old-world trait of character, or moral code the backwoodsman may have taken with him into the mountains—it is quite sure that that instinct, that trait of character, that moral code are living forces in him to-day. The late war was, however, the chief cause of feuds. When it came, the river-bottoms were populated, the clans were formed. There were more slave-holders among them than among other Southern mountaineers. For that reason the war divided them more evenly against themselves, and set them fighting. When the war stopped elsewhere, it simply kept on with them, because they were more isolated, more evenly divided; because they were a fiercer race, and because the issue had become personal. The little that is going on now goes on for the same reason, for while civilization pressed close enough in 1890 and '91 to put an end to organized fighting, it is a consistent fact that after the failure of Baring Brothers, and the stoppage of the flow of English capital into the mountains, and the check to railroads and civilization, these feuds slowly started up again. When I started to the Cuban war, two companies of State militia were on their way to the mountains to put down a feud. On the day of the Las Guasimas fight these feudsmen fought, and they lost precisely as many men killed as the Rough Riders—eight.

Again: while the feud may involve the sympathies of a county, the number of men actually engaged in it are comparatively few. Moreover, the feud is strictly of themselves and is based primarily on a privilege that the mountaineer, the world over, has most grudgingly surrendered to the law, the privilege of avenging his private wrongs. The non-partisan and the traveller are never molested. Property of the beaten faction is never touched. The women are safe from harm, and I have never heard of one who was subjected to insult. Attend to your own business, side with neither faction in act or word and you are much safer among the Kentucky mountaineers, when a feud is going on, than you are crossing Broadway at Twenty-third Street. As you ride along, a bullet may plough through the road ten yards in front of you. That means for you to halt. A mountaineer will come out of the bushes and ask who you are and where you are going and what your business is. If your answers are satisfactory, you go on unmolested. Asking for a place to stay all night, you may be told "Go to So and So's house; he'll pertect ye"; and he will, too, at the risk of his own life when you are past the line of suspicion and under his roof.

There are other facts that soften a too-harsh judgment of the mountaineer and his feud—harsh as the judgment should be. Personal fealty is the the corner-stone of the feud. The mountaineer admits no higher law; he understands no conscience that will violate that tie. You are my friend or my kinsman; your quarrel is my quarrel; whoever strikes you, strikes me. If you are in trouble, I must not testify against you. If you are an officer, you must not arrest me, you must send me word to come into court. If I'm innocent, why, maybe I'll come.

Moreover, the worst have the list of rude virtues already mentioned; and, besides, the mountaineer is never a thief nor a robber, and he will lie about one thing and one thing only and that is land. He has cleared it, built his cabin from the trees, lived on it and he feels that any means necessary to hold it are justifiable. Lastly, religion is as honestly used to cloak deviltry as it ever was in the Middle Ages.

A feud leader, who had about exterminated the opposing faction and had made a good fortune for a mountaineer while doing it, for he kept his men busy getting out timber when they weren't fighting, said to me, in all seriousness:

"I have triumphed agin my enemies time and time agin. The Lord's on my side and I gits a better and better Christian ever' year."

A preacher, riding down a ravine, came upon an old mountaineer hiding in the bushes with his rifle.

"What are you doing there, my friend?"

"Ride on, stranger," was the easy answer. "I'm a-waitin' fer Jim Johnson, and with the help of the Lawd I'm goin' to blow his damn head off."

Even the ambush, the hideous feature of the feud, takes root in the days of the Revolution, and was borrowed, maybe, from the Indians. Milfort, the Frenchman, who hated the backwoodsman, says Mr. Roosevelt, describes with horror their extreme malevolence and their murderous disposition toward one another. He says that whether a wrong had been done to a man personally or to his family, he would, if necessary, travel a hundred miles and lurk around the forest indefinitely to get a chance to shoot his enemy.

But the Civil War was the chief cause of bloodshed; for there is evidence, indeed, that though feeling between families was strong, bloodshed was rare and the English sense of fairness prevailed, in certain communities at least. Often you will hear an old mountaineer say: "Folks usen to talk about how fer they could kill a *deer.* Now hit's how fer they can kill a *man.* Why, I have knowed the time when a man would hev been druv outen the county fer drawin' a knife or a pistol, an if a man was ever killed hit wus kinder accidental by a Barlow. I reckon folks got used to weepons an' killin' an' shootin' from the bresh endurin' the war. But hits been gettin' wuss ever sence, and now hits dirk an Winchester all the time." Even for the ambush there is an explanation.

"Oh, I know all the excuses folks make: Hit's fair for one as 'tis fer t'other. You can't fight a man far an squar who'll shoot you in the back. A pore man can't fight money in the courts. Thar hain't no witnesses in the lorrel but leaves, an' dead men don't hev much to say. I know hit all. Looks like lots o' decent young folks hev got usen to the idee; thar's so much of it goin' on and thar's so much talk about shootin' from the bresh. I do reckon hit's wuss'n stealin' to take a feller critter's life that way."

It is also a fact that most of the men who have been engaged in these fights were born, or were children, during the war; and were, in consequence, accustomed to bloodshed and bushwhacking from infancy. Still, even among the fighters there is often a strong prejudice against the ambush, and in most feuds, one or the other side discountenances it, and that is the faction usually defeated. I know of one family that was one by one exterminated because they refused to take to the "bresh." The last one killed was a good-looking generous young fellow, eighteen years of age. He was urged to either leave the country or take to the bush for his enemy, who had taken to the bush for him. He would rather live in the mountains for a year and die, was the boy's answer, than live to be an old man anywhere else; and he would rather die than shoot a man in the back. In less than a year he was shot while drinking from a spring.

Again, the secret of the feud is isolation. In the mountains the war kept on longer, for personal hatred supplanted its dead issues. Railroads and newspapers have had their influence elsewhere. Elsewhere court circuits include valley people. Civilization has pressed slowly on the Kentucky mountains. The Kentucky mountaineer, until quite lately, has been tried, when brought to trial at all, by the Kentucky mountaineer. And when a man is tried for a crime by a man who would commit that crime under the same circumstances, punishment is not apt to follow.

Thus the influence that has helped most to break up the feud is trial in the Bluegrass, for there is no ordeal the mountaineer more hates than trial by a jury of bigoted "furriners."

Who they are—these Southern mountaineers—is a subject of endless conjecture and dispute—a question that perhaps will never be satisfactorily solved. While there are among them the descendants of the old bond servant and redemptioner class, of vicious runaway criminals and the trashiest of the poor whites, the ruling class has undoubtedly come from the old free settlers, English, German, Swiss, French Huguenot, even Scotch and Scotch-Irish. As the German and Swiss are easily traced to North Carolina, the Huguenots to South Carolina and parts of Georgia, it is more than probable, from the scant study that has been given the question, that the strongest and largest current of blood in their veins comes from none other than the mighty stream of Scotch-Irish.

Briefly, the theory is this. From 1720 to 1780, the settlers in southwest Virginia, middle North Carolina and western South Carolina were chiefly Scotch and Scotch-Irish. They were active in the measures preceding the outbreak of the Revolution, and they declared independence at Abington, Va., even before they did at Mecklenburg, N.C. In these districts, they were the largest element in the patriot army, and they were greatly impoverished by the war. Being too poor or too conscientious to own slaves, and unable to compete with them as the planter's field hand, blacksmith, carpenter, wheel-wright and man-of-all-work, especially after the invention of the cotton gin in 1792, they had no employment and were driven to mountain and sand-hill. There are some good reasons for the theory. Among prominent mountain families direct testimony or unquestioned tradition point usually to Scotch-Irish ancestry, sometimes to pure Scotch origin, sometimes to English. Scotch-Irish family names in abundance speak for themselves, as do folk-words and folk-songs and the characteristics, mental, moral, and physical, of the people. Broadly speaking, the Southern mountaineers are characterized as "peaceable, civil, good-natured, kind, clever, naturally witty, with a fair share of common sense, and morals not conscientiously bad, since they do not consider ignorance, idleness, poverty, or the excessive use of tobacco or moonshine as immoral or vicious."

Another student says: "The majority is of good blood, honest, law-abiding blood." Says still another: "They are ignorant of books, but sharp as a rule." Says another: "They have great reverence for the Bible, and are sturdy, loyal, and tenacious." Moreover, the two objections to this theory that would naturally occur to anyone, have easy answers. The mountaineers are not Presbyterian and they are not thrifty. Curiously enough, testimony exists to the effect that certain Methodist or Baptist churches were once Presbyterian; and many preachers of these two denominations had grandfathers who were Presbyterian ministers. The Methodists and Baptists were perhaps more active; they were more popular in the mountains as they were in the backwoods, because they were more democratic and more emotional. The back-woodsman did not like the preacher to be a preacher only.

Scotch-Irish thriftiness decayed. The soil was poor; game was abundant; hunting bred idleness. There were no books, no schools, few church privileges, a poorly educated ministry, and the present illiteracy, thriftlessness, and poverty were easy results. Deed books show that the ancestors of men who now make their mark, often wrote a good hand.

Such, briefly, is the Southern mountaineer in general, and the Kentucky mountaineer in particular—as a remnant of pioneer days, as a relic of an

Anglo-Saxon past and as a peculiar type that seems the invariable result of a mountain environment the world over. Or, rather, such he was until fifteen years ago and to know him now, you must know him as he was then, for the changes that have been wrought in the last decade affect localities only and the bulk of the mountain people is, practically, still what it was one hundred years ago. Still changes have taken place and changes will take place now swiftly; and it rests largely with the outer world what these changes shall be.

The vanguards of civilization, railroads, unless quickly followed by schools and churches, at the ratio of four schools to one church, have a bad effect on the Southern mountaineer. He catches up the vices of the incoming current only too readily. The fine spirit of his hospitality is worn away. He goes to some little "boom" town, is forced to pay the enormous sum of fifty cents for his dinner, and when you go his way again you pay fifty cents for yours. Carelessly applied charity weakens his pride, makes him dependent. You hear of arrests for petty thefts sometimes, occasionally burglaries are made, and the mountaineer is cowed by the superior numbers, superior intelligence of the incomer, and he seems to lose his sturdy self-respect.

And yet the result could easily be far different. Not long ago I talked with an intelligent young fellow, a young minister, who had taught among them many years, exclusively in the Kentucky mountains, and is now preaching to them. He says, they are most tractable, more easily moulded, more easily uplifted than the people of a similar grade of intelligence in cities. He gave an instance to illustrate their general susceptibility in all ways. When he took charge of a certain school every boy and girl, nearly all of them grown, chewed tobacco. The teacher before him used tobacco and even exchanged it with his pupils. He told them at once they must stop. They left off instantly.

It was a "blab" school, as the mountaineers characterize a school in which the pupils study aloud. He put an end to that in one day, and he soon told them they must stop talking to one another. After school they said they didn't think they could ever do that, but they did. In another county, ten years ago, he had ten boys and girls gathered to organize a Sunday-school. None had ever been to Sunday-school and only two knew what a Sunday-school was. He announced that he would organize one at that place a week later. When he reached the spot the following Sunday there were seventy-five young mountaineers there. They had sung themselves quite hoarse waiting for him, and he was an hour early. The Sunday-school was founded, built up and developed into a church.

When the first printing-press was taken to a certain mountain town in 1882, a deputation of citizens met it three miles from town and swore that it should go no farther. An old preacher mounted the wagon and drove it into town. Later the leader of that crowd owned the printing-press and ran it. In this town are two academies for the education of the mountaineer. Young fellows come there from all over Kentucky and work their way through. They curry horses, carry water, work about the houses—do everything; many of them cook for themselves and live on two dollars a month. They are quick-witted, strong-minded, sturdy, tenacious, and usually very religious.

Indeed people who have been among the Southern mountaineers testify that, as a race, they are proud, sensitive, hospitable, kindly, obliging in an unreckoning way that is almost pathetic, honest, loyal, in spite of their common ignorance, poverty, and isolation; that they are naturally capable, eager to learn, easy to uplift. Americans to the core, they make the Southern mountains a store-house of patriotism; in themselves, they are an important offset to the Old World outcasts whom we have welcomed to our shores; and they surely deserve as much consideration from the nation as the negroes, for whom we have done, and are doing so much, or as the heathen, to whom we give millions.

I confess that I have given prominence to the best features of mountain life and character, for the reason that the worst will easily make their own way. It is only fair to add, however, that nothing that has ever been said of the mountaineer's ignorance, shiftlessness, and awful disregard of human life, especially in the Kentucky mountains, that has not its basis, perhaps, in actual fact.

First, last, and always, however, it is to be remembered that to begin to understand the Southern mountaineers you must go back to the social conditions and standards of the backwoods before the Revolution, for practically they are the backwoods people and the backwoods conditions of pre-Revolutionary days. Many of their ancestors fought with ours for American independence. They were loyal to the Union for one reason that no historian seems ever to have guessed. For the loyalty of 1861 was, in great part, merely the transmitted loyalty of 1776, imprisoned like a fossil in the hills. Precisely for the same reason, the mountaineer's estimate of the value of human life, of the sanctity of the law, of a duty that over-rides either—the duty of one blood kinsman to another—is the estimate of that day and not of this; and it is by the standards of that day and not of this that he is to be judged. To understand the mountaineer, then, you must go back to the Revolution. To do him justice you must give him the awful ordeal of a century of isolation and consequent ignorance, in which to deteriorate. Do that and your wonder, perhaps, that he is so bad, becomes a wonder that he is not worse. To my mind, there is but one strain of American blood that could have stood that ordeal quite so well, and that comes from the sturdy Scotch-Irish who are slowly wresting from Puritan and Cavalier an equal share of the glory that belongs to the three for the part played on the world's stage by this land in the heroic rôle of Liberty.

8

The Anglo-Saxons of the Kentucky Mountains:
A Study in Anthropogeography

Ellen Churchill Semple

Of all the environmental determinist essays regarding Appalachian culture, none was more widely quoted than Ellen Churchill Semple's "The Anglo-Saxons of the Kentucky Mountains: A Study in Anthropogeography." Indeed, it has been stated that "this brief article has fired more American students to interest in geography than any other article ever written" (Charles C. Colby in an obituary for Semple published in *Annals of the American Association of Geographers,* December, 1933). The essay is also important from a folklore viewpoint because, although Semple's emphasis is that of the cultural geographer, her concern is with traditional culture. Moreover, much of her discussion deals with matters of primary interest to folklorists—traditional housing, food, crafts, religious beliefs, dialect, and customs. Semple's knowledge is provincial about some of these traditions. For example, the statement that the infare custom in 1901 was practiced only in the Kentucky mountains is inaccurate. Equally specious is her contention that mountain English is Elizabethan, although many others have made the same claim. It is correct because Elizabethan English is essentially modern English and, so, every English-speaking person is, in a sense, using Elizabethan English. Semple's statement is misleading in its implication that the mountaineers spoke in a totally archaic tongue. Like any conservative society, the Kentucky mountaineers used many older linguistic forms but they did not go around speaking like sixteenth-century Englishmen.

Of great interest are Semple's comments on music, in particular her assessment that "women are the chief exponents of mountain minstrelsy." Experiences of some subsequent collectors, who have been more concerned with ballads and folksongs than Semple, seem to support her claim. For example, a majority of the singers from whom Cecil Sharp collected in the years 1916 to 1918 were women. Yet, if Semple's opinion was correct, the situation has changed in recent years, for most of the folksingers recorded during the four decades since World War II have been men, many of

Reprinted from *The Geographical Journal* 17 (June 1901): 588–623. Also reprinted in *Bulletin of the American Geographical Society* 42 (August 1910): 561–94.

them having extensive repertoires. For example, in the 1950s Leonard Roberts collected one hundred songs and other folklore from two eastern Kentucky brothers whom he identified by the pseudonym Couch.

Ellen Churchill Semple (1863–1932) was the daughter of a well-to-do Louisville family, their wealth enabling her to attend Vassar College where she took both undergraduate and graduate degrees. While working on her M.A. degree Semple encountered the writings of the German cultural geographer Friedrich Ratzel, a scholar very much in vogue during the 1880s. Ratzel developed a thesis that culture was automatically shaped by environment; in other words man was controlled by his climate and geography and was totally powerless against them. Semple traveled to Germany to study under Ratzel but, because women students were a rarity in German universities of that era, she was not allowed to enroll; she had to be content with listening to Ratzel's lectures. This contact was sufficient, for Semple saw the geographer's views as the theoretical stance for which she had been looking. "The Anglo-Saxons of the Kentucky Mountains" was her seventh publication, but her most significant one up to that date. While following Ratzel's thinking closely, she does alter the view slightly by considering culture as part of the environment. This difference is important because it means that, unlike topography and climate, culture is malleable. As Henry Shapiro notes in *Appalachia on Our Mind,* p. 142, this distinction appealed to "persons active in benevolent work who found there explanation and a program for action neatly combined."

In 1901 Semple also published another article on Appalachia, "Mountain Passes: A Study in Anthropogeography," *Bulletin of the American Geographical Society* 33: 124–37, 191–203. For information on Semple see Charles C. Colby, "Ellen Churchill Semple," *Annals of the American Association of Geographers* (December 1933): 229–40 and John K. Wright, "Miss Semple's 'Influences of Geographic Environment': Notes toward a Biobibliography," *Geographical Review* 52 (July 1962): 346–61.

*   *   *

In one of the most progressive and productive countries of the world, and in that section of the country which has had its civilization and its wealth longest, we find a large area where the people are still living the frontier life of the backwoods, where the civilization is that of the eighteenth century, where the people speak the English of Shakespeare's time, where the large majority of the inhabitants have never seen a steamboat or a railroad, where money is as scarce as in colonial days, and all trade is barter. It is the great upheaved mass of the Southern Appalachians which, with the conserving power of the mountains, has caused these conditions to survive, carrying a bit of the eighteenth century intact over into this strongly contrasted twentieth century, and presenting an anachronism all the more marked because found in the heart of the bustling, money-making, novelty-loving United States. These conditions are to be found throughout the broad belt of the Southern Appalachians, but nowhere in such purity or covering so large an area as in the mountain region of Kentucky.

A mountain system is usually marked by a central crest, but the Appalachians are distinguished by a central zone of depression, flanked on the east by the Appalachian mountains proper, and on the west by the Alleghany and the Cumberland plateaus. This central trough is generally designated as the Great Appalachian Valley. It is depressed several hundred feet below the highlands on either side, but its surface is relieved by intermittent series of even-crested ridges which rise 1000 feet or more above the general level, running parallel to each other, and conforming at the same time to the structural axis of the whole system. The valleys between them owe neither width nor form to the streams which drain them. The Cumberland plateau forms the western highland of the Great Valley in Eastern Kentucky, Tennessee and Northern Alabama. This plateau belt reaches its greatest height in Kentucky, and slopes gradually from this section to the south and west. Its eastern escarpment rises abruptly 800 to 1500 feet from the Great Valley, and·shows everywhere an almost perfectly straight skyline. The western escarpment is very irregular, for the streams, flowing westward from the plateau, have carved out their valleys far back into the elevated district, leaving narrow spurs running out into the low plains beyond. The surface is highly dissected, presenting a maze of gorge-like valleys separating the steep, regular slopes of the sharp or rounded hills. The level of the originally upheaved mass of the plateau is now represented by the altitude of the existing summits, which show a remarkable uniformity in the north-east—south-west line, and a slight rise in elevation from the western margin towards the interior.

About 10,000 square miles of the Cumberland plateau fall within the confines of the state of Kentucky, and form the eastern section of the state. A glance at the topographical map of the region shows the country to be devoted by nature to isolation and poverty. The eastern rim of the plateau is formed by Pine mountain, which raises its solid wall with level top in silhouette against the sky, and shows only one water-gap in a distance of 150 miles. And just beyond is the twin range of the Cumberland. Hence no railroads have attempted to cross this double border-barrier, except at the north-east and south-east corners of the state, where the Big Sandy and Cumberland rivers have carved their way through the mountains to the west. Railroads, therefore, skirt this upland region, but nowhere penetrate it. The whole area is a coalfield, the mineral being chiefly bituminous, with several thousand square miles of superior cannel coal. The obstructions growing out of the topography of the country, and the cheap river transportation afforded by the Ohio for the Kanawha and Monogahela river coal have tended to retard the construction of railroads within the mountains, and even those on the margin of this upland region have been built since 1880.

Man has done so little to render this district accessible because nature has done so little. There are here no large streams penetrating the heart of the mountains, as in Tennessee, where the Tennessee river, drawing its tributaries from the easternmost ranges of the Appalachians, cuts westward by flaring water-gaps through chain after chain and opens a highway from the interior of the system to the plains of the Mississippi. The Kentucky streams are navigable only to the margin of the plateau, and therefore leave this great area without natural means of communication with the outside world to the west, while to the east the mountain wall has acted as an effective barrier to communication with the Atlantic seaboard. Consequently, all commerce has been kept at arms' length, and the lack of a market has occasioned the poverty of the people, which, in turn, has prohibited the construction of high-roads over the mountains of the Cumberland plateau.

It is what the mountaineers themselves call a rough country. The steep hills rise from 700 to 1200 feet above their valleys. The valleys are nothing more than gorges. Level land there is none, and roads there are almost none. Valley and road and mountain stream coincide. In the summer the dry or half-dry beds of the streams serve as highways; and in the winter, when the torrents are pouring a full tide down the hollows, foot trails cut through the dense forest that mantles the slopes are the only means of communication. Then intercourse is practically cut off. Even in the best season transportation is in the main limited to what a horse can carry on its back beside its rider. In a trip of 350 miles through the mountains, we met only one wheel vehicle and a few trucks for hauling railroad ties, which were being gotten out of the forests. Our own camp wagons, though carrying only light loads, had to double their teams in climbing the ridges. All that had been done in most cases to make a road over a mountain was to clear an avenue through the dense growth of timber, so that it proved, as a rule, to be just short of impassable. For this reason the public of the mountains prefer to keep to the valleys with their streams, to which they have given many expressive and picturesque names, while the knobs and mountains are rarely honoured with a name. We have Cutshin creek, Hell-fer-Sartain, Bullskin creek, Poor Fork, Stinking, Greasy, and Quicksand creek. One trail leads from the waters of Kingdom-Come down Lost creek and Troublesome, across the Upper Devil and Lower Devil to Hell creek. *Facilis decensus Averno,* only no progress is easy in these mountains. The creek, therefore, points the highway, and is used to designate geographical locations. When we would inquire our way to a certain point, the answer was, "Go ahead to the fork of the creek, and turn up the left branch," not the fork of the road and the path to the left. A woman at whose cabin we lunched one day said, "My man and me has been living here on Quicksand only ten years. I was born up on Troublesome."

All passenger travel is on horseback. The important part which the horse plays, therefore, in the economy of the mountain family recalls pioneer days. Almost every cabin has its blacksmith's forge under an open shed or in a low outhouse. The country stores at the forks or fords of the creek keep bellows in stock. Every mountaineer is his own blacksmith, and though he works with very simple implements, he knows a few fundamental principles of the art, and does the work well. Men and women are quite at home in the saddle. The men are superb horsemen, sit their animals firm and erect, even when mounted on top of the meal-bag, which is the regular accompaniment of the horseman. We saw one day a family on their way to the country store to exchange their produce. The father, a girl, and a large bag of Indian corn were mounted on one mule, and the mother, a younger girl, and a black lamb suspended in a sack from the saddle-bow on the other. It is no unusual thing to see a woman on horseback, with a child behind her and a baby in her arms, while she holds an umbrella above them.

But such travel is not easy, and hence we find that these Kentucky mountaineers are not only cut off from the outside world, but they are separated from each other. Each is confined to his own locality, and finds his little world within a radius of a few miles from his cabin. There are many men in these mountains who have never seen a town, or even the poor village that constitutes their county-seat. Those who have obtained a glimpse of civilization have gone done the head-waters of the streams on lumber rafts, or have been sent to the state penitentiary at Frankfort for illicit distilling or feud murder. The women, however, cannot enjoy either of these privileges; they are almost as rooted as the trees. We met one woman who, during the twelve years of her married life, had lived only 10 miles across the mountain from her old home, but had never in this time been back home to visit her mother and father. Another back in Perry county told me she had never been farther from home than Hazard, the county-seat, which was only 6 miles distant. Another had never been to the post-office, 4 miles away; and another had never seen the ford of the Rock-castle river, only 2 miles from her home, and marked, moreover, by the country store of the district.

A result of this confinement to one locality is the absence of anything like social life, and the close intermarriage of families inhabiting one district. These two phenomena appear side by side here as in the upland valleys of Switzerland and other mountain countries where communication is difficult. One can travel for 40 miles along one of the head streams of the

Kentucky river and find the same names recurring in all the cabins along both its shores. One woman in Perry county told us she was related to everybody up and down the North Fork of the Kentucky and along its tributary creeks. In Breathitt county, an old judge, whose family had been among the early settlers on Troublesome, stated that in the district school near by there were ninety-six children, of whom all but five were related to himself or his wife. This extensive intermarriage stimulates the clan instinct and contributes to the strength of the feuds which rage here from time to time.

It is a law of biology that an isolating environment operates for the preservation of a type by excluding all intermixture which would obliterate distinguishing characteristics. In these isolated communities, therefore, we find the purest Anglo-Saxon stock in all the United States. They are the direct descendants of the early Virginia and North Carolina immigrants, and bear about them in their speech and ideas the marks of their ancestry as plainly as if they had disembarked from their eighteenth-century vessel but yesterday. The stock is chiefly English and Scotch-Irish, with scarcely a trace of foreign admixture. Occasionally one comes across a French name, which points to a strain of Huguenot blood from over the mountains in North Carolina; or names of the Germans who came down the pioneer thoroughfare of the Great Appalachian Valley from the Pennsylvania Dutch settlements generations ago. But the stock has been kept free from the tide of foreign immigrants which has been pouring in recent years into the States. In the border counties of the district where the railroads run, and where English capital has bought up the mines in the vicinity, the last census shows a few foreign-born, but these are chiefly Italian labourers working on the road-bed, or British capitalists and employees. Four of the interior counties have not a single foreign-born, and eight others have only two or three.

Though these mountain people are the exponents of a retarded civilization, and show the degenerate symptoms of an arrested development, their stock is as good as any in the country. They formed a part of the same tide of pioneers which crossed the mountains to people the young states to the south-west, but they chanced to turn aside from the main stream, and ever since have stagnated in these mountain hollows. For example, over a hundred years ago eleven Combs brothers, related to General Combs of the Revolutionary army, came over the mountains from North Carolina. Nine of them settled along the North Fork of the Kentucky river in the mountains of Perry county, one went further down the stream into the rough hill country of Breathitt county, and the eleventh continued on his way till he came into the smiling regions of the Bluegrass, and there became the progenitor of a family which represents the blue blood of the state, with all the aristocratic instincts of the old South; while their cousins in the mountain go barefoot, herd in one-room cabins, and are ignorant of many of the fundamental decencies of life.

If the mountains have kept out foreign elements, still more effectually have they excluded the negroes. This region is as free from them as northern Vermont. There is no place for the negro in the mountain economy, and never has been. In the days of slavery this fact had momentous results. The mountains did not offer conditions for plantation cultivation, the only system of agriculture in which slaves could be profitably employed. The absence of these conditions and of the capital wherewith to purchase negroes made the whole Appalachian region a non-slave-holding section. Hence, when the rupture came between the North and South, this mountain region declared for the Union, and thus raised a barrier of disaffection through the centre of the Southern States. It had no sympathy with the industrial system of the South; it shared the democratic spirit characteristic of all mountain people, and likewise their conservatism, which holds to the established order. Having, therefore, no intimate knowledge of the negro, our Kentucky mountaineers do not show the deep-seated prejudice to the social equality of blacks and whites which characterizes all other Kentuckians. We find to-day, on the western margin of the Cumberland plateau, a flourishing college for the coeducation of the Bluegrass blacks and mountain whites; and this is probably the only geographical location south of the Mason an Dixon line where such an institution could exist.

Though the mountaineer comes of such vigorous stock as the Anglo-Saxons, he has retained little of the ruddy, vigorous appearance of his forebears. The men are tall and lank, though sinewy, with thin bony faces, sallow skins, and dull hair. They hold themselves in a loose-jointed way; their shoulders droop in walking and sitting. Their faces are immobile, often inscrutable, but never stupid; for one is sure that under this calm exterior the mountaineer is doing a great deal of thinking, which he does not see fit to share with the "furriner," as he calls every one coming from the outside world. The faces of the women are always delicately moulded and refined, with an expression of dumb patience telling of the heavy burden which life has laid upon them. They are absolutely simple, natural, and their child-like unconsciousness of self points to their long residence away from the gaze of the world. Their manners are gentle, gracious, and unembarrassed, so that in talking with them one forgets their bare feet, ragged clothes, and crass ignorance, and in his heart bows anew to the inextinguishable excellence of the Anglo-Saxon race.

The lot of a mountain woman is a hard one. Only the lowest peasantry of Europe can show anything to parallel it. She marries between twelve and fifteen years a husband who is between seventeen and twenty. The motive in marriage is very elemental, betrays little of the romantic spirit. Husband and wife speak of each other as "my man" and "my woman." A girl when she is twenty is put on the "cull list," that is, she is no longer marriageable. A man is included in this undesirable category at twenty-eight; after that he can get no one to take him "except some poor wider-woman," as one mountain matron expressed it, adding, "gals on the cull-list spend their time jes' bummin' around among their folks." During a ride of 850 miles, with visits at a great many cabins, we met only one old maid; her lot was a sorry one, living now with a relative, now with a friend, earning her board by helping to nurse the sick or making herself useful in what way she could. The mountain system of economy does not take into account the unmarried woman, so she plunges into matrimony with the instinct of self-preservation. Then come children; and the mountain families conform to the standard of the patriarchs. A family of from ten to fifteen offspring is no rarity, and this characterizes not only the mountains of Kentucky, but the whole area of the Appalachian system. In addition to much child-bearing, all the work of the pioneer home, the spinning and weaving, knitting of stockings, sometimes even the making of shoes and moccasins, falls on the woman. More than this, she feeds and milks the cow, searches for it when it has wandered away "in the range," or forest, hoes weeds in the corn, helps in the ploughing, carries water from the spring, saws wood and lays "stake and ridered" fences. A mountain woman who had a husband and two sons, and who had been employed all day in making a fence, lifting the heavy rails above the height of her own head, replied in a listless way to the question as to what the men did, with, "the men folks they mostly sets on a fence and chaw tobacco and talk politics."

The mountain woman, therefore, at twenty-five looks forty, and at forty looks twenty years older than her husband. But none of the race are stalwart and healthy. The lack of vigour in the men is due chiefly to the inordinate use of moonshine whiskey, which contains 20 per cent more alcohol than the standard liquor. They begin drinking as mere boys. We saw several youths of seventeen intoxicated, and some women told us boys of fourteen or fifteen drank. Men, women, and children looked underfed, ill nourished. This is due in part to their scanty, unvaried diet, but more perhaps to the vile cooking. The bread is either half-baked soda biscuits eaten hot, or corn-pone with lumps of saleratus through it. The meat is always swimming in grease, and the eggs are always fried. The effect of this shows, in the adults, in their sallow complexions and spare forms; in the children, in pimples, boils, and sores on their hands and faces. This western side of the mountains, moreover, has not an abundant water-supply, the horizontal strata of the rocks reducing the number of springs. Hence all the mountain region of Kentucky, West Virginia, and Tennessee shows a high percentage of diarrhoeal disease, typhoid, and malarial fever.

The home of the mountaineer is primitive in the extreme, a survival of pioneer architecture, and the only type distinctly American. It is the blind or windowless one-room log cabin, with the rough stone chimney on the outside. The logs are sometimes squared with the hatchet, sometimes left in their original form with the bark on; the interstices are chinked in with clay. The roofs are covered with boards nearly an inch thick and 3-feet long, split from the wood by a wedge, and laid on, one lapping over the other like shingles. The chimneys, which are built on the outside of the houses, and project a few feet above the roof, lend a picturesque effect to the whole. They are made of native rock, roughly hewn and cemented with clay; but the very poorest cabins have the low "stick chimney," made of laths daubed with clay. In the broader valleys, where the conditions of life are somewhat better, the double cabin prevails—two cabins side by side, with a roofed space between, which serves as a dining-room during the warmer months of the year. Sometimes, though rarely, there is a porch in front, covered by an extension of the sloping roof. In some of the marginal counties of the mountain region and in the sawmill districts, one sees a few two-story frame dwellings. These are decorated with ornamental trimming of scroll-saw work in wood, oftentimes coloured a light blue, along the edges of the gables, and defining the line between the two stories. The regulation balcony over the front door and extending to the roof has a balustrade of the same woodwork in excellent, chaste design, sometimes painted and sometimes in the natural colour. These houses, both in their architecture and style of ornamentation recall the village dwellings in Norway, though not so beautiful or so richly decorated. But the usual home of the mountaineer is the one-room cabin. Near by is the barn, a small square log structure, with the roof projecting form 8 to 10 feet, to afford shelter for the young cattle or serve as a milking-shed. These vividly recall the mountain architecture of some of the Alpine dwellings of Switzerland and Bavaria, especially when, as in a few instances, the roofs are held down by weight-rocks to economize hardware. Very few of them have hay-lofts above, for the reason that only a few favoured districts in these mountains produce hay.

The furnishings of the cabins are reduced to the merest necessaries of life, though in the vicinity of the railroads or along the main streams where the valley roads make transportation a simpler problem, a few luxuries like an occasional piece of shop-made furniture and lamp-chimneys have crept in. One cabin which we visited near the foot of Pine mountain, though of the better sort, may be taken as typical. Almost everything it contained was home-made, and only one iron-bound bucket showed the use of hardware. Both rooms contained two double beds. These were made of plain white wood, and were roped across from side through auger-holes to support the mattresses. The lower one of these was stuffed with corn-shucks, the upper one with feathers from the geese raised by the housewife. The sheets, blankets, and counterpanes had all been woven by her, as also the linsey-wolsey from which her own and her children's' clothes were made. Gourds, hung on the walls, served as receptacles for salt, soda, and other kitchen supplies. The meal-barrel was a section of log, hollowed out with great nicety till the wood was not more than an inch thick. The flour-barrel was a large firkin, the parts held in place by hoops, fastened by an arrowhead at one end of the withe slipped into a slit in the other; the churn was made in the same way, and in neither was there nail or screw. The washtub was a trough hollowed out of a log. A large basket was woven of hickory slips by the mountaineer himself, and two smaller ones, made of the cane of the broom corn and bound at the edges with coloured calico, were the handi-work of his wife. Only the iron stove with its few utensils, and some table knives, testified to any connection with the outside world. The old flint-lock gun and power-horn hanging form a rafter gave the finishing touch of local colour to this typical pioneer home. Daniel Boone's first cabin in the Kentucky wilderness could not have been more primitive.

Some or most of these features can be found in all mountain homes. Some cabins are still provided with hand-mills for grinding their corn when the water-mills cease to run in a dry summer. Clay lamps of classic design, in which grease is burned with a floating wick, are still to be met with; and the manufactured product from the country store is guiltless of chimney. Every cabin has its spinning-wheel, and the end of the "shed-room" is usually occupied by a hand-loom. Only in rare cases is there any effort to beautify these mountain homes. Paper flowers, made from old newspaper, a woodcut from some periodical, and a gaudy advertisement distributed by an itinerant vendor of patent medicines, make up the interior decoration of a cabin. Sometimes the walls are entirely papered with newspapers, which are more eagerly sought for this purpose than for their literary contents. Material for exterior decoration is more accessible to the mountain housewife, and hence we find, where her work-burdened life will permit, that she has done all she can for her front yard. Poppies, phlox, hollyhock, altheas, and dahlias lift their many-coloured blooms above the rail fence. Over the porch, where there is one, climb morning-glory, sweet potato vines, and wild mountain ivy; and from the edge of the roof are suspended home-made hanging baskets, contrived from old tin cans, buckets, or anything that will hold soil, and filled with the various ferns and creepers which the forest furnish in great beauty and abundance.

A vegetable garden is always to be found at the side or rear of the cabin. This is never large, even for a big family. It is ploughed in the spring by the man of the household, and enriched by manure from the barn, being the only part of the whole farm to receive any fertilizer. Any subsequent ploughing and all weeding and cultivation of the vegetables is done by the women. The average mountain garden will yield potatoes, beets, cabbages, onions, pumpkins, and tomatoes of dwarf size. Beans are raised in considerable quantities and dried for winter use. The provisions for the luxuries of life are few. Adjoining every garden is a small patch of tobacco, which is raised only for home consumption. It is consumed, moreover, by both sexes, old and young, and particularly by the women, who both smoke and "dip" snuff, making the brush for the dipping form the twig of the althea. In a large gathering like a funeral, one can often see girls from twelve to fourteen years old smoking their clay or corn-cob pipes. A young woman who went through the mountains last summer to study the conditions for a social settlement there, found the children at a district school amusing themselves by trying to see who could spit tobacco-juice nearest a certain mark on the school-house wall, the teacher standing by and watching the proceeding with interest.

Sugar is never seen in this district, but backwoods substitutes for it abound. Almost every cabin has its beehives, and anywhere from ten to twenty. The hives are made from hollowed-out sections of the bee-gum tree, covered with a square board, which is kept in place by a large stone. The bees feed in the early spring on the blossoms of the yellow poplar, but in the western counties, where this tree is rapidly being cut out of the forest for lumber, honey is no longer so abundant. But the mountain region, as a whole, produces large amounts of honey and wax. Pike county, on the Virginia border, produced over 60,000 lbs. of honey in 1890. Maple sugar is gotten in considerable quantities from the sugar maple, which abounds. As one rides through the forests, he sees here and there the rough little log troughs at the base of these trees, the bit of cane run into the hole bored through the bark for the sap, and at long intervals a log sugar-house with its huge cauldron for reducing the syrup. Maple sugar is used only as a sweetmeat. The mountaineer puts his main reliance for sweetening on sorghum molasses, which he makes from the sorghum cane. Two acres of this will provide an average mountain household with sorghum molasses, or "long sweetening," for a year. They eat it with their "pone" bread and beans; coffee thus sweetened they drink with relish, though to the palate of the uninitiated it is a dose. Sugar, or "short sweetening," is a rarity.

Conditions point to agriculture as the only means for the Kentucky mountaineer to gain a livelihood. Mineral wealth exists in abundance in this section, but the lack of transportation facilities prevents its exploitation; so the rough hillsides must be converted into field and pasture. The mountaineer holds his land in fee simple, or by squatter claim. This is based, not upon title, but merely on the right of possession, which is regarded, moreover, as a thoroughly valid basis in a country which still preserves its frontier character. Large tracts of Kentucky mountain lands are owned by persons outside the state, by purchase or inheritance of original pioneer patents, and these are waiting for the railroads to come into the country, when they hope to realize on the timber and mines. In the mean time the mountaineers have been squatting on the territory for years, clearing the forests, selling the timber, and this with conscious impunity, for interference with them is dangerous in the extreme. Every lawyer from the outside world who comes up here to a county courthouse to examine titles to the land about, keeps his mission as secret as possible, and having accomplished it, leaves the town immediately. If further investigation is necessary, he does not find it safe to return himself, but sends a substitute who will not be recognized.

The pioneer character of the region is still evident in the size of the land-holdings. In the most mountainous parts near the eastern border-line the farms average from 160 to 320 acres; in the western part of the plateau, from 100 to 160 acres. Of the whole state, the mountain counties show by far the largest proportion of farms of 1000 acres and over. Pike county has sixty-six such. Mountaineers in two different sections told us that the land on the small side creeks was better, and there farms averaged about 200 acres; but that on main streams, like the North Fork of the Kentucky river and Poor Fork of the Cumberland, the farms were usually 600 acres, because the soil was poorer. The cause for this was not apparent, unless it was due to exhaustion of soil from long tilling, as the valleys of the main streams, being more accessible, were probably the earliest settled.

Only from thirteen to thirty per cent of the acreage of the farms is improved; the rest is in forest or pasture. Land is cleared for cultivation in the old Indian method by "girdling" or "deadening" the trees, and the first crop is planted amidst the still standing skeletons of ancient giants of the forests. Indian corn is the chief crop raised, and furnishes the main food-supply for man and beast. Great fields of it cover the steep mountain sides to the very top, except where a farmer, less energetic or more intelligent than his fellows, has left a crown of timber on the summit to diminish the evil of washing. The soil on the slopes is thin, and in the narrow V-shaped valleys there is almost no opportunity for the accumulation of alluvial soil. Hence the yield of corn is only from ten to twelve bushels to an acre, only one-third that in the rich Bluegrass lands of Central Kentucky. But population is so sparse that the harvest generally averages forty bushels *per capita.* In these "upright" farms all ploughing is done horizontally around the face of the mountain, but even then the damage from washing is very great, especially as the staple crop forms no network of roots to hold the soil and requires repeated ploughing. In consequence, after two successive crops of corn the hillside is often quite denuded, the soil having been washed away from the underlying rocks. The field then reverts to a state of nature, growing up in weeds and briars, and furnishing a scanty pasturage for cattle. Level land is very scarce, and is to be found only in the long serpentines of the main streams; but even here, from long cultivation and lack of fertilizers, a field is exhausted by two crops, and has to "rest" every third year. Clover is almost never seen. The mountaineers maintain it will not grow here, although on our circuit we did see two fields.

Of other cereals beside corn the yield is very small. Some oats are raised; but rye, wheat, barley, and buckwheat are only occasionally found. One or two rows of broom-corn provide each cabin with its material for brooms. Sometimes a small quantity of hay, poor in quality, is cut from a fallow-field for winter use. The yield in all the crops is small, because the method of agriculture employed is essentially extensive. The labour applied is small, limited to what is possible for a man and his family, generally, too, the feminine part of it, because his sons found their own families at an early age. It is almost impossible to hire extra labourers, because this element of the population, small at best, finds more profitable and steadier employment in various forms of lumber industry. The agricultural implements used are few, and in general very simple, except in the vicinity of the railroad. In remote districts the "bull-tongue" plough is in vogue. This primitive implement is hardly more than a sharpened stick with a metal rim; but as the foot is very narrow, it slips between the numerous rocks in the soil, and is therefore adapted to the conditions. Natives in two different sections told us that "folks fur back in the mountains" resort to something still simpler—a plough which is nothing but a fork of a tree, the long arm forming the beam, and the shorter one the foot.

The mountains of Kentucky, like other upland regions, are better adapted to stock farming; but, as the native has not yet learned the wisdom of putting his hillside in grass to prevent washing, and at the same time to provide pasturage, the stock wanders at will in the "range" or forest. There sheep thrive best. They feed on the pea-vine, which grows wild in the dense woods, but will not grow on cultivated land. One native explained that the sheep liked the "range," because they could take refuge from winter storms and the intense noonday heat of summer in "the stone houses." In answer to the inquiry whether he constructed such houses, he answered with the characteristic reverence of the mountaineer, "No; God made 'em. They're God's houses—just caves or shelter places under ledges of rock." About half of the mountain sheep are Merino and English breeds, but they have deteriorated under the rough conditions obtaining there. While the average yield per fleece for the whole state of Kentucky is over 4 lbs. of wool, for the mountain counties it is only 2 lbs., and in some localities drops to 1⅓ lb. These sheep are naturally a hardy stock, and are often bought up by farmers from the lowlands, taken down to the Bluegrass and fattened for a few months, and sold at a profit.

Sheep are the only product of the mountain farm that can find their way to an outside market and do not suffer from the prevailing lack of means of transportation. In regard to everything else, the effort of the native farmer is paralyzed by the want of a market. If he fattens his hogs with his superfluous corn, they are unfit to carry their own weight over the 40 or 50 miles of rough roads to the nearest railroad, or they arrive in an emaciated condition. So he contents himself with his "razor-back" pigs, which climb the hills with the activity of goats and feed with the turkeys on the abundant mast in the forests. Cattle also are raised only for home use. Steers are used pretty generally for ploughing, and especially for hauling logs. Every cabin has one cow, occasionally more. These can be seen anywhere browsing along the edge of the road, where the clearing has encouraged the grass. In the late summer they feed greedily on "crap grass," or Japan clover (*Lespedeza striata*), which springs up wherever there is a patch of sunlight in the forest. Knowing that dairy products are natural staples in almost all mountain countries of the world, as we penetrated into this district we made constant inquiries in regard to cheese, but everywhere found it conspicuous by its absence. However, on our returning to civilization, the census reports on mountain industries revealed the surprising fact that just one county, in the south-western part of the district and on the railroad, was cheese-producing, and that it made 6374 lbs. in 1889. The mystery was explained on referring to the statistics of population, which showed that this county harboured a Swiss colony of 600 souls. In the state of West Virginia, also, where the topography of the country is a repetition of that of eastern Kentucky, no cheese is produced; but, on the other hand, considerable quantities are made in all the mountain counties of Tennessee and Virginia. These states, again, are alike in having, as their geographical structure, the broader inter-montane valleys between the chain-like linear ranges of the Great Appalachian depression. In 1889, Lee County, Virginia, produced 8595 lbs. of cheese; while just over Cumberland mountain, which forms its western border, Bell County, Kentucky, produced not an ounce.

In spite of the hard conditions of life, the Kentucky mountaineer is attached to this rough country of his. Comparatively few emigrate, and many of them come back, either from love of the mountains or because the seclusion of their previous environment has unfitted them to cope with the rush and enterprise of life in the lowlands. One mountaineer told us that, though it was a poor country, "the men mostly stays here." Another who had travelled much through the district in his occupation of selecting white oak timber for a lumber company, estimated that about one man in five emigrated; such generally go to Missouri, Arkansas, and Texas. We met several who had been out West, but the mountains had drawn them back home again. The large majority of the population, therefore, stay in their own valley, or "cove," as they call it, divide up the farm, and live on smaller and smaller estates, while the cornfields creep steadily up the mountains. The population of these twenty-eight counties with their 10,000 square miles area was about 220,000 in 1880, or over twenty to the square mile; that in 1890 was 270,000, showing an increase of 25 percent. As the ratio in the past decade has risen, there is now a population of 340,000, or thirty-four to the square mile, while for the state at large the ratio is fifty-four. This growth of population is to be attributed almost entirely to natural increase; and as the accessions from the outside are practically limited to the foreign element, only two or three thousand all told, employed in the coal-mines and on the railroads, so large a percentage of increase precludes the possibility of much emigration. Cities there are none, and the villages are few, small, and wretched. This is true also of the county-seats, which, in the interior counties, average only from 300 to 400 souls; while those of the marginal counties and located on railroads encircling the mountain districts sometimes rise to 1500, but this is rare.

In consequence of his remoteness from a market, the industries of the mountaineer are limited. Nature holds him in a vice here. As we have seen, a few of his sheep may find their way to the railroad, but his hogs are debarred by the mountains from becoming articles of commerce. The same is true of his corn, which is his only superabundant crop; and this, therefore, by a natural economic law, the mountaineer is led to convert into a form having less bulk and greater value. He makes moonshine whiskey, and not all the revenue officers of the country have succeeded in suppressing this industry. At our first camping-place, only 15 miles from the railroad, we were told there were twenty illicit stills within a radius of 5 miles. Two women, moreover, were pointed out to us who carried on the forbidden industry; their husbands had been killed in feuds, so they continued to operate the stills to support their families. Living so far from the arm of the law, the mountaineer assumes with characteristic independence that he has a right to utilize his raw material as he finds expedient. He thinks it laudable to evade the law—an opinion which is shared by his fellows, who are ready to aid and abet him. He therefore sets up his still in some remote gorge, overhung by trees and thickly grown with underbrush, or in some cave whose entrance is effectually screened by boulders or the dense growth of the forest, and makes his moonshine whiskey, while he leaves a brother or partner on guard outside to give warning if revenue officers attempt a raid. It is a brave man who will serve as deputy marshal in one of these mountain counties, for raiding a still means a battle, and the mountaineers, like all backwoodsmen, are fine marksmen. In Breathitt County, called "Bloody Breathitt," four deputy marshals have been killed in the past six months. The moonshiner fully understands the penalty for illicit distilling, and if he is caught, he takes his punishment like a philosopher—all the more as there is no opprobrium attached in his community to a term in the penitentiary for this crime. The disgrace falls upon the one who gave testimony against the illicit distiller; and often a mountaineer, if summoned as a witness in such a case, leaves his county till the trial is over, rather than appear for the prosecution. Most of the moonshine is sold within the mountains. The natives, physically depressed by lack of nourishment and by the prevalent diseases of the district, crave stimulants; so the demand for spirits is steady. Not content with the already excessive strength of moonshine whiskey, they often add pepper or wood-ashes to make it more fiery. The result is maddened brains when under its influence, and eventually ruined constitutions.

Forests of magnificent timber cover the Kentucky mountains, and supply the only industry which brings any considerable money from the outside world, because the only one which can utilize the small, rapid streams for transportation. The steep-sided valleys are productive of valuable hardwood timber. Many varieties of oak, walnut, poplar, chestnut, maple, ash, and tulip trees grow to magnificent size. Log-rolling begins in the fall after the Indian corn harvest, and continues through the winter till March. The logs are deposited along the banks of the streams to wait till a "tide" or sudden rise supplies enough water to move them. Sometimes, where a creek or "branch" is too small to carry its prospective burden, the loggers build across it a "splash dam," behind which logs and water accumulate to the requisite point, and then the barrier is knocked loose, when tide and timber go rushing down the channel. On the main streams of the Kentucky, Big Sandy, Licking, and Cumberland, the logs are rafted and floated down to the saw-mills in the lowlands. All the headwaters of these rivers are marked out to the traveller through the mountains by the lumber stranded from the last "tide" and strewn along their banks.

Some of the wood within a day's hauling of the railway is worked up in a form ready for commerce, but generally with great waste of good material. The fine chestnut oaks are cut down in large quantities simply to peel off tan-bark, while the lumber is left to rot. Railroad ties are cut and shaped in the mountains from the oak and hauled to the railroad. The making of staves of white oak for whiskey-barrels is also a considerable industry. The trees are sawed across the length of the stave, and split by wedges into billets, which are then hollowed out and trimmed into shape. This last process is performed by an implement run sometimes by steam, generally by horse-power, for in the latter form it is more readily transported over the rough mountain roads from place to place, as the supply of white oak is exhausted. These staves bring $32.00 a thousand delivered at the railroad. The mountain labourer working at stave-making or at the portable saw-mills earns 75 cents a day, while the usual wages for farm hands in this district are only 50 cents.

The trades in the mountains are the primitive ones of a pioneer community—cobbler, blacksmith, and miller; but even these elemental industries have not been everywhere differentiated. Many a cabin has its own hand-mill for grinding corn when the water-mill is too remote. Many a native still makes moccasins of calf or raccoon skin for himself and his family to spare the more expensive shoes; and it is a poor sort of mountaineer who cannot and does not shoe his own horses and steers. Here is reproduced the independence of the pioneer home. Spinning and weaving survives as an industry of the women. In some few localities one can still see the flax in every stage, from the green growth in the field to the finished homespun in 100-yard pieces; or, again, one sees a cotton patch in the garden, a simple primitive gin of home invention for separating the fibre, and understands the origin of the cotton thread in the linsey-woolsey cloth of domestic manufacture which furnishes the dresses for women and children. Cotton and flax spinning, however, have died out greatly during the past few years, since the introduction of cheap cotton goods into the mountain districts. Spinning of woolen yarn for stockings is still universal, with the concomitant arts of carding and dyeing; while the weaving of linsey-woolsey for clothes or blankets is an accomplishment of almost every mountain woman. One native housewife showed us her store of blankets, woven by her mother and herself. They were made in intricate plaids of original design and combination of colour, and the owner told us she worked without a pattern and without counting the threads, trusting to her eye for accuracy. Many of the dyes, too, she made herself from certain trees, though a few she bought at the country store. The home-woven counterpanes are very interesting, because the designs for these have been handed down from generation to generation, and are the same that the Pilgrim Fathers brought over to New England. But the mountain woman puts forth her best taste and greatest energy in making quilts. In travelling through this section one looks out for some expression of the aesthetic feeling as one finds it in the wood-carving of the Alps and Scandinavian mountains, the metal-work of the Caucasus, the Cashmere shawls of the Himalayas, and the beautiful blankets of the Chilcat Indians. Gradually it is borne in upon him that quilt-making amounts to a passion among the women of the Kentucky mountains; that it does not merely answer a physical need, but is a mode of expression for their artistic sense; and there is something pathetic in the thought. They buy the calico for the purpose, and make their patch-work in very intricate designs, apparently getting their hints from their own flower-gardens; at any rate, the colours in certain common garden flowers were reproduced in some quilts we saw, and the effect was daring but artistic. Quilt-making fills the long leisure hours of the winter, and the result shows on the open shelves or cupboard which occupies a corner in every house. Passing a one-room cabin on the headwaters of the Kentucky river, we counted seventeen quilts sunning out on the fence.

The only work of the women which brings money into the family treasury is searching for ginseng, or "sang-pickin'," as the mountaineer calls it. This root is found now only in the wildest, most inaccessible ravines; but the women go out on their search barefoot amid the thick brush and briars, taking their dogs along to keep off the rattlesnakes. They also gather "yel-low root" (*Hydrastis canadensis*), which with the ginseng (*Panax quin-quefolium*) they dry and then barter for produce at the nearest store, the former at the rate of 40 cents per pound, the latter at 3 dollars. Most of the trade in the mountains is barter, for money is as scarce as in genuine pioneer countries, and the people are accordingly unfamiliar with it. A native who came over the mountains from some remote cove to sell eggs to a camping party this past summer, was offered a dollar bill for his pro-duce, but refused to accept it, as he had never seen one before, his experi-ence having been limited to silver dollars and small change. At another place we found that the people were reluctant to take the paper currency of the issue of 1892, anything so recent having not yet penetrated into their fastnesses. But the lack of money does not prevent them from being eager traders, especially in horseflesh. One of the attractions of Sunday church-going to the men is the opportunity it offers for this purpose. A glance at one of these little mountain churches when meeting is going on reveals the fitness of the occasion. The people have gathered from every direction for miles around; they have come on their best horse, and now every tree on the edge of the clearing has become a hitching post. Groups form outside before and after the service, satisfying their social craving, and, with the few topics of conversation at their command, talk naturally drifts upon the subject of their "beasties," with the inevitable result of some trading. Their trading propensity carries them so far that they often trade farms as they would horses, no deeds being executed.

As the isolation of his environment has left its stamp upon every phase of the outer life of the mountaineer, so it has laid its impress deep upon his inner nature. The remoteness of their scattered dwellings from each other and from the big world beyond the natural barriers, and the necessary self-reliance of their pioneer-like existence, has bred in them an intense spirit of independence which shows itself in many ways. It shows itself in their calm ignoring of the revenue laws, and in their adhering to the principle of the blood-feuds which inculcates the duty of personal vengeance for a wrong. In consequence of this spirit of independence, and of its antecedent cause in their slight dealings with men, our Kentucky mountaineers have only a semi-developed commercial conscience. They do not appreciate the full moral force of a contract; on this point they have the same vague ideas that most women have, and from the same cause. At all times very restive under orders, when they have taken employment under a superior, their service must be politely requested, not demanded. If offended, they throw up their job in a moment, and go off regardless of their contract and of the inconvenience they may occasion their employer. Every man is accustomed to be his own master, to do his own work in his own way and his own time. And this brings us to another curious characteristic of the mountaineer, also an effect of his isolation. He has little sense of the value of time. If he promises to do a certain thing on a certain date, his conscience is quite satisfied if he does it within three or four days after the appointed time. For instance, some mountaineers had promised to furnish horses for our camping party, which was to start from a certain village on July 15; when that day came half a dozen horses had failed to appear, but their places were supplied and the party moved off. During the succeeding week, delinquent mountaineers dribbled into town with their horses, and were surprised to find they were too late, explaining that they did not think a few days would make any difference.

Living so far from the rush of the world, these highlanders have in their manner the repose of the eternal hills. In the presence of strangers they are quite free from self-consciousness, and never lose their simplicity or directness. There is no veneer about these men; they say exactly what they think, and they think vigorously and shrewdly. Endowed with the keen powers of observation of the woodsman, and cut off from books, they are led to search themselves for the explanation of phenomena or the solution of problems. Though hampered by ignorance, their intellects are natively strong and acute. Conscious of their natural ability, conscious too that they are behind the times, these people are painfully sensitive to criticism. Cut off so long and so completely, they have never been able to compare themselves with others, and now they find comparison odious. They resent the coming of "furriners" among them, on the ground that outsiders come to spy upon them and criticize, and "tell-tale," as they put it, unless they are convinced that it is some commercial mission or a political campaign that brings the stranger. His suspicions allayed, the mountaineer is the most generous host in the world. "Strangers, won't you light and set? Hitch your beasties. This is a rough country, and I'm a poor man, but you can have all I've got." This is the usual greeting. If it is a question of spending the night, the host and his wife sleep on the floor and give the guests the bed. In a one-room cabin, the entertainment of strangers involves inconvenience, but this discomfort is never considered by the Kentucky highlander. When he says, "You can have everything I've got," this is no lip-service. At one cabin where we spent the night, when we were making our toilettes in the morning, the daughter of the house, with infinite grace and simplicity, offered us the family comb and her own tooth-brush. Hospitality can go no further. This quality the Kentucky mountaineer has in common with the inhabitants of all remote, untrodden regions where inns are rare. But if he refuses to be reimbursed for his outlay and trouble, he is repaid in part by the news which the stranger brings, and the guest is expected to be very communicative. He must tell everything he has seen or heard on his jour-ney through the mountains, and must meet a whole volley of questions of a strictly personal nature. Inquiries come as to his age, married or unmar-ried condition and the wherefore, his health, ailments, symptoms, and remedies.

The mountaineer has a circumscribed horizon of interests; he is little stirred by the great issues of the day, except those of a political nature, and for politics he has a passion. A discussion of party platforms or rival candi-dates for office will at any time enthrall him, keep him away for a whole day from the spring ploughing or sowing. As we have explained, since the mountains presented conditions for agriculture as little adapted for a slave industrial system as did those of New England, when the conflict of the systems of the North and of the South came to an issue in the Civil War, the mountain sections of the southern states took the side of New England, and went over almost bodily into the Republican party. Such was their zeal for the Union, that some of the mountain counties of Kentucky contributed a larger quota of troops, in proportion to their population, for the Federal army than any other counties in the Union. The enthusiasm of those days survives in that section to-day in their staunch adherence to the Republican party. The spirit has been encouraged also by the fact that topography has defined the mountain section as one of the political divisions of the State by a kind of common law of both political parties in their conventions and in common parlance. Although more sparsely populated than any of the others, the mountain division, from its greater local unity, is relatively much stronger in party conventions, since its delegate vote is more likely to be a unit. In consequence of this fact, it is sure to get a fair proportion of its men as candidates upon the State ticket, and its party vote can be counted upon with considerable accuracy. Knowing, therefore, that they are a strong factor in the politics of the State, it is not surprising that the Kentucky mountaineers should find therein a great interest.

Men, who, from the isolation of their environment, receive few impressions, are likely to retain these impressions in indelible outline; time neither modifies nor obliterates them. Thus it is with the Kentucky mountaineer. He never forgets either a slight or a kindness. He is a good lover and a good hater; his emotions are strong, his passions few but irresistible; because his feelings lack a variety of objects on which to expend themselves, they pour their full tide into one or two channels and cut these channels deep. Like all mountain-dwellers, they love their home. They love the established order of things. Their remoteness from the world's great current of new ideas has bred in them an intense conservatism, often amounting to bitter intolerance. For instance, they were so outraged by the divided skirts and cross-saddle riding of some of the women of our party, that in one county they were on the point of blocking our way; in another, they were only dissuaded from a raid on the camp by a plea from a leading man of the town for the two Kentucky women of the party who used side-saddles, and everywhere they gave scowling evidence of disapproval. There were no jeers; the matter was to them too serious for banter or ridicule. Nor was their feeling, as we shall see later, an outgrowth of a particularly high and delicate standard of womanhood; it was more a deep-seated dislike of the unusual. Painfully lax in many questions of morals, they hold tenaciously to matters of form. The women who came into our camp at different times to visit us, in spite of a temperature of 90° Fahr., wore red woolen mitts, their tribute to the conventions.

The upland regions of all countries are the stronghold of religious faiths, because the conservatism there bred holds to the orthodox, while the impressive beauty and grandeur of the natural surroundings appeals to the spiritual in man. Such a religion, however, is likely to be elemental in character—intense as to feeling, tenacious of dogma, but exercising little or no influence on the morals of everyday life. This is the religion of the Kentucky mountaineer. By nature he is reverential. Caves are "God's houses," sun time is "God's time," indicated by the noon-mark traced with charcoal on the cabin door. A God-fearing man has the unlimited respect of every one in the mountains. A preacher is a privileged person. Wherever he goes he finds free board and lodging for himself and his horse, and his horse is always shod free. In that lawless country, a man who shoots a preacher is ever after an object of aversion, and there is a general assumption that the murderer will not live long—either a superstition or a generalization from the experience that often some individual constitutes himself an arm of the Almighty to punish the offender. One who is a preacher must be "called" to the work, and must serve without pay. The "call" does not presuppose any previous preparation for the profession, and naturally involves some modern substitute for Paul's tent-making to earn a livelihood. The result in the Kentucky mountains is sometimes amazing. Preachers there have been known to be whiskey distillers. Some have been seen to take one or two drinks of liquor while delivering a sermon. We attended an outdoor "meetin'" conducted by one whose widowed sister ran a moonshine still. The best are farmers or country storekeepers. All are more or less ignorant, some densely so. We heard one man preach who could neither read nor write. At a meeting of some sectarian association in the fall of 1898, a mountain preacher advanced the opinion that the old blueback spelling-book gave all the education that a preacher needed. The style of preaching that appeals to the mountaineer is purely hortatory. It begins in a natural tone of voice, but, like all highly emotional speech, soon rises to rhythmical cadences, and then settles to a sustained chant for an hour or more. Any explanatory remarks are inserted parenthetically in a natural voice. This, and only this, stirs the religious fervour of the mountaineer. A clergyman from one of our cities who was doing missionary work among these people was met with the criticism after his service, "Stranger, I 'lowed to hear ye preach, and ye jest talked."

Though his religion is emotional and little suggestive of a basis in rationalism, yet the mountaineer takes his mental gymnastics in vigorous discussion of dogma. This seems to be the one form of abstract reasoning open to him—an exercise natural to the Teutonic mind. He is ignorant, remember, therefore positive and prone to distinguish many shades of belief. Sects are numerous. There are four recognized kinds of Baptists in the mountains. Denominational prejudice is so strong that each denomination refuses to have anything to do with another. A Methodist refuses to send his children to the Presbyterian mission school in his neighborhood, though it is far superior to anything else at his command, and costs him nothing. For this reason the work of the various Home Mission boards in the mountains has achieved only limited results as to number. Only undenominational work, like that of a social settlement, can reach all the people of one locality; and in view of the sparsity of the population, this is a vital matter.

In spite of the intensity of religious feeling, the number of communicants of all denominations forms only from five to fifteen per cent of the total population. The mountains of Eastern Kentucky show the largest area of this low percentage in the United States, east of the Missouri river and the Indian territory. It may be due to the lack of churches and of any church organization where the preachers are "called" and do not form a distinct profession. Baptists, Disciples of Christ, and Methodists are most profusely represented. The sparsity of population with the diversity of sects permits religious service only once a month, when the circuit rider comes. This devoted man leaves his farm or store on Friday, and goes "creeter-back" over the mountains to each of his distant charges in turn. The district school building, in lieu of a church, answers for the meeting. Service is held on Saturday morning, and again on Sunday, for many of the congregation have come such a distance they feel entitled to a double feast of religion. They stay at the nearest cabin, which takes them in with their horses. After the Saturday sermon, the secular affairs of the church are attended to, as the mountaineer considers it unseemly to transact any business, even the disciplining of a delinquent member, on Sunday, although outside the sacred precincts he trades horses and indulges his taste for conviviality. Religion is something to be kept assiduously apart from common everyday living.

The fact that the profession of a mountain preacher is only an avocation with its consequent secondary claim upon his time, the fact of the severity of winter weather for horseback travel, and of the impassability of the roads at this season both for pastor and people, render church worship intermittent in this upland region, and at the same time explain the curious custom of the mountain funeral. This never takes place at the time of interment, but is postponed for months or years. It is desirable to have the ceremony at a time when the roads are passable, when the preacher will not be detained by the harvesting of his corn crop, and when there can be a great gathering of kinfolk, for the clan instinct is strong among these people, and a funeral has its cheerful side in the opportunity for social intercourse it affords. Sometimes a long arrear of funerals has to be observed, if adverse circumstance for several years have prevented a family gathering. At one cabin we visited, the woman of the house told us she was getting ready for a big gathering at her place on the first of October, when the funerals of five of her relatives were to be preached. A university man, travelling through the mountains to make some scientific research, told us he had recently heard a sermon preached in honour of an old man who had died a year before and of a baby girl who had departed this life in 1868. The prominence given to funeral sermons in the season of good roads lends a sombre cast to the religion of the mountaineer, and strengthens in him a fatalistic tendency which is already one of his prominent characteristics, born doubtless of the hopelessness of his struggle with natural conditions. This feeling is so strong that it goes to astonishing lengths. It frankly condemns missions and Sunday schools as gratuitous meddling with the affairs of Providence. An Episcopal bishop recently, on arriving in a mountain village, heard that one of the families there was in great distress, and went immediately to make a visit of condolence. When he inquired as to the cause of their grief, he learned that a ten-year old son had disappeared the evening before, and they had reason to suppose he had been lost in a large limestone cave which ran back 2 miles under the mountain not far away. In answer to his question if their search had been fruitless, he learned they had made no attempt at search, but "if he's to die, he's to die" came the wail, with pious ejaculations as to the will of God. In a few moments the man of God was striding along the trail to the cave, a posse of men and boys armed with candles and lanterns pressing close upon his heels, and in two hours the lost child was restored to the bosom of its family.

The morals of the mountain people lend strong evidence for the development theory of ethics. Their moral principles are a direct product of their environment, and are quite divorced from their religion, which is an imported product. The same conditions that have kept the ethnic type pure have kept the social phenomena primitive, with their natural concomitants of primitive ethics and primitive methods of social control. Such conditions have fostered the survival of the blood-feud among the Kentucky mountaineers. As an institution, it can be traced back to the idea of clan responsibility which held among their Anglo-Saxon forefathers; and it is this Old World spirit which animates them when the eldest man of a family considers it a point of honour to avenge a wrong done to one of his kindred, or when a woman lays upon her sons the sacred obligation of killing the murderer of their father. In a community that grows from within by natural increase, hereditary instincts are strong, and clan traditions hold sway. But if the blood-feud was decadent among the colonial ancestors of our Kentucky mountaineers, the isolation of this wild upland region was all-sufficient to effect its renascence, and to-day in some counties it is a more powerful factor of social control than the courts of law. The mountains, by reason of their inaccessibility and the sparsity of their populations, saw a great prolongation of pioneer days and pioneer organization of society, where every man depended on his own strong arm or rifle to guard his interests and right his wrongs. When the law invaded this remote region, it found the feud established and the individual loath to subordinate himself to the body politic. This individual was justified to himself by the almost universal miscarriage of justice. For the administration of the law is almost impossible in a feud case. It is next to impossible to convict a murderer in his own county, because the jury, and often the witnesses are intimidated by the party of the defendant, and will fail to render a verdict of guilty; or, if the murder was committed to avenge some real wrong, the mountain jury, trained by tradition in their peculiar ideas of family honour, feels itself in sympathy with the criminal and acquits him. This they do without compunction, for they have as yet only a rudimentary conception of the sacredness of the law. The court often tries a change of venue, but the cost of this is particularly burdensome in a poor community, and the change is made to an adjoining county, where sympathy with mountain methods still holds.

As a last resort, a rescue party of the defendant's relatives will make its attempt to defeat justice. An episode of the Howard and Baker feud, which raged during the summer of 1899 in Clay County, was the trial in Knox County of a Baker lad who had killed one of the opposing faction. Forty-two Bakers, armed with rifles and smokeless powder, came over the mountains to attend the trial, and openly established their "fort," or headquarters, in the county-seat. The boy, though clearly guilty, was acquitted, received his gun from the sheriff, and started off that night to the scene of hostilities, attended by his kindred as a guard of honour, not as a rescue party. The consequence is, if a man is killed in a quarrel, his relatives, knowing from long experience the helplessness of the law, take the matter of punishment into their own hands, and at their first chance shoot the murderer. But the desire for personal vengeance is always present. In the same Howard and Baker feud, Tom Baker shot to death William White, an ally of the Howards and brother of the sheriff, as likewise kinsman of the county clerk, jailer, and judge. Naturally reluctant to give himself up to officials who were his personal enemies, Baker took to the hills until State Troops were sent to the county, when he gave himself up to them. They pitched tent in the court-house yard, with a Gatling gun in position for action, and Tom Baker was placed in a tent in the centre, while no one was allowed to enter the military lines. But one day his guards brought Tom Baker for a moment to the door of his tent for a breath of air, and in that instant a shot, fired from the house of the sheriff, found its way to his heart. And the mountaineers openly exulted that a hundred trained soldiers could not protect a man who had been marked out as a victim.

The exciting causes of these feuds are manifold and often of a trifling nature. A misunderstanding in a horse trade, a gate left open and trespassing cattle, the shooting of a dog, political rivalry, or a difficulty over a boundary fence may start the trouble. The first shooting is sometimes done in the madness of moonshine intoxication. These mountaineers are men who hold life as light as a laugh, and to such anything is sufficient provocation to shoot; so the first blood is easily shed. The feud once started, a long and bloody war ensues, often for several years, in which waylaying, shooting from ambush, and arson are regular features. Sometimes pitched battles, engaging a hundred men or more, or a protracted siege of a factionist stronghold varies the programme. In the recent Howard and Baker feud, the principals were men of prominence, influence, and means, so they were able to command a number of followers. The main allies of the Howards were the White Family, who have furnished members of the United States Congress, State Senate, and House of Representatives, and have controlled the offices of the county for fifty years. In the French and Eversole feud, which raged at intervals for many years in Perry County, the best people of the county were drawn into one or the other faction. And yet throughout this section there are those who deplore the reigning lawlessness.

In all mountain regions of the world crimes against persons are far more frequent than crimes against property. So in the Kentucky uplands the former are frequent, the latter rare. There is no real disgrace attached to killing an enemy or a government officer who attempts to raid a moonshine still. There is little regard for the law as such, little regard for human life; but property is sacred. If a mountaineer is asked what, in the eyes of the mountain people, is the worst crime a man can commit, the answer comes, "Horse-stealing. If a man up here steals a horse, his best friend would not trust him again with fifty cents." Here speaks the utilitarian basis of his ethics in the almost impassable roads and trails of a pioneer country. To further inquiry he replies, "And the next worst thing is to steal logs out of a stream—indeed, to steal anything." The mountaineer is honest, scrupulously so. If a log from a lumber-camp is stranded on his field from a subsiding flood in the river, he rolls it into the water at the next rise; or if this is impossible on account of its weight, he lets it lie and rot as a matter of course, for it never occurs to him to cut it up for his own use. He never locks his door. If a robbery occurs, the punishment is swift and sure, for the hue-and-cry is raised up and down the valley or cove, and the escape of the culprit is almost impossible. Primitive in their shortcomings, these mountain people are primitive also in their virtues. The survival of the clan instinct has bred in them a high degree of loyalty; and their free, wild life, together with the remoteness of the law, has made them personally brave. They carry themselves with a certain conscious dignity which peremptorily forbids all condescension. Every man recognizes man's equality; there are no different classes. The consequence is the prevalence of that democratic spirit which characterizes the mountains of Switzerland and Norway.

In only one respect do the mountain people show marked moral degradation. There seems to be no higher standard of morality for the women than for the men, and for both it is low. This is true throughout the Southern Appalachians. The women are modest, gentle, and refined in their manners, but their virtue is frail. The idealism of youth keeps the girls pure, but when they marry and take up the heavy burdens that mountain life imposes upon them, their existence is sunk in a gross materialism, to which their environment offers no counteracting influence. Furthermore, the one-room cabin harbours old and young, married and single, of both sexes.

The Kentucky mountaineers are shut off from the inspiration to higher living that is found in the world of books. Isolation, poverty, sparsity of population, and impassability of roads make an education difficult, if not impossible; the effect of these conditions is to be seen in the large percentage of illiterates in this section. Of the women over twenty-five years old and men over forty, 80 per cent can neither read nor write. It is quite the usual thing to meet men of clear, vigorous intellects and marked capacity in practical affairs who cannot sign their own names. One mountaineer gave it as his observation that only one-half of the men over twenty years in his county could read. With the children it is somewhat better, because with the natural increase of population more district schools are established, and distances are therefore shortened for the tramp from cabin to school-house. To children who must go barefoot, or wear home-made moccasins, or who can afford not more than one pair of store shoes a year, the question of distances is a vital one, especially in the winter. The district schools are in session for five months, from August 1 till Christmas. The number of pupils at a school ranges from fifty to a hundred of all ages from six years to twenty, and all are in charge of one ignorant, often inexperienced teacher. All start in at their work in August, but it is soon interrupted for a week, because the instructor has to leave to attend the Teachers' Institute at the county-seat. On October 1 the older boys and girls are withdrawn from school for two weeks to help get in the harvest. Then November comes, and with it in alternative years certain important state and county elections. If the teacher is a man, being one of the few educated men of the section, he is probably a candidate for one of the county offices, or a member of his always numerous family connection aspires to the State legislature. In either event the teacher, with a mountaineer's sense of the importance of politics, closes school for ten days before the election in order to take part in the campaign. The middle of November the little flock reassembles, and the work of education goes on. But soon the fall rains come, and then the cold and snows of December. First the youngest and frailest are kept at home. but the older and sturdier ones continue, all the more eagerly now because they have the undivided attention of their instructor. The day comes, however, when the intense cold, combined with their own sad want of stout shoes and warm clothes, keeps even the most ambitious at home, and the teacher, with a sigh of relief or regret, locks the school-house door two weeks before the term is over. And the children, with no books at home on which to exercise their attainments, lose almost all that they have gained. And that all is little at best.

The district school of the Kentucky mountains is, in general, a rough log-cabin more or less crudely equipped according to the sparsity or density of the surrounding population. Some are entirely without desks, rude, uncomfortable benches of rough mountain manufacture taking their places. We saw no maps, and instead of blackboards, the unplaned planks of the inside of the walls had been stained a dark colour for a space of 12 feet. In some of the back districts, where hardware is at a premium, the children are summoned from recess by a big wooden rattle. If the physical equipment of the school is primitive, the mental is almost as crude. The standard of education for the teachers is not high. Some of them have not progressed farther than the multiplication table in arithmetic, and all use ungrammatical English. Their preparation for teaching in general consists of the course of instruction at the district school and a few months' training at the so-called normal school of the county-seat. At a recent meeting of the Teachers' Institute in one of the mountain counties, when the subject up for discussion was "Devotional exercises in schools," it transpired that, of the fifty-six public school teachers present, only one in eight knew the Lord's prayer, a majority did not know what it was or where it came from, a majority did not own a Testament, and only two or three were the proud possessors of a Bible. Such ignorance is pitiable, but pitiable chiefly because it means lack of opportunity. Many of such teachers are half-grown boys and girls, who are in this way trying to earn the money, always so scarce in the mountains, "to go down to the settlements" and get an education. When their desire for knowledge is once aroused, they are strong, persistent, and ready to face any obstacle to get an education. Their vigorous minds, unjaded nerves, and hardened bodies combine to make them victors in the struggle. One boy of fourteen started out from his hillside home with his little bundle of clothes slung over his shoulder and 75 cents in his pocket, and tramped 25 miles over rough mountain trails to Berea, where the nearest school and college were. While taking the course there, he supported himself by regular jobs of various kinds, and maintained an excellent standing in his classes. When a mountain lad comes down to the State University at Lexington, it is a foregone conclusion that he is going to carry off the honours. We find at work in him the same forces that give success to the youth from the Swiss Alps and the glens of the Scotch Highlands, when these too come down into the plains to enter the fierce struggle for existence there. For the Kentucky lad, the change has meant a stride over an intervening hundred and fifty years.

The life of the Kentucky mountaineer bears the stamp of the eighteenth century. His cabin home is rich in the local colour of an age long past. The spinning-wheels for flax and wool, the bulky loom in the shed-room outside, the quaint coverlet on the beds within, the noon-mark on the door, and, more than all, the speech of the people, show how the current of time has swept by and left them in an eddy. The English they speak is that of the Elizabethan age. They say "buss" for kiss, "gorm" for muss, "pack" for carry, and "poke" for a small bag. Strong past tenses and perfect participles, like "holp" and "holpen," and the syllabic plural of words ending in *st*, like "beasties," are constantly heard. The Saxon pronoun "hit" survives not only in the upland regions of Kentucky, but also of the Virginias, Carolinas, and Tennessee. With the conserving power of the mountains has come into operation also their differentiating influence within their boundaries. Every valley has some peculiarity of vocabulary or speech which distinguishes it from the community across the adjoining range. The mountaineers have, therefore, criticized the dialect in John Fox's stories of this region, because they are not judges of the dialect of any locality but their own.

Survivals of speech are accompanied also by survivals of customs. In the mountains, the "rule of the road" when two horsemen or wagons meet is to turn to the left, as in England. Another relic of old Scotch or English custom we find in the "infare" or "infair," after a mountain wedding. This is the dinner given at the home of the groom's parents the day after the ceremony. It was observed in the rural districts of all Kentucky and Indiana up till fifty years ago, but now is adhered to only in the mountains. A more remarkable case of survival was discovered in 1878 by Prof. Nathaniel S. Shaler, of Harvard, on the borders of Virginia and Kentucky. There in a secluded valley he found men hunting squirrels and rabbits with old English short-bows. "These were not the contrivance of boys or of to-day, but were made and strung, and the arrows hefted in the ancient manner. The men, some of them old, were admirably skilled in their use; they assured me that, like their fathers before them, they had ever used the bow and arrow for small game, reserving the costly ammunition of the rifle for deer and bear."

Though these people came into the mountains with eighteenth-century civilization, their isolation and poverty not only prevented them from progressing, but also forced them to revert to earlier usages which at the time of their coming were obsolescent. This is the explanation of the feud, as has been shown above, of the use of the hand-mill and short-bow, and especially of the old English ballad poetry which constitutes the literature of these mountain folk to-day. This has survived, or, more properly, flourished in its medieval vigour because it has not felt the competition of books. The scant baggage of the pioneer immigrants from colonial Virginia and Carolina could not allow much space for books, and the few that did make the trip across the Appalachian mountains were used up, from much reading and handling, by one generation. Poverty and inaccessibility prevented an invasion of new books from without, and from within there was no competition from newspapers. There are to-day twenty contiguous mountain counties, covering altogether an area of 6,000 square miles, not one of which can boast a printing-press. Under these circumstances, the Kentucky mountaineer reverted to his ancestral type of literature and revived ballad poetry. This has now been handed down from lip to lip through generations, the slightly variant form and phrase only testifying to its genuineness. The ballad of "Barbara Allen," popular in Great Britain three hundred years ago, and known now in America only to the musical antiquarian, is a stand-by in several of the mountain counties. The tragic ballad of "Little Sir Hugh," or "The Jewish Lady," as it is variously called, traces back to the Prior's Tale of Chaucer. The lengthy ballad of "Lord Bateman," or "The Turkish Lady," shows unmistakable identity with the poem of the same name in Kurlock's "Ancient Scottish Ballads," though the Scotch version is longer.

Animated by the spirit of minstrelsy, the mountaineers have composed ballads on the analogy of the ancient. These are romantic or heroic and of narrative length. We heard a woman sing a native ballad of fifty-two stanzas, entitled "Beauregard and Zollicoffer," which recounted the deeds of these two generals of the Civil War. The music for all these ballads is in a weird minor key, and is sung in a nasal tone. As far as we were able to judge, the women are the chief exponents of mountain minstrelsy, and the accuracy of their memories for these long poems is suggestive of Homeric days. Spain and Sicily are perhaps the only other parts of the civilized world, at least in Europe and America, where modern folk-songs are still composed in the form of ballad poetry.

The whole civilization of the Kentucky mountains is eloquent to the anthropogeographer of the influence of physical environment, for nowhere else in modern times has that progressive Anglo-Saxon race been so long and so completely subjected to retarding conditions; and at no other time could the ensuing result present so startling a contrast to the achievement of the same race elsewhere as in this progressive twentieth century.

9

Life in the Kentucky Mountains.
By a Mountaineer

Samuel Johnson

Of the numerous accounts of life in the southern Appalachians published during the years prior to World War I, few were by mountaineers themselves. Indeed, only one such essay gained any widespread readership, the article reprinted here. About its author, Samuel Johnson, no biographical details are known beyond those contained in this account of life in the Kentucky mountains. Even his exact place of residence is unknown, indeed place names seem to be carefully avoided here. Evidently Johnson, if that was his real name and not a pseudonym, was of middle age, and articulate. His insider's view is valuable not only for the attitudes expressed but for the discussion of various customs, entertainments, courting procedures, and the work ethic. In addition, Johnson deals with music and presents various dialect terms, all given in context.

"Jack rocks" or "hull gull" is an American version of a game that dates back to the time of Xenophon (434–355 B.C.). It is played by three or more players who stand in a circle. A player addresses his left-hand neighbor asking him to guess a number of counters (beans, grains of corn, marbles, nuts, or similar items). The second player guesses, two guesses sometimes being allowed. If the guess is four, and the real number six, the first player responds, "Give me two to make it six," and so on until all the counters have been gained by one player. The number allowed to be taken is often limited, by agreement, to six or ten. Goebel refers to the martyred governor of Kentucky, William Goebel, who was assassinated in 1900.

In 1913, five years after Johnson's article, twenty-seven year old Josiah Henry Combs, later to become a noted folksong scholar, published *The Kentucky Highlanders from a Native Mountaineer's Viewpoint.* Combs was much more highly educated than Johnson, eventually receiving a Ph.D. from the Sorbonne, and his pamphlet is more academic than Johnson's. That does not mean it is necessarily more valuable; indeed, in one respect, Johnson's is the more important, albeit shorter, publication. "Life in the Kentucky Mountains" is more spontaneous than Combs's pamphlet, and

Reprinted from *Independent* 65 (July 9, 1908): 72–82.

unlike *The Kentucky Highlanders,* the work of one who had never lived outside his own folk culture.

* * *

The farthest back I can remember is when I was a wee chap in cotton dresses pulling after my mother and begging for a biscuit. Sometimes I would beg for hours and hours when I knew there wasn't one in the house. Biscuits were a rarity with us.

I was the seventh of a family of eight—four boys and four girls—Bill, Dick, Josie, Sarah, Becky, Martha, Sam and Joe. Joe was the baby; the largest biscuit and the prettiest piece of meat always went to him.

The house where I was born and lived till I was four years old was a little log cabin of one room, far up a deep, long hollow, four miles from any schoolhouse or church, surrounded by a dense forest of trees and entwining grape vines. In those days the country was very different from what it is now. A great deal of land that is now cleared and settled was in woods. We were sometimes so far from any postoffice that even tho a letter were directed to us, we would never get it.

When I was five years old and commenced wearing pants, I thought I was beginning to be a man, and Joe and I would shoulder our little wooden guns and go out to "fight the Indians." While the rest of the children were at school Joe and I would have great times together, hunting chestnuts and chinquapins and gathering wild flowers. We were not left to ourselves many weeks and months tho, for father would get behind in his work and the older boys would have to quit play and assist him, while the girls would have to help mother with her pumpkin and apple butter and jams. As the school was in most all cases very far off, and the creeks so wild, they were afraid to send the smaller ones alone. I would be glad when they didn't go, so we could all be together!

Altho I managed to obtain a rough knowledge of some of the free school branches, yet "book-learning" in those days had no fascination for me. While the children of the "land owners" wore their nice, new suits and pretty caps and shoes, I had to wear my "jeans" pants, "hickory" shirt, bark hat and go barefooted, and this contrast would cause me a feeling of great shamefulness, and tended to corroborate the theory that "such fellows as me were never intended to learn anything." I was a swift runner, an excellent ball player and expert wrestler—but for "book lore"—I left that for the "other fellow."

My happiest days were those spent at home in winter, after supper, before the fire on the old puncheon floor. Us boys and girls would gather around in a circle and play "Jack rocks" or "hull gull." For hours and hours this merry sport would continue till a gruff voice would command us to bed. Sometimes some of the neighbors' children from over in the next hollow would come in and join us in our little games.

When I was about ten years old Dick traded for an old banjo, and every night after his day's work was done, he would take it down from where he kept it hung on the wall and thump on it for hours at a time, trying to make a note on some tune he had heard. This did not suit father, who always went to bed as soon as supper was over; and when the nights got warm Dick would take him a chair and go out and sit against a tree and pick till far into the night. While Dick was away to his work, and I was not in school, I would slip the banjo out into the woods and go over those notes Dick had learned. One day he caught me at this, but when he saw I could play equally as well as himself, he never afterward objected to me using it.

We never lived at one place long at a time, except when father would take a lease for several years on one tract. Joe and I were always glad when it came "moving time," so we could have new woods to explore, new trees to climb and new caves to rummage. At no time, tho, were we ever fortunate enough to be in close range of any schoolhouse or church.

As soon as my sisters would become grown they would hire out to the farmers of the valley, at from twenty-five cents to a dollar a week. Then some fellow would take a liking to them, and before I was grown they had all married off.

My father was a great hunter, and always kept a good hunting dog, which we all loved dearly. During the fall of the year father and Bill and Dick would work hard all day and hunt the greater part of the night. Joe and I thought if we could ever get big enough to go hunting our greatest ambition would be realized; and one of the most regrettable things of my life is that little Joe's ambition was never realized. Before he was seven years old he took with diphtheria, which he caught at school, and became its victim after an illness of only a few days. If he had had the proper medical treatment he could have been saved; but father had had bad luck that year and because he had not been able to settle up an old account he owed for previous treatment, the doctor feigned sickness and wouldn't come. It threw a gloom over the little household and saddened us for several years.

After quitting school, life was somewhat strange and lonesome to me, for little Joe was not there to keep me company. For a while after my day's work was finished I would get my arithmetic and slate and work examples till bed time; but I kept running on sums that I couldn't work, and as there was no one to help me, I gradually began to lose interest, until I finally gave up altogether. Instead, I would pick up my gun and call old "Tray" and stroll out thru the woods in quest of the possum and the coon. If the night was cool and game scarce, I would sometimes build up a fire and old "Tray" and I would gather around it and look out over the dark, mysterious valley and the world beyond, till far into the night. I would talk to him and tell him what a peculiar, curious world it was we were living in, and I always thought old "Tray" could understand that I was talking about, for he would draw himself closer up to the fire, and with his tongue protruding out the side of his mouth, gaze down into the valley with a dreamy, far-away expression.

If the night was dark, warm and damp we would often get as many as three or four possums and one or two coons, which I would skin and stretch on boards and sell to the country store for shoes, clothing, powder, lead and many other necessaries of life. This was almost my only financial source.

To add to my many other misfortunes and loneliness, Dick had taken away his banjo, when he went down to Tennessee to get him a job. I was thrown so completely at sea in this last misfortune that I decided I must have one of my own, and one night, on one of my midnight rambles, I called on one of my old school chums and swapped him a "Bull Dog" pistol to his "home made" banjo. At the time I thought this was the greatest bargain anyone had ever made.

The noise never seemed to bother my mother very much, as she appeared to take an interest in the different tunes I was learning—sitting quietly in her corner knitting, she would watch me from over her spectacles. But father always did regard it as a nuisance and something that was altogether uncalled for.

So when the pleasant moonshiny nights of spring and summer came on, like my older brother, I would take my banjo and chair and go out and tilt back against the crib or a tree and pick till far into the night. Old "Tray" would lay out in front of me with his head resting on his paws, and whenever I would stop he would wag his tail, raise his head and blink his eyes to tell me how well he was appreciating the music, and to encourage me on.

Thanksgiving, Christmas and New Years, was the time of all times with me. All during the spring and summer I would study about the good times I would have when that period came round—of the girls I would hug and the boys I would "beat." But my one fad in these sports was my old banjo. However great the distance and dark the night, I would take my old banjo and start for any and every "party" or "dance" I could hear of. As long as there was no one present that could beat me, I would play for them, while they went thru their game of "Boston" or "Snap." (I always would rather pick than to do anything alse, and if I had any hugging or kissing to do, preferred to do it on the quiet.) It was not long till I got to be the best banjo picker there was in the country, and I managed to save me up some money from the sale of my fur, and this, with what I sold my old one for, ordered me a good "store" instrument. It was not long till my fame spread and I was sent for far and near to make music for school exhibitions and all sorts of entertainments thruout the country.

At these "parties" I made the acquaintance of a Miss Lizzie Blarney, the daughter of a widow washerwoman (of the sturdy old Irish stock). She knew more "calls" and could dance more new "steps" than any one else, and was always the life of the crowd and favorite at all of the dances and "plays." Falling in love with her seemed to be the most natural thing of my life. When it would come her turn on the floor I would always tune my banjo till it would ring as clear as a bell, and I had a natural incentive to do my best on all of my "favorite" tunes; and when she would smile at me it would make me feel mighty glad the "other fellow" wasn't the banjo picker!

The next spring after I met her they moved on old man Brown's place (i.e., she and her mother and two younger brothers) just across the valley, in plain view from where we lived; and that summer, besides keeping even on the neighbors' washing, ironing and scrubbing—going far and near over the valley, working from early till late, receiving their thirty or forty cents stipend, and being paid in "hog's heads," "back bones," a "turn of corn"; or, when the old lady would keep persistently reiterating the dire need of "Lizzie a new dress," "Bobby a pair of shoes," she could manage to procure an "order to the store"—they also tended several acres of corn, and to me their cabin, surrounded by this foliage of white tassels, presented a beautiful and bewitching spectacle, and I began to secretly cherish and admire the thrifty and persevering qualities of the Blarney family.

That fall and winter during the holidays I would make it convenient to be around where Lizzie's hat and shawl were, when the "play" had concluded, and ask her "if any one had made any arrangements to take her home," and tell her "if she didn't have any particular objections I would just as soon go around that way."

After the "plays" had all "died out" old "Tray" and I would go over in that direction hunting (tho we rarely ever got any game). I remember very well the first night I went over in there (i.e., after the holidays) I never could quite understand just how Lizzie and "the folks" regarded my suit, and I sat on a log, some hundred yards back of the house, with my gun across my lap, looking far out over the golden, moonshiny valley, and wondering why life had become so miserably to me. Old "Tray" came and laid his head on my lap as if to tell me: "Old Pal, I'm one that won't go back on you." How I did love old "Tray"! For several hours I sat stroking his velvet ears, pouring out my troubles to him. At last he seemed to understand, for he pulled himself loose from me, and gazed out thru the timbers in the direction of the house, and whined piteously. Old "Tray" had solved my problem for me, for it was not long ere I became a familiar figure at the

Blarney fireside; and when the old lady was busying with her household duties and the boys were not keeping too close guard, such an exchange of kisses!

One night I was somewhat later than common in getting started from home, and to make it still worse, my father got me to go by one of the neighbors and return some meal we had previously borrowed; and, as it so happened, Mrs. Blarney and Lizzie had been off doing some washing that day, and being tired and sleepy, had retired somewhat earlier than usual. When I got there, all was darkness and solitude. Thinking some accident might have happened to them, I rapped on the door. Old Mrs. Blarney's voice broke out clear and audible on the still night air: "Mister Johnson, if you want to court my gal, you have to come earlier." That was warning enough!

In the early spring Lizzie and I were married—she being eighteen and I nineteen—and I took a five years' lease on a piece of land on the ridge some two miles down the valley from the scene of our old homes. This tract at the time was nothing but a jungled mass of forest. I went to work with all the zeal of a pioneer woodsman, cutting down trees to build me a house; riving my own boards, splitting logs into halves and dressing them down with my ax into puncheons for the floor, and then, after "chinking" it securely, I had as comfortable a cabin as any mountaineer could wish for. Then Lizzie and I bundled up our belongings into a two-horse wagon load, and betook ourselves to our new home.

The first year was a rather tough one for us, for building my house threw me so late with my clearing that I only got about five acres cleared off, and was nearly till June getting the corn planted. However, I managed to pull thru somehow, with not any more than $25 to the debit side of my account! At the end of the next year I was even with my creditors, and with a horse, cow, a crib of corn and some vegetables stored up for winter besides. At the end of the five years I had the entire thirty-five acres cleared off, and besides a team of horses, cow, hogs, chickens and winter's supply of feed; I also had $250 stored away in our old chest. (About half of this I made swapping horses, fattening hogs and selling off calves.) This amount we put into the farm where we are now living.

Those first five years of married life, tho hard, yet were not without their joys. Often after my day's work in the woods was done, I would take my boy on one knee and my banjo on the other, and while Lizzie was "cleaning up" the supper dishes, sit and rehearse the old tunes of the Christmas holidays, looking out thru the open door into the bleakness of the night building pyramids for the future. I sometimes think they were about the happiest days of my life.

This little farm we are now living on (and where we have lived since our lease was out) contains about a hundred acres. That part which lays in the valley (about twenty-five acres) is considered fairly good for all farming purposes. At the time we bought it, there was about twenty-five acres in pasture and the rest was in timber. Now we have it all cleared off and in grass and under cultivation, except about twenty-five acres.

It cost us $10 per acre, $250 down and $125 per year for six years, with interest. About six years ago we sold off timber to the amount of $500, which we used in repairing the house, fencing and fixing up generally.

While I have made what I consider a pretty fair success in life—brought up a family honestly and successfully, and given them many modern advantages, and have a comfortable home in which to spend my old days, I cannot overestimate the important part my wife has played in the matter. In fact, as I sometimes tell myself: "It was Lizzie that did it, not me."

Like her mother—an untiring worker and economical housewife. Many a morning she would hurriedly wash up her dishes and hoe her row of corn by my side, thruout the long Spring and summer days, stopping only to cook our noon and evening meals. She it was that saw that the extra dollar was laid away for a rainy day. And besides all this—laying aside the matter of a comfortable home and farm as of insignificant importance—I yet owe her a larger debt of gratitude than I shall ever be able to repay.

Lizzie had had some educational advantages; tho meager, yet it was enough to enable her to grasp an idea of what it was and what it meant to be educated. Most of this knowledge she obtained while they were living with one of her uncles, at the village, before they moved to the Brown farm. And even here at this latter place she attended two terms of the country school—(what time her mother could do without her).

So after we were married she kept expostulating with me about subscribing for some papers and buying some books and "trying to keep up with the times." But manhood had brought on a fuller conviction of the old doctrine of my forefathers, and I was firmly settling it in my mind that "the woods was the only place for me." And when she would say: "Sam, have you ever ordered those papers and books yet?" she would cut me to the core and wound me unmercifully.

After many misgivings, much contemplation, arguments and reasoning, I finally gave in; and, thanks to my wife, I now have a fairly good understanding of what is going on, and what has went on, and slowly but surely the old prejudice for "book knowledge" has vanished away.

And in purchasing the land for a home I let the matter of school and church house be of first importance. Here we would be within a mile of both, and I thereupon decided that no pains would be spared to give my children as good an education as my means would allow. No, I did not expect to make an Abraham Lincoln out of them, but I thought I could at least get them to the point where they could earn a living without having to work as hard as I did for it.

Dear reader, if I were to draw these notes to a close at this point I could possibly be able to portray for you as beautiful a picture of home life and contentment as it has probably been your lot to read of. But in this autobiography it is not my intention to offer you a balm for your imagination or a soothing ointment to all your prejudice. As near as I am able to do so, I intend to give you absolute facts—my own genuine autobiography—of an undistinguished Kentucky mountaineer.

Not long after I married, my father got killed in an election row, down near the village where he lived. They had had trouble at that place at the previous election, and my father, with several others, had been notified to "be on guard and stand for their rights." That day they, sure enough, tried to work their same old game of voting men who were not entitled to vote, and marching some of the "weak-kneed" mountaineers up and voting them their way. My father was well known thruout the country as one who would not give an inch to any man. He would do almost anything to avoid a difficulty, but when he was imposed upon, or saw others imposed upon, his anger knew no bounds.

When the mountaineers made their "stand" that day, a cry went up: "Watch Dan Johnson," and my father was shot dead in his track, while reaching for his revolver. But when the smoke cleared up three men were found dead on the porch of the little house used for a poll booth, and the rest were routed from the town. The mountaineers then appointed their judges, and the process of voting proceeded according to law. Of course it created some little disturbance in the neighborhood; but then it was not long in blowing over.

I shall never forget old "Tray"'s actions after my father's death.

That evening I went up to take the news to mother and to stay with her for the night, and as I walked up to the house he did not come bouncing to meet me, as was his usual custom, but just regarded me in a very serious and indifferent manner. As I went about doing up the little chores, feeding the hogs and chopping wood, I noticed that he was very restless, going from place to place and very ill at ease; this the more strange because old "Tray" was not an eye-witness of the village tragedy, and because it was nothing unusual for my father to go off and stay for two or three days at a time.

That night after I went to bed, feeling, of course, very sad and dejected, my mother sitting in the corner sobbing plaintively, old "Tray" was out behind the crib uttering the most mournful howls that ever I heard come out of the mouth of a dog. And he kept this up till far into the night.

Poor "Tray"! He disappeared shortly after my father was killed. Not long after that a traveler, passing thru from Tennessee, described such a dog as that, that was wandering among the mountains there. And that is all I could ever learn of him.

After my father died my mother came to live with me; but this was not for long, for a year had hardly past till we laid her beside her husband and little son at the Jarvis graveyard. Poor mother! She never ceased to speak of little Joe and father. Often she would take out little Joe's clothes and smooth them across her lap with a tender affection, and when her eyes would fall on father's old hat or coat she would break out and cry. Death seemed to come to her as her only relief.

Next election I wrote Bill and Dick, and buckling on our six-shooters we took an early start for the little town that had marked such a sad epoch in our lives.

I was not going for the express purpose of killing some one, for I knew the penalty of the law too well for that, and if there is one thing I have tried to avoid more than anything else it is the thoughts of having wilfully and maliciously transgressed the laws of our land. I have no particular objections to the law if it is a just one and properly applied, but I do object to discriminating laws and the unjust application of the just ones; to a law that will allow one man the right of suffrage and deprive another on purely political principles.

Our presence on the grounds that morning seemed to throw an awe over our adversaries—the ballot-box stuffers and political tricksters—and I was greatly in hopes that everything would go off quietly and smoothly without the usual row.

Abut ten o'clock I began to notice the presence of whiskey on the grounds—several red faces and an occasional outburst of laughter or a loud oath. (I had cautioned my brothers very carefully on this point and had their promise to refrain from taking but one dram on this occasion.)

Soon some of them began huddling together in groups of three and four. Some of them would look at me with a haggard, wolfish expression, while others would talk in low monotones near their ears. Of course I was curious to know what new motive they were brewing, so I posted one of my friends to go over and lounge near them, in a very unconscious manner, and find out what they were talking about. Pretty soon he returned and reported what he had heard: "Fire! fire—fire at the first signal! Let's clean them up at one volley!"

I then saw I had no time to lose, and I said to him: "Go back there and tell those fellows when they see me advancing to fall in line." I beckoned to my brothers, who came up with quick steps and dropped in on each side of me.

The red faces and stiff collars were not long in catching my meaning, for they came together in one band by the time I commenced advancing.

It was my purpose to strike while the iron was hot and before any one was hurt, for I knew that one shot fired meant a dozen or more killed; to explain to them what it meant to raise a row at such a time as that, and to effect a compromise if it was possible to do so. No sooner had I came with some fifteen steps of them than they broke out in a tumult of loud oaths, and I soon saw that I would have no opportunity to reason with them about the matter. I could see their hand working nervously toward their guns. A cry went up: "Kill Big Sam Johnson" (so called on account of my immense weight and height, being at that time six feet and two inches high and weighing one hundred and eighty-five pounds. I also had a cousin "Sam Johnson," who was not near so large as me so they called me "Big Sam.") Instantaneously our twelve forty-fives were leveled at their head. I was too quick for "my man," for I had my gun on him ere he had his more than half-way up.

"Down," I says, "down with it, or you are a dead man."

As soon as I saw we had the "wire" edge off of them, I said: "Boys, I think this matter has gone far enough, for it seems that there can't be an election held here without some one getting killed. We don't want to have trouble with you, but we are going to have justice or death; understand me—justice or death! You people have been in the habit of running things at this place as you please—of sending us old agriculture report books in lieu of official ballots, and when we do get good tickets, of voting your men and knocking ours out, and we are not going to stand it any longer. My father sacrificed his life for this cause, and I stand here ready to put mine into the bargain if you want it."

At that an exclamation of oaths broke out behind and around me.

"Gentlemen," I says, "I just give you thirty minutes in which to vote and get away from here." And they did, without another word. That was the last row that ever occurred at that place.

The great press will speak in horrible terms of the "lawlessness of the mountaineers," but us poor mountaineers, as far as the press is concerned, have no retaliation. Unschooled and unlearned, we must sit quietly back and bear it all in silence. Our only retaliation to speak of is the muzzle of our guns; when all else fails us we at least have that left us. We cannot invite the wise judge and commonwealth's attorney to a dinner of wines and champagnes, write him out a fat fee and say: "When this you see, remember me."

We have no aristocratic family to boast of, and in what other way can we protect and uphold what honor we do have than thru these "automatic friends" of ours?

Tho the election laws are bad enough as they stand, and the old Goebel law has served its purpose well, there is not now the political chicanery in this county there once was.

But I have never yet drawn blood nor had blood drawn from me, nor do I ever intend to have if there is any other alternative. Very early I seemed to have been possessed with a sense of extreme cautiousness, combined with my frank fearlessness, that has probably been the means of my salvation in this way.

I am now fifty years old, in tolerably fair health, tho my locks are getting somewhat gray. I have been elected to two offices—constable and deputy sheriff. They are talking of running me for sheriff next time, and I think I will run. After that I want to be elected to the Legislature, and see how they make laws at Frankfort before I die.

Of my brothers and sisters only three are living—Bill, Sarah and Martha. Dick was killed from ambush several years ago in the lower end of the county. Some said he had taken a part in that Baker and White feud, but I always thought it was done thru an old grudge against my father. Josie and Becky died of typhoid fever somewhere down in Breathitt County.

Bill comes up every year or so (he owns a scrap of land in Letcher County) and we discuss the events of the day and political matters together. The last I heard of Sarah and Martha they had moved over in West Virginia, near the coal-mining region, and their husbands and boys were working in the mines.

All of my seven children are married and gone, except Lillie and little Dan. Two are teaching school, two own a store together, at the village, and one took a business course and is now working in a bank at Jackson.

My old banjo is still hanging on the wall, tho somewhat battered and worn and with its fourth "hide." And often when the nights are warm and moonshiny, while Lizzie is sitting in her corner knitting (a bit changed than when she used to trip the "light fantastic" at the country dances!), and Lillie and Dan are working their sums in arithmetic and algebra, I take my old banjo and go out and tilt back against the woodshed and play to old "Tray" Junior, who lays curled up at my feet.

And however well read I get to be, and whatever honor is accorded me in this world—and tho Goebel laws may come and Goebel laws may go—I will still be just "Big Sam" Johnson ("what hain't afeered uv nuthin'," as the little mountaineer chaps are wont to say), and I guess that's about all the Lord intended me to be.

10

The Virginia Mountaineers

John H. Ashworth

While the "contemporary ancestors" thesis of Frost with its assumption of a homogeneous mountain culture found great acceptance it also found strong opposition from some quarters. Among those who took exception to it were John H. Ashworth (1879–1942), an economist who in 1913 was completing his Ph.D. at Johns Hopkins University. A native of southwestern Virginia, Ashworth taught in rural schools in his home area from 1897 to 1911. Most of his post-graduate school career was spent at the University of Maine from which he eventually retired as head of the economics department. Though he never did any further writing on the Appalachian mountaineer, Ashworth, like Josiah Combs, knew the subject both from an insider's and an analyzing outsider's viewpoint. His special position made him aware that many of the claims of those who saw Appalachian mountaineers as Elizabethans were false, indeed preposterous. Considering his background in political economy it is hardly surprising that he relied largely on statistical tabulations rather than ethnographic fieldwork to advance his arguments. Yet, despite his figures and tables, his essay is more descriptive than analytic.

In assigning blame for the misconceptions commonly held about Appalachian life Ashworth makes some excellent points; even more than seventy-five years later his arguments seem quite modern and convincing. He correctly notes that novels and short stories rather than systematic scholarly investigations are to a great extent responsible for the mistaken ideas. Furthermore, he is accurate in saying that the works of John Fox, and other popular writers, are set in a past era and should not be accepted as typical of present conditions. Ashworth is also correct in stating that many writers have pandered to certain stereotypes by seeking out colorful stories of moonshining and uncivilized life. For various reasons, missionaries, engineers, prospectors, and others have added to the generally distorted concept of mountain life. Ashworth doesn't claim that everything about mountain life is idyllic but he concludes that "there has been much generalizing from few particulars." His mention of the Allens

Reprinted from *The South Atlantic Quarterly* 12 (July 1913): 193–211.

refers to a 1912 courtroom fracas in Hillsville, Virginia in which the family of Sidney Allen started shooting in reaction to a jail sentence. About two hundred shots were fired and the judge, the sheriff, and prosecuting attorney were all killed. Eventually two members of the family were executed and Sidney Allen was given a lengthy jail sentence. Two ballads, "Sidney Allen" and "Claude Allen," about these events became traditional.

*   *   *

The ordinary picturesque portrayal of the Southern mountain folk in newspapers, magazines, missionary literature and missionary expositions forms a very striking contrast to these mountain people as seen in real life and is extremely amusing to those who are familiar with the prevailing conditions in the Virginia highlands. These vivid representations, or rather misrepresentations, are usually not limited to the mountain districts of any particular state, but include, *en masse,* all the inhabitants of the Southern Appalachians.

Let us view first the Virginia mountaineers as they have been presented—along with other Southern highlanders—through the editorial columns of some of the leading newspapers and magazines of the United States. Quotations from a few of the thousands of comments on the Virginia court massacre at Hillsville will suffice.

From the New York *Evening Mail* we quote: "These Virginian and Kentuckian and Tennessean outlaws are the most zealous and earnest conservatives in the world. They regulate their lives by immemorial customs. To them all "book-l'arnin'" means revolution and subversion.

The Baltimore *Sun* suggests the following prescription for this diseased section of country: "There are but two remedies for such a situation as this, and they are education and extermination. With many of the individuals, the latter is the only remedy. Men and races alike, when they defy civilization, must die. The mountaineers of Virginia and Kentucky and North Carolina, like the red Indians and the South African Boers, must learn this lesson."

The Kansas City *Star,* in speaking of the mountainous sections of North Carolina, Tennessee, Kentucky, Virginia, and West Virginia informs its readers that: "There are whole counties without railroads, telegraphs, telephones or even churches."

The *Literary Digest* of March 30, 1912, says: " . . . We have on our hands another national problem of no mean magnitude—the problem of bringing the 3,000,000 isolated inhabitants of our southern mountains back into the procession of civilization and progress from which they have been separated for generations." Two prominent features of this quotation should be noted: (1) The three million people spoken of include practically the entire population of the Southern Highlands; (2) That these three millions of people are not within the scope of civilization.

In an *Outlook* editorial of June 22, 1912, "The College and the Sheriff," Berea College[1] and the Hillsville[2] court tragedy are discussed. We quote from this editorial: "Five or six miles from Berea the turnpike ends and the trail or path begins. From that point the traveler walks or rides astride. He finds himself in a great mountain region in which two million people have lived by themselves for generations.... If ever a college held a great light aloft in a dark place that college is Berea.... The cure for the numerous lawlessness of the feud is not an army of sheriffs: it is Berea College. Lawlessness ends wherever the college gets a foothold."

More astounding than the above tragedy-inspired sayings are the following quotations from *The Southern Mountaineers,* written by John Fox, Jr., which was published in Scribner's in 1901 and later in *Blue Grass and Rhododendron.* He says: "The first generation after the Revolution had no schools and churches. Both are rare and primitive today. To this day, few Southern Mountaineers can read, write, and cipher; few indeed can do more." ... "And it is really startling to realize that when one speaks of the Southern Mountaineers, he speaks of nearly three millions of people who live in eight states—Virginia and Alabama and the Southern states between."

The mountaineer of missionary literature and of missionary expositions is no higher type of the uncivilized man than is the mountaineer of the newspapers and magazines. We take the following from *The Highlanders of the South,* a book written by Samuel H. Thompson and used in the study course of the stewards who had charge of the mountain section of the missionary exposition called the "World in Baltimore."[3] "Shirts, trousers, coat, shoes, socks and hats constitute the wardrobe of the average Southern mountaineer. Very few of them wear underclothes." From what the author terms, "Some statistics relating to an isolated township of average conditions, in a border country of the southern Appalachians," we take: "Illegitimacy: sixteen and two-thirds percent of parents illegitimate, eight percent of children illegitimate." In one of the closing paragraphs of the book we find: "You would be surprised to have a Methodist preacher take you far up in the mountains where the moral relations of the sexes are hardly more sacred than among lower animals.... Many, many, such communities have no preacher at all. Many such homes are bare even of the commonest furniture and home-comforts, not having even a comb for the hair."

The people who attended the "World in Baltimore"—also, as I am informed, those who saw the "World in Cincinnati" and the "World in Boston"[4]—were given the following information regarding Southern mountain life. The scene: A little cabin containing an old bed of prehistoric model; some apples, beans and pepper-pods strung on strings, hanging on the outside walls of the cabin; the following articles scattered about the room: reel, spinning wheels, loom, oven, candle-moulds, hand wool cards, wooden tray and rolling-pin; and some pots swung over an open fire near the cabin. What was told to visitors by the stewards in charge? That the people of the Southern Appalachians live just as they lived a hundred years ago; that they card their wool, spin it, weave their cloth, knit their socks and stockings—all by hand; that they bake their bread in an oven; do their cooking over an open fire; and mould their own candles, which, with the pine torch, serve to illuminate their cabins. By questioning the stewards one received the following information: This exhibit represents the home life of practically all the people of the Southern Appalachians; the articles seen here are in every well-stocked home; the cabins rarely have but one room, though sometimes the better homes have two, one above the other, the upper one being reached by ladder from the outside; improved farm machinery and telephones are not in use anywhere; there are some mail routes, but most of the communities do not get sufficient mail to justify the establishment of routes; a few mission churches have been established, but no other churches are found; the few public schools that exist are almost worthless; little is known of medical skill, there being no physicians except the mountain herb doctor. By referring to our *Guide Book to the Exposition,* we learn that the section represented here "Includes the mountain masses and enclosed valleys of nine states. . . . The two Virginias and Tennessee may be said to have the largest section of this territory. . . . The whole region is 101,880 square miles in area." Also, that "Lack of transportation and trade, scarcity of money, and timid shrinking from an attempt to invade the outside world—these and like conditions have held the mountaineers fast in their fateful environment." In speaking of the lines of uplift, we read: "As a third and a most indispensable agency of uplift, the missionary forces of the churches must through their self-sacrificing service and transforming ideals create a new life among the Southern mountaineers. This is being done through the establishment of schools and churches and model homes of missionaries through the region by many of the home boards of Northern churches." Note here, first, as in other citations, the broad expanse of territory included: "The mountain masses and enclosed valleys," which in area are "101,880 square miles"; secondly, the location of the largest section of said territory is the two Virginias and Tennessee; thirdly, that the situation is such that even the establishment of model homes is necessary.

Inasmuch as the foregoing pictures of mountain life have been largely an outgrowth of events occurring on Virginia soil, and since accuracy is more easily attainable in a definite study of a particular territory, the reader is now invited to a careful consideration of some facts pertaining to the seventeen extreme southwestern counties of the "Old Dominion." The region embraced in these counties is that part of the state so often referred to as the uncivilized mountain section and extends from the counties of Wise and Lee, the scene of John Fox's *Trail of the Lonesome Pine,* to Carroll county, the home of the Allens. In order that the statistical facts may serve as an index to the actual social, religious, educational and economic conditions of the remotest of these counties, it is necessary to give specific data by counties rather than for the section as a whole. In the tables given, there may be some minor errors, but the facts have been very carefully collected and are approximately correct.

That the other figures given may be studied and applied intelligently, the area and population of each county is given in table 10-1.

Table 10-1. Area, Population, Physicians, Lawyers, Normal-School Attendance and High Schools

Counties	Area Sq. Mi.	Popula-tion	Physi-cians	Lawyers	Teachers Attend Summer Normal, 1909	No. High Schools	Total Value High School Property
Bland	352	5,154	6	3	11	3	$ 5,000
Buchanan	492	12,334	4	8	13	1	15,000
Carroll	445	21,119	8	6	74	1	23,000
Dickenson	324	9,199	5	13	39	2	10,000
Floyd	383	14,092	12	8	59	1	4,500
Giles	349	11,623	12	10	21	4	30,000
Grayson	438	19,856	13	11	95	8	50,000
Lee	433	23,840	12	12	70	5	50,000
Montgomery	394	21,470	20	13	32	5	50,000
Pulaski	338	17,246	15	11	22	4	15,000
Russell	503	23,474	23	14	40	2	32,000
Scott	535	23,814	18	10	91	7	38,000
Smythe	444	20,326	12	6	21	5	50,000
Tazewell	557	24,946	33	27	34	5	67,500
Washington	605	39,077	25	20	87	15	50,000
Wise	413	34,162	21	41	67	7	140,000
Wythe	474	20,372	21	15	47	5	78,000
Total	7479	342,001	260	227	814	80	$708,000

Since the number and the ability of professional men, especially of physicians and lawyers, forms a good index to the progressiveness of a county, the number following each of these professions is given in the above table. The physicians included in the enumeration are graduates of medical schools and have passed the examination given by the State Medical Board of Examiners. Likewise, the lawyers included have passed the State Bar Examination, and the majority of them are university trained men and will compare favorably with the lawyers of any section of the state. Approximately, there is one physician for every thirteen hundred, and one lawyer for every fifteen hundred of population.

The high school figures were obtained from division superintendents of schools and from the high school report issued in 1910 by Dr. Payne, of the University of Virginia. Normal School data were obtained from the report of the State Superintendent of Public Instruction.

The schools referred to here are recognized state high schools, and the majority of them prepare their pupils for college entrance. In these schools, with two exceptions, elementary work is given, but the entire time of from one to five teachers in each school is devoted to high school work. The term of all schools having high school departments is eight or nine months, and the course of study is that outlined by the State Board of Education. Practically all the high school principals are men holding A.B. degrees from good colleges, while the teaching force usually consists of women who have had either college or normal training. In addition to the work given in the state high schools, many district schools give one and two years of high school training.

The majority of high school buildings are constructed according to modern plans. The above estimate of their value is very conservative. Similar property in the city or away from a section having abundant building material would be valued at something like double the value given in the table.

In the three Summer Normal Schools held each year in this part of Virginia, the teachers receive training under those who stand among the educational leaders of the state. I have been unable to get complete recent data with respect to the elementary schools, but the large attendance at the Normals strongly indicates a progressive educational spirit. A very large percentage of all the women teachers have received training in the State Normal Schools at Farmville and Harrisonburg.

Dr. Abbot's reference to Berea College as "a light held aloft in a dark place" illustrates a common mistake made by sincere men who assert that the education of the mountain boys and girls depends predominantly upon the mountain mission schools. Such institutions as we have mentioned are vigorous and growing, have the confidence and respect of the people, and are doing most effective work in higher education in the mountain districts.

In addition to the denominations represented in table 10-3, other church organizations, each having from two to twelve pastors working in various localities, are the Methodist Episcopal, German Baptist, Episcopal,

Table 10-2.   Colleges

[Information obtained from the Report of the Commissioner of Education for 1911. Some deficiencies in this report have been supplied from other sources.]

	Colleges	No. of Faculty	No. of Students	Value of Property
Male:	Emory and Henry College	13	226	$208,579
	Virginia Polytechnic Institute	49	500	683,750
Female:	Sullens College	26	284	125,000
	Intermont College	74	725	176,000
	Martha Washington College	20	173	125,000
	Stonewall Jackson Institute	14	102	66,500
	Marion Female Institute	—	—	60,000

Table 10-3.   Ministers in Charge of Churches

[Data obtained from ministers of the various denominations.]

Counties	M. E. South	Miss'n'ry Baptist	Presbyterian	Christi'n	Luth'ran
Bland	4	1	1	1	1
Buchanan	3	1	1	0	0
Carroll	3	2	1	1	0
Dickenson	2	3	0	0	0
Floyd	2	3	0	0	1
Giles	4	2	1	3	1
Grayson	7	3	0	0	0
Lee	7	3	1	2	0
Montgomery	7	2	4	1	2
Pulaski	5	2	2	3	1
Russell	5	4	0	0	0
Scott	5	2	1	0	0
Smythe	8	4	2	0	2
Tazewell	11	3	3	7	2
Washington	7	9	8	3	3
Wise	9	4	2	1	0
Wythe	8	3	1	2	3
Total	97	51	28	24	16

Holiness, and the Catholic. The Primitive Baptist Church has a large following in three or four counties, but we do not know the number of ministers belonging to this organization. Approximately, this mountain section has one minister for every eleven hundred people. These ministers are fairly well distributed throughout the district, no part of which is unevangelized. The annual conference reports for 1910 show the following financial data of the M. E. Church, South, in this territory: Churches, 386; value of churches, $657,570; parsonages, 77; value of parsonages, $185,500; money raised for various church purposes, $243,766.

Table 10-4. Banking

[Figures taken from a bankers' directory (*Credit Company of Chicago and Illinois*) for 1912. In a few instances, corrections have been made so as to conform to recent changes.]

Counties	No. of Banks	Paid-Up Capital	Surplus	Deposits
Bland	1	$ 11,000	$ 17,000	$ 65,000
Buchanan	1	25,000	11,000	125,000
Carroll	2	48,000	38,200	189,000
Dickenson	1	25,000	25,000	150,000
Floyd	2	55,000	44,000	223,000
Giles	5	79,000	38,100	386,000
Grayson	4	145,000	21,800	393,000
Lee	4	75,000	58,300	386,000
Montgomery	6	232,000	217,000	1,134,500
Pulaski	4	139,000	106,100	674,000
Russell	4	115,000	34,500	363,000
Scott	3	73,500	30,400	493,000
Smythe	4	146,000	166,000	609,000
Tazewell	7	350,000	200,000	1,200,000
Washington*	10	575,000	319,400	3,083,000
Wise	6	275,000	123,000	1,126,000
Wythe	6	170,000	141,400	689,000
Total	70	$2,623,500	$1,387,700	$10,355,000

Table 10-5 forcibly contradicts the loosely made assertions that southwest Virginia has no commercial facilities and no means of finding out what is going on in the world.

Rural free delivery and star mail routes penetrate nearly every nook of this section. According to government regulation, the 205 rural carriers must handle at least 615,000 pieces of mail each month. This amount is greatly augmented by the 138 daily star routes. The fact is not to be overlooked that all the leading towns get their mail by railway service.

The community without phone service is rare, indeed. The figures

*Including Bristol City, which is partly in Tennessee.

Table 10-5.   Rural Mails, Phones and Railroads

[Data as to mails obtained from Department of Rural Mails; that pertaining to phones taken from tax book of the Virginia Corporation Commission. Miles of railroad were calculated from railway timetables.]

Counties	Mails		No. Miles Phone Wire	No. Miles Railroad
	No. Star Routes	No. R. F. D. Routes		
Bland	4	5	139	10
Buchanan	12	0	51	15
Carroll	12	17	747	35
Dickenson	15	0	75	0
Floyd	7	22	534	0
Giles	7	3	337	70
Grayson	14	22	25	10
Lee	4	23	429	100
Montgomery	9	9	836	75
Pulaski	4	11	697	45
Russell	11	12	210	50
Scott	7	13	158	80
Smythe	5	18	335	37
Tazewell	12	10	437	54
Washington	5	19	1,421	72
Wise	9	4	862	85
Wythe	1	17	762	58
Total	138	205	8,055	796

given in the table refer to chartered lines only. Besides these, there are hundreds of miles of private lines which connect with the lines of chartered companies. Thus, in Grayson county there are only twenty-five miles of phone line owned by a chartered company, yet an investigation reveals the fact that there are about thirty-five hundred phones in the county.

Five great railway systems enter this section, namely: the Norfolk & Western, Virginian, Southern, Louisville & Nashville, and the Carolina, Clinchfield & Ohio. The table includes only passenger lines. Lumber and mineral roads are numerous in some sections.

So far, I have let statistical facts refute the many unfounded assertions concerning the Virginia mountaineers. But, since some things cannot be told in figures, a few general remarks, based on thirty years' experience in this section, may not be amiss. However, I shall make no attempt to describe minutely the mountaineer, to enumerate what he eats and drinks, nor to say wherewithal he is clothed. For any description of the mountain-folk of Virginia as a homogeneous people of a single type is misleading.

There are many classes of mountaineers, the rich and the poor, the good and the bad, the learned and the ignorant, the cultured and the boorish. Where is a section of country of which this not true?

The "typical home" of the "mountain whites," the rough and ill-kept cabin, which appears so often in current literature, is preposterous. Such may be a typical cabin, although the unrepresentative, the worst cabin of all, is usually shown; but cabins constitute only a small percentage of the homes. Beautiful dwellings, worth from two thousand to five thousand dollars, are in most every community, while residences costing from five thousand to twenty thousand and even thirty thousand dollars are not at all uncommon. How absurdly false, then, is the statement that "There is being a general uplift through the establishment . . . of model homes of missionaries through this region by many of the home boards of Northern churches."

The colonial household articles, which are said to be in every well-stocked mountain home, can scarcely be found at all. Those who are fortunate enough to possess them, value them, not as articles of common use, but as heirlooms. The classic spinning wheel, the reel, the bake-oven, and the candle moulds, which are so familiar in literature, have, except in rare instances, become relics of the past, and the mountain children know of their use only through stories told them by their parents and grandparents. It is true that there are scattered here and there, individuals who own and operate the hand-loom in order to supply with home-woven carpets many who prefer this kind to any other, though more costly modern coverings are in general use. In my day I have never known of the hand-loom being used for any other purpose.

Improved farm machinery—mowers, rakes, grain drills, and reapers—are in common use everywhere. Of course, many of the leading farmers have mountain lands where these machines cannot be operated, yet, for the most part, such land serves for grazing purposes, the valley land only being cultivated. In some sections, where mining and lumbering are the chief industries, can be seen little patches of corn and garden truck which are cultivated with small though not primitive tools. Such cultivation represents the avocational rather than the vocational farmer. The same thing is true of the border land of good farming communities where dwells the laborer on his little plot of ground which he takes pride in cultivating. Yet, in the main, he obtains his living from the nearby farmer for whom he works.

The poor of the Virginia mountains have opportunities as good as, perhaps better than, the poor of the cities. Poverty, squalor, and degradation, such as one can see in the slums of any large city, is very uncommon among the mountain people of Virginia. There, the poor are not segregated. All classes attend the same churches and the same schools. The farmer sits at the table with his laborers, and all partake of the same kinds of food. The landowner and the tenant visit and mingle with each other on terms approaching equality. Under these conditions, poverty is not so galling nor such a barrier to those aspiring to better their fortunes.

To the statement, that "The moral relations of the sexes are scarcely more sacred than among the lower animals," I have no statistics to offer in refutation. I merely enter a protest that such assertions are vile and slanderous. If there is any one virtue in which the mountain people excel, it is in the high standard of morality which pervades the sex relationship. Race purity is, likewise, zealously preserved. The cohabitation of whites and negroes would not be tolerated by the whites of the remotest mountain sections.

Many uncomplimentary remarks have been made concerning the character of the religion and the worship of the people. Religion is said to be the propelling force actuating the feudist and the "moonshiner." This is false. These classes, while in no sense atheistic, constitute the worst element of mountain society and have nothing to do with church work. The ministry, on the whole, are educated, enlightened, and progressive. The emotional revival, whether for better or worse, is rapidly passing away. Just a word about the Primitive Baptists, who are quite numerous in a few counties, and who have been the targets for many darts. Their religious beliefs we will not discuss. As a people, they are plain and simple in habits and noted as law-abiding citizens. Many of their ministers are men of ability and occupy prominent positions in their localities.

As yet, only slight reference has been made to that important character, the "moonshiner." From the publicity given him, it is no wonder that the belief is abroad that Virginia mountaineer and "moonshiner" are synonymous terms. The truth is, the temperance sentiment in the mountain sections is as strong, or stronger, than in any other part of the state. In these seventeen counties, whisky is legally sold in only three towns, and in one of these the will of the people, as expressed at the polls, was overruled by a legal technicality. The anti-saloon sentiment is said to be a result of competition between the saloon-keeper and the illicit distiller. This is not true. The prohibitionist is no friend of the "moonshiner." By most of the people, whisky drinking is condemned, regardless of whether it is made legally or illegally. However, illicit distilling in a few counties is common, not that the citizen-body uphold it, but because the mountain glens offer favorable retreats for the few who wish to carry on this unlawful occupation.

Recent history shows that this part of Virginia has been furnishing her quota of the prominent men of the state. This "outlaw" section gave five prominent generals to the Confederate army, namely: Generals J. E. B.

Stuart, William E. Jones, John B. Floyd, William Terry and James A. Walker. Since the war, this "lawless" region has continuously been represented on the bench of the State Supreme Court, Judges Stapleton, Richardson, Phelgar and Buchanan having held this position. During the same period this mountain section has produced four attorney-generals, namely: Taylor, Blair, Ayers, and Williams; three lieutenant-governors: Walker, Kent, and Tyler; and one governor: J. Hoge Tyler. One of the men most prominently suggested as next governor is Henry C. Stuart, a mountaineer. At one time, both United States senators of Virginia—Judge John A. Johnston and Colonel Robert E. Wythers—were from southwest Virginia. Dr. George Ben Johnston, perhaps the best known surgeon of Virginia, is a product of her mountain soil.

Since this is a mountain region and highway construction costly, there are many rough, bad roads. But, the fact that there are two hundred and five rural mail routes in these seventeen counties, is sufficient to convince any reasonable person that trails are not the only mountain highways. For the government regulation as to the establishment of rural routes is: "It is required that the roads traversed by rural routes be in good condition, unobstructed by gates, unless such gates are made to open automatically: that there be no unbridged creeks or streams not fordable at all seasons of the year." That the people are alive on the good roads question, is indicated in the report of the Virginia Highway Commission for 1912, which shows that of $3,853,000.00 of bond issues for highway improvement in the state $2,484,000.00 is accredited to the mountain counties which we are studying. Since this report was made, about $500,000.00 more has been voted by these counties for the same purpose.

According to the census of 1910, there are in this section 33,431 native white illiterates, or, approximately, one person out of every ten is classed as illiterate. This is a bad showing, but strikingly different from Fox's assertion—"that few mountaineers can read and write." This illiteracy is due to past, not to present, conditions. Because the state had no free school system until 1870, and because of the impoverished conditions and local strife growing out of the Civil War, the mountain youth for more than a quarter of a century had little opportunity to secure even an elementary education. That the high rate of illiteracy is an inheritance of the past, surviving in the old and middle-aged, is indicated by the fact that, though the population is rapidly increasing, the number of illiterates, with the passing of the older generation, is gradually growing smaller. Thus, the population of the section increased more than fifty-four thousand from 1900 to 1910, yet the number of illiterates during this period decreased more than four thousand.

After talking to a friend in a strain very similar to that in which I have been writing, he amused me by saying: "What you tell me may be true; but you have not told about the real mountaineers." He could not be made to believe but that in large territories the predominating type of manhood is he of the coonskin cap, dressed in home-spun, and carrying his favorite companion, the old mountain rifle.

To the dubious reader, let me say that I have not avoided the real question, but have taken as a basis a block of territory commonly referred to as the abode of the "uneducated," the "uncivilized," and the "lawless." In applying the term mountaineer to all the inhabitants of the section, I have merely adopted the common usage. I have refrained from describing *the typical* character, because he does not exist. But to satisfy the doubting Thomas, I will say that there is a low stratum of society, representatives of which can be found in almost any neighborhood. Here are ignorant and worthless human beings, but they are not cut off from civilizing influences; even the few who are scattered here and there in the mountain coves, are within easy reach of schools and churches.

Dickenson and Buchanan are the most mountainous, and, in development, the most backward counties of this region; yet, a census made of Clintwood, a village in Dickenson, twenty-five miles from the railroad, and having a population of three hundred and forty people, revealed the fact that sixteen per cent of its adult population were college and university graduates. Six of this number hold degrees from the University of Virginia, and among other schools represented are: University of Chicago, University of Ohio, William and Mary College, and State Normal School at Farmville. Practically the same conditions prevail at Grundy, in Buchanan county. In this little mountain hamlet reside ministers, lawyers, physicians, teachers, and business men, not only college-trained but possessing culture and the spirit of progress in a high degree.

If the popular conception of Virginia mountain life does not correspond to the actual facts, then arises the question: Why these misconceptions? An intimate relation to the section and people of whom I write, and a careful study of many things which have been said and written about them, have convinced me that, whether followed through ignorance or otherwise, unscholarly methods of study account for much of the false information that has been disseminated.

The first unscientific method to be noticed is that of describing past conditions and ascribing these conditions to the present. Many who write and speak of this section, base their assertions on old antiquated jokes and stories told by our fathers years ago, and upon works of fiction which refer to conditions long since past. Much stress is laid upon Fox's novels in their characterization of this section and its people. No account is taken of the fact that the time of the *Little Shepherd of Kingdom Come* dates back to and before the Civil War, and that the *Trail of the Lonesome Pine* carries us back twenty-five years. What can be more unscientific than the acceptance of highly colored descriptions of persons and events of more than a quarter of a century ago as applicable to the present? There has been a persistent refusal to recognize the prodigious strides made in industrial, and consequently in other, lines of development during the last twenty-five or thirty years, and the blind assertion is made that "They live just as they did a hundred years ago." An example of this was seen at the missionary exposition in Baltimore, where the *Little Shepherd of Kingdom Come* was advertised as one of the most popular missionary books of the day.

The extent to which one may be misled by this judging of the present by the past may be seen by a comparison of the school system of Wise county twenty-three years ago with the system of today. Then there were about thirty schools in the county and about the same number of teachers. The schools were taught in rough log buildings, and the total school fund was $7,000. Now, according to the superintendent's report, there are seventy-seven schools, employing one hundred and sixty-one teachers. The buildings are modern, several of them having cost from twenty to thirty-five thousand dollars each. For the year ending September, 1911, the total sum spent on schools in the county was $116,649.91. Similar advances have been made along other lines.

Again, in describing mountain conditions there has been much generalizing from few particulars. The picturesque, the unique, and the uncommon persons and things are thrown on the screen of publicity as "typical." A Virginia "moonshiner" kills a revenue officer. Newspapers would have one believe that all the mountain people are "moonshiners." The people of a large section of country are denounced because of the crime of an individual. When the Allens shot up the Hillsville court, three million people were condemned for the act; but when the gunmen of New York City killed Herman Rosenthal, only those intimately connected with the crime were censured.

The question arises: Are these false deductions and conclusions arising from unscientific methods of procedure the outcome of ignorance or of unscrupulous misrepresentations? This is a delicate question; but I do not hesitate in saying that both ignorance and dishonesty have played a part.

In addition to those who write ignorantly about what they have neither seen nor heard, different classes of persons continually visit the mountains and keep alive the old stories concerning the life there. To three classes of these, we will give some attention: (1) the newspaper reporter and the magazine writer, (2) the civil engineer and the prospector, (3) the so-called mountain missionary.

The newspaper reporter from abroad visits the mountains after some extraordinary crime. He knows the popular conception of mountain life and what his readers are expecting. He improves his opportunity by displaying his imaginative powers and giving the world some startling news.

When the storm center has passed away and while the echoes of the newspaper article still linger, the magazine writer arrives on the scene to investigate the conditions which have led to such a crime. He, too, wants to give his readers something to feast upon. He knows what he wants to write, but he must appear to make an investigation. In the mountains, as elsewhere, it is easy to find what one is looking for. A production more literary than the newspaper article appears. It is the same old story of a people a century behind the times.

Many tales of hair-breadth escapes from the "moonshiner" and of the uncivilized life among the mountains come from engineers and prospectors who frequent the mountain section. They usually come into contact only with the few who live in or near the mountains. Often, perhaps, they describe life as they believe it to be from what they see; but they do not see enough to judge correctly. However, the following incident which came under my observation less than a year ago shows that the stories circulated by the engineer and the prospector are not always true.

An engineer corps boarded at a refined and cultured home in a progressive community. Into this home came regularly a leading daily newspaper and some four or five leading magazines. Imagine the landlady's surprise and chagrin, after her boarders had departed, when she came across an open, unmailed letter, a part of which read something like this: "Tell me what is going on in the world. What has become of the Allens? You know we never see a newspaper or magazine up here."

Are the reports given out by those working in, or investigating, the region as a mission field also unreliable? Yes; they make mistakes similar to those made by others, and some of them grossly misrepresent the true situation. So-called missionaries, working in Tennessee and Kentucky, do not hesitate to describe Virginia mountain life, though they have never been there. If newspaper reports be true, a lady connected with the recent Baltimore missionary exposition sent an appeal to Governor Mann in behalf of the Allens, asking him to pardon them because they had never had any religious or civilizing influences and were not to be judged by the same standards as other people.

Many methods used by some school and church people to awaken sympathy and to obtain money at the North are dishonorable and contemptible. Here is a story which did not occur in Virginia, but it illustrates my point. This story was told me by an educated and responsible minister, and I vouch for it.

A missionary of the Northern Presbyterian Church was working in Cumberland county, Tennessee. He regularly preached at several places, including Grassy Branch, one of the best communities in the county. Nearly all the people there own their homes and live in comfort. In this neighborhood are three churches—Baptist, Methodist, and Presbyterian. Another minister connected with Maryville College visited him in order to go over a part of his work. Instead of following the public road through Grassy Cove—a fine community—they took a path around the side of the cove—no doubt to deceive the visiting clergyman—and went to the home of a family known as the most careless and indifferent family in the whole community. This family lived in a log house, satisfied with few comforts and conveniences, though they could have lived much better had they tried. These two ministers came to this home unexpectedly and asked the privilege of taking a picture of the house and family, with the request that the family would not change their clothes. This picture was to be used in the north to illustrate the life of the "Mountain Whites," the object being to raise money.

This not at all an extreme case. Many who profess to teach others the way of life are very active in slandering a country and its people. They secure the most uninviting pictures possible, as well as out of date household utensils and articles of clothing found only in garrets. We have already seen for what purpose these are used. One might as well judge Fifth Avenue life in New York from the worst scenes obtainable on the East Side as to judge Virginia mountain life by photographs of scenes not typical but very, very rare.

Another common mistake is the misuse of the term mission field as applied to this territory. Is a country which is completely evangelized and well supplied with good churches and educated ministers to be classed as a mission field because certain denominations do not happen to be strong in that particular region, and, in order to maintain ministers, must supplement their salaries from mission funds? Practically all the appeals for mission money and mission workers for the "mountain whites" come from religious organizations which have very little foothold in the Virginia mountains. Too often is the mission money supplied by northern churches used to build churches where churches are plentiful rather than to give the gospel to those who have it not.

With the rapid development of the mountain resources, new towns are springing up, and in such towns help is needed in keeping the church abreast of the times. But this assistance can best be given by those church bodies which are well established in the mountains, and which are ever ready and alert to extend the gospel. New York City has her mission churches, and it would be folly for the church organizations of the Virginia mountains to send special missionaries to New York to organize and run city mission churches separate and distinct from the work being done by the New York churches. Just so it is not necessary for New York, Boston or any section of country to send missionaries to southwest Virginia.

In this Virginia territory there are no real mission schools. Several denominations have colleges, and the Missionary Baptists and Presbyterians have some preparatory schools. These schools are the results of the efforts of local enterprising citizens under the direction of their respective churches, which, through their educational boards, give some assistance. If these be mission schools, then all denominational schools are mission schools.

If aid is to come from outside, let it be given to the established colleges of the section that they may keep pace with the great onward march of education. Their endowments must come largely from outside sources, for, while there are wealthy farmers and grazers in the district, there are no financial magnates. To say that our colleges are greatly handicapped from lack of endowment does not mean that they are not doing a great work, and that our people are ignorant and unprogressive. Some of the greatest educational institutions of the country find it necessary to make special campaigns in order to secure sufficient endowments. Although Johns Hopkins University, University of Virginia, Randolph-Macon College, and Goucher College have made such campaigns, no one thinks of calling them mission schools.

It has been my purpose to correct wrong impressions, not to laud the mountain people. They have great social, religious, and educational problems to solve, but these problems, while perhaps in some respects different from, are not greater than the problems which confront the people of other sections of our country. The mountain population have neither crowning virtues nor peculiar vices which strikingly differentiate them from other rural Americans.

Notes

1. Berea College is in Kentucky.

2. Hillsville is in Virginia—more than a hundred miles from the Kentucky border.

3. An exposition under the auspices of the Missionary Education Movement, in which practically all the churches of the city took part. In one immense building were scenes representing the life of the various mission fields. Stewards in charge explained the customs, religious life, etc., of each territory represented. The exposition lasted five weeks and was visited by about 150,000 people.

4. I have been informed that the attendance at the Boston Exposition was 500,000.

11

Elizabethan America

Charles Morrow Wilson

Charles Morrow Wilson (1905–1977) was a writer, newspaper correspondent, political analyst, public relations specialist, produce company executive, and an expert on international affairs. Born in Fayetteville, Arkansas he spent most of his adult life in Vermont but claimed that the Ozarks always remained his homeland, "my very special America." Wilson demonstrated the truth of his assertion by writing *The Bodacious Ozarks* (1959) and *Stars Is God's Lanterns: An Offerin' of Ozark Tellin' Stories* (1969), and the novels *Acres of Sky* (1930), *Rabble Rouser* (1936), *Ginger Blue* (1940), and *A Man's Reach* (1944), all of which are set in the Ozarks. In addition, his 1934 nonfiction work, *Backwoods America,* dealt with the Ozarks and southern Appalachia. Wilson also treats the two regions in "Elizabethan America"; in fact, the connection between the two mountain areas is the main virtue of the essay. Wilson was the first to assert in print that the Ozarker and his Appalachian counterpart were of the same stock. Like other writers who concerned themselves with the "arrested culture" of the Appalachian mountaineer, Wilson utilized folk speech as a major part of his argument. Although his reasoning is just as faulty as that of others making the same point, Wilson differs from many similar writers in one regard: he had much more field contact with the "Elizabethans," although his principal collecting was done in the Ozarks, rather than in Appalachia.

There is no biography of Wilson, but there is biographical information in his twenty books. His papers, which are quite extensive, are available at the University of Arkansas, Fayetteville.

* * *

Reprinted from *Atlantic Monthly* 144 (August 1929): 238–44.

I

We know a land of Elizabethan ways—a country of Spenserian speech, Shakespearean people, and of cavaliers and curtsies. It is a land of high hopes and mystic allegiances, where one may stroll through forests of Arden and find heaths and habits like those of olden England.

We are speaking of the Southern highlands—Appalachia and Ozarkadia. Putting it generally, Appalachia includes the four western counties of Maryland, the Blue Ridge hills, the Allegheny Ridge country of Virginia, Eastern Kentucky, Eastern Tennessee, Western North Carolina, Northwestern South Carolina, Northern Georgia, and Northeastern Alabama—an area of about a hundred and twelve thousand square miles, approximately that of New York and New England combined, or of England, Ireland, Scotland, and Wales put into one. And by way of an appendage there are the Ozark hills of Southern Missouri, Northwestern Arkansas, and the southeastern tip of Oklahoma, a country in dimensions near a hundred and fifty by two hundred miles, or, roughly, about the size of New York State. The people of Appalachia generally call themselves mountain folks, those of the Ozarks, hill people. The Southern highlands have between six and seven million people, which is somewhere about the population of England during the days of Shakespeare. Nearly 86 per cent of the Southern highlanders are rural people, which is approximately the ratio which held in Elizabethan England.

Husbandmen and ploughmen of Shakespeare's England and present-day upland farmers could very likely have rubbed shoulders and swapped yarns with few misunderstandings, lingual or otherwise; for Elizabethan English, as well as Elizabethan England, appears to have survived magnificently in these isolated Southern uplands.

The speech of the Southern mountains is a survival of the language of older days, rather than a degradation of United States English or a falling away from blunt-edged journalese. Mountain speech has little slang or sauciness. While it does, of course, show local differences a plenty, a surprisingly large number of old ways, giving a quaint and delightful flavor of olden England. Illustrations are plentiful enough. The most casual of listeners will become conscious of the preponderance of strong preterits in mountain speech: "clum" for "climbed," "drug" for "dragged," "wropped" for "wrapped," "fotch" for "fetched," and "holp" for "helped"—all sound Elizabethanisms, to be found in Shakespeare, Lovelace, or King James's Bible. The Southern uplander says "fur" (for) with Sir Philip Sidney, "furder" with Lord Bacon and in common with Hakluyt, "allow" for "suppose." Like Chaucer, he forms the plurals of monosyllables ending in *st* by adding *es*—"postes," "beastes," "jystes" (joists), "nestes," and "ghostes."

Shakespeareanlike, he probably calls a salad a "sallet," a bag a "poke," says "antic" for "careful," and "bobble" for "mix-up." Like Piers Plowman, he says "heaps of people," and Spenserlike says "mought" for "might," rimes "yet" with "wit," and says "swinge" for "singe." He keeps such Elizabethan pronunciations as "sence," "ag'in'," "scriptur," "ventur," "natur," "yit," and "yander." He still "toles" hogs with corn, and, like Gower, comments upon "a sighte of feynold flowers." He gets up "afore daylight" to make a "soon start," "rives" oak blocks into shingle boards, carries a "budget" on his back, looks out for "quiled-up" snakes, and on particular occasions uses a "handerker."

Theseus, in *A Midsummer-Night's Dream,* commends the "pert and nimble spirit of mirth." Ephraim Kilgew may reasonably testify that he is raising up a pert bunch of young 'uns. Like Othello, the hillman "spends" his opinions. He most likely says "dorts" for "sulks," "dauncy" for "ailing," "chat" for "gravel," "swarve" for "crowd together," and "tinsey" for "tiny."

Southern uplanders have a charming capacity for making words and phrases fit the want of an occasion, to express thoughts which are still mobile. Elizabethanlike, their speech is still rollicsome and fluid.

> "The mill war consider'ble damnified."
> "Can I get over that road?"
> "Well, I don't jest edzactly know. Some places the rain has gouted it out mightily, You'll have to surround them places."
> "I done been and had dinner."
> "Sheep is natured like deer."
> "B'ar is destructious. They kill hawgs."
> "Hit'll take two slugs er buckshot to moralize Forgy Dell."
> "I ain't saw Tom in forty year. I can't hardly memorize him."
> "If it don't disfurnish ye none, I'll pay fur that ham-meat later on."

Comparatives and superlatives are generally formed by adding a final "er" or "est," regardless of the length of the word: "endurabler," "fast-runnin'er," "fiddlin'est," "preachin'est," and "hogkillin'est." Just as "wealth" is a collective of "weal," to a majority of uplanders "stealth" is what one steals, "spilth" is what one spills, and a "blowth" is a mass of blowing things or blossoms. They take the *y* from "yeast," but add it to "earn"; "queer" is usually "quare"; "care," "keer"; "chair," "cheer"; "crop," "crap." Extra *r*'s frequently invade such words as "warter," "orter," "arter," and even make a way into names, such as "Caurdle" and "Orsborne."

The Chaucerian "hit" is frequently substituted for "it," but by no means invariably. The choice seems to be governed by an instinct for euphony. Like Spenser, they say "swarve" for "swerve," and, like the immaculate Alexander Pope, "jine" for "join."

Elizabethan exactness of thinking is easily discernible in upland speech. They talk of cow-brutes, ham-meat, lard-cracklin's, of tooth-dent, church-houses, biscuit-bread, and rifle-guns.

> "Was the new baby at your house a boy?" "Yessur, hit was a boy, and I reckon hit's a boy yit."
> "Does that jug hold a gallon?" "W'y, no, not hardly. But hit'll hold quite a content."
> "I'm clearn'n' a field to raise my bread."

II

Broadly speaking, the Southern highlanders are an Old England folk. English and Scotch-Irish, whose forebears came forth from Elizabethan England, a nation of young life which had just found its prime, a nation of energy and daring, a nation leaping from childhood into manhood. And the spirit of Elizabethan England has long survived the weathering of time. The first settlers brought with them Elizabethan ways of living, and these ways have lasted in a country of magnificent isolation, one little touched by the ways of a modern world.

Southern uplanders do not have the Elizabethan's wealth, galleries, or his mechanics and autocracies of high living. They are rather the counterparts of rural Elizabethans, "folk of plain and splendid ways."

"All the corn we make our bread of groweth on our own demesne ground. The flesh we eat is all of our own breeding. Our garments, also, or much thereof, are made in our own home. Our own malt and water maketh our drink." Thus went a good husbandman's boast of self-sufficiency.

It goes in much the same way with the Southern uplander. He gambles squarely upon the benevolence of soil, growth, and weather. He plants crops, hunts game, catches fish, and harvests fruits and berries with a basic idea of self-sufficiency. His wife cooks, churns, makes the clothes, keeps the home, and picks the geese for feather beds. Coffee, baking soda, kerosene, sugar, and lamp chimneys are virtually the only commodities to be bought at the village store. And if times are hard he can use maple or molasses sweetening, make parched-wheat coffee, and sit about in the firelight; or, more expedient still, go to bed at dusk. He cuts elm and ash for cart parts and ploughs, hickory for axe handles, and apple wood for saw rounds, much as was the "presidence" in the days of fair Bess.

Countrysides have their midwives, their herb doctors, their basket makers, their carders, and their millers. Water mills still turn which have ground their community's grain for fully a century, and farm boys continue to ride toward them, with bags of shelled corn swung over their horses' withers—shirts open, lips pursed for whistling, bodies asway to the leisurely, plodding gaits of their mounts.

Trevesses's *Good Plowmen,* as a polaris for rural life in Old England, has this to say of the country fare:—"Look weekly of custom and right / For roast meat on Sundays and Thursdays / at night." But the rest of the week pease and bacon washed down by a draft of cider or good homebrew ale, made the husbandman's ordinary dinner. To the haymaking field he and his workers took with them a bottle or two of good beer, with an apple pasty, potted butter, churn-milk bread and cheese. The well-to-do ate wheat bread and maschet. The poor ate bread made of rye or barley, and in time of dearth, beans, pease and oats.

The culinary outlay of a modern-day uplander offers a pretty consistent parallel. Sunday calls for meat, pork or beef roast, chicken, squirrel, or fried wild turkey or fish or rabbit. The settler will probably have a meat dinner or two during the course of the week. But the Elizabethan countryman's stand-bys of pease and bacon hold general following among mountain people; pole beans or bunch beans, picked green in season and "shilled" and kilned for winter use; corn-meal breads, with flour breads the occasional luxury; and pork meat, bacon, jowls, sausage, ham-meat, backbone, spareribs, and shoulder joints, boiled, fried, stewed, or baked—those are the hill-man's day-in and day-out dependables. Except in the pasture, country beef is generally scarce. Hogs represent the easiest source of meat. The standing motto regarding pigs is to raise plenty and eat plenty. Mongrel sows are astonishingly prolific. The pigs range at large, get their growth from eating herbs and acorns, and have only to be "topped off" with corn at slaughtering time. Frequently a hill family will slaughter twenty or thirty shoats for a season's meat. We know a patriarch in the vicinity of Hawg Eye, Arkansas, who regularly slaughters twelve pigs for the nurture of each of his twelve offspring—a hundred and forty-four a year. Now, since four of his daughters and three of his sons are married and moved farther on up the creek a way, the benevolent old squire can hardly reckon how he is going to range enough hogs to provide for the coming harvest of grandchildren.

Nicholas Vreton tells of rural England of old:

> August brought the harvest and the end of the husbandman's year, a merry time wherein honest neighbors make good cheer. The sun dries up the standing ponds. Now begin the gleaners to follow the corn cart, and a little bread to a great deal of drink makes the traveller's dinner; the melon and the cucumber are now in request, and the oil and the vinegar give attendance to the sallet herb.
>
> The pipe and the tabor is now lustily set on work, and the lad and the lass will have no lead in their heels. The new wheat makes the gossip cake and the bride cup is carried

above the head of the whole parish. The fermenty pot welcomes home the harvest cart and the garland of flowers crowns the captain of the reapers. Then come the brisking nights of autumn with new revelry. The young folks, smiling, kiss at every turn in the dance; the old folk sit about talking and laughing; the children dance for a garland or play at stoolball for a tansey and a banquest of curds and cream. There is much drinking of old nappy ale and casting of sheep eyes, much exchanging between men and maidens of pairs of gloves or pretty handerkers.

In Elizabethan America, October brings the corn harvest and the end of the tenant's year. But the tilling season is pretty thoroughly over by late July or early August. Flails have almost altogether lost their place as the yield of wheat barley and buckwheat continues generally decreasing. Corn huskings and county fairs offer the uplanders their autumnal daytime diversion.

Then comes the regular run of the season's merrymakings—hay rides, fish, giggings, possum hunts, candy pullings, and quiltings. And if you should chance to be roaming about in the vicinity of a back-hill meetinghouse on a Saturday night, it is altogether probable that you will first hear a vague, far-off pounding noise, and on coming nearer you will gradually come to identify the squeak of a fiddle. Inside you will see gyratory merriment—big and little, young and old, executing square dances, flings, and reels, sedate and otherwise; virtually everyone in the frolic, whole-heartedly, from toe to top hair. And then there are the moonlight picnics and pie suppers, where frolic holds sway and foodstuffs are consumed in splendid profusion.

III

As a people the Southern highlanders are surprisingly free from awkwardness and uncouthness. Theirs is an unpresuming dignity, a quiet courtliness, unspoiled by the conventional forms of etiquette and politeness. Theirs is a genuine, unhurried serenity. They are a folk who can afford old-time, homely ambitions.

The other day we were asking about an upcountry acquaintance:

"Do I know Uncle Bog Sellers? Why, this creek were named fur him. He been right puny this winter, but he's perter now. You see, he'd killed ninety-nine b'ar in his lifetime, and war fixin' fur another hunt when he tuck sick with a misery in the stummick. The doctor told him he'd got to die. But Uncle Bog, he prayed the good Lord to raise him up to kill jest one more b'ar—and, shore 'nough, He done it."

We know another upcountryman in Taney County, Missouri. His name is Elijah Shrum. In his young days Lige was commonly taken as being worthless, merely because he seemed to have an insuperable aversion to following the guiding end of a bull-tongue plough. So Lige took up treasure hunting as a life's occupation. He spent better than forty years at searching for bountiful treasure. He followed down marker trails, prowled through the backmost recesses of innumerable caves, digging and delving, following out generally the path of high romance. Mr. Shrum has not, at this writing, unearthed the manifold treasure, but he still figures to find it—to unearth, one of these days, an iron-bound chest altogether too heavy for one man to hoist. So he continues high-heartedly at the search, and the years have in no way dimmed his ardor.

We know another searcher after stars, a dwarf named Sammy Blankhall. For twenty-odd years he ran a store near Eagle Rock, and did well enough, too, until one night his store burned to the ground, leaving him not only penniless, but heavily in debt. We took a tramp together the other day. He showed me into the one-room log cabin which he calls home. In the far corner of it was a bin filled with bushels and bushels of hulled black walnuts. Sammy explained that he isn't stout enough to swing an axe, nor has he the heft to follow a plough, and so he is paying off his debt to the wholesale grocery house by picking out walnut kernels and selling them to town confectioners. Sammy is sixty-four. By the time he is seventy he reckons he will have paid out the whole of his indebtedness.

The uplander's vital philosophy resembles that of the Elizabethan's in that it is usually more proverbial than speculative. Both were doubtless prone to agree with Launcelot Gobbo that it "was not for nothing that my nose fell a-bleeding on Black Monday last at six o'clock i' the morning." Lore of spells and magic, strange fantasies of moon destinies, ill omens and bringers of wealth and fertility, still hold sway in the Southern back hills. When ordinary means fail, the hillman is at edge more likely to consult a witch doctor than to call a skilled veterinarian when the old cow gives "quare" milk and "won't no butter come."

Here is a somewhat typical story of magic coming from the Cumberland country:

Old Doc was a-walkin' along with his wife. They was both elderly, and she says, "Let's go up to this home and git a light for our pipes." Folks didn't have matches none to speak of in them days; many a time I've walked a mile to a neighbor's with a shovel to borry fire. Well, they found a child that screamin' an' kickin' as bewitched.

So Doc told 'em to git him two new pins that hadn't never been stuck in cloth, an' a bottle. He puts the pins in the bottle and sets it on the mantelshelf. Then he got a shingle and drawed a picture of a woman and told the man to set it up ag'in' a stump and shoot it just at sundown.

About a week atter that, Doc was comin' by ag'in, an' he inquired about the child. Then he axed had anybody died suddintly, and they told him an old woman across the holler had died with a shriek everwhen the man shot the picture with his rifle-gun. And the bottle on the mantelpiece busted in a thousand pieces, and they never did find ary one of them pins.

Just as the Elizabethan countryman took the blood of an elephant mixed with the ashes of a weasel as a cure for leprosy and dead moles as a cure for baldness, believed in love charms and the avenging power of a wax figure pierced through with a needle and put to melt before the fire, so the Southern mountaineer will drive a spike through the heart of a tree to make it fruitful, or devise tonics or healing potions from cobwebs or iron rust.

Some of them will tell you that the moon and stars are eternal lamps set out to show the signs and the seasons, and that the lay of the Milky Way predicts the direction of the prevailing winds for a period of a lunar month. The set of the horns of the moon indicates rain or prevailing dry weather. The set of the oak leaves and the habits of fireflies they take as ready barometers. When cattle munch restlessly at pasture, or barn owls whoop in the daytime, or snake trails show in the dust, they begin making ready to stack the hay or tote in the fodder, for the signs say rain. In the wintertime, if the household Tabitha sits with her tail toward the fire, or if the wind whistles through the orchard land, they figure to fetch in a few extra armloads of firewood—cold weather is coming. Grain crops, beans, and vegetables they plant during the light of the moon, because these are sunlight crops, but they plant potatoes in the dark of the moon, since potatoes are tubers, growing in underground darkness. They take medicine and cures under a waning moon, so that their ills may also wane. Very generally they split rails, chop post timber, rive boards, and slaughter hogs when "Ma Moon" is appropriately set. They "witch" for water with forked twigs of willow or peach wood. There are treasure finders who witch for buried gold and silver by slipping a silver dime or a piece of gold into the fork of their twig. So their folkish ways go. As a race they place inestimably more confidence in elves than in elevators.

IV

When it comes to folk romancers and romantic rascals, the Southern highlands again smack of Merry England. Not too specifically speaking, the moonshiners are the upcountry Robin Hoods. They have their Friar Tucks, their Maid Marians, their Little Johns, their Greenwood revels, and their Sheriffs. They hold Saturday night gambles and gambols in palatial chambers of mountain caves.

The run of moonshiners are, professionally speaking, a cave people, but their homes are the open hills. It is true, too, that some of the young

radicals make their runs in the open brush, trusting their fortunes to isolation, legal degression, ready defense, and a fast get-away. But the old-timers
continue to labor underground and to jubilate in the open wildwood or
wherever the spirit directs.

The ethical stand of a moonshiner is closely akin to that of the forest
poacher in the days of Queen Bess. Moonshining began merely as a household economy. The first settlers lacked means and utensils for canning or
evaporating their surplus of fruit and produce. Their potatoes, parsnips, and
turnips could be "holed up" in the field for winter use; cabbage they put
to kraut, meat was salted and smoked; but for saving their surplus of fruits
and berries they trusted to alcoholic preservation. They made brandies of
their cherries, peaches, blackberries, and pawpaws; they made alcoholic
preserves of their plums and apples, made "sweet rum" from their sorghum
"seconds," and put their surplus of corn, rye, and barley to the making of
paralyzing stimulants.

The world grew up about them, leaving them still in a country of young
frontiers. Roads were few and far-scattered. They are yet. Back-hill travel
routes usually follow the stream beds, and this involves sundry fordings and
blockades. Commodities bulky as grain, or perishable as fruit or eggs or
butter, were next to impossible to market. And a hillman needs a little cash
money now and then, even as you and I. A gallon of corn in the keg may
fetch more cash than an acre of corn in the ear. Just as the poachers of olden
England slew the Queen's deer and made ready to take the consequences,
so the "blockaders" of Elizabethan America crush their corn, set their
"beers," make their runs, keg their wares, swig their surplus, and "let go
roll—life, and a dollar for the fiddler's toll."

Moonshiners have no time for mincing or bickering about professional
casualties. Should one be killed or lamed by an enforcement officer—well,
that is all in the day's labor. And if it appears expedient to plug a "law" in
the back where the suspenders cross, or to shove one over a high wild bluff
with only moonlight, mountain air, and limestone ledges below, then that,
too, is part of the game of swap. But the chances are that the moonshiner
will pay his debts, give milk and meal to the widow lady, prove helpful at
births and buryings, and, once convinced of your harmlessness, take you
into his home with a hospitality which is nothing short of princely.

So moonshining has come to be a hardy trade. Liquor is hard to make
by the hill-country recipe. Corn must be shucked and shelled and cracked
in tub mills or with hickory mauls or pestles. The distilling must be done
in a creek bed or beside an underground stream, for running water offers
the only means of refrigeration. If vaporization is too slow or too fast, then
all is not well with the product. To make a first run requires from thirty-six

214 Charles Morrow Wilson

to forty-eight hours of firing, which means that the moonshiner must be on his toes, alert and laboring, virtually every minute of that time. And there are the hazards and hardships and luckless slips.

While the moonshiner draws out his thread of romance, he cannot forget that its spool is tethered to handcuffs, jail houses, penitentiaries, and buryin' grounds. His candle is lit at both ends, and it burns with a clear blue flame.

III

Change Comes to the Appalachian Mountaineer

12

Change Comes to the Appalachian Mountaineer

Mary French Caldwell

Most of the writers dealing with the "problem" of Appalachia have been concerned with how to bring the mountaineer into the "civilized world." Most of the earlier commentators saw the mountaineer's culture as homogeneous and arrested in its development but, beginning in the century's second decade, increasing numbers of observers saw the situation in a different light. Appalachian residents were still thought to have a uniform culture that was anachronistic in many respects but one that was definitely changing. In 1916 B. H. Shockle wrote about "Changing Conditions in the Kentucky Mountains," complaining that change was not always for the better. He lamented that certain forces, if left unchecked, would bring about the "disappearance of this race of true Americans as a unit." Two years later, in 1918, Margaret T. McGuire asserted that much of what Shockle feared had already come to pass when, in a *Ladies Home Journal* article, she discussed "The Passing of the Backwoods: They Vanished Overnight, Never to Return."

Mary French Caldwell (1896–?) was a native of Catlettsburg, Tennessee who spent most of her professional career working for the Tennessee Department of Education. Earlier she spent a brief period as a newspaper reporter, working for *The Knoxville Journal* during World War I. Her national reputation is based on numerous publications dealing with Southern educational, political, social and economic subjects, and Tennessee history. As a young woman she was a strong advocate of women's suffrage and took great pride in being the youngest female delegate to the first Tennessee Democratic convention in which women participated.

Most writers lacked McGuire's confidence that the mountaineer's traditional culture was gone but there was no doubt that it was being transformed. Industrialization, the groundwork for which was laid in the last decades of the nineteenth century, began in earnest in the early twentieth century and necessitated change. Many observers viewed industrialism as a mixed blessing, often expressing their feelings in terms similar to those found in "Change Comes to the Appalachian Mountaineer." Caldwell's

Reprinted from *Current History* 31 (February 1930): 961–67.

survey of conditions in the 1920s leans toward ethnocentrism, as indicated by her obvious distaste for faith healers, whom she inaccurately refers to as a religious sect, and Holy Rollers (a derogatory name for fundamentalist religious groups whose meetings are characterized by extreme emotionalism and physical agitation). There are also some inaccuracies in her statements regarding folklore. For example, "Possum Up a Gum Tree" and "Sourwood Mountain" are not technically ballads for they don't tell a narrative story. Nevertheless, there is no reason to doubt the authenticity of the material she reports for she evidently knew the mountaineer at firsthand. It is also evident that Caldwell shared the "them" and "us" attitude towards mountain people that numerous other writers adopted.

*   *   *

A Southern mountain boy, bearing an opossum as a birthday gift to the President of the United States, focused the attention of the nation on the picturesque subject of the "mountain white." The little community on the Rapidan, in Virginia, from which this boy hailed, a few weeks later was the scene of an informal parley between two Anglo-American chiefs, with the world news organizations turning their spotlights upon it. News articles on the MacDonald visit contained vivid descriptions of the natural beauty of this region and of a people who still use quaint words reminiscent of the Elizabethan era.

Earlier in the season President Hoover and the young mountain boy discussed schools, opossums, elections and things in general with the same grave informality which characterized the conversation with Great Britain's Prime Minister. Who can foretell which parley has greater potentialities for the good of our country, if President Hoover, the government and the people of the United States should give them equal attention. Already, not satisfied with heading a committee to raise $1,250 to build a schoolhouse for that little community, President Hoover has set in motion the machinery of government to end illiteracy not only in the Southern mountains but throughout the country. On Nov. 16 Secretary of the Interior Wilbur announced with the President's official sanction the appointment of the Advisory Committee on National Illiteracy, consisting of nineteen men and three women, comprising educators, legislators, publicists and editors from all parts of the country. Since this undertaking will embrace all elements in our population, it holds out wonderful possibilities. Suppose, for instance, that with literacy foreign-born illiterates should be taught some of the loyalty and patriotism of the so-called "mountain whites." Might not the undeveloped man and woman power of the nation thus be made of use to promote national and international welfare in a manner no less beneficial than the results accruing from new pacts of peace between the nations?

The education of the Anglo-Saxon population of the South is a matter very close to the heart of the nation. These people have in their veins the blood of the builders of the nation, in their minds the native intelligence of the Anglo-Saxon, and in their hearts a deep loyalty to their country and an abiding faith in God. If they are sometimes illiterate, narrow-minded, provincial and a trifle "hide-bound," at least they are not Communists or atheists, and the ease with which their minds may be developed is amazing.

But, as the appointment of the Advisory Committee on National Illiteracy indicates, to give the "mountain whites" full opportunity for development, private educational enterprise is inadequate for the purpose. The ideal of popular education presupposes that it is a government's duty to educate its citizens, and since this is true, the child in the isolated mountain community has as much right to schooling provided by the State as the child in the city and the rich farming sections. Numbers of mountain schools have been established by women's federated clubs, patriotic organizations, church societies and individuals. Many of them have been successful, but if the effort which has been expended in establishing and maintaining them had been applied to one great, concerted effort to develop a public school system adequate to meet the needs of the people, a large part of the problem would already have been solved.

Causes of Illiteracy

Illiteracy is not always caused by lack of schoolhouses. In fact the boy on the Rapidan lives in a county which has three high schools, seventeen elementary schools for white children and twelve elementary schools for negroes. Where are the young men whose thirst for learning was so great that they went penniless to the nearest schools to "work their way"? Where are the boys who were willing to walk twenty miles to borrow books? Where are the Lincolns who studied by the light of pine torches and used charcoal for pencils? Schooling is not convenient for every family in the nation, but it should not be impossible for ambitious parents to find some way to have their children taught to read and write. Schoolhouses must then be provided and teachers hired for certain classes of people, and truant officers must be sent to compel parents, in the name of the law, to send their children to school. Only by the enforcement of rigid compulsory attendance laws, coupled with financial aid for the poorest families, can illiteracy be eliminated.

The Southern mountain sections do not have adequate school facilities, but a great stride is being made in the right direction. A few years ago there were no passable roads in the mountains, and even today there are many isolated communities. The consolidated school, with the school bus on the highways, is doing much to improve conditions, and the smaller schools, where consolidation is not practicable, are being made more efficient. Teachers' salaries are being raised; standards are higher and terms are growing longer.

The mountainous sections are hard to reach and still harder to handle after they are reached because of their sparse population and the rugged nature of the country. Reaching these communities is, however, a part of the work of the public school system, and most Southern States are conducting programs which are meeting with great success. Tennessee's new plan provides for a State fund to supplement county funds for educational work, and under it the richer counties have cheerfully submitted to being taxed to provide better school facilities for counties which cannot finance good schools. This plan was accompanied by a law making Tennessee's minimum school term eight months. North Carolina, with a splendid program to combat illiteracy, in addition to her improved schools, is doing important work, and other Southern States have equally ambitious plans in operation. Thus are times changing in the mountains; in fact, change is inevitable, for the processes which will replace the primitive existence common to many mountain communities begin as soon as passable roads establish communication with the outside world. The mountaineer is quick to meet new conditions. When he has a chance to earn money, his family soon adopts the current style, and he acquires a Ford, a radio and a high school education for his children as soon as he is able.

"Poor mountain whites" is the term applied to the dwellers in the Appalachians, and most writers select the illiterate dwellers of one-room, tumbledown log shanties for their portrayals of the mountaineer. Too often they give the impression that only people of this class live in the mountains and adjacent districts, and that entire States have suffered the arrested material development which isolation and a rugged country have forced upon the mountaineer. The late Dr. George R. Stuart, a famous evangelist and lecturer of the Southern Methodist Church, used to tell an amusing story of one of his visits to Boston to deliver a lecture. At the close of his speech Dr. Stuart was greeted effusively by a lady who had been a member of his audience. "Oh, Dr. Stuart," she pleaded, "do tell us about your poor mountain whites." Replied Dr. Stuart, in his courteous, dignified manner, "Madam, I am one of them." Dr. Stuart was one of the finest examples of the type of man the Anglo-Saxon population of the Southern Appalachians can produce. He was descended from a long line of mountain people, and became one of the America's leading pulpit orators.

Dr. Stuart's statement applies not only to men and women who have sprung from mountain families but also to a large portion of the remainder of the population of Tennessee and neighboring States. Even today only a negligible part of the population is foreign-born, or even of foreign extraction. The people who dwell in the fertile valleys and in the cities are of the same stock as the mountain families, but they have had the advantage of broader cultural and material development. Family names are often identical, and, barring the slight difference made by urban polish, types are surprisingly similar. The Scotch-Irish type which was predominant in Andrew Jackson's day has by no means passed away; indeed, it has been touched very little by the great stream of immigration which has flooded other parts of the country and has almost obliterated the racial characteristics of the founders of the nation. With the Scotch-Irish there is mixed a small percentage of descendants from the early Pennsylvania "Dutch" and French immigrants, with, perhaps, a sprinkling of other nationalities. The racial type has changed very little, however, and these people from both the highlands and the lowlands are still vigorous and are taking an important part in the affairs of the nation.

Since the appointment of Dr. P. P. Claxton as Commissioner of Education for the United States by President Taft in 1911, a Tennessean has occupied this position. When President Harding selected a successor for Dr. Claxton he chose Dr. J. J. Tigert, another Tennessean. Both were educated in Tennessee. William Gibbs McAdoo, Secretary of the Treasury under Woodrow Wilson, Director of Railroads during the war period of government control, and builder of the Hudson Tunnels, was born while his family was with Confederate refugees in Georgia, but he is by inheritance and training a Tennessean. In the legal profession Tennessee has such representatives as Justice Sanford, born in the Tennessee mountain region; Justice McReynolds of the United States Supreme Court, and Martin W. Littleton, a leader of the New York bar. One of the cotton kings of America was Samuel M. Inman, born in the Tennessee mountains. Norman H. Davis, distinguished in international affairs, and Frank L. Polk, Acting Secretary of State in 1918, are Tennesseans. Richard T. Wilson, multi-millionaire, whose descendants married into the Vanderbilt family, and Admiral Farragut were Tennesseans. The present commandant at West Point was born in Tennessee. Among the Tennesseans who have won national prominence in art is George de Forest Brush, who was born at Shelbyville. In sculpture Belle Kinney is known for her figures on the pediments of Nashville's replica of the Parthenon; and Nancy Cox-McCormack has received special recognition for the bust of Mussolini which she recently completed. Editors and publishers produced by Tennessee include such men as Adolph S. Ochs, publisher of *The New York Times;* Henry Watterson, and Dixon L. Merritt, editor of the *Outlook.* Among the Tennessee writers in the public eye at present are: Bruce Barton, Grantland Rice, Opie Read, Roark Bradford, E. B. Stribling, Maristan Chapman, and others. The Clemens family, to which Mark Twain belonged, lived in the Tennessee mountains until shortly before the birth of the great humorist, and several scenes of *The Gilded Age* are laid in that district. The American Medical Association has of recent years had two presidents from Tennessee, the late Dr. John A. Witherspoon and Dr. W. D. Haggard. John E. Edgerton of Tennessee was president of the National Manufacturers' Association.

Isolated Communities

If a predominantly Anglo-Saxon population can produce such leaders, the people of remote mountain districts, who are of the same stock, may be depended upon to develop a superior type of citizen when they are reached by modern progress. Until the past decade their isolation has been practically unbroken. Their customs and living conditions have changed very little, and their speech is still sprinkled with quaint, obsolete words used in England three centuries ago. This old English, combined with words of their own coining and current American terms, has formed a dialect which is peculiarly their own. The use of "hit" for "it" and the dropping of the final *g* are two of the most noticeable characteristics of the mountaineers' speech. "Holp" is often used for the past tense of "help" and "seed" for past of "see." "You-all" is frequently used, and is always plural. "You-uns," which is similar in meaning to "you-all," is sometimes used, but I have never heard the "we-uns" which some writers put into the mouths of their mountain characters.

Old customs and superstitions still persist, the old English ballads are still sung; and life in some of the cabins is quite as primitive as it was when the first pioneers came over the mountains, breaking the way to the West. Food is usually cooked on a wood stove, although a few cabins still have only a fireplace; wood is often hauled on a kind of sled with crude runners of hard wood; and some mountain families are quite as averse to bathing as Englishmen were in Queen Elizabeth's day. Many of the superstitions which persist until the present day are those which have to do with planting; for instance, some seeds must be planted on the "dark" of the moon and some on the "light." Good Friday is considered a lucky day for certain kinds of planting. Ghosts and witches exist only in tales handed down from other days, but hundreds of superstitions still cling to various affairs of life. Early infancy is surrounded by its peculiar superstitions, and woe to a mother who allows her baby to look in a mirror before it is a year old—it will surely die before the year ends. Too often ignorance of infant care makes this prophecy come true.

The ballads are numerous and varied in nature. Many of them date back to the England of three centuries and more ago. Some of them, such as *Possum Up de Gum Tree* and *Sourwood Mountain,* are humorous. Others are filled with bloodthirsty tales of jealousy, murder, trials and hangings; examples of this type are *The Twa Sisters, The Twa Brothers* and *The Cruel Mother*. The most beautiful are the love songs with their plaintive melodies and invariably sad stories. *Lord Lovel* is an interesting example of the love song. Its hero is a lord who returns from his travels to find that his sweetheart has died. It concludes with these lines:

> Go dig my grave, Lord Lovel he said,
> Go dig my grave, says he,
> For I have no longer in this world to stay,
> For the loss of my Lady Nancy.

No single fact can explain the existence of the people in these mountain communities, although a number of theories have been developed concerning their origin. Some historians say that they are the descendants of those who could not keep up with the westward-moving stream of pioneers. Others believe that they were fugitives from justice and deserters from the armies of both the Revolutionary and Civil War periods. A few writers advance the theory that they are descended from English peasant stock, while the planters and city builders were descended from the Cavaliers, but it took sturdier material than the Old World aristocracy to build all the country west of the mountains. William Blount, Territorial Governor of Tennessee, was one of the few leaders of Cavalier ancestry; John Sevier was French Huguenot; Andrew Jackson, James K. Polk and Andrew Johnson were Scotch-Irish and other leaders were of this same general strain.

The urge for settlement of the West, which began when the first pioneers pushed over the mountains into Tennessee and Kentucky, continued steadily until the United States, under a Tennessee President, James K. Polk, acquired Texas, California and Oregon, which then included territory out of which other Western States have been carved. Tennesseans were leaders during the Mexican War and in the settlement of Texas. Sam Houston, a former Governor of Tennessee, was Governor of the Texas Republic. David Crockett was another picturesque figure of this period. Thomas Hart Benton, who figured prominently in national affairs as United States Senator, grew to manhood in Tennessee.

Regardless of his past history and his present condition, the mountaineer is going to be an important factor in the growth of the Southern Appalachian section. Both industrial and agricultural development are beckoning him and the rugged mountain country is being gradually opened up. He represents a reserve of man-power quite as important as the potential electric power in the streams which rush down his mountainsides. It may be rather a difficult task to harness this manpower, and it is possible that outside capital will undertake to exceed its rights in this respect, as well as in connection with electric power, but if the South is truly awake it will guard its human beings as jealously as it guards its streams.

Rising Tide of Industrialism

The rising tide of industrialism in the South, particularly in the region of the mountains where unlimited electric power is available, is bringing many changes. Perhaps in two or three more decades the mountain type, as it is now known, will have entirely disappeared, for intermarriage with outsiders and changes which must be made to meet the progress which is being thrust upon them, will prevent the mountain people from escaping certain alterations in their mode of life. The new textile mills, the artificial silk plants and the other industries which have come South seeking cheap, intelligent labor, have encountered the growing pains of labor troubles. But they have been of no more serious nature than strikes in other parts of the country.

The foreign capitalist will learn in dealing with this type of labor that he will have intelligent workers who may be had, for a while at least, at a rate materially lower than is common in other parts of the country. But he will find, also, that these people, who are quick to learn their work in the factories, will not take long to discover their lower wages. The mountaineer has a very definite sense of honor in regard to personal property, and he can not easily be converted into a Communist. His mountain cabin never knew the need of a lock, but let the person beware who takes something from him. He has no foolish ideas about confiscating the mill he works in, but if the labor agitators succeed in making him believe that he has just cause for grievance against his employer, trouble will surely develop.

Economic Conditions

The annual income of many families in the mountains is so small in dollars and cents that it would mean abject poverty and even starvation in the city. For this reason the wages first offered to the mountaineer in the mills seem like a fortune. It does not take him long, however, to learn that city wages must meet city prices, and very often he finds that he has forsaken his easygoing life in the open for long hours of labor which improve his condition very little, if any. And so it is doubtful if, under the most satisfactory conditions, the greatest good will result from converting these people into industrial workers. Naturally, many of them will be attracted to the towns, but a satisfactory rural development should be sufficient to keep the bulk of the population on the small farms, to help produce food for the growing army of workers.

The new agricultural industries—creameries, cheese plants, canneries and poultry and fruit shipping concerns which deal directly with the farmer, seem to offer far greater opportunities for normal development to the mountain people, as well as to farmers in all parts of the South. During the past decade fruit growing in Southern mountain sections has gone forward by leaps and bounds. Canneries are offering markets for both fruits and vegetables; creameries and cheese plants are encouraging the development of small dairy herds; and poultry raising has become a real business instead of merely furnishing "egg money" for the farm wife. Weaving, basketry and other handicrafts are being developed in the homes, and the tourists who visit national parks and mountain resorts, as well as gift shops, furnish a market for these wares. On every side marketing and farm demonstration work are important phases of community development. The mountain farmer is being taught to make the most of his steep acres through crops particularly suited to his soil. Grazing land and water are plentiful in the mountains; the choicest of peaches, apples and grapes may be grown on incredibly steep hillsides; chickens can always be raised and many profitable garden and field crops can be produced, even though the area which it is possible to cultivate is not large. It is of necessity the land of the small farmer, but it need not be a land of want. Good roads are the only thing which make production above the amount required for family use profitable. Even today many mountain communities cannot reach market with their produce, but roads are being thrown out like magic ribbons and the isolated communities are gradually tied to the rest of the world.

Conditions in the mountains today are still far from ideal. The death rate is unnecessarily high; illiteracy is far too common, and religious sects, like the Holy Rollers and faith healers, prey upon ignorant, superstitious minds. There is a crying need for physicians, nurses, teachers and sane, level-headed ministers of the gospel. But contact with the mountains is being established, and however we may look at it, the mountaineer is standing face to face with the modern world. What he will do with it and what it will do with him are interesting subjects for speculation, but the States which seize this opportunity and offer to him the greatest and best chances for development will be richly repaid.

13

The Mountain Handicrafts:
Their Importance to the Country
and to the People in the Mountain Homes

Allen Eaton

Much of the discussion about Appalachian improvement suggested the need for help from outside. It could hardly be otherwise since those making the hint regarded the mountaineer as being outside the pale of civilization; to be brought into the fold required assistance from persons already on the inside. Even so, most proposals implied that outside intervention should be as limited as possible. One of the more popular schemes to help mountaineers and at the same time preserve the integrity of their culture was through creating interest in crafts. This revival began in the mid-1890s and gained momentum in the twentieth century eventually leading to the creation of craft guilds. In 1923 during a fourteen-month tour of Scandinavian countries, Olive Dame Campbell visited a cooperative crafts shop. This experience started her thinking about the possibility of establishing a similar organization in Appalachia. It was 1929 before the guild was formally established at a meeting in Asheville, North Carolina. This group, the Southern Highland Handicraft Guild, is still in existence today.

The paper reprinted here is an address given by Allen Eaton (1878–1962) at the Guild's initial meeting. Eaton is primarily remembered today for two books on crafts. His *Handicrafts of the Southern Highlands* (1937) is still the only comprehensive volume of Appalachian crafts; *Handicrafts of New England* (1940) is its northern counterpart. For some time prior to 1929 Eaton had worked closely with Mrs. Campbell and others interested in establishing the Guild. His 1929 speech gives the thrust of Eaton's emphasis. Despite the implication that traditional crafts were his concern he did not restrict his thinking in that way—any handicraft, be it traditional or not, was fair game. The same emphasis is seen in the subsequent development of the Guild which has generally forsaken the folk for the folksy, then forsaken the folksy for the "finer arts." Another aspect of crafts stressed by Eaton, given greater emphasis in his book, is the

---

Reprinted from *Mountain Life and Work* 6 (July 1930): 22–30.

value of crafts for therapeutic and recreational purposes. Thus, it may accurately be said of Eaton that his major concern is with the "rewards" rather than the traditions of crafts.

* * *

This afternoon we are to complete the work begun a little over a year ago, bringing into closer association the several handicraft centers of the Southern Mountains. I say "we," for I like to think of this as an organization broad enough to include in its membership all those who are interested one way or another in conserving and continuing the handicrafts; and you have in your plans made a place for persons like me by creating a type of membership to be known as "Friends of the Guild." I hope it will not be long until there will be scores, yes, hundreds of people throughout the country who are enrolled as "Friends," for it is my conviction that there is hardly a limit to the number of people in our country who will become interested in the things for which this organization stands, and will by their subscriptions and in other ways help to carry on its work.

I am going to try to tell you some of the reasons why I think the handicrafts of the mountains are of great importance to all of us wherever we happen to be. But before getting to this I have promised to say something about the steps that have already been taken toward the organization which is to be completed today; and I am glad to do this because it has been my privilege to sit in on the three meetings preceding this one, in which plans for the handicraft guild have been considered. I will be glad to sketch briefly what has thus far been done.

The first meeting was held at Penland, North Carolina, on December 27 and 28, 1928, in the Weavers Cabin on the top of Conley Ridge, near the Appalachian School. Here a few people came together to ask themselves if it would be possible, through some kind of cooperative association, to advance the general cause of the handicrafts in the mountains, without in any way interfering with the individual work that had been or might be done. It was clear that no one wanted to interfere with any one else, but it was also clear that each one felt that in union there should be strength and that there were a number of ways in which a broad cooperative organization might be helpful. Here at Penland, for the first time as far as I know, a list of handicraft centers was prepared, showing about forty places in different parts of the mountains where some work in the handicrafts was being done. Eight of these centers were represented in the conference. The conclusion reached at Penland was unanimous for recommending to the next meeting of the Conference of Southern Mountain Workers, which was to be in Knoxville, April 2–5, 1929, that steps be taken to bring these handicraft workers into some kind of cooperating organization.

At the Knoxville conference in April we took up the discussion where it had been left at Penland, and out of it emerged a unanimous recommendation by the Conference that Miss Helen Dingman, Executive Secretary, be authorized to take the necessary steps toward completing the organization. Pursuant to these instructions another meeting was called for December 28, 1929, at the The Spinning Wheel, Beaver Lake, North Carolina, where the form the organization should take was quite fully discussed and twenty-two handicraft producing centers were agreed upon as eligible for charter membership. Several committees were appointed, including one on constitution and bylaws, and further authority was given to proceed with the organization, as it is proposed to do this afternoon.

At the meeting held at The Spinning Wheel on December 28th, it was decided to bring together at this conference some examples of the handicrafts from the centers which had been suggested for membership, and this is the exhibit which some of you have seen and about which you will hear more later this afternoon.

Let me say in passing that I think in your efforts to form a handicraft association you have set one pattern for the Guild that ought to be followed in the future, that of having at least two meetings each year: one at the conference and the other at one of the producing centers. If my contacts with the handicraft workers should never be extended beyond those made at Penland and Beaver Lake, I still would have such pleasant and definite impressions of the work and the people that it would always seem to me a privilege to do anything I could to encourage this useful and beautiful work.

We could not possibly have had, it seems to me, a more appropriate place for our first meeting than that of the Weavers Cabin, on the high ridge above Penland. This cabin build by Miss Lucy Morgan and her weavers you shall hear more about this afternoon, but it will long remain for me one of memory's most beautiful pictures, as with the snowflakes falling outside and the log fire blazing within, a small group of us gathered around the hearth that winter afternoon to talk over the possibilities which are today about to be realized.

And equally appropriate was the place of our last meeting, The Spinning Wheel, at Beaver Lake, in the old log cabin which Miss Clementine Douglas found somewhere in the neighborhood and which she moved and made over, with no loss of character, but a positive gain in comfort and convenience, into a workshop and exhibition room of rare charm. Here we had a still larger group of friends, but there was a good strong mountain chair for every one who joined our circle, and the great old wooden loom in the corner by the fireplace was piled high with coats and hats from many places.

This log cabin is an excellent example of mountain architecture, and only a few steps away is the weaving room with its big family of looms.

Hanging on the walls were masses of beautifully colored yarns, and these, with weavings on the looms in all stages of progress, made a glowing picture of mountain handicrafts that I shall long remember. These visits to Penland and Beaver Lake, with a few other glimpses of workers, both leaders and craftsmen, have impressed me deeply with the vital and important place of the handicrafts in the life of this mountain region.

The handicrafts are a measurable part of the culture of the mountains, and they should be the concern of all people everywhere who believe, as I do, that no invention of any time can bring to a man, woman, or child a satisfaction which equals that of creating with his own hand something which he thinks is useful and beautiful. It is because I think that the preservation of the handicrafts and their encouragement to higher levels should interest all Americans, whether in or out of the mountains, that when Miss Dingman asked me what I would suggest as a subject for this afternoon's discussion, I gave her the rather inclusive one that is printed on the program, "The Mountain Handicrafts: Their Importance to the Country and to the People in the Mountain Homes."

One of the first reasons why the handicrafts of the mountains should interest the people of our country is that their practice is making it possible for many to live in the mountains who would otherwise have to move out. Every influence which makes possible the continuation of life in the mountains of the Southland contributes just so much to the preservation of American rural life. I know there are those who think that it would be better for the mountaineer if he moved out of the mountain home into the city or into some industrial center where, as a machine tender or as some other contributor to mass production, he might become a regular wage earner. Indeed there are those quite bent on forcing the change. There is not time for a discussion on this point, but may I express the conviction that one of the privileges which ought to be preserved to Americans for a little longer is that of deciding for themselves where they shall live. As to the mountaineer, before we decide to move him from the mountains to the town, yes, even before we press upon him the economic standard of life which seems essential to us, let us make an honest, unprejudiced study of his life and his culture. It is just possible that we should find values which we would not have him exchange for our program of averages even if he were willing to do so. I am glad that most of us who work with mountain people are not bent on moving them out of the mountains, or on keeping them in, but rather on helping them to make life fuller and better wherever they may be.

Students of American life are alarmed at the rate at which for several years our people have been moving from the country to the city. We seem, in point of population, to be changing from a rural to an urban nation.

Whatever advantages may be in the new conditions—and there are un-doubtedly some—the most thoughtful students are seriously asking what this change will mean to our future. And they are asking the question because they know that what we are as a nation has been largely an out-growth of our rural life. Not only has our population until recent years been predominantly rural, but rural life has contributed largely to leadership in all fields of endeavor. The growth and strength of our cities of today has been determined more by the forces from without than by the forces from within. And this feeding from without has been from rural communities, mainly native Americans, but partly through immigrants, many of them from the rural districts of Europe. Although about two-thirds of all our people are now living in cities, it is probably not too much to say that more than half of the acknowledged leaders in our nation have come from the country districts.

I am not trying to make a case against city life. The only point I am trying to make is that what we are and what we have achieved as a nation can be traced largely to rural life and rural influences, and that the majority of men and women who have led us and who are doing so now have spent their formative years in a rural environment, either in the country or in small towns. These are the reasons why students are watching this great population shift with concern. Whatever contributes to the stability of our rural life, as the handicrafts in the mountains certainly do, is a matter in which the whole country should be interested.

The second reason why the handicrafts of the Southern Mountains should interest our people throughout the country is that they make an important contribution to rural culture. One purpose of the exhibition across the hall is to furnish evidence to the conference of its conviction that there is a distinct mountain culture of which the handicrafts are an important part. But we should think of this mountain culture as belonging not alone to the region with which we are especially concerned, but as being a part of the rural heritage of America.

In speaking a moment ago of the handicraft exhibition as furnishing evidence of a mountain culture, I was thinking entirely of the objects which have been sent in from the different producing centers throughout the highlands. However, I would like to refer briefly to another feature of the exhibition of which many of you have expressed appreciation, that is the portraits of mountain people which have been loaned to us by one of America's foremost photographers, Doris Ulmann of New York City; and the interpretations of the mountain cabins by the gifted photographer, Charles A. Ferrill, now of Greensboro, North Carolina. It is because these artists see in the mountain people and their modest habitations something very worthy that they bring us these fine interpretations; it is because they share our view that there are unique qualities of culture in this mountain country that they have gone far from the beaten path to record them.

And finally the handicrafts are important to the whole country because they furnish objects of use and beauty for the homes of countless people who may never get within this mountain region at all.

I believe that an increasing number of home-makers are following the excellent advice of the great English craftsman, William Morris, who said: "Have nothing in your home which you do not know to be useful or believe to be beautiful." The endeavor to follow such a good rule is sure to lead to discrimination in the furnishing of any home. In case of American homes it is quite certain to lead to a knowledge of and interest in the handicrafts of these mountains, for there is no rural section of our country where so many useful and beautiful things for home use and decoration are made by hand at such reasonable prices as in this mountain region. And so I think we who live far from the mountains will look increasingly to you to help us make our homes more attractive, more interesting, and more expressive of the culture of our native land.

Let us now turn to the importance of the handicrafts to the people in the mountain homes, for after all it is here that we shall find their greatest justification.

The first and most obvious measure of the value of the handicrafts is their economic return, the money which they bring to those who practice them. Just because this measurement is so obvious I shall dwell on it for only a moment here and use the remainder of my time in discussing other values not so well understood or so widely acknowledged, but of very great importance. If we were compelled to rest our case alone on the economic return from the handicrafts it would be possible to fully justify it. Information by no means complete, which a few of those in charge of this work have given me, indicate a return to the workers in the mountain homes far in excess of what my guess would have been. The figures alone would challenge the consideration of any good business man, and would far exceed any estimates that I have ever heard before. But if we knew the exact figures, impressive as they may be, they would not alone suggest the full meaning of the earnings to the workers, for the dollar that comes into the mountain home is a dollar of unusual value. It does more than the average dollar in the city. There could be no better way to make a complete case for our cause than to describe how the earnings from the handicrafts are spent. However, many in this audience are familiar with these facts, and for those who are not, I am glad to commend an article in the January, 1928, issue of *Mountain Life and Work* entitled "THE SPINNING WHEEL," written by Miss Helen Dingman. If you would gather still more information on this vital point you will be able to get it first hand from any of the several handicraft leaders who are with us here today. We shall therefore leave this very basic consideration of what the earnings from the handicrafts have meant to home life in the mountains and to the many boys and girls who have been able to gain an education through them, and we shall turn to some of the other reasons why they are so important.

The values of which I wish now to speak cannot be measured in terms of money. They are not material values, but rather spiritual in the broad sense of that word; that is they contribute to the life, to the growth, and to the development of the individual, and to the community. And these values are perceivable only to those who know the workers and their work. Therefore I thought you would enjoy getting some of this information first hand, and I have asked a few members of our Handicraft Guild to speak directly to you of some of the things which I have in mind. Five friends have agreed to help me out with this, the most important part of my talk. They will speak on the worth of the handicrafts as follows: Their Cultural Value; Their Social Value; Their Traditional Value; Their Therapeutic Value; and Their Educational Value.

In the circle of friends who gathered at The Spinning Wheel last December to consider the formation of the Handicraft Guild was one to whom we often turned for answers to questions growing out of our discussion. As fresh in her quiet enthusiasm as the youngest in the group, Miss Frances Goodrich was in point of experience the oldest advocate of the handicrafts for the mountain people. In fact she was the pioneer not only to see the need of the handicrafts but to start them, and what is still more inspiring, she has continued to encourage them to this present moment.

Miss Goodrich has seen more clearly than many of us, beyond the economic value of this work into its cultural side. I have, therefore, asked her to tell us a little of her pioneer work and of the contributions of the handicrafts to mountain culture. There is no need to introduce Miss Goodrich to this Conference, but in presenting her I have thought I might bring you what a few days ago was indeed good news to me, the fact that Miss Goodrich has written a book on her experiences in these mountains and it is to be published by the discriminating Yale Press. When I read of this I at once wrote for a copy of the book, but instead I received a letter explaining that it would not be published until autumn. For my information they included in the letter a short statement which Miss Goodrich has made, and which I would like to read to you both as a delightful announcement of this promised book and also as a fitting foreword in presenting her to you: "It was in the Fall of 1890 that I went into the Southern Mountains to help in a country school and to be as far as I might a good neighbor. Going to teach, I remained to learn. Out of what was taught me, of crafts, of country ways and of life has come this book, HOMESPUN."

> Miss Goodrich told how forty years ago she had come as a teacher into the mountain country near Asheville, North Carolina. Her first interest was in the children. Rural schools were not then well developed but were bringing the children knowledge and enlightenment. The men got out occasionally and saw something of life. The women did not. They were shut-ins and it was for them especially that something must be done.
>
> First they needed a way to earn. There was a beautiful craft which was dying out. Miss Goodrich saw a coverlet made by a mountain woman. That was the start. (They have that very coverlet today.) If this weaving could be developed it would bring in money and preserve the craft. They set to work, a few of them, and began to make coverlets. Progress was slow at first, but the great return came as these mountain women found a new interest in life, became producers recognized in the community and at the country store, were able to purchase family necessities which had always been out of their reach, and came to feel that they were no longer isolated and shut in but that they were themselves a part of the workers of the world. They felt deeply the satisfaction of making something beautiful that was recognized as worth while by their own people and by the people in far off places. They would not claim it outwardly, but they were inwardly conscious that in making these coverlets and other beautiful things they were contributing something, be it ever so little, to the culture of the mountains.
>
> Out of the need for encouraging this work and finding an outlet for the weaving and other crafts, the Allanstand Industries grew and developed. The folks up on Laurel say that through these mountain industries the name of Allanstand has become known throughout the United States.

One of the great immeasurable values of the mountain handicrafts is their social value, the way in which they bring the workers together and often draw in other members of the neighborhood. If we had no other record of the social value of the handicrafts than that in Penland it would be quite sufficient to prove our case completely. I have asked Miss Lucy Morgan, of Penland, to tell whatever comes to her mind about the social doings of her weavers, but I would like before presenting her to give you a little of the background there as I had an opportunity to see it in connection with that first meeting of those interested in forming the Southern Mountain Handicraft Guild.

Within a radius of thirty miles of Penland in the mountain homes are about forty looms, generally one in a cabin, but sometimes two. As we sat in the Weavers Cabin the morning after our conference, a young mountain girl came in to get some weaving supplies. The warm morning sun had melted the snow of the night before, and as she stood by the open fireplace drying out her clothes and visiting with Miss Morgan, I finally made out that she was the girl whose excellent weaving, along with that done by her mother, I had seen earlier in the day. And Miss Morgan had, through the window of the cabin, pointed out to me the spot seven and a half miles away behind the Blue Mountain where they lived. This girl explained that last week her father had lost one of his span of mules and she was afraid of an accident to the other if she rode him across the mountain; so she had walked. She had not been sure that she could get the supplies needed, but—there are no telephones in this region—she thought she would come over to see, especially as there was some weaving she was just longing to get to. Before noon she had started back with about 40 pounds of yarn and warp, which, except for the first half mile, when I was going her way, she toted over the mountain alone.

Weaving has meant something to this family, especially to the mother who can now stay at home and care for the children. With her loom by the fireplace in their mountain cabin she can make even a little more than she used to make before weavin' came into her life. She used to go out into the woods and do a man's work, felling trees, shaping them into crossties, loading them on the wagon, and hauling them out to the railroad miles away.

I refer to the girl and her mother not only because they are so deft and dependable in their weaving, but because they also helped in the building of the Weavers Cabin, which in addition to being a workshop, is a social center for the weavers and their friends. Miss Lucy Morgan is going to tell us how the handicrafts develop sociability among the mountain folks at Penland.

Miss Morgan told of how a few years ago no one was weaving anymore in the region of Penland and in the hope of reviving an old art she went to Berea, learned weaving, and brought two looms back with her. One of the older women took one of the looms, and Miss Morgan furnished her with materials and stayed with her until she could weave by herself. When the weaver finished her first piece, Miss Morgan sold it for twenty-three dollars. From then until now there have been more people asking for looms than could be kept busy.

It was the weavers and their families who joined in building the Weavers Cabin, where once a week during the summer months, the weavers, their families, and their friends gather to plan their handicraft work and for social times such as they never knew before. When the Cabin was built they had a "log-raising" which is to this day looked back upon as the social event of recent years. The neighbors gave logs, stone for the fireplace, so many days of work, each doing what he or she could to make the Cabin possible. Then on the great day the men "raised" the logs and the women gave a big dinner.

At the Cabin are discussed not only weaving problems, but also the neighborhood problems such as new roads, telephone lines, and other community matters. Then when a new weaver is to start, some neighbor will go and help her put on her warp, and another neighbor will help teach her how to weave. They all teach each other and thus there is a great deal of neighborliness. Since the weaving has been going on, some women have met who have not seen each other since childhood, although they have lived only a few miles apart. Efforts are made to get people who used to weave to come out to these gatherings, and sometimes the Penland School truck is sent after them. One woman who

Figure 13-1. Mountain Loom at Berea College, about 1900 (*Southern Appalachian Archives, Berea College*)

Figure 13-2. Mountain Woman at an Old-Time Loom
(*Southern Appalachian Archives, Berea College*)

had not been out for eight years sent back word that she was afraid of the Ford and of
the mule and wagon, but that she would come on their sled.

Bonnie Willis, a student at Berea, whose mother was the first one to take up weaving
at Penland, wrote a play last year on The Life of the Weavers. It was in three parts. Part
I, The Passing of Old Things; Part II, Weaving Planned; Part III, A Scene in the Weaving
Cabin. It was played by the weavers at Penland. Dr. Koch of the University of North
Carolina drove down to see it, and this time the play was given on the porch of the
Willis cabin. The foot-lights were behind the posts of the porch. Dr. Koch asked, "Are
they talking or are those lines they have learned?" They were lines they had learned. He
said, "I can't believe it, for they are just talking their everyday language."

It is always a pleasure to me to learn of the handing down of American
traditions from one generation to the next. There is more of that in these
mountains than any one would guess. In the exhibition across the hall, in
the center of the main wall is a beautiful quilt which was made by Mrs.
Andy Hatcher of Ware's Valley, Tennessee, on a little farm that has been in
the family since 1795. I have not had the pleasure of meeting Mrs. Hatcher
or of learning just how unbroken has been the practice of the handicrafts
in their family, but some day I hope to know.

I do have the pleasure, however, of knowing another family represented in this exhibition in which the torch of the handicrafts has never
been lowered from the early colonial days to this 27th of March, 1930. This
is the Dougherty family of Russellville, Tennessee. The three sisters whose
textiles and rugs are shown in the exhibition learned weaving, spinning,
and coloring with native dyes from their mother, who in turn had learned
the crafts from their grandmother just as that generation was passing from
the hand work of the homestead to the machine industries of the cities. In
their home at Russellville the Doughertys have many examples of the handicrafts associated with the family and neighborhood from the early colonial
days, and in this spacious old house are several hand looms on which are
being made textiles that go out into every part of this country. It is our
privilege this afternoon to have with us the mother, Mrs. Leah Dougherty,
and two of the daughters, Miss Sarah Dougherty and Mrs. Rebecca Hyatt. I
have just this minute learned that they are leaving at once to make the
Russellville train. Since I don't want them to miss it I am going to ask Miss
Sarah Dougherty to speak to us for as long as she can, and afterwards while
she is catching her train I will introduce her to you.

Miss Dougherty said that her mother, her married sisters, and she represented three
generations of weavers in their home in Russellville. Miss Dougherty was compelled to
leave the hall in order to catch her train home. As she and her mother and sister, Mrs.
Hyatt, were leaving Mr. Eaton introduced them all to the Conference; and when they had
gone an account of their interesting and important work in the handicrafts was given,
of which there were several examples in the Guild exhibition.

The therapeutic or curative value of the handicrafts is a subject that has interested me for a long time. There are authentic records of cases in our hospitals, asylums, and prisons, in which patients have through a practice of the handicrafts been literally made over physically and mentally. I did not expect in my brief contact with the mountain people to find examples of the therapeutic value of the handicrafts, but Mrs. N. W. Johnson, of Crossnore, has told me of an experience in point which she has had and which I want her to pass on to you. This was the case of a large family in which there was a dull child. It is this child's story which Mrs. Johnson will tell you. I am especially glad to have this testimony from one who is not a physician, a trained nurse, or a specialist in occupational therapy, but an instructor in the handicrafts at Crossnore, with a keen sense of observation and a great fund of common sense.

> Mrs. Johnson told of a family of thirteen in which the brother who was crippled came to the school to learn weaving. He did it well, and he and the children thought they would like a loom for their mother. The family lived over the hill and there was no wagon road to their cabin; so the children came over and, each one carrying a part or two, took the loom over the hill to their home, and put it together. The children learned to weave—all but one, the oldest girl of seventeen, who was considered too dull to learn anything that required concentrated effort or memory. She was only in the third grade. The family had always had her work outside in the field. When she was sent to the store for anything, one of the smaller children would go along to do the buying. She told Mrs. Johnson she wanted to learn to weave, but she could not do anything; she was afraid to try.
>
> One day Mrs. Johnson heard someone passing make the remark that Z—— was dumb. The girl flushed. Mrs. Johnson thought to herself that if Z—— could flush about this remark she was not hopelessly dumb. Upon this she began to build. The next time Mrs. Johnson started to teach her to weave she told her she knew she could do it, and informed her also that although she had pulled that "dumb stuff" over others she couldn't over her. The girl brightened up and seemed pleased at this rather questionable compliment. She seemed to feel encouraged to take hold. Slowly she learned to weave. Then Mrs. Johnson gave her things to do, a spool of thread to take home to her mother. The first time she laid the thread down on the way and forgot it. But Mrs. Johnson did not send one of the other children to get it; she sent her back for it. Later she could go to the store and get things for the school and bring them back. And what she learned in her weaving, she kept. With this basis of accomplishment to give her confidence, she kept on, and when Mrs. Johnson asked her to show someone else how to do something in weaving a new light seemed to break for her. Life had a new interest, a vital one, and now she often helps others with their weaving.

We have just had a glimpse of the value of the handicrafts in the development of a mentally handicapped child. I wish we had the time to discuss the place of the handicrafts in the broad field of child education. This we cannot do today, but we shall have time to hear of a very interesting and original experiment in adult-education which Miss Clementine Douglas and her girls are working out at Beaver Lake, North Carolina. I am sorry Mr. Lester of the Carnegie Corporation could not have remained over to hear this talk. In his excellent address on "Adult Education: Its Basis and Background in the United States," which he delivered on the evening of March 26th, he referred specifically to the importance of developing an educational program out of an established interest. He stated this principle in better words than these, but I think he meant the same thing. Miss Douglas will tell us how with their daily work as a center these weavers are making fascinating excursions into history, geography, art, and other fields.

> Miss Douglas, of The Spinning Wheel, told how her weavers through their own think-ing out had insisted that they take up the study of weaving. Some of them had gone to Opportunity School at Berea and had come home with the idea that whatever work one was doing was important and that from this work as a center it would be possible to reach out to all the world.
>
> So the study began, and since Miss Douglas had a very small choice weaving from Italy one of the early excursions was to that sunny land. The weavers not only went back into the history of weaving, of which there are so many records in Italy, but they have had something to do with current events. One of the girls gave this terse but comprehensive sketch of Mussolini's career: "He said, you just lay off Italy for awhile and I will manage it." Other studies of Italy have been made, also of Greece, and other European countries.
>
> Miss Douglas gave her group an account of the very beginning of weaving, after which it was decided to include the Spinners as sisters of the Weavers, and now the quest for traces of both will go along together. Through books, maps, charts, and pictures the study continues, leading every way. There are pictures of the temples of Egypt, and a photo-graph of a mummy who was a sister weaver shows that the wrapping had a flat—she had tramped her treadle too much.
>
> And so the search goes from one age and country to another age and country as the thread of weaving is followed, and it seems as if through the quest for weaving alone it would be nearly possible to learn everything there is to know about the world.

In closing, may I say a few words aside about the handicraft exhibition. This exhibition as you know is the first one to be given by the Southern Mountain Handicraft Guild. One of the purposes of it was to give us all a better idea of the things that are being made in the mountains. Thirty-two different centers sent in examples of their best work, and on the main wall of the exhibition room is arranged at least one example of the handicraft work from each of these places. It has been a very interesting experience to see these objects and to help arrange them. My opinion of the impor-tance of the mountain handicrafts has been confirmed. I would like to take this opportunity to thank the committee which has done the work and made the task of arrangement both easy and pleasant for me. The Exhibition Committee consists of Miss Evelyn Bishop of Gatlinburg, Miss Marguerite Butler of Brasstown, and Mrs. Mary Sloop of Crossnore. Since Mrs. Sloop could not come, her associate Mrs. N. W. Johnson has taken her place here.

This then completes the formal program and we will without delay resolve ourselves into a meeting of the Southern Mountain Handicraft Guild, to which you are all, whether or not you are members, invited to remain.

14

Life in a Blue Ridge Hollow

Margaret A. Hitch

A popular activity that accelerated beginning in the 1930s was that of describing life in a specific mountain community or communities, usually selected because of their isolation. Beginning with Mandel Sherman and Thomas E. Henry's *Hollow Folk* (1933) these "community studies" became common fare for books. An earlier, and more modest, example of this approach is Margaret A. Hitch's "Life in a Blue Ridge Hollow."

Hitch's report of her stay among the people of Corbin and Nicholson Hollows in Virginia's Blue Ridge Mountains is typical of the genre. The community is extremely isolated, indeed "one of the most isolated in the Blue Ridge." While basically subscribing to the idea that mountain culture was homogeneous, Hitch, and others, noted that there were differences between one hollow and another, apparently without pondering what those differences meant for their assumption of homogenized Appalachian culture. Many aspects of everyday life, such as meals, education, sources of income, homes, lack of modern facilities, and how such traditional crafts and skills as basket making and apple butter making are utilized in the community, are discussed in some detail. But Hitch's main concern is that of most writers doing community studies, namely the change to be brought about by rapidly increasing contact with the outside world. In the case of Corbin and Nicholson Hollows such change would happen more quickly than for most other isolated communities because the Shenandoah National Park was soon to take over the entire region. It is instructive to compare Hitch's essay with Sherman and Henry's *Hollow Folk*, which is a study of a community in the same general vicinity.

*   *   *

Reprinted from *The Journal of Geography* 30 (November 1931): 309–22.

A Mountain School

"Books, books!" came the call, bringing to an end the game of Prisoners' Base played by a group of mountain children beside a little log school near the head of one of the numerous hollows of the beautiful Blue Ridge. The school yard, however,—if such it might be called, delineated by hill, thorn bushes and burned over forest—has seen little use as a play ground, for these isolated children first learned of games from the teacher of the preceding term. Moreover, school days here have been few.

Unattractive and uninviting tho this bleak little building may be to the itinerant of wider acquaintance, to the mountain folk of the community its faults are not glaring for they know nothing better. To them it brings a contact with something beyond their mountain fastness, one of their few glimpses of the "outside." Within, the bareness is somewhat dispelled by the bright pictures adorning the walls. But even their cheerfulness cannot conceal or counteract the meagerness of furnishings and equipment: no teacher's desk or chair, no shelf or drawer for books and supplies, five desks for some score of children, four rough benches (one serving the teacher as chair and desk), a blackboard limited to one wall, a map of the world (Mercator's projection), a defective stove, a water pail, a wash basin.

The call to "books" amid even these tools of learning has sounded all too seldom as is attested by the inability of most of the parents to read or write. Twenty-two years ago, six years ago, two years ago, the past summer and autumn—these are the only times when school terms were held in this community during the past half century. And none save the last term (of eight months) has exceeded three months in length.[1] The teacher of one term was a fourteen-year-old fourth grade girl, who married and thereupon closed the school before the term was completed. At a meeting held one night in the little school house during the sixth, and supposedly final, month of the past term, the patrons signed a petition for an additional two months of school.[2] Of the fourteen present eleven signed with a cross, only three being able to write their names. This community, isolated and untutored, is a part of the Old Dominion state, the first settled, and lies within seventy-five miles of the nation's capital, being included in the Proposed Shenandoah National Park.

Life in a Small, Secluded Hollow

These mountain people are suspicious of strangers and somewhat unapproachable, but after I had spent a day at school every family knew the teacher had a visitor, and when a few days later we proposed visiting some of the homes in Corbin Hollow below the Thoroughfare Mountain school (the hollow from which about half of the school children come) all homes were opened to me as to the teacher. This hollow is said by men who know the mountain districts of the state to be one of the most isolated in the Blue Ridge. Some of the earlier settlers went into the hollow to avoid the draft for the Civil War. The land which they later abandoned was taken up by the present owners, whose descendants make up the population. The land is held by "possession right," without deeds.

One afternoon after school we made our way down into the hollow along a foot path for there is no road, or need for one. The narrow trail was stony, steep, and rough. On either side the close undergrowth clutched our clothing while above towered the tall forest trees, here and there among them a lonely chestnut bearing few nuts, since most of its limbs were killed by the blight. This winding, green, tunnel-like trail led us down nearly 500 feet in the half mile to the first cabin.

On the steep slope above the cabin, in a semi-clearing where the underbrush gave way a little from the trail, we came unexpectedly upon four or five shocks of corn. This was the only corn "field," apparently, cultivated by the family living in this cabin. The log cabin itself, standing on the bank of small, tumbling Brokenback River, was badly in need of repair. Its one room and makeshift furniture spelled the acme of discomfort. A garden of sorts meandered among the boulders and fallen trees, a pumpkin vine and cabbages being most in evidence. Apples cut for drying were spread on one of the boulders altho we saw no fruit trees.

Further down the hollow, as we followed the course of the stream with the forest on either side, we came to other mountain homes. In the small clearing beside each, reaching up the steep slope, was a patch of corn, so necessary in the food supply of these people. Late "snaps" from their gardens, if the rains came, would be dried to eke out the winter's food.[3] Here, too, were the apple trees, old and uncared for, bearing inferior fruit. Near one cabin a few bee "gums," housing captured wild bees, gave promise of an occasionally gratified sweet-tooth. A patch of parsnips growing in one small garden was destined to be used in making wine, the only use known here for parsnips until the teacher came.

Only one family of the seven or eight in this hollow possesses a cow. Two families have a few chickens; none has a pig. Nor is there a horse or other beast of burden in the hollow. A horse here would be chiefly a matter of luxury which these people can ill afford. Their gardens and hillside corn patches are worked with a hoe, or, on occasion, if not too steep to be plowed, a horse may be borrowed for a few hours from a more prosperous family on the mountain slope above the head of the hollow. As for hogs, there is no surplus of food here to provide for them.

The most substantial cabin of this hollow stands in such a position on the slope that it commands a most engaging view thru a gap in the mountains and over the Piedmont. At night one may watch the lights of autos skimming along a highway between populous towns of the "outside," yet sit within this secluded, backward hollow so difficult of access.

Life in a Richer, More Open Hollow

In this same mountain district are other hollows less secluded, hollows into which roads—albeit poor ones—lead, and which, in comparison, look like prosperous farming communities. One of these, years ago, gained the name of Free State Hollow because, thru its inaccessibility, it served as a haven for those seeking, for any reason, freedom from the laws of the state. It is now, for the most part, called Nicholson Hollow, since most of the people living within it are named Nicholson. Into this hollow the teacher of the little log school and I trekked late one afternoon. Having crossed the intervening ridge, we followed the shoulder of the mountain, and descended thru the thick forest, first along a winding road, then by a "short cut" path. Suddenly the forest ended and we found ourselves perched on the upper edge of a clearing, high on the mountain side.

From our vantage point a splendid view of this section of the hollow lay before and below us. In comparison with the region just left this presented a distinctly cultural landscape. Woods there were, to be sure, notably a band of varying width marking the course of the stream, while from this strip occasional lateral arms reached out to join the thick forest cover of the higher slopes. But the greater portion of the lower slopes was occupied with orchards, corn fields with the corn now in the shock, hayfields or pastures, and here and there a cabin with a little group of farm sheds and a garden. The slopes, many of them, were quite as steep as the cultivated patches of Corbin Hollow (seemingly far too steep for soil maintenance); but this hollow was wider and more open than the smaller one, affording within it other slopes less steep. Here there permeated an air of energy and effort wholly lacking in the smaller hollow where shiftlessness and laziness seemed so evident.

The farm on whose cleared margin we stood comprised about fifty acres, about half of it being under cultivation. With the exception of a strip, perhaps forty feet wide, of comparatively level land bordering the deeply cut little river, its area was made up of steep hillside. The owner later assured us that he used a horse in cultivating all his cleared land. Nevertheless, the degree of the slope was such that we descended his fields and orchards with caution, avoiding the path, a veritable chute, deep in dust powdered by pine logs cut on the higher slopes and recently marketed in a Piedmont town. Near the upper limits of this clearing were a dozen or more young peach trees, while on the lower slope just back of the cabin was an apple orchard. This little cabin was in good repair, the owner even having begun to cover the logs with hand rived clap-boards like those used for the roof. In the little front yard surrounded by a paling fence, an elevated platform held apples cut for drying. The occupants of this cabin, a man and his wife, were twenty-four and twenty-one years of age, respectively. They had been married seven years.

The farms in this hollow vary in size from about 25 acres to 200 or more. Corn is by far the most important crop, tho some rye and potatoes are grown. There is, therefore, scant opportunity for crop rotation. One man had grown corn in the same field for seven consecutive years. When a farmer considers the yield too small, he turns his corn field into pasture or allows it to revert to forest. He then starts a new clearing, girdling the trees in order to kill them. A new field is spoken of as a "deadenin'." Some of the farmers complained that "Land is goin' back fast" and "Crops ain't good like they used to be."

Practically every family in this larger hollow has one or two horses, two own automobiles (purchased second-hand, of course), and one owns a truck. However, the most usual form of transport within this mountain area is by means of a horse drawn "slide," or sled, which is found on most of the farms, and which operates more easily over the numerous rocks and steeps than a wagon does. The slide is also cheaper to obtain and to keep in repair. It is home-made, and when a "shoe," as the runner is called, becomes worn, the owner goes to the woods and makes a new one. There are pigs, too, in this hollow; not many, but one or more on practically every farm. The mountaineers, however, claim they do not care for ham, tho they use other parts of the hog. As hams are among the few things which may be sold from these mountain farms, the money they bring doubtless has some effect upon the local taste for ham.

Very large families are the exception rather than the rule in these mountain districts altho one man in Nicholson Hollow told us he was the father of eighteen children, eleven of whom were at home at the time of our visit. The oldest, about seventeen years of age, was churning. Six were helping their father, on Saturday morning, bring in fodder from the field.

The meals which we shared with one of the families in this hollow during our two days' stay there, while somewhat lacking in variety of food, were well cooked and the food abundant. Breakfast, the most diversified meal, was the only one at which meat was served—once canned corn beef (from the nearest store, about three miles down the hollow) with fat back, and again chicken. There were also fried white potatoes, corn bread, biscuits, apple sauce and coffee At noon the main dish and only one aside from the breads (similar to breakfast) and apple sauce, was a large platter of boiled sweet potatoes served hot. At supper the remnant—half or more—of this same dish, cold, constituted the meal, with the addition of the breads and apple butter. At every meal there was an abundance of good butter, cream, and milk.[4] Only five of us sat at the table altho there were more in the family and there was unoccupied space at the table. Before most of us had finished the meal, the young housewife, who was serving, said to one of the children, "If you are thru, you can get up and I'll wash your plate so someone else can come."[5] This family owned an auto and a truck.

Apple butter making is another point of difference between these two hollows. In the smaller, more primitive one this stage of civilization apparently has not been reached, apple drying being their limit for preserving the fruit. In the larger hollow the making of apple butter is the general order and is, sometimes at least, in the nature of a social event. The cooking is done out of doors. A fire-place of stones and mud is built and over it the iron, copper-lined kettle, twenty gallons or more in size, is suspended by means of a horizontal pole resting upon two upright poles. The boiling continues for twenty-four hours with constant stirring of the butter, hence there is excellent opportunity for a social gathering with something to do. Two people usually stir at a time, and of course there must be relays. Sometimes families join in a "boiling." When the apple crop fails, or is markedly short, some of the families make pumpkin butter in lieu of apple butter. The manner of cooking and the equipment used are the same.

A dozen yards down the slope in front of the cabin where we stayed for two days was a spring which supplied water for the household, and over which a little "spring house" was built, serving as the farm refrigerator. Most of the families in these mountain districts are dependent for their water supply upon springs, near which their cabins are usually built. There is but one well in even this larger and relatively prosperous hollow, and no cistern. During a prolonged dry season, as the summer and autumn of 1930, many of the springs dry up and water must be brought from greater distances, usually up a hill. A few of the springs were claimed by their owners to maintain a regular flow thru all seasons. Water works and plumbing are unknown, of course; likewise toilet facilities of any sort; and screening.

Sources of Cash Income

The cash income in these mountain communities is decidedly meager, and naturally varies greatly among the inhabitants, according to their individual ability, resources, and industry. Logging, carried on to a limited extent, has already been mentioned. Some of the men leave the district for shorter or longer time, finding work cutting wood or building trails and roads. In apple picking season, and occasionally at other times, they may find a few weeks' employment in the Shenandoah Valley.

When other employment fails, a few men who have become proficient in the art make baskets. There is a limited sale for these articles among other mountaineers, but the chief market is of course outside the mountains. A man and his two young sons living near the little school have realized $30 from baskets made during the past winter. So far as the material is concerned, however, spring time, when the sap is running, is the most advantageous season for making the baskets. The oak saplings, of which the baskets are made, are split into strips which are then soaked in a spring branch for some days in order to soften them for weaving. These oak strips are also utilized in other ways in the household equipment—for seats in the home-made chairs, and for binding the broom corn to the handle in making brooms. These light weight, home-made brooms were in evidence in several cabins, and in one garden a few rows of broom corn still were standing.

One of the most enterprising men of the region has an orchard of a few hundred trees from which he dried about 1300 pounds of apples during the past season. In other seasons he has dried even more. This man's farm lies nearer the Piedmont than the other farms visited, and he is more accessible to a market. He sold his fruit to two country merchants whose stores are three and six miles distant from him, respectively. The store six miles away is in the Piedmont. Seven cents a pound was the price received for most of the dried fruit. Apples from another orchard even nearer the Piedmont have been, in some seasons, boxed and shipped to city markets. Only a few of the men in this mountain region are attempting to spray and prune their fruit trees, most of the product, consequently, being of an inferior class. There would seem to be opportunity for further orchard development here should the area not be taken over for the proposed park.

Mountain tradition, of course, credits some income to whiskey, condensed product of the hillside corn patch. Such may be the case here. Rumor was not lacking that some of the men had interests in a still "on the Ridge." Indeed, in one home we visited, revenue officers a few months previous had found the equipment for a still under the kitchen floor. There was, moreover, evidence of at least some home consumption of this product in the district.

Effects of Isolation

The scarcity of the contacts which the people of these communities have beyond their mountains is reflected in various ways. Even in Nicholson Hollow, which boasts a road thruout its length and has received more

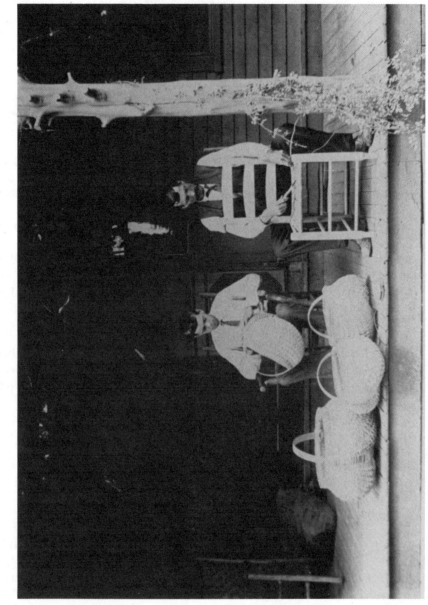

Figure 14-1. Baskets and Chairs: Practical Southern Mountain Folk Arts
(*Southern Appalachian Archives, Berea College*)

school advantages than Corbin Hollow,[6] the people have little concern for happenings other than those directly related to their own lives. Few of the inhabitants read with a facility which enables them to obtain their news thru the medium of a newspaper. Thus, with neither books, papers, nor news of the world at large to occupy them, their interests are limited almost wholly to their own and neighboring communities. The people whom they know personally comprise their world. And most of these, particularly the neighbors within their own community they know very well indeed, including all their affairs. With attention so little divided it is not surprising that jealousies, misrepresentations, and distrust are met with.

Their diction includes words and expressions of a past generation. In conversation with the children at the little school it was frequently necessary to have more than one child repeat what another had said before it became intelligible to me. One day in response to an exclamation over the beauty of the mountains a little girl said, "There must ain't no mountains where you live." A fourteen-year-old girl upon seeing at school the picture of a train for the first time asked what it was. She had never seen a train. Few, if any, of the children have seen one, altho under certain atmospheric conditions, one can hear at the little school the whistle of a locomotive in the Shenandoah Valley. Some of the children in the smaller hollow have never seen an automobile.

Since practically no "new blood" comes into any given district in the mountains, relationships are quite complicated. Upon asking how three men, patrons of the little school, were related the following answer was received: "Oscar is Bailey's nephew; Oscar's wife and Bailey's wife are sisters, and are also nieces of Fennell; Fennell's wife was a sister to Bailey and to Oscar's father." On another occasion in reply to an inquiry regarding the ownership of a certain apple orchard apparently very well cared for which came into view on a distant mountain side, the mountaineer addressed answered, "Pete and Paul." In a district where most of the inhabitants have the same last name, the use of it is more or less superfluous.

"Outside" Contacts Affect Changes

Contacts of the mountaineers with the outside world are increasing, however. Some changes have already taken place and others are creeping in. With but one exception, all the homes which we visited in the mountains were built with fire-places—chimneys of stone and mud. Yet in practically every cabin a box stove was in use at the time of our visit and the fireplace closed. The stove is not so picturesque, certainly, as the open fire, but affords far more comfort in cold weather.

Last spring one of these mountaineers, the father of several children, traded his only horse for a $10 phonograph and sixteen records. He said his children wanted it so badly. The year's crop was already planted, but the cultivation had to be done with a hoe. In a cabin in Corbin Hollow a phonograph was played proudly for us by the owners. It had been obtained in exchange for two barrels of corn and the crop of fodder.[7] Radios, too, have been introduced. Thru some philanthropist a limited number of these are now installed in certain centralized cabins in the mountains to serve the respective communities. One evening we attended a gathering of neighbors in Nicholson Hollow to listen to the radio. "Amos 'n' Andy" hold no interest for these isolated people who have practically no acquaintance with the Negro race.[8] Their choice was for a program whose subject matter knows no mountain barrier—music.

In some instances people living outside the mountains are making use of mountain land and thus introducing contacts. Farmers from the "Valley," the usual way of referring to the Shenandoah Valley, have fenced certain areas and are using them as summer pastures for cattle. We passed thru one such tract between Thoroughfare Mountain school and Nicholson Hollow. About forty-five head of cattle had been pastured here thru the summer on approximately 275 acres. Usually the cattle may be kept in the mountains until the end of October, but because all the springs had dried up and there was, consequently, no water for the cattle, they had to be taken out last fall a month early. The cattle were driven to the valley farm of their owner where they would be fed thru the winter. The parts of this tract thru which we passed had the appearance of affording very poor pasturage in even a good season. The owner of a similar tract told me that the cattle get much of their living there from the undergrowth, as much perhaps as from the grass.

Another means of outside contact which is developing in this region is thru the hikers and vacationists. In increasing numbers they are being attracted by the scenic beauty, the facilities of a nearby resort, and the construction of the Appalachian Trail.

Future Outlook

The future of this region may be in marked contrast to its past. The National Park Commission for several months has had men at work appraising the private property in the proposed park area as a basis for remuneration should the region actually be taken over for a federal park. Some of the mountaineers are making tentative plans for leaving their mountain homes; one family has already left. The owner of perhaps the largest holding in Nicholson Hollow hopes to be able to buy a certain Piedmont farm. His son has an offer for permanent employment with a "Valley" farmer for whom he has picked apples. One of the problems confronting the authorities in converting this region into a park is the satisfactory disposition of the people now living within the area. The mountaineers doubtless will have difficulty in adjusting themselves to other environments. One family sold their farm in Nicholson Hollow a few years ago and moved to a town in West Virginia; but they were dissatisfied and within six months had returned to the hollow and purchased another farm. Another family lived for a time in Culpeper, Virginia, but after a few months they, likewise, returned to the mountains where they have since remained.

If plans for the proposed Shenandoah Park materialize, this region should become one of the most popular national parks since it is within a two-day drive, or less, of a large percentage of the country's population. In all probability within another decade a new era will have begun in these mountains and the day of the Blue Ridge mountaineer will have passed.

Notes

1. The greater part of the school terms in these mountain communities have been three-month summer terms (vacation schools). In summer it is easier for the smaller children to climb the mountain trails and attend school, tho the older children are to some extent kept at home then to work. However, the choice of the season for the school terms has been primarily an adjustment to finance rather than to climate. The state pays two-thirds of the salaries of vacation school teachers, the county alone bearing the expense of other terms. Therefore, the county school officials have been interested in satisfying the mountaineers with short summer schools. The patrons in these districts are now demanding longer school terms.

2. This was the second extension asked for this term.

3. The usual manner of drying string beans in the mountain districts is merely to lay them in the sun for a few days, on the lower slope of the roof or elsewhere. One of the better housekeepers, however, living above the head of the hollow, has another method. She had threaded the full pods thru the center, spacing them an inch or so on the string. In the shed where they were drying there were perhaps 200 or 300 strings of beans hanging from roof to floor.

4. In one of the homes in Corbin Hollow the evening meal was in the process of preparation at the time of our visit. It consisted of a pot of boiled cabbage and a thick hoe-cake cooked on a griddle. At a meal some days later with family in another community—a family of more education and apparently with certain outside contacts—we were served a greater variety of vegetables, and even pie and cake. These mountain folk know nothing of making light bread. On a few occasions when it was served to the children at school it was highly prized by them.

5. A dearth of dishes was apparent, too, in a smaller hollow. Funds had been provided the teacher whereby she might supplement the meager lunches of the children. Frequently condensed milk was used in this preparation, and so keen became the competition among the children of the several families for the one or two empty cans available at one time

that a system for their distribution had to be devised. The cans were wanted for cups at home.

6. For the past seven years or more Nicholson Hollow has had a school term each year of from three to eight months duration. One teacher scarcely qualified for fourth grade, but the others held teachers' certificates. The school equipment, however, is even less than that of the Thoroughfare Mountain school. As there is no school building, school is held in the church. This is an unsatisfactory arrangement from the standpoint of equipment and supplies as they cannot be cared for adequately or safeguarded. About five years ago the church authorities refused to give the key of the building to a young man who had been appointed to teach, because he was not of their particular religious sect. At another time they demanded the key after school had been in session for several weeks.

7. Acute food shortage in this cabin followed a few months later.

8. There was neither need nor wealth for slaves in the mountain section of Virginia. Nor has there been any attraction here for the free Negro.

15

Changes in the Dietary Habits of Remote Mountain People since 1900

Lester R. Wheeler

While many of the writers on Appalachian folklife briefly discussed foodways few focused exclusively on the subject. The first food studies date only from the first decade of the twentieth century and, although folklorists have recently become more interested in food lore, there are still only a handful of publications on the subject. To date, most studies of traditional Appalachian cookery have been carried out not by folklorists but by nutritionists and psychologists such as Lester Rosin Wheeler (1894–1978). Dr. Wheeler, a Tennessee native, was for nearly two decades a member of the faculty of East Tennessee State University, Johnson City. He spent the last twenty years of his academic career at the University of Miami, Coral Gables, Florida. A pioneer in reading education, Wheeler had a special interest in rural, racial, and sociological problems in the southern Appalachians, particularly as evidenced in the more isolated regions of the mountains.

Wheeler's paper on foodways was the last in a series of studies based on his work among remote mountain people. His findings, particularly about the use of milk and honey, may be surprising to some readers but they should keep in mind Wheeler's own caution that his comparison is to a degree faulty. Wheeler's other studies of isolated mountain people include "Intelligence of East Tennessee Mountain Children," *Journal of Educational Psychology* 23 (May 1932): 351–70; "The Physical Status of East Tennessee Mountain Children," *Human Biology* (December 1933): 706–21; and "A Study of the Remote Mountain People of the Tennessee Valley," *Journal of the Tennessee Academy of Science* 10 (1935): 33–36. Although it says little about Appalachia, Sam Bowers Hilliard's *Hog Meat and Hoecake: Food Supply in the Old South, 1840–1860* (Carbondale: Southern Illinois University Press, 1972) is a useful resource on Southern foodways. Thomas A. Adler's "Bluegrass Music and Meal-Fried Potatoes: Food, Festival, Community" in Theodore C. Humphrey and Lin T. Humphrey, eds., *"We Gather Together": Food and Festival in American Life* (Ann Arbor: UMI

Reprinted from *Journal of the Tennessee Academy of Science* 10 (July 1935): 167–74.

Research Press, 1988), pp. 195–204, is an interesting article dealing with food and a type of music with strong Appalachian connections. Ferne Shelton's *Southern Appalachian Mountain Cookbook* (High Point, North Carolina: Hutcraft, 1964) is just a recipe book but one of the genre that includes some comments on traditional foods.

* * *

As part of an inquiry into the socio-living conditions of mountain people of the Southern Appalachians, the author has recently investigated the dietary habits of four hundred twenty-eight mountain families in remote sections of Eastern Kentucky, East Tennessee, and Western North Carolina. The degree of remoteness is indicated by the distance these families live from a post office and paved roads. The average distance to a paved road is ten miles, with a range form zero to forty. The average distance to a post office is two miles, with a range from zero to twenty-one.

During the winter and early spring of 1933–1934 these data were collected in two ways. First, an objective questionnaire pertaining to the food habits of the family was filled out by the oldest child in each family represented above the third grade in remote mountain schools. Second, actual dietaries were kept for seven days by two hundred ninety-six of these children under the supervision of the teachers. A careful record was kept of what each child had to eat for breakfast, dinner, and supper. It is hoped to follow this survey with a quantitative study in order to answer some of the problems pertaining to the nutritive value of the mountain diet. No attempt is made to give a detailed discussion of the investigation, but rather to present one phase which seems of particular interest at this time.

When the results of this survey are compared with previous investigations within the same areas, some interesting interpretations can be made as to the changes that have taken place since 1900. While early diet studies are very subjective and inadequate for minute comparative purposes, certain general trends can be studied which may be significant.

The earliest investigation the author has been able to locate was a quantitative study made by Wait in 1901–1905 (1909). While a few of the families in his investigation lived in remote areas, many of them were located in a fertile valley village only a few miles out from Knoxville. This fact, together with the small number of cases, should be considered in studying the comparisons. The difference between Wait's study and the present one is probably greater than the figures indicate, for the remote sections of today are compared with a prosperous valley of 1900.

We have taken what information we could gather from Wait's study to represent the decade of 1900. While in some instances an overlapping occurs in the actual time various investigators collected their data, it seems safe to assume that Kephart's observations (1913) are fairly representative of the decade of 1910, Campbell (1921) and Roberts (1922) for 1920, and our data for 1930. From these sources we have attempted to trace the changes in dietary habits of the remote mountain people. Although discrepancies are found among these studies, in general there appear some consistent trends in the comparisons so that a general picture of the changes can be shown.

Wherever it was possible to obtain from previous studies definite information as to the use of various foods, we have attempted to show the general trends. Unless authors indicated the prevalence of foods in terms of percentage of families or dietaries using them, the graphs are designated thus: "very common," 75 to 100 per cent; "common," 50 to 75; "less common," 25 to 50; and "rare," 0 to 25 per cent. Graphs constructed from subjective observations should be interpreted with reservations.

Milk

In 1901–1905 Wait found that, while buttermilk was commonly used, only 14% of the dietaries contained whole milk. Horace Kephart, in 1913, maintained that many families went without milk a great part of the year. Roberts states that during the winter of 1919–1920 buttermilk was often served and that eight-one per cent of the children had whole milk. She found less than one per cent using condensed milk, and powdered milk was unknown. Campbell's study in 1921 appears to disagree somewhat with Roberts' findings. He maintained that many families in the mountains had milk the year round and that "numbers" were without it in winter and summer. He added that while milk and buttermilk were found in the diet of the more prosperous families, they were conspicuously absent among the middle and lower classes. Because Roberts gives more definite information, we have used her figures, realizing that they may not be typical for the whole area.

When we compare Roberts' data with ours, there appears an increase since 1920 of 14% in the number of families using whole milk during the winter, or an increase of about one per cent a year for the past 15 years. A smaller increase of 10% is indicated when we compare Roberts' data with the total mountain area. Considering all the comparisons, it appears that the use of whole milk has increased from "rare" in 1900 to "very common" in 1930. It seems that, although buttermilk is used slightly less than whole milk, it ranks as one of the common foods in the mountain diet. In 1920, according to Campbell, only the more prosperous had milk and buttermilk. Today 91% use whole milk, and 81% buttermilk, which indicates an increase in the use of milk. It seems that today milk is as commonly used by the middle class of mountain families as it was by the prosperous class fifteen years ago.

No mention was made of condensed or powdered milk prior to Roberts' study in 1920. In the Kentucky area there has been an increase in the used of condensed milk from eight-tenths of one per cent in 1920 to 21% today, and a three per cent increase in the use of powdered milk. Our data show less use of condensed milk in the Tennessee and North Carolina areas; the average for the total area is nine percent. Milk preparations are rarely used in the remote mountain areas.

Cereals

Corn bread and biscuits have been very common in the mountain diet since 1900, and they are now the most popular forms of cereal foods used. Wait found an excessive amount of corn meal and white flour used in the dietaries; he states that 78% of the remote dietaries were made up of these two items. Kephart in 1913 mentions corn bread as very common. Roberts reported in 1920, 100% of the Kentucky families used corn bread, 96% biscuits, 29% lightbread, and 4% whole wheat bread. Campbell reported in 1921 that corn bread was the most common bread found in the mountains, biscuits were common in the better families, and lightbread was very unusual.

Investigators before 1920 made no mention of any cereal foods except corn meal and white flour. Roberts found in 1920 that 69% of the Kentucky families used oatmeal. Our data show in 1934 that 75% of the Kentucky families were using oatmeal, and 71% of the families in the total area. In Kentucky the general use of lightbread has increased from 29% to 61%, or has more than doubled since 1920. We found less use of lightbread in the other areas, but the trend indicates its use has probably increased from a rare to a common food. While whole wheat bread is still rarely found, a significant increase in its use since 1900 is indicated. Rye bread, not mentioned in any of the previous studies, is used by nine per cent of the families today. Campbell stated that hominy was used extensively in the better families; we found it used during the winter months by 61% in North Carolina and by 41% of the families of the total area. Other cereal foods such as macaroni, cream-of-wheat, and uncooked cereals were used occasionally in 1934, but were not mentioned in previous investigations.

In general it appears that corn bread and biscuits continue to take first place among the cereal foods of the mountain dietaries, that oatmeal has been commonly used since 1920, and that there has been a significant increase in the use of lightbread, whole wheat bread and rye bread.

Fruits and Vegetables

Wait found fresh fruits seldom used even in summer, and no dried, canned, or jellied fruit. His findings indicate that fruits were rarely used in 1900. In 1910 Kephart did not mention fruits in the diet. Roberts states that in the winter of 1920, 95% of the Kentucky families had blackberries, and "a few" apples and peaches were eaten. Campbell in 1921 said that berries and apples were plentiful throughout the mountains and in some sections peaches were abundant. We have found in 1934 that berries, apples, and peaches are commonly used the year round and are very common during the summer and fall. If summer and fall use rather than year round average were used, no decrease would appear since 1920.

Campbell states that grapes were plentiful in 1920, and we have found in 1934 that they are used by over half the families during the summer and fall. Campbell maintained that "a few" watermelons were found; we have found 67% of the families using them in the summer. Campbell listed persimmons as plentiful during the fall, and we found over a third of the families using them. As previous investigators have made no mention of oranges, lemons, etc., which would have to be purchased from the store, we have assumed they were not used during the earlier decades. Our data indicate that today an average of 31% of mountain families make occasional use of this class of fruit.

There appears to be no significant change since 1900 in the use and variety of vegetables. Potatoes and onions appear very common the year round, and cabbage, tomatoes, and beans are commonly used. Wait found white and sweet potatoes the most common vegetables and he mentions the use of onions, cabbage, tomatoes, beans, and turnips. In 1913 Kephart said that potatoes were common, but that not enough were raised to last the family through the winter. He mentioned cabbage and field beans as the two other common vegetables. Campbell in 1921 stated that the most common vegetables were white potatoes and green beans; those less common were sweet potatoes, beets, cabbage, dried green beans, field corn, a few squash, pumpkins, and tomatoes which were becoming more widely used each year. Roberts' list for Kentucky diets showed the same general trend except for tomatoes which she found among the most commonly used vegetables.

In 1934 we found only white potatoes and onions very commonly used the year round, but lettuce and cucumbers were very common during the summer. Those commonly used the year round are sweet potatoes, cabbage, beans, beets, and pumpkin. Greens, green corn, and possibly sweet peppers are common during the summer. Less commonly used are sauerkraut, parsnips, peas, and squash. Cauliflower, celery, asparagus, carrots, okra, and spinach are rarely used. There is evidence that a limited amount of vegetables, as well as fruits, is purchased from stores. For example, we found that 18% of the families occasionally buy lettuce during the winter.

Meat, Fish, Eggs, Etc.

There has been practically no change to the use of pork since 1900. Wait found it extensively used in 1901, and Kephart and Campbell agree that hog meat, salted and cured, made up the greatest part of the meat diet in 1910 and 1920. Roberts found that 60% of the Kentucky families were "salt meat users" and 24% "fresh meat users." Our data show that 75% of the families in Kentucky used fat meat, 43% used cured lean meat, and 44% used fresh pork. During the winter 70% of the families served sausage, liver, and souse meat.

There appears to be no significant change in the use of poultry and eggs since 1900. While most families have poultry, chicken and eggs are rarely eaten. No poultry was served on the dietaries studied by Wait, and only 12% served eggs. Campbell stated that chicken was the only meat common besides pork, and eggs did not form as great a factor in the diet as they should. Roberts stated that while 85% of the families had chickens, eggs were rarely eaten. Our data show that while 81% had poultry, only about a fourth of the families served eggs or chicken.

There appears to be an increase of 14% in the use of beef since 1900. Wait found beef occurring in 30% of the diets in his study, a figure probably too high to represent the remote mountain area. Wait collected many of his dietaries from a fertile valley where grazing was abundant and good beef cattle could be raised. Kephart and Campbell stated that beef was rarely eaten. We have found beef used by 44% of the families in 1934. An increase appears in the use of fish from three per cent in Wait's study to approximately 40% in 1934. Very little salt fish is used, but considerable canned fish is found, especially in the Kentucky area. Kephart, Campbell, and Roberts made no mention of the use of fish. In 1900 Wait found game on 4.5% of the diets. Because of the prosperous valley families in this study, there may have been a wider use of fresh fish and game in the remote sections than his figures indicate. Campbell mentioned that variety was occasionally furnished to the mountain diet by squirrel, opossum, rabbit, and lamb. We found that only 18% of the families use lamb, but about 50% make some use of game during the fall and winter months. Campbell stated that no cheese was used in the mountain diet. Today we find nearly a third of the families occasionally serving cheese. Nuts, which Campbell said were commonly gathered for fall and winter use, are used today by over half the families.

Fats and Sugars

Previous studies have given us a rather confusing and indefinite picture of the use of lard and butter. Wait stated that butter was fairly common in 1900 and that lard was ordinarily replaced by butter. Kephart in 1913 gives a different opinion. He observed that the average mountain man despised butter and rarely ate it. Roberts reported the 85% used butter in the Kentucky mountains, and Campbell stated that it was common in 1921, but of a poor flakey quality. In 1934 we found butter used by 91% of the families the year round, and lard used by 83%. Vegetable shortenings, not mentioned by previous investigators, are used today by 43% in Tennessee, 62% in North Carolina, and 11% in Kentucky, indicating an increase of its use for the total area of about 38%.

Wait made no mention of sugars in his study. Kephart mentioned the wide use of honey. Campbell stated that molasses, jellies, and honey were common and that maple sugar was occasionally used. Roberts reported a wide use of molasses in Kentucky. No mention was made in these earlier studies of the use of white and brown sugar. In 1934 we found that white and brown sugar are very commonly used by mountain families in addition to a common use of molasses. Our data show that honey has decreased from a common food in 1910 to the less common class in 1930. There has also been a significant decrease in the use of maple sugar, syrup, etc., during the past decade.

Summary

1. The dietary habits of 428 families living in remote mountain sections today have been compared with previous investigations and the changes studied.

2. Milk, rarely found in the dietaries in 1900, is very commonly used today. Buttermilk, commonly used since 1900, is served almost as frequently as whole milk. While a slight increase is found since 1920 in the use of condensed and powdered milk, these prepared milk foods are rarely used in the remote mountain areas.

3. No marked change appears in the wide use of corn bread and biscuits since 1900. Oatmeal has been commonly found since 1920, and there has been an increase in the use of lightbread, whole wheat and rye bread.

4. While the variety of fruits has changed little since 1900, there has been a marked increase in the use of berries, apples, and peaches. The use of oranges, lemons, etc., purchased from the store has increased 31% since 1920. There appears to be no significant change since 1900 in the use and variety of vegetables.

5. Pork has maintained first place among the meat foods since 1900. Even though the average family has poultry and eggs, they rarely make use of them in the diet. Beef, rarely served in remote areas before 1920, is used by 44% of the families today. An increase is found in the use of fish, especially canned fish in the Kentucky area, and the use of cheese has increased 31% since 1920.

6. To-day butter and lard are very common in the mountain diet. Evidence from previous studies indicates that butter was common in 1900, while lard was rare. Vegetable shortenings are common in North Carolina, less common in Tennessee, and rarely used in Kentucky.

7. White and brown sugar, not mentioned in any of the previous investigations, are today very commonly used. Molasses remains a common food. Since 1920 there has been a decrease in the use of honey, maple sugar, and syrups.

8. Since 1900 there has been no significant change in the use of corn bread, biscuits, pork, poultry, eggs, vegetables, and molasses.

9. An increase is found in the use of milk foods, oatmeal, whole wheat, rye, and lightbread, fruits, beef, fish cheese, lard, vegetable shortenings, white, and brown sugar.

10. A decrease appears in the use of honey, maple sugar, and syrups.

16

Shingle Making on the Lesser Waters of the Big Creek of the French Broad River

Edmund Cody Burnett

In contrast with the type of "folk crafts" that usually get displayed at the Southern Highland Handicraft Guild and similar organizations are folk crafts, that is traditional objects that are primarily made for non-esthetic reasons. Most general writings dealing with Appalachian culture mention traditional crafts but relatively few studies of this aspect of mountain folklife exist; even smaller are the number of works dealing with traditional building crafts. One of the earlier such works is Edmund Cody Burnett's essay tracing the history of shingle making in one eastern Tennessee valley. Burnett's paper is in many respects an admirable study, providing an excellent brief account of the actual process involved in making shingles, the material used, conditions dictating the location of shingle mills, and marketing of the finished product. His article, unfortunately, relies basically on the author's memory rather than on interviews with former shingle makers. Moreover, despite the use of several anecdotes, Burnett's concern is with the process rather than the people making the product. Finally, the title notwithstanding, the focus here is on sawed shingle making and only incidentally with shaved shingles.

Edmund Cody Burnett (1864–1949) was a prolific and multi-talented scholar. A native of Alabama with three degrees from Brown University, Burnett taught at several colleges in such varied fields as literature, Greek, mathematics, and history, but his major publications were in the area of political science. Most of his professional career was spent as a staff member of the Carnegie Institution's Department of Historical Research. After his retirement in 1936 he moved to Del Rio, Tennessee, a small community in the eastern part of the state.

* * *

Reprinted from *Agricultural History* 20 (October 1946): 225–35, by permission. © 1946 by the Agricultural History Society.

It has been said, and with some marks of verity, that, with the first wagon train to a projected settlement on the frontier, went a Baptist preacher. But, when he arrived at his destination, he found a Methodist preacher already on the spot, sitting on his saddlebags, his horse hitched to a tree, waiting for the caravan of settlers. I do not know that the enterprising denizens of Big Creek Valley in Tennessee had bunches of shingles stacked beside the railroad ready to be loaded on the first train out, but they might well have done so. That first train, so it would appear, pulled out from the station then called Big Creek, now known as Del Rio, at 5:30 on the morning of August 11, 1868. For the time being Big Creek was the terminus of the road, but trains had been operated between Morristown and Clifton, the present Newport, since the fifth of the preceding February.[1] Therefore, the aforesaid enterprising denizens had had a full six months' notice of the coming opportunity. Certainly little, if any, time was lost in making full use of it.

Neither is it possible at a distance of eighty years save two to determine when the first sawmill outfit arrived at Big Creek, but is it certain that such an outfit was among the earliest hauls of the Cincinnati, Cumberland Gap, and Charleston Railroad into that valley, whose people were eager to be up and doing—doing something besides clawing a scant living, mainly in the form of corn, from meager coves and steep hillsides. At all events the railroad began almost immediately to gather from the rich forests of that small valley of the Appalachians a goodly harvest.

The lumbering business in general has flourished in the valley and the region roundabout from the summer of 1868 to the present day, but the story here told is limited to that of one tree and one of its products during a period of a little over a decade. The tree is the white pine, the product shaved shingles, and the period 1868–1880.

Besides the white pine, five other trees have played stellar parts in the economic history of the valley. These are the walnut, the poplar, the oak, the hemlock (alias spruce, or spruce pine), and the chestnut, with a little maple thrown in for good measure. Latterly another tree has pushed its way to the front, not so much from obscurity as from disrepute and scorn. This is the pine known over the country as black pine, jack pine, old field pine, scrub pine, and bastard pine. It was not even esteemed for firewood, if anything else was available. In recent years, however, this renegade among the pines has attained a place in the economic world as pulpwood. Even in our small segment of the mountains it brought in a good many thousands of dollars during World War II.[2]

It was the walnut tree that for several generations supplied the wood for most of the furniture, fashioned by the community's own cabinet workmen. To sleep in a bed made of anything but walnut was to lower self-respect. Not until walnut became scarce and the railroad brought factory-made furniture of oak and other woods, at the same time extinguishing the craftsmanship of the woodworker, could a housewife with any measure of pride resign herself to the inevitable decay of the times. In my youth there were still a good many noble walnut trees to be seen. In our schoolyard, which was also our churchyard, stood as fine a group of walnut trees as the eye has ever beheld. I sometimes persuade myself that both religion and education have sadly declined since they were cut down.

Oaks of several varieties, especially the white oak (*Quercus alba*) and the red oak (*Quercus rubra*), were abundant in our forests. The red oaks were particularly prized as rail timber, and it required many trees to supply the miles of rail fences that were necessary on every farm of considerable size. The oaks that I have myself seen made into rails on our farm, if they were still standing, would fetch far more than the entire farm without them. White oak, a tougher wood and less easily split, was occasionally made into rails, but it was especially valued as wagon timber, although there was no substitute for tough hickory for axles. In my youth very little oak in our community was converted into lumber.

In those early days the timber made into lumber was chiefly poplar, for magnificent poplars grew in every cove and hollow, and poplar lumber was in great demand. It was soft and smooth and could be had in almost any desired length and width clear of knots. The largest of these poplars within easy reach of the river were particularly sought after to be made into canoes or dugouts. There was always need of one or more canoes wherever a ferry was maintained; besides, every family along the river must have a canoe for its own use. Trees as much as 4 feet in diameter at the stump abounded, and trees 5 or 6 feet in diameter, though not common when I can first remember, were still to be found here and there. I well remember one canoe that must have been made from a tree close to 6 feet in diameter, for its hold was something like 5 feet wide. It had been skillfully and beautifully carved, with an ornamental prow and stern, suggestive of the viking ships, pictures of which I had seen. Time came when, for the ferry at Big Creek, search had to be made far and wide for a poplar big enough to make even a passable canoe. A few years more and resort was of necessity to a canoe make of plank. Dugouts became only a memory.

What was almost universally called spruce, sometimes spruce pine, in our mountains, until the lumberman from up north came along and called it hemlock, is actually assigned by the botanists to the hemlock family, and the particular variety in our forests is termed by them *Tsuga canadensis*.[3] Submissively we yielded to the name hemlock for the lumber, but that same tree, old or young, when it adorns the grounds of our dwelling places, we will call spruce until it shall be gnawed down by the tooth of time. It was a late comer in the lumber business, for the grain is seldom straight, and the wood is coarse and brittle, qualities that limit its serviceability even for rough framing. In our locality its history is chiefly limited to its use for tanbark and pulpwood. When a tannery was established in our county, hemlock trees by the thousands were felled for their bark alone, and the trunks were left lying in the woods to rot. The demand for the wood in the pulp business did not come until the supply of trees in our valley had almost entirely disappeared. Deep in the mountains, however, there were, and still are, immense growths. At the present time many carloads of huge logs, mostly wind-shaken, are being shipped from Del Rio.

As an ornamental tree our Appalachian spruce (hemlock to you) plays an important role, although chiefly in its youth. Grown in the open its cone-like symmetry and beauty are surpassed by few if any of the genuine spruces. Properly trimmed it has its place among the ornamental shrubs and makes a beautiful evergreen hedge.[4] In our region it is the favorite Christmas tree. Not far outside our valley, close by the eastern end of the Great Smoky Mountains National Park, is an extensive nursery devoted chiefly to the growth of spruce from seedlings gathered by the thousands from the nearby forest.

The wood of the chestnut was not esteemed for any purpose except fence rails, and for that purpose only comparatively young trees were serviceable. In the localities where chestnut trees abounded, it was a common sight to see acres of them deadened preliminary to clearing the land, and many crops might be raised before all the dead trees were removed. Only after thousands upon thousands of these trees had been piled and burned or had rotted into the soil, did the call come for chestnut wood for its valuable acid. Chestnut acid wood has, nevertheless, for a good many years been the source of many a living in our mountains.

About 4 miles from the railroad, numerous long hollows converge and their several streams unite to make the one called Big Creek. Geographically speaking, the place is a miniature Pittsburgh. It required no superlative genius to fix upon this spot as a suitable location for a sawmill, and a sawmill outfit, including a newfangled circular saw, was among the earliest deliveries of the railroad. It was characteristic of East Tennesseans that the place should be immediately dubbed Slabtown.[5]

This sawmill was not the first in the valley, although it was, I believe, the first to use a circular saw. This type of saw was a comparatively new device, having come into use only about the middle of the nineteenth century. The earlier sawmills had been the gate or sash type, that is, a straight saw, somewhat like a hand saw, though power driven. The stark old skeleton of such a mill, roofless and with the straight-up-and-down saw in place, rusting away, was a familiar sight to me in my early boyhood. Its site, just below a natural waterfall, was only about a mile and a half from my home, on land once owned by my grandfather and now in my own possession. Every vestige of the old mill, except a rock wall, has disappeared, but a nearby barn has planks still bearing the marks of that old saw.

Naturally, with water power available almost anywhere along any of the creeks, Slabtown did not retain its monopoly of the sawing business. Before many years had passed another mill was erected in the upper reaches of one of the long gorges, and because of the outfit's prevailing color the place was called Blue Mill. And it is called that to this day, although the mill has long since gone, and only the sky above is blue.

Even with two mills busy, however, lumber making was bound to have been on a comparatively small scale. It was only when portable steam-driven mills came into use, as they did a few years later, that lumbering in our mountains attained really large proportions. It was almost at the same time that the shingle mill, a mill for sawing shingles, was introduced, bringing to a close the era of the shaved shingle. By that time, moreover, the growth of virgin white pine, which had been the basis of the shaved-shingle business, had been pretty well exhausted.

It was, in fact, the magnificent white pines that supplied the first impulse to the development of the business in shaved shingles in the region the moment the railroad gave access to a market for the product. Like hemlock, or spruce, essentially a tree of northern latitudes, the white pine ranges from Newfoundland to Manitoba, southward to Illinois, and follows the Appalachians throughout their extent. At the time of which I speak, the hills and mountains through which flow the multitudinous streams that race and ripple to their confluence in one or the other of the two Big Creeks for their ultimate deliverance to the French Broad River had a growth of white pine said to have been unsurpassed in all the southern Appalachians. Indeed, the white pine, although not without its preferences of soil and environment, was, and still is, one of the most characteristic trees indigenous to the region.

The white pine under favorable conditions grows to a height of 100 or 120 feet, with a diameter of 3 to 4 feet, or exceptionally to a height of 250 feet, with a diameter of 6 feet.[6] Whether our early shingle makers found trees of that exceptional size I do not know, but trees 150 feet high and 4 feet or more in diameter were not, I think, exceptional among the virgin stands, although it is doubtful whether trees of that size are now to be found anywhere in our valley.[7]

Scarcely any one, it seems, can write about the white pine without heaping the measure of enthusiasm to the brim. The great authority, Charles Sprague Sargent, asserted that the white pine is "the most valuable timber-tree of northeastern America." Then, being historically minded, he added:

"*Pinus Strobus* has played a conspicuous part in the material development of the United States and Canada. Great fleets of vessels and long railroads have been built to transport the lumber sawed from its mighty trunks; and men have grown rich by destroying it, building cities to supply the needs of their traffic, and seeing them languish as the forests disappear."[8]

Turning from such a scene of desolation to a forest still unslaughtered, Sargent exclaimed: "The most beautiful Pine-tree of eastern America, our sylvan scenery owes the peculiar charm which distinguished it from that of all other parts of the world to the wide-spreading dark green crowns of the White Pine, raised on stately shafts high above the level of the forest roof and breaking the monotony of its sky-line." Another writer has even offered the white pine a queenly crown: "Tall, stately, with massed lacy-looking foliage of slender, blue-green needles in graceful, airy tassels, the white pine is a very regal Queen of the Forest."[9]

To the mind of another enthusiast, one whose eyes have caught not only the grace and beauty of the individual tree but whose soul is attuned to the orchestral symphony that comes from a grove of white pines when the breezes are astir, the white pine is "the graceful goddess of the tree family." Sorrowfully he calls to mind that our pioneer ancestors, even as they strove to build a nation, "sacrificed" many of these noble trees for log cabins, barns, mills, stores, and other utilitarian purposes, taking comfort the while that "the queens among them were marked for the masts of great sailing ships."

It is, of course, the glory of the undesecrated, the unspoiled forest that inspires this same writer's song of praise:

> The white pines wear a beautiful dress of delicate needles arranged in groups of five. Their slender branches sweep out horizontally, with tips that often curve upward. The needles have small but distinct whitish lines on the lower surfaces. The imbricated, brownish cones are things of beauty from time of formation until the scales obey Nature's law and open their hearts, that the winged seeds may sail away on currents of air.
>
> The goddess of the trees sings a constant song among her branches. When the breezes are strong, her soft aria is rich and full. There are those who think the pine is plaintive and melancholy; perhaps that is because she prefers gentleness and quietness in a world that's noisy and blatant. As the green-clothed branches sway and move, they seem to be talking among themselves; sometimes almost whispering; again, their conversation is animated and cheerful. The tall pines know the cycle of earth's seasons. Through winter blizzards, spring rains, summer heat and the frosty starlight of autumn they live in poise and graciousness. The pines stand calmly and speak gently in a world where men make cacophony and confusion.[10]

Apart from the crowded forest, the white pine, like the Appalachian hemlock, has long played an important part in ornamental landscaping, although it can scarcely rival the youthful spruce for beauty and symmetry.

The denizens of our hills were, however, little concerned with the beauty of the white pine, whether in the deep forest or in the front yard, and probably not at all with the music of her wind-swept branches. Some of them had, no doubt, heard of the use of the tall trees for masts, but probably not one of them had ever looked upon the sea or beheld a ship at sail.[11] To them the big tree meant so many feet of lumber or so many shingles, in exchange for which they might obtain the necessities and comforts of life.

For the people of our valley, the years following the Civil War were very hard. For most of them the necessities were scant and comforts were scantier. The majority of them were barely able to produce on their small farms of coves and hillsides sufficient corn for their bread and possibly for fattening a hog or two, although for the latter purpose the mast of the woods furnished a very important part. Corn bread and bacon, particularly in winter, constituted their principal diet. Wheat bread was everywhere a luxury; for one thing, because they could not grow sufficient wheat for their support, and, for another, because, if their supply of bread ran short, one day's work in the valley would earn them a bushel of corn, whereas it required two to earn a bushel of wheat.

These, then, were the fundamentals of the shaved-shingle business: the abundant trees, the universal needs, and the sudden opening of a market. But there was another potent factor in spurring shingle making into immediate and almost universal activity. The business called for little capital. The necessary tools were the ax, the saw, the frow, the mallet, the drawing knife, and auger. Almost anybody could acquire these. Two essentials, not difficult to make, completed the equipment: a shaving horse and a press.

The shaving horse was a slab of timber, usually hewn out, about 8 feet long, 8 inches wide, and 4 inches thick, with 2 short legs at one end and 2 longer ones at the other, giving the horse, or bench, a slope that greatly facilitated the use of the drawing knife. Through a mortise near the higher end of the bench ran a lever, hinged on a wooden pin and having at the upper end a square-chinned knob for gripping the board, while attached to the lower was a pedal by means of which the workman's foot applied the necessary power for holding the board in place. The workman sat astride the shaving horse and, for his own comfort and for the protection of his trousers, he made himself a sort of saddle, or padded seat, like as not a piece of old quilt, topped with a sheepskin.

The press for bunching the shingles consisted of a frame, essentially a box with one end open, in which the shingles were laid, thin ends overlapping, until the required number of layers for a bunch had been laid. By means of a hand lever the bunch was compressed until it could be securely clamped. The clamp consisted of two small sticks of timber, 2 or 3 inches in diameter, one at the bottom, the other at the top of the bunch, the two being held together by smaller sticks, like the rungs of a chair. With the invasion of the shingle mill a different type of compress was introduced, one that made bunching a much easier process. The compression was by means of a wheel and screw.

Two standard widths of sawed shingles, the only type of wooden shingle known to many people of this generation, have prevailed in different localities, the 4-inch and the 5-inch. In our locality, so far as I recall, only the 4-inch sawed shingle was ever made. The shaved shingle, on the other hand, though it was counted by inches, might be of any width from 2 to 12 inches. Indeed many a shingle maker seemed to take pride in making his shingles as wide as practicable, and all of them liked to have exceptionally wide shingles with which to dress the outside of their bunches—much as the apple packer selects his finest apples for the top layer of his barrel or basket. In short, the shingle maker and his drawing knife were the veritable arbiters of the shingle's format; accordingly, as in every handicraft, the product bore the impress of the artisan's individuality.

In the matter of length there could not of course be the same freedom of choice. A roof made of shingles of irregular width might, according to some tastes, be lacking in harmony, but, if the shingles were properly made and well laid, only a straight-laced mind and a sour soul could find fault with it. Lengths, however, must be uniform. Three standard lengths have prevailed, 16, 18, and 20 inches. Our shingles, both shaved and sawed, were uniformly 18-inches long.

Sawed shingles were usually put up in bunches of 250; which is to say, 25 courses, each course being 10 shingles with overlapping ends. Latterly they have been marketed to some extent in smaller bundles. Shaved shingles, on the other hand, were almost invariably put up in bunches of 500, the count, as I have indicated, being by inches and not by individual shingles. Only rarely were they to be seen in so-called quarter bunches. Just why our shingle makers should have made their bunches so large is a question I am unable to answer. They were so heavy that two men were required to lift them on and off the wagons and to load them into railroad cars.

Just who, if any one in particular, is to be credited with having initiated the shingle business on so extensive a scale, is another thing that history will probably never tell us.[12] Very likely it was the storekeepers, my father, for one, who found the market. What we do know is that shingle making is a very old handicraft, maybe antedating Noah's ark, and that shaved shingles on a small scale for local use had been made in our settlement since the early days. We also know that, in that unspoiled era, our woods were fairly asquirm with handicraftsmen of many kinds.

The first stage of shingle making is, of course, felling the tree, which in those days was normally done with the ax alone. The white pine, as it grows in the forest, tends to drop its lower limbs, with the result that, when the bark of the tree is removed, belts of knots, often very small, are revealed all along the trunk of the tree. These belts of knots must be sawed out as it is only between them that a clear shingle may be obtained. To the modern lumberman this is a great waste of timber, and even the maker of sawed shingles paid little regard to the knots.

It was only in sawing the tree into blocks that the shingle maker needed assistance, that is, some one to pull the other end of the crosscut saw. Even that was not absolutely necessary, for a man could hang his hat on the other end of the saw to balance it and still do a pretty good job of sawing.

Next, with frow and mallet, the blocks were rived into boards of a thickness to make a shingle a good half inch at the butt.[13] Shingles of less thickness were sometimes made, but they were not in good repute. With a pile of boards beside him, the shingle maker seized his drawing knife, bestrode his wooden steed, and went proudly and joyfully to work.

No one who has ever watched a shingle maker shaving a shingle can doubt that he takes a genuine joy in his work. The wood is straight grained, soft, and light, qualities that make white pine one of the most prized woods for interior finishing. Its lightness in particular has created the tremendous demand during the recent war for white pine for boxing and crating. When to these qualities is added another quality, that of durability, white pine becomes a superb wood for shingles. As evidence of the durability of the shaved shingle made from virgin white pine, this chronicler offers a single instance. Our house was covered with such shingles in 1874. Forty years later the roof was still perfectly good so far as its main purpose was concerned; only the exposed butts of the shingles had become weathered and frayed. Second-growth white pine was said to be not so durable. Maybe some dendrologist can explain the reason.

As for the softness of the wood, there was never a man in all that country with a sharp pocketknife who did not love just to whittle a white-pine shingle. To see a man sitting on a nail keg on the store porch or beside the stove inside the store whittling a white-pine shingle was to see a man who, for the time being at least, was in love with life. Or, if you care to go back into the mountains for evidence, to see a man sitting on his own doorstep calmly shaving a shingle while waiting for the doctor to arrive, or the baby, was to learn what power for sweetness as well as for light lay in a sliver of white-pine wood.

There was a certain preacher, so the story goes, who composed his sermons while whittling a shingle; and so powerful was his oratory that he could shake sinners out of their shoes and make them feel that they were hair-hung and breeze-shaken over the pit; but, when white-pine shingles were no longer to be had, he lost in great measure his power to convict and convince. In another, but closely related domain, the shingle played its part in behalf of righteousness and the good life. Most parents kept one or more neatly shaped paddles (in or about the same repository where they kept the bottles of paregoric and castor oil) expressly for the promotion of family discipline. Who of our community brought up in the era of the white-pine shingle does not have a sharply etched memory of such a paddle?

The shingle maker, as he drew his sharp drawing knife through the soft wood and watched the shavings gracefully curve and fall at his feet, knew in his soul what it was to enjoy life, liberty, and the pursuit of happiness. Gentle thoughts floated down to him from where the top of the tree used to be, or from far beyond, and, though he might not be a preacher or a speaker, or even a plain argufier, he felt the inspiration to expound and exhort. At least he could, and often did, compose the soft answer that turneth away the aggravating wrath of a wifely scolding. Indeed it is averred that the most irascible of tempers, given a sharp knife and a white-pine shingle, became subdued to the gentleness of a zephyr.

As a craftsman the shingle maker had to make a good shingle. However varied the width, the shingles must be of uniform thickness at the butt, must be shaved on both sides to a smooth even finish, and must be tapered evenly to the sixteenth of an inch at the other end. The edges likewise must be straight and true. A story has come out of the Maine woods that a good shingle shaver could toss a shingle into the air and shave another before that one came down.[14] That kind of a shingle, with a lick and a promise, might have been good enough for Maine, but our folks would not have used it for anything but a chicken house, and even then they would have felt that they owed an apology to the chickens.

My own first introduction to the shingle business was at almost the identical spot at which I had first encountered the new railroad. Our house was about half a mile from the Big Creek depot and hard by the road over which all traffic from up the valley and out of the mountains had to pass. About a mile above us branch roads led off to the west and the south, and 3 or 4 miles farther up the creek the road branched every which way. The road along the creekside was as rocky a road as it was ever the lot of wagon wheels to roll over. In fact, the soil of those creek bottoms is as tightly packed with boulders large and small as a primeval glacier and the age-long wash of waters could pack it. The rumble of one wagon over that road could be heard for a mile or more; the rumble of a dozen was like the approaching battle of Waterloo.

Not infrequently, from whatever part of the forest region they came, a dozen, or maybe two dozen or more, wagons loaded with shingles came lumbering and rumbling by our house one right after another. It was just such a rumble that one morning caught the ears of the small boy playing in the back yard. Increasing in intensity as it drew nearer, the noise became more than the chugging of heavy wagons over a rocky and uneven road. There were overtones of harsh voices giving commands to the oxen that drew the loads. The small boy scampered to the roadside to peer through the crack of the fence.

The progress of a yoke of oxen from one place to another, when drawing a load, is notoriously slow. I have sometimes thought in later life that they must put the snail to shame. Away up the road I could see them coming, raising dust and making a lot of noise, and, after a long time, there was one wagon and team, with their big load of shingles, right there before my eyes, while behind it as far as I could see came other wagons, all drawn by yokes of oxen. What a wonderful sight it was! Never in after years did I look upon a parade of elephants, zebras, camels, and other strange beasts with a greater thrill, although I could scarcely "hear my ears" for the jumble of noises, which now included the creaking of wheels on ungreased axels and the straining of the big bunches of shingles on the hickory withes with which they were tied to one another and to the wagon.

Some of the drivers, as they passed, said "Howdy, Bud," and some of them winked at me. And probably the next breath would be used in saying things to the oxen—like as not in monosyllabic explosives. As the days and weeks went by I gathered in a lot of vigorous old Elizabethan English through that crack in the fence, words that I would never have learned from either Smith's or Pineo's grammar, or even from Webster's school dictionary.

It was not just oxen under a yoke and pulling a wagon that stirred me to gaze and to wonder. It was those long caravans of oxen under the yoke straining at their heavy loads of shingles, sometimes with women and children scrooched on top of them, and the rough bearded drivers, raucously calling their commands to the oxen, or jawing back and forth to one another, that gave me a never-ending thrill.

One day when, from my private box in the grandstand, I was watching a train of wagons go by, I saw a sight that to me was almost as astounding as if I had beheld an elephant or a camel drawing an oriental chariot. Trailing along behind the ox teams, with their heavy creaking wagons, was a single ox, a little muley ox, a scrubby runt of a thing that scarcely looked as if he belonged to the cattle breed. I had seen a muley before, for once there had been one on our farm, though not for long. No self-respecting farmer would suffer a muley, the most despised of the cattle kind, to remain on his premises any longer than might be necessary to beef him, to sell him, or to give him away. The horned cattle seemed to feel the same way about it. To be hornless was not only a disgrace but was often regarded by the herd as a capital offense. If, therefore, the farmer himself failed to remove the muley to a safe place, that abominated scrub, that low-bred outcast, was likely to be eliminated by a well-directed thrust of a contemptuous horn. Yet right there before my eyes was one of these outcasts, looking for all the world as if he were ashamed to be seen in the society of respectable oxen.

What was also astonishing to my eyes, the muley did not wear a yoke but was harnessed somewhat after the manner of a horse—as nearly as could be, considering the way he was made; and he was drawing a small wagon, the least wagon by far that I had ever seen on the road, one that even to my young eyes appeared to have been very crudely made. Moreover, on the wagon were two quarter-bunches of shingles, bunches only half the size of those on the big wagons. Ox, wagon, load, and all were on a diminutive scale. Even the driver, as the picture now rises before me, was but a runt of a man. Logic and the fitness of things required that he should be; therefore, to every slithering skepticism respecting the correctness of my memory, I say, avaunt! In these latter days, when some of the muley tribe have become "high-caste" cattle, taking their places amongst the aristocracy of the bovine race, and the nice smooth horn in which the farmer once took such pride has itself come under condemnation, I sometimes wonder whether the muley of that earlier generation, if he could have envisioned this transformation, would not have faced his frowning world with confidence and courage.

The shingle makers sold their shingles to the Big Creek storekeepers and took in exchange such goods as they desired or were obtainable. Cash transactions were almost unknown. Money was so scarce that even the fairly well-to-do often had difficulty in paying their taxes. Almost the entire business of the stores was done by barter. The entire value of the shingles might be taken up at once, or credit might be entered on the store's books, purchases to be made from time to time as desired. Perhaps oftener than otherwise it was the other way about. The shingle maker purchased on credit and later paid the account in shingles, sometimes supplemented by eggs, feathers, and chickens.

A few years ago a fire destroyed a set of store accounts covering fifty or sixty years. Among those lost books was one of exceptional character. One of those storekeepers, Swan L. Burnett, a generous soul, gave credit over a long period to a good many people from whom he had little or no expectation of ever receiving pay, although every now and then, as he has told me, he had occasion to draw the book forth from its hiding place in his safe to enter an unexpected payment. It was labeled the "S. A. Book," those being the initial letters of two short Anglo-Saxon words, customarily used in our neck of the woods to designate a worthless person.

The storekeepers found good markets in towns and cities within reach for all the shingles that the country could furnish. Knoxville was, naturally, one of the principal markets, although many carloads went to Chattanooga and beyond. In fact, Chattanooga once figured in an episode that juts out like a rugged promontory in the story of Big Creek and its shingle business.

For a long time freight rates for carload shipments were specific, without regard to the size of the car. Accordingly the bigger the car the more shingles could be shipped for a given sum. At first that made little difference, as the standard car had a capacity of only 20,000 pounds. Before long, however, cars carrying 30,000, and a little later, 40,000 pounds, came into use. The introduction of cars having a 60,000-pound capacity came later.

Suddenly my kinsman, Swan L. Burnett, began to find that deductions were being taken from the proceeds of his shipments on account of extra freight charges for excessive weight. The railroad company, having fixed the maximum carload, was weighing cars in Chattanooga, a hitherto unheard-of practice. Thereupon my kinsman decided to utilize the river for transportation. The one obstacle was the falls, 5 miles down the river, but he convinced himself that a raft could be constructed which, under proper guidance, could be made to shoot the principal channel successfully. The raft was built accordingly and loaded with shingles, the equivalent of several carloads, a crew of men signed on, and a certain Sunday morning was set for the launching.

The crew numbered, as I remember, some eight or ten men. I distinctly recall that the captain was William ("Bill") Moore, a hustling lumberman, who lived up the creek a few miles. My friend, J. W. D. Stokely, has supplied the names of five others of the crew: William Cannon Bryan,[15] a neighbor of Moore, Daniel Evans, William Murphy, Millard Robinson, and Scott Westall, all dwellers in the hill country. The names of the others appear to have been lost beyond recovery. Whether there was a first mate, second mate, or bos'n I know not.

The launching was on a Sabbath morning and at about the hour for services in the nearby church. There were, as may well be imagined, those who, because of this profanation, were inclined to prophesy the failure of the expedition, if not some dire disaster. But they were not blatant about it, and the local church remained absolutely empty. There was plenty of piety in our community for all practical purposes, but our folks were not prone toward the pietistical. The assemblage that gathered on the riverbank would have filled three churches to capacity and then spilled over. Everybody who lived at Dry Fork or Slabtown was there, for most of the crew came from up that way, and their families and friends had to bid their brave men good-bye as they departed on their long and hazardous journey. In fact, all up and down the river and the two big creeks and their forks, prongs, and branches as well, people were obedient to the urge to look upon one of the rarest sights ever offered them. That journey through treacherous waters to far-away Chattanooga was as dramatic, as romantic, as was the voyage of a clipper ship from Old Salem to China.

At length the raft was pushed form the shore and began to float gently down the stream. From the shore many voices shouted "Good-bye, Bill!" "Good-bye, Dan!"—and all the rest of them—and hands and hats were waved in farewell. From the raft came crisp good-byes and hurried glances toward their folks, but most of the crew were too deeply absorbed in their immediate tasks even to turn their faces toward the shore. Watching the scene were women with anxious faces. Even as a small boy, to whom the whole thing was only a show, though a rare one, I sensed that anxiety. For a few minutes the raft floated smoothly as the men aboard pushed and guided it with poles. Then suddenly it stopped. It had stuck on a rock bar or shoal. Evidently the heavily loaded raft drew more water than had been expected, for the existence of the shoal was well known and had figured in all the calculations. The raftsmen tried with might and main to push the raft farther out into the river where the water was deeper, but in vain. Thereupon the captain gave a command, and every member of the crew, including the captain himself, leaped into the river. Not being even fresh-water tars, not one of the crew, I am sure, responded with an "aye, aye, sir," but they did obey without a moment's hesitation. They shoved their poles under the raft where it had grounded and lifted with might and main. Again and again they tried, pausing now and then to get their wind, but nothing happened except that one end of the raft settled more and more firmly on the river bottom, while the other sank deeper and deeper into the water. They began to try first one device and then another. Probably not one of them had ever had an hour's experience in rafting; and being up-creekers probably none of them had had much, if any, experience with a ferryboat. From what I saw of rafting many years later on the Kentucky River, I am convinced that a crew of experienced Kentucky River raftsmen would have gotten that raft off the shoal or more likely would never have grounded it in the first place.

All day long, nevertheless, the raftsmen did not relax their efforts, except for intervals of needed rest. At noon the crowd on the shore thinned out somewhat but came flocking back after hurried dinners, although for the majority dinner was too far away. The present chronicler did not have far to go to gulp down some sustenance but speedily trotted back to the riverbank and the crowd of onlookers. All through the afternoon the struggle went on. Meanwhile distant dwellers, by ones and twos and threes, took their reluctant departures. About sundown, entirely unconscious of the fact that I was destined to become the sole historian of the affair but acutely conscious of a duty to bring up the cows, I painfully dragged myself away. I yearned mightily to see that raft go floating freely and smoothly on the slow current until it disappeared in the bend of the river. But even if it should be loosened from the shoal before dark, there was not the least likelihood that the ticklish plunge over the falls would be risked until daylight.

Early the next morning I hastened back to the scene. The captain and his crew had departed, the crowd had melted away, and only one or two other early risers had come to take a look. One end of the raft still rested firmly where it had grounded on the troublesome shoal, while the other end appeared also to have sunk to the bottom of the river, and what might be called the after deck of the raft was awash. Whether the author of the scheme had passed the night tossing on a bed of chagrin I could not know. He was not given to weeping and wailing, but I have no question whatever that at that moment he was seeking what comfort he might from a gnashing of teeth.

A few days later a crew set to work to tote the shingles back to shore. It was no small task, for the toters had to wade a distance of 30 or 40 yards through water up to their waists. When, after a few weeks, the shingles had sufficiently dried, they were loaded aboard cars and shipped. The railroad got its extra freight money after all, and I imagine some of the railroad people got a lot of fun out of the incident. As for the shipper, a man never wont to harbor gloom or to nurse his wrath to keep it warm, he too, in due time, like the vigilance committee that apologized to the widow for hanging her husband by mistake, freely acknowledged that the joke was on him. Although I am not able to date this incident, I am confident that it was after the shingle mill had pretty well driven the shingle shaver out of business.

The first shingle mill in the community was set up at Slabtown about 1880 by a man named John Marshall, an Englishman by birth. He had, I believe, lived in Massachusetts for a time and then at Knoxville, but he finally found his way into our valley and went into the lumber business. Traditions of Marshall's career in our midst still linger in the valley. Primarily a lumberman, he occasionally nevertheless occupied a pulpit, although whether licensed thereunto by any church I am unable to declare. His bent, as I recall, lay in the direction of exhorting rather than expounding.

Marshall's shingle mill at Slabtown was long operated by Charles S. Goodnough. A little later one was set up farther back in the mountains, at the place which came to be called Blue Mill. The latter was operated by L. D. Goodnough, brother of Charles S. Descendants of the Goodnoughs still live there. These shingle mills quickly doomed the shaved-shingle business. The shingle mill was to shingle shaving what the threshing machine was to the old-time flail on the barn floor.

By that time the better of the virgin white pines had been used up, so maybe, after all, the sawing of shingles meant progress. Sawed shingles, nevertheless, did not compare with shaved shingles in serviceability. The timber now available was inferior in quality, and little or no effort was made at the shingle mill to eliminate knots. A small knot at the thin end of a shingle made little or no difference but any kind of knot at the end exposed to the weather might be fatal to a roof. A consequence was that the merchants had to break down a large proportion of the bunches of shingles taken in trade, sort out the defective ones, and rebunch those that were merchantable.

All in all, the business in sawed shingles flourished for a quarter of a century; then that too dwindled away. All the white pine that was fit for shingles had been used up, and it would be another generation before a new growth was ready for use. Much of this second growth has in recent years been converted into lumber, but few, if any, trees have attained the size or maintained the quality that the early shingle shavers found in such abundance and attacked so eagerly. Today, in the region where shingles were once the main source of livelihood, wooden shingles are a thing of the past. True, a good many roofs in the valley and in the hills roundabout still carry covers of wooden shingles, but the shingles are invisible, hidden beneath sheets of galvanized iron, or maybe of asphalt. As old Sam Singletree expressed it to me last summer: "This country used to live on shingles. We et shingles for breakfast, shingles for dinner, and shingles for supper; and in betwixt and between we whittled 'em, jist to pass the time. Now you couldn't find a shingle on all Big Creek, either to pass away the time a-whittlin', or to paddle a young'un."

Notes

1. For a summary of the evidence see this writer's article, "The Railroad Comes to Big Creek," Railway and Locomotive Historical Society, *Bulletin*, October 1946, which also provides a sort of crow's-eye view of the valley of Big Creek on the French Broad River.

2. The article cited in note 1 includes (note 7) some figures on outgoing shipments and railroad freight earnings at Del Rio in a recent period. During the recent war some $65,000 in war bonds were purchased by the patrons of the Del Rio post office, while an amount, probably in excess of that figure, was withheld from salaries of local citizens. A man who hauls acid wood out of the mountains purchased $8,000 worth. The post office of Del Rio is the only one in Cocke County that received the following citation: "For Patriotic Cooperation Rendered in Behalf of the War Finance Program This Citation Is Awarded the Patrons of Del Rio, Tenn., Post Office. Given under My Hand and Seal the 22 Day of Jan. 1945. Henry Morgenthau, Jr." The first plaque to be placed on a piece of

war material (a quarter-ton truck) in the State of Tennessee was from Del Rio. It bears the inscription: "Presented to the U.S. Army by the Citizens of Del Rio." These facts were furnished by Miss Nannie F. Jones, postmaster of Del Rio.

3. See Charles Sprague Sargent, *The Silva of North America,* 12:63–68 (Boston and New York, 1898), and *Manual of the Trees of North America,* 43–44 (Boston and New York, 1933).

4. According to ibid., 65, *Tsuga canadensis* has been a favorite ornament in the parks and gardens of the United States and Europe for a century and a half. As early as 1691, one of the trees, the gift of John Banister of Virginia, was growing in the London gardens of Bishop Compton. In beauty and stately grace, remarked Sargent, *Tsuga canadensis* "has no rival among the inhabitants of the gardens of the northern United States, when, with its long lower branches sweeping the lawn, it rises into a great pyramid dark and sombre in winter and light in early summer, with the tender yellow tones of its drooping branchlets and vernal foliage." Ibid., 66.

5. It was also characteristic of the folks roundabout that, when, in the course of years, Slabtown was by way of becoming a metropolis and took steps to have itself constituted a post office in its own right, the residents of the vicinage cast about for a name more refined than Slabtown, a name less indicative of the rough and raw. What more appropriate than to honor the pioneer, and still dominating, family of Goodnough? The head of that family was, however, a modest man and a man of commendable pride. To call it Goodnough was to tax everybody's credulity, including his own. "Just call it Nough," said he. And Nough it became, and Nough it remained, until rural free delivery wiped it off the postal map. In the years that have followed old Slabtown has shouldered its way back to the front and horned Nough into the ditch, from which it will probably never be able to scramble.

6. Sargent, *The Silva of North America,* 11:17, and *Manual of the Trees of North America,* 3–4.

7. The white pine grows taller in the forest than it does in the open. Most of the exceptionally tall white pines in our woods have drawn the lightning and so have perished. A fair example of what a white pine will do within a lifetime such as my own is one that was planted in our front yard in 1875 and died in 1943. As nearly as can now be determined, its height was about 110 feet and the diameter of the stump 3 feet 4–1/2 inches. A companion tree of approximately the same size continues to flourish 30 feet away.

8. *The Silva of North America,* 11:21.

9. Charlotte Hilton Green, *The Trees of the South,* 469 (Chapel Hill, 1939).

10. Quoted from an editorial in the *New York Times,* Jan. 29, 1945, with the gracious permission of Charles Merz. See also the editorial, "Green Ladies," in Washington, D.C., *Sunday Star,* Apr. 14, 1946.

11. George William Huntley, Jr. *A Story of the Sinnamahone* (Williamsport, Pa., Williamsport Printing and Binding Co., 1936) is characterized in its preface as "Unwritten history of the old white pine days on the Sinnamahoning from 1865 to 1885."

12. I have an impelling desire to preserve here for posterity—even though posterity may not care a knotty sawed shingle for the gift—the names of some of the principal makers of shaved shingles which have been supplied by my fellow pilgrim J. W. D. Stokely. He knew personally most, if not all, of the men here named, and I knew several of them. To

give the list an alphabetical order, there was the Arrowood family, James and his three sons, W. M., John, and Henry; Ben, Ira, and Nige Ball; Mordecai Bible; Adam, Royal, Matthew, John, and Solomon Black; Hugh Clark; William, Robert, and Nathan Davis; Benjamin, James, John, Burt, and Isaac Ford; Isaac, Dennis, and William Green, with Isaac's five sons, James, W. M. Reuben, Milburn, and John; Andrew and Calvin Holt; Wyatt, John, Wiley, and William Jones; David and Lee Knight; John, James, Gooler, William, and Green Rose; Abijah and Thomas Simmons; William, Cobb, Joel, Louis, and Lawson Smith; George Sparks; Edward and Reuben Teague. Most of these men resided in what is known as the Grassy Fork settlement.

Concerning these men Stokely further remarks that most of them had a useful trade. The Smiths, for instance, were blacksmiths and also gunsmiths. The Simmonses were coopers and made such things as water kegs, washtubs, kraut stands, and barrels. The Fords manufactured looms, spinning wheels, and corded bedsteads, a type of bedstead that has gone almost entirely out of use. The Teagues were also skilled woodworkers, their products including such things as bread trays, butter bowls, and measures of various sizes. In short, it was a community of skilled artisans.

W. V. Jones, lord of many acres at the head of the valley, believes that the Goodnough brothers, Charles S. and L. D., who came from the white-pine region of Pennsylvania about 1868, started the shaved-shingle business in our valley.

13. In short, all the shingle maker has thus far done is to make boards, essentially as would be done if they were intended to go directly on a roof without benefit of drawing knife. Boards (or "shakes" as they are called in some localities), usually made of oak, were still much used in our country, even in the era of the shaved shingle. But our folks would have been ashamed to call a board a shingle, as some people elsewhere seem to do. Says Stanley F. Horn, in *This Fascinating Lumber Business*, 177–78 (Indianapolis, Bobbs Merrill Co., 1943): "To a limited extent throughout the South there is a local use of hand-split hardwood shingles (locally called 'boards') usually made from some species of oak, preferably the *Quercus acumuniata*, which goes by the common name of shingle oak because of its adaptability to this use. The total hand-rived production is small, and it is one of the last remaining vestiges of the old handicraft processes." Here and there in East Tennessee one may still see an old roof of oak boards, with their ends cupped up, reminding one forcibly of Friesland ("Frizzly") chickens.

14. Richard G. Wood, *A History of Lumbering in Maine*, 1820–1861, p. 174 (Orono, 1935), mentions that the shingle maker was called a "shingle weaver." Others, however, speak of the term as applied to the process of bunching or bundling, the "shingle-weaver" being the person who bunches the shingles. The term was never used in our country. See also James Elliott Defebaugh, *History of the Lumber Industry of America*, 2:89 (Chicago, 1907).

15. Of the crew Bryan was the only one who subsequently "made history," and that was not naval history. He had a post office named for him. You would never guess its name, and even when I tell you it was Punkton you would never guess why. The tale is of the following tenor. The man carried on his shoulders a very large round head, from which most of the hair had disappeared in his early manhood. "Punkin Head," somebody jibed, whereupon everybody began to call him "Bill Punk," a name that he was soon taking in his stride, without grumbling, if not with pride. Time came when a post office was to be set up in Punk's community, and the Post Office Department in Washington called upon the postmaster at Big Creek to recommend a name for it. The postmaster who happened to be the same Swan L. Burnett who had fathered the project of rafting shingles to

Chattanooga, recommended Punkton. Thus it was that Bryan left his footprints on the sands of time. To be sure, he made other small segments of local history, but it is not now meet to record them.

W. V. Jones thinks that Charles S. and L. D. Goodnough built the raft, though they did not sign on for the voyage.

IV

**Rethinking Usages:
The Age of Functional Studies**

17

Ordeal by Serpents, Fire and Strychnine: A Study of Some Provocative Psychosomatic Phenomena

Berthold E. Schwarz

Perhaps because many of the early observers of Appalachia, such as John C. Campbell, came from church backgrounds the subject of traditional religious practices in the region has received considerable attention. Much of the work has involved the so-called folk religions, by which is meant fundamentalist, literalist churches featuring highly emotional services. That view is misleading because all churches have elements of folk tradition in their worship practices and beliefs. Thus, there is folk religion but not specific denominations that are folk religions *per se*. Another reason for the appeal of the "folk churches" is that they are simply more exotic to the observers than the conventional denominations. Until recently, a majority of those commenting on the subject have been from outside the region and inclined to think of Appalachia as exotic *per se*, so they have sought what they considered most colorful, sometimes finding it in churches whose beliefs and practices are most distant from their own.

One group that has aroused special interest, but few studies, is that of the various fundamentalist churches practicing snake handling, drinking of poisons, and ordeals by fire as demonstrations of their faith. In the following essay by psychiatrist Berthold E. Schwarz (1924–) an attempt is made to account for the relative lack of fatal or ill effects from the dangerous acts performed by believers. Schwarz tries to determine the rational explanations, concluding that, in essence, the church's practitioners are made immune, or nearly so, by a degree of religious ecstasy they reach while engaging in possibly fatal acts. He does, however, overlook some purely physical explanations of the phenomena he describes. For example, in the discussion about fire handling it should be noted that smearing the hands and feet with fuel oil would make them much less likely to ignite when held over a flame than dry hands and feet put "in the midst of the flames." Because of vaporization the fuel oil would act as a protective coat until by convection and diffusion it became combustible.

For further information on the snake-handling cult see Keith Kerman, "Rattlesnake

Reprinted from *Psychiatric Quarterly* 34 (July 1960): 405–29.

Religion," in Lealon N. Jones, *Eve's Stepchildren: A Collection of Folk Americana* (Caldwell, Idaho: The Caxton Printers Ltd., 1942), pp. 93–102; for one anthropologist's approach to the topic see Weston La Barre, *They Shall Take Up Serpents: Psychology of the Southern Snake-Handling Cult* (New York: Schocken Books, 1969; revision of a work originally issued in 1962); and for one folklorist's approach to the topic see Ellen J. Stekert, "The Snake-Handling Sect of Harlan County, Kentucky," *Southern Folklore Quarterly* 27 (December 1963): 316–22. There are also at least four films dealing with the topic: *The Holy Ghost People* (Producer Blair Boyd—1968); *They Shall Take Up Serpents* (Producer Tennessee Arts Commission—1972); *The People Who Take Up Serpents* (Producer Gretchen Robinson—1974); and *They Shall Take Up Serpents* (Producer Scott Siegler/WKYC-TV, Cleveland, Ohio—1974).

For more on Appalachian religious beliefs and practices see W. D. Weatherford and Earl D. C. Brewer, *Life and Religion in Southern Appalachia* (New York: Friendship Press, Inc., 1962); Earl D. C. Brewer, "Religion and the Churches," in Thomas R. Ford, *The Southern Appalachian Region: A Survey* (Lexington: University of Kentucky Press, 1967; reprint of a work originally issued in 1962), pp. 201–18; and Loyal Jones, "Studying Mountain Religion," *Appalachian Journal* 5 (Autumn 1977): 125–30.

* * *

The Free Pentacostal Holiness Church is a religious sect* located in the mountainous, rural regions of eastern Kentucky, Tennessee and parts of Virginia and North Carolina. The basic tenets of their beliefs conform to fundamentalist, literal interpretations of the Bible. Their members, who are mostly farmers and coal miners, are descendants of the early English and Scotch-Irish colonists, and have strait-laced Calvinist backgrounds and traditions. Their speech is provincial and includes many words and expressions that Shakespeare used and that are found in the King James version of the Bible. Few have had formal education extending beyond elementary school. They are hardy people, who come from large families, and whose life histories illustrate a fierce struggle with the ravages of nature, disease and often extreme difficulties of earning a living. Their mountain culture is a patriarchy. The men work, hunt, and frequently go on their evangelical missions, while the women stay in the background and keep busy in their homes, with cooking, cleaning and attending to the needs of their large families. Many of the "Saints"** had childhoods where one or both of their parents, siblings or other relatives died of disease, or in mining accidents or "shooting matches." Not a few have had, or have, pulmonary tuberculosis. Some

---

*Subsequently referred to as Holiness in this paper.
**"Saints" is a term used to denote those consecrated church members who have extraordinary faith and gifts. In some respects they may be considered to be "ministers."

of the leading saints had crimes of violence, bootlegging, whoremongering and other "sins" in their backgrounds before they were "saved."

Most of the members do not attend motion pictures, and they abstain from alcohol, coffee, tea, tobacco, drugs and even soda pop. They battle temptation and sin with the certain knowledge of an approaching judgment day, the imminent second coming of the Messiah, and the end of the world. The realities of Satan, of sin, and of the vivid fire and brimstone of Hell strike terror in their hearts. Their faith tolerates no adultery, delinquency, lying or other forms of "backsliding." A member dedicates his whole life to "the living faith." Such are the rigors of this faith, however, that it is the exception when a member has all or even part of his family—his spouse, children, parents or siblings—as fellow-worshipers. Although the Holiness brethren attempt to convert and save souls, they use persuasion, rather than the "shooting-match approach."

It is customary for them to attend church at least two nights a week, and frequently every night. Interpreting various Biblical passages as direct commands of God, the Holiness members severely test their faith and identification with Biblical personages through "miracles," or ordeals by serpents, fire and strychnine. In this way, it can be conjectured, their previous impulses to "sin" are suppressed and repressed, while at the same time the grim threats and realities of everyday living are denied and mastered. By these highly symbolic ordeals, there is also a triumph over feelings of helplessness, and in the fierce struggle with nature and the often calloused, persecuting, cognitive outside world. The successful ordeal, spectacularly dramatized before their peers and before "unbelievers," becomes an acceptable outlet, and a substitute for what was often past violent, antisocial behavior. The ordeals constitute narrow escapes from torture and death. The proof and expiations afforded by the "miracles" justify the faith that there will be rewards in Heaven for the suffering and for sacrifices on earth. With the intense concentration of all their individual and collective energies epitomized in the ordeals, the Holiness people see themselves as "the [true] children of God"; and the great threat of life, bodily death, is transposed into an eternal spiritual existence. The constant repetition of this theme in their revivals protects them from doubt ("backsliding"), but, like an obsessive mechanism, it generates further need for the reassurance and propitiation of their ambivalently loved and feared Father. As an ancient religious practice of great affective force, the ordeals might then portray in microcosm all the vicissitudes of man's relationship to his fellow-man and his mystical awe of the infinite macrocosm. Other intermittent phenomena claimed by various members of Holiness have been the power of prophecy, clairvoyance, prolonged fasting and, in the knowledge of one saint, the levitation of "a bearded [backwoods] patriarch."

This report is based on four field-trip studies during the past year of several Holiness churches, and comprises first-hand observation of the various charismatic phenomena occurring during the services. The investigative techniques also included, when feasible and indicated, the use of a tape recorder, photoflash and motion picture cameras, a stopwatch, and chemical analysis of different specimens. There were psychiatric examinations of six of the saints of the church. In none of the saints who were examined, was there any evidence of current neurotic, psychotic, or psychosomatic reactions, or of pathologic dissociative behavior. In general, the individual psychopathology of Holiness people was not markedly different from that of people in other sects. It is of interest that—unlike typical mystics who, in the words of one authority, "have been women, unmarried or experienced in an abnormal sex life"—the Holiness saints, by the size of their families, appear to be very active and sexually potent. However, this report is not particularly concerned with any specific details of psychopathology in individual members and reserves any further dynamic formulations for future communications.

Through the catharsis of testifying before a congregation, without the inhibiting mediation of a preacher between God and themselves, the Holiness people act out their conflicts with the often-tragic realities of their lives. The particular dissociated states of ecstasy and exaltation that occurred concomitantly with the phenomena of the ordeals were apparently necessary accompaniments. These states might be viewed as violent upheavals of the unconscious, with totally unabashed shame. At these times, all affects and imagerial contents are forthrightly displayed. The Bible comes to life. In contrast to this overwhelming display of emotion during services, however, the Holiness members express few fantasies in their everyday living. Even in their dreams, which are seldom recalled, the manifest content is reported to be about "church services, handling serpents, fire" and the like.

A typical revival meeting begins at 7:30 p.m. and lasts three hours or longer. It takes place in a church, which is usually a simple, square wooden frame building, or may be a concrete-block house. A meeting may even be in a private home. The churches are situated along rural roads, high in the mountains or deep in the hollows, and sometimes are only accessible by a rocky creek-bed road. Inside they are clean and are furnished with plain wooden pews and an altar. In the middle of the room is an iron coal stove. The walls have inscribed on them various Biblical passages and religious mottoes like "Jesus Saves," "Jesus Never Fails," and "Give Me My Flowers While I Live." Often there may also be a large funeral-parlor calendar with a picture of Jesus admonishing the congregation to "Go to Church," a crucifix, similar to that associated with Roman Catholic churches, and sometimes photographs of Holiness saints holding rattlesnakes and copper-heads. The services are attended by 15 to 125 people. The men are clean-shaven and neatly dressed in colored pants or blue denim overalls and shirts. They sit on one side of the church and the women on the other. The women use no cosmetics, jewelry or artificial beauty contrivances. Most of them wear brightly colored cotton calico or gingham dresses. At a large service, there are usually one or two women breast-feeding their babies. The congregation is about evenly divided between the sexes and has members of all ages.

When the brothers and sisters* arrive, they go among the congregation and onlookers to greet fellow-members cordially. At times the saints, who are always males, hug and kiss each other with the greeting, "How are you, Honey?" The service starts with a stirring mountain hymn that is frequently original with the Holiness Church. Everyone sings at the top of his voice—to the accompaniment of one to four guitars, clashing cymbals and tambourines. This singing is followed by prayer. The members kneel down, in a loud, chaotic, pandemonium of voices, individually thank God for His mercy and favors, and beseech His help for healing and for the ordeals of faith that will shortly follow. Then different members preach and testify; they confess their sins and repent; they recite their personal life experiences and compare them with their fellows' experiences and to appropriate parts of the Bible. They gradually or suddenly go into frenetic states depending on "the power of the Lord in moving [on them]." Their exaltation superficially resembles mania. At these times, they shout, scream, cry, sing, jerk, jump, twitch, whistle, hoot, gesture, sway, swoon, tremble, strut, goosestep, stamp, and incoherently "speak in new tongues" (Mark 16.17, Acts 2.1–13). The glossolalia sounds like: "ma-ma-ma-ma-ma."

When in deep dissociated trances the members appear as if they were intoxicated, and their faces are very similar to those seen with reactions induced by mescaline and LSD 25. They describe the depersonalization phenomena as: "I feel high in the spirits" ... "happiness in the bones" ... "a shield has come down over me" ... "I've got conviction" ... "I lose sight of the whole world" ... "I can't tell if my head and face are all together" and "I can't stand under the power of God." When at the apparent climax of ecstasy, but only when "the Lord moves [them]," the worshippers impulsively turn to the screened, flat, wooden boxes containing the venomous serpents and take them out for handling. Occasionally, the "coal oil" torches or carbide lamps are ignited and the flames applied to their bodies.

---

*"Brothers and sisters" refer to the Holiness-baptized male and female members of the congregation, who participate in some of the ordeals.

In rare instances, only the most faithful of the saints will open a bottle of strychnine, dissolve some in a glass of water and drink it.

In their comments on unsuccessful ordeals by unbelievers, the saints agreed that the "faith" would hold only when the members obeyed the inner command or impulse. In many respects, this is not unlike the apparent prerequisite for a successful telepathic experiment, with which the writer is acquainted. Success in that case seemed to depend on transmitting only when the agent genuinely felt in the mood, and then using his presumably autonomous or autochthonous affect-laden ideas or complexes. In both instances, then, (the ordeals and telepathic experiments) critical cognition was in abeyance, or was secondary to the immediate emotional constellation.

If a member of the congregation claims he is ill or knows of someone who is ailing (it once happened that an infant was present who had a congenital deformity), the members gather around the afflicted, anoint with olive oil, "lay on" their hands and loudly pray for divine intercession and healing. Both because of their rigid moral code and their vulnerability to persecution, the brothers and sisters carefully refrain from the laying on of hands during the healing rites below the shoulders of any member of the opposite sex. In their vivid descriptions and testimonials the Holiness people claim to have cured diseases that physicians had diagnosed as hopeless: cases of what might have been tuberculosis, carcinomatosis, breast tumors, "skin cancer of the jaw," acute adenitis, poliomyelitis, other forms of paralysis, "sleeping sickness," and convulsive disorders. In a study of one of the saints, it appeared that he had a history that seemed to be compatible with a clinical diagnosis of a coronary occlusion, with either two recurrent attacks, and/or bouts of acute congestive failure. He reported that, while in the hospital and in severe distress, he was visited by members of his congregation who prayed for him. Following this moving experience, he immediately assumed his excessively exuberant physical devotions and usual form of life without any apparent untoward affect, but, on the contrary, with subjective (and objective?) improvement. Because of the enigmatic, spectacular nature of some of their ordeals, and the fervor of a faith seldom seen nowadays in perhaps more sophisticated urban circles, some of the Holiness "cures" might be profitably studied from the psychosomatic viewpoint. Although rare, there are some well-documented cases in the medical literature of spontaneous resolution of various forms of proved malignancy. If one could actually find any similar cases among the Holiness people, an intensive psychiatric study might reveal another connection between the emotions and anatomical body changes.

Ordeal by Serpents

With the Biblical injunction of Jesus "to take up serpents" (Mark 16.18, Luke 10.19) and Paul's experience of shaking off a viper "fastened on his hand," (Acts 28.3) the Holiness members handle venomous rattlesnakes and copperheads that are caught in the surrounding mountains and fields by "unbelieving sinner boys" or by saints who inspiringly trudge these regions, put their bare hands in the rock dens, and pull the serpents out. If not bitten, and if able to handle the snakes, the worshippers then gain "victory" (over the Devil). During the actual ceremonies one to four poisonous snakes are held in the hands, around the neck, on the head, or close to the lips of the members. Although the women also handle serpents, this ordeal is performed for the most part by the men. The snakes crawl around their hosts and are seemingly adapted to the rhythmical swaying and chanting of, "Thank you Jesus, thank you Jesus, Gloree, Gloree, Bless him Lord, bless him." Some of the serpents are gently molded into different positions by the saints. The serpents maintain these particular, and sometimes, bizarre attitudes for variable periods, and appear to be cataplectic. One brother held a rattlesnake (approximately four feet in length) in the mid-trunk region, and as he stamped around the congregation, shouting his praises to the Lord, the reptile hung limply, seemed to be cataplectic, and showed no response until the worshipper paused and became silent for a few seconds. Invariably on these occasions, the serpent would start to wiggle, writhe, and then ominously rattle. It should be noted that the rattlesnakes seldom rattled when being handled during the ceremonies, but they frequently made a collective racket when their cages were disturbed. Although the author personally observed more than 200 instances of serpent handling, he has not witnessed a bite.

Many of the saints have been bitten. Two, in particular, claim to have been bitten more than 50 times, and two others, more than 30 times each. One claims to have handled serpents more than 2,000 times in his career without once being bitten. When a Holiness member is bitten, medical treatment is refused. The saints use no definitive treatment and rely solely on their "faith in the Lord" for a cure.

Four saints studied knew, among them, of only 18 Holiness people who had died of snake bites in 31 years. They cited examples of men and women in their 70s and 80s who survived bites. Although there are instances of children, as young as four years of age, handling the serpents at the services, and also other instances where infants inadvertently handled serpents in private homes, no member of the Holiness Church knew of any case when a child was bitten. A saint asserted that, when a person is bitten there is a free flow of blood and intense swelling and pain. From their combined experiences, the saints believe that the mortality and morbidity does not depend on the site of the bite, since they have been bitten on the faces, necks, hands and lower extremities without any significant difference in the final outcome. However, some of the brothers and former members of the faith were observed to have snake-bite complications of auto-amputation of digits and parts of hands.

Three brothers, who, in their collective lifetime experiences, have been bitten more than 100 times, and, on some occasions, two to three times almost simultaneously, concluded that: "A rattlesnake bite gives numbness, difficulty in walking, talking, weakness and a 'drunken-like' feeling, like having a shot for a tooth-pulling. A copperhead bite doesn't have these effects but feels like fire and there is much more swelling. The poison makes you hot and the blood thin. You [can] bleed to death." In the cases of these three saints, there were apparently never any sequelae. It was difficult to ascertain how frequently bites occurred through the years, the species of snakes involved, the sizes or estimated ages of the snakes, how many members subsequently received medical treatment, and the final outcome.

When a bitten member suffers complications or dies, it is because "he didn't have enough faith." As an example of the relationship between their beliefs, their faith and the ultimate results of handling serpents, many persons told how one famous saint successfully handled serpents for 30 years until he believed a sister's prophecy of his own approaching death from a snakebite. As prophesied, he was bitten and died. Although the history could not be verified in all the salient details, it was stated that this saint had received similar bites throughout his career without any fear of dire results or any lasting complications.

Discussion

What is it that might account for the apparent ability to avoid being bitten when in such intimate contact with these dangerous reptiles? In some way, it might be related to the magnitude of dissociation or trance. Indirect evidence in support of this supposition is the fact that those who have been bitten the least number of times appear to be very gentle and kind people who only handle the serpents "when the Lord really moves on us; this is not for show. God won't let 'em open their mouth. The snake would dart at me but hit can't open hit's mouth." The saint who was alleged to have handled serpents more than 2,000 times without being bitten was a particularly kind and gentle individual. On the other hand, those who have been bitten many times are, perhaps, not so cautious and gentle in handling the serpents. Some frequently handle snakes in their homes or in church without "the command of the Lord," or the deep dissociative state. One brother who once handled 26 serpents at the same time was, of course, more likely to be bitten, and he was bitten. Nevertheless, he suffered no complications. The particular minister who was never bitten in 2,000 experiences said that he quaked in terror on seeing or handling harmless garter snakes or black snakes when he was not in a trance.

Many of the snakes appear to react in a fashion analogous to other animals observed in various states of hypnosis (Totstell-reflex), that is, from a light drowsy-like state to complete cataplexy. The saints reported one unusual and enigmatic situation where it was alleged that two particular sisters frequently handled rattlesnakes that died (of fright?) during the ordeal. It is plausible then to conjecture that the rhythmic stimulation to the serpent, combined with its possible terror during the experience, might produce, in the snake, reactions varying from relative inertia and drowsiness to cataplexy and even death. ·

Practical considerations in the evaluation of the treatment of snake bites in medical practice might make it worth while to determine the mortality and morbidity of untreated rattlesnake and copperhead bites in the Holiness members. For instance, from some of the historical data of members incurring repeated and even multiple simultaneous snake bites—and where no tourniquets, cruciate incisions, antisera, transfusions and the like were used—questions might be raised about current therapy and the pathophysiology of snake bites. However, this should not be construed to mean that current established therapeutic procedures should be abandoned or radically modified. After further investigation and documentation of untreated snake bites in Holiness members, however, might there be some value in doing careful immunologic studies? Possibly Holiness donor-blood or some of its derivatives (globulin fraction?) could be studied for possible use in the therapy of those envenomed people who are sensitive to hyperimmune horse protein or directly allergic to the venom itself. Perhaps performing such suggested studies on Holiness blood would yield different results than similar tests reported by Parrish and Pollard. In the case of the Holiness people, some of the saints have been bitten many more times, much more frequently, and more often have had multiple bites than the subjects reported by these two authors. Furthermore, since most of Parrish and Pollard's severely envenomed cases had received large amounts of antivenom, the active immunity in this group might be expected to be lower than that in the Holiness group—if the factor of immunity is involved in the Holiness group. The material presented would seem to point to the importance of the bitten saints' attitudes and "faith." In any event, these potential by-products of this investigation are of secondary importance, compared to the fact that human beings in states of exaltation can generally handle poisonous snakes without being bitten, and that, most frequently, when bitten, they do not die. The real question that should be asked is how? Or why?

Ordeal by Fire

In the ancient history of many Western peoples, the ordeal by fire plays a prominent role. In medieval Europe, the Christian clergy officiated at ordeals, which included boiling water and oil, red-hot iron and burning logs, to determine the guilt or innocence of people. The legal term, *judicium ferri,* was derived from these particular rites, and the still prevalent custom of taking an oath in court can be ascribed to related ordeals. Eventually, the fire ordeal became so dangerously prevalent that the church outlawed it in the Fourth Lateran Council in 1215. Nevertheless, the rites persisted; and, for instance, in 1725 during the bloody French Reformation, it was reported that "a convolutionary called *'La Salamandre'* remained suspended for nine minutes over a fiery brazier, clad only in a sheet, which remained intact in the flames." At approximately this time in America, the French missionaries reported that the Indians of the St. Lawrence River region and Great Lakes, had various fire ordeals, including successful handling of hot coals and stones, plunging their arms into boiling water, and walking through fire. In many similar forms, the fire ordeal was widespread in other cultures and parts of the world for centuries and exists today or did very recently in Ceylon, the Fiji Islands, Hawaii and India. In the 1860s, the famous medium, D. D. Home, is alleged to have handled hot coals many times and once "kneeled down, placed his face right among the burning coals and moved it about as though bathing in water." Another more recent event occurred in New York City some years ago when a Hindu mystic, Kuda Bux, was reported to have safely walked over charcoal that was measured to be burning at 1220° Fahrenheit.

This part of the present study concerns the first-hand observation of thirteen members of the Holiness sect and their experiences with fire handling. They base their ordeal on various parts of the Bible (Isaiah 43.2, Daniel 3. 25), and, as with the serpents, they usually take to the fire at a climactic furor in the revival. At such times a rag wick placed in a milk bottle or tomato juice jar full of "coal oil"* is ignited. The flames are orange-yellow and shoot eight to 24 inches high. The worshippers slowly move their outstretched open hands and fingers over the midpoint of the

---

*Kerosene.

flames for times ranging from three to five seconds or even longer. Frequently, one turns the burning torch horizontally and puts the proximal flame to the palm of his hand for five seconds or longer. On three occasions, two of the saints put their exposed toes and the soles of their feet directly in the flames for five to 15 seconds. As noted with the fingers, the flames were observed to pass through the interdigital spaces. In one instance, the most faithful saint smeared fuel oil over hands and feet, and then proceeded to hold them in the midst of the flames for more than 10 seconds. Although there was some thick white smoke, the fuel oil on the skin did not burn. The saint then cupped the palm of his hand and tired to ignite the little pool of fuel in it with the blazing torch, but it only flickered a few times. As controls, an iron poker and a wooden dowel, that had fuel oil sprinkled on the surfaces, quickly burst into flames when in contact with the torch. On 13 occasions, five different women moved the midpoint of the torch flame backward and forward directly under their elbows, forearms and upper arms for a few seconds—or longer. One of the women had chronic blotchy erythema of the exposed parts of her body (actinic dermatitis), and she claimed that this condition developed every spring and persisted throughout the summer until fall. There was no change in her condition, locally or diffusely, before or after the ordeal. Once a sister handed the flaming torch to an old man sitting in the back of the church. Apparently moved by the fervor of the services, he acquired an immunity for the first time, applying the flames to his hand without burning. On three occasions, three different women held the blaze to their chests, so that the flames were in intimate contact with their cotton dresses, exposed necks, faces and hair. This lasted for longer than a few seconds. Twice, at separate times, one of the "most faithful of the saints" slowly moved the palmar and lateral aspects of one hand and the fifth finger in the midpoint and tip of an acetylene flame (produced by the reaction of calcium carbide and water in a miner's headlamp). He did this for more than four seconds, and then repeated the procedure, using the other hand. Later that same evening, he alternately applied each hand again to the acetylene flame for slightly longer periods. Once this saint, when in a relatively calm mood, turned to a coal fire of an hour's duration, picked up a flaming "stone coal" the size of a hen's egg and held it in the palms of his hands for 65 seconds while he walked among the congregation. As a control, the author could not touch a piece of burning charcoal for less than one second without developing a painful blister.

In all these fire ordeals, except one, there were, apparently, no evidences of painful reactions; and there was no erythema, blistering, charring, singeing, suggestive odor of a burn, or gross change in sweat production. Just once, when a brother handled the torch, there was a slight singeing and an associated odor, where some hair on the dorsal distal forearm burned. In no instance though, was there ever any evidence that clothes had been either scorched or burned. Although some of the men had calluses on their palms and soles, others, including "the most faithful saint" did not. The women, of course, had no calluses on their forearms, arms, necks or faces. In no case, was any change found before or after the fire ordeal, upon examining the affected body parts for superficial touch, pain and temperature sensitivity, or astereognosis. On the occasion when the most faithful saint immersed his oil-soaked hands and feet in the flames, he washed his hands shortly before the ordeal. As a control, the author could not keep his own hand closer than 3 cms. to the "coal oil" torch flame at its base for longer than one or two seconds without pain or the danger of getting burned. Other control attempts, under ordinary circumstances and simulating the ordeal, were impossible to complete, because of almost instantaneous pain and the risk of incurring severe burns.

Careful history-taking of these people revealed no discrepancies in their accounts of the fire ordeal, and brought forth more interesting and suggestive data. For instance, "the most faithful saint" inaugurated his gift 26 years ago by rushing to the hearth, balancing—with his hands—red-hot logs on his shoulders, and walking around the congregation without any ill effects to his person or clothes. Another minister* is alleged to have jumped up on a red-hot iron stove, to have sat on it, and to have put his exposed feet and legs among the glowing coals while he delivered his sermon. A third saint has a reputation for putting his head and neck in a red-hot stove for "many seconds or a few minutes." However, no observer claimed to have actually timed this. The same man is also reported to have had a welder's acetylene torch applied to his outstretched upper arm for many seconds, and also later to his forehead, against which was placed a piece of paper which instantaneously disintegrated. In neither case was there any burn to his skin or shirt.

The fire ordeal has been undertaken by male and female worshippers from seven to 80 years of age. It is alleged to be a not uncommon practice to hand red-hot coals among the congregation during winter service ("it feels like velvet") and for "the young girls to hug the red-hot stovepipes and pass around a hot [glass] lamp chimney." Also, on occasion, the fire immunity has been seemingly conferred by the saints on newly-converted spectators at the services.

An interesting story was provided by one brother who reported applying the "coal oil" torch flame to the palm of his hand for several seconds with complete immunity until he noticed that a piece of wick was breaking

*Or "saint." They are ordained in their own church.

off. This trivial incident was enough to cause him to awaken from his trance and engender anxiety. At this point, he suffered a very discrete and localized blistering burn. The surrounding area that had previously been in contact with the flames during the trance, and had been of no apparent concern to him showed no burn.

In a like manner, a sister who had, during previous ordeals, frequently handled a hot glass chimney, developed blistering burns when one evening while at church, the electric power failed and she, in a reflex action, grabbed the brightly burning kerosene lantern that was hanging on the wall. She was not entranced at that particular moment. The fact can, therefore, be noted that when Holiness members are not entranced, they, like everyone else, suffer burns, are afraid of poisonous snakes and possibly are more frequently bitten by them.

Various brothers and sisters emphasized their accounts by telling how "sinner people" when intoxicated with alcohol, or disbelieving what they saw, attempted to duplicate the feats, suffered bad burns of the skin, hair or clothes. As an example, a scoffing brother of the most faithful saint, had his finger for a fraction of a second in the acetylene flame and rapidly developed blisters in the exposed area. There have been reports in the literature of similar experiences where those "without the faith," or not in complete trance, have been severely burned. Some of these people were ministers, of other sects than the fire-handlers, who tried to prove the trials fraudulent. They apparently considered them to be superstition or heresy, or perhaps felt the need to expose as hoaxes something that differed from, or threatened, their own convictions. However, it can be surmised that there was a close connection between their not being in receptive, dissociative states (their lack of "faith") and their suffering serious burns.

Discussion

It appears to be fact that some people in a state of religious ecstasy and faith can have varying degrees of immunity to burns on their body and their clothing. However, what explanation for these phenomena, if any, can be offered? It should be frankly admitted that careful critical studies ought to be undertaken, so that the collateral historical data can be scrutinized, and the observed data can be further explored and measured. The problems in a study of this kind are manifold. One must establish rapport, obtain cooperation, and then adjust to quick-moving, ever-changing conditions. The fire ordeal studied here is part of a church service, and there is much compulsive and excessive motor activity. In addition to these factors, there is the problem of measuring flame temperatures, distance from flame, time of exposure, the particular part or parts involved, the effects of movement on such a part, and at all times, the apparently fundamental relationship to the underlying and varying degrees of ecstasy or dissociation.

Despite the many drawbacks of the present field-trip observations, which are admittedly not comparable to well-controlled laboratory investigations where the data are accurately measured there still exists the fact of varying degrees of fire immunity and no satisfactory explanation. In this regard, for those who would insist upon strict laboratory controls during the fire ordeal, one should recall the previously-noted example of the man who, while in a trance, became aware that the burning wick was breaking and thus came out of his trance and suffered a burn, when moments before this, flames had licked his hand without effect. Similarly, interjecting the body of an overzealous experimental interference (with its necessary demands for frequent and strict controls and checks) may sabotage the trance, taint the results, lead to false conclusions, and expose the participants (and observer?) to serious bodily harm.

The patent freedom from pain in the fire ordeal is not unusual when consideration is given to the related conditions of spectacular hypnotic anesthesias and the categorical emotional aspects of pain perception. Although no striking chemical changes have been associated, to date, with hypnotic anesthesias, such anesthesias are incontestable facts, and, similarly, the religious dissociations might also have no readily identifiable chemical changes. Hypnotic anesthesia has been studied with scalp electro-encephalography, and, in one instance, with depth electrography, but in neither case has there been a clear-cut major electrophysiological change in comparison to control states. Even though the formidable technical obstacles could be overcome, it would then be reasonable, by analogy, not to anticipate any gross electrographic changes during the fire ordeal.

The fact that there is absence of pain does not explain the immunity to burning, but it also does not necessarily mean that the two phenomena are unrelated. Evidence in favor of some neural factors, however, is provided by experiments where blistering has been produced during the hypnotic trance and by some studies by Sevitt on guinea pigs, which led him to conclude that: "burns [that] just produced a definite increase in capillary permeability in the intact skin, failed to affect the capillaries of the denervated skin." He also noted the observation that transection of the spinal cord decreased inflammatory edema and degree of hemoconcentration after burning. In any event, it is difficult to see how these rather scanty data could be transposed and sufficiently magnified to account for the high immunity to burning in the fire ordeals.

Kolb has shown how the presence, absence or degree of pain is closely related to meaningful past life experiences, current attitudes, symbolic values and whatever conscious and/or unconscious significance the pain-

associated situation or body part might have for the patient. In a comparable way, it can be supposed that the success of the fire ordeal depends on
the worshipper's experiences, beliefs and particular body image. The Holiness worshippers are compelled to apply the flames to the bodily parts
when and where "the Lord moves on them." Since, from suckling infancy
and childhood, many of the Holiness people have witnessed or heard about
such ordeals from relatives and friends, it is reasonable to suppose that in
their minds there can be no question about the reality of such phenomena,
or for that matter, other "miracles" mentioned in the Bible. "It is a matter
of having enough faith and living the right kind of life." To the worshippers,
it is the unbelievers or "sinner boys" who are strange and illogical; they act
"rationally," and of course do not really expect fire immunity, and are
subsequently burned. Therefore, for the believer, success, freedom from
pain, and complete immunity to the fire is anticipated; and the results
conform to this projected body image.

The effects which, in more ordinary situations, would be expected to
occur do not result. Thus, there are: (1) lack of effect of the flame on the
skin during the trance (when, seconds after, a localized burn resulted when
the individual came out of the trance); (2) the lack of burn when the flame
was applied to the forehead (while a piece of paper interposed between the
flame and forehead disintegrated in the fire); and (3) the failure of "coal
oil," smeared on the hands and foot of the believer, to ignite when the torch
was applied (while similar "coal oil" smeared on a poker and wooden dowel
burst into flame in similar circumstances).

A Holiness member's faith has the strength of an incorruptible obses-
sion. As an example of this, and of indifference to worldly matters, one saint
(perhaps wisely?) refused much material wealth for "going on the stage
with his wife and baby" (to perform the fire ordeal). The members are
always careful to refrain from doing anything which would compromise
their convictions and jeopardize their exaltation and gifts. For instance, it
is reported that one member successfully handled fire until he returned
from military service and tried to resume his ordeals, when he was badly
burned. "He lost faith in the service; didn't live the right kind of a life."
Those who participate in the most unusual feats must keep at them compul-
sively so as not to develop fear and lose ability. Being totally immersed in
his faith means that a member is ready to leave his job, family and personal
comforts at almost any time that the "Lord moves" (him) and go to evangel-
istic revival meetings, bedside prayers for healing, and so forth.

Although the believers' attitudes toward strangers varied between
wholehearted acceptance and co-operation to suspiciousness and with-
drawal, these disparate factors never seemed to alter their exaltations significantly or change the frequency, content or magnitude of the phenomena

from one meeting to another. When in exaltation, they are in another world, and, as frequently noted with mescaline and LSD 25 reactions, they are relatively unresponsive to the distracting external stimuli of their immediate environments.

Another possible concomitant to the trance might be an increased efficiency of circulatory cooling mechanisms. However, this would not seem to be a plausible explanation because the "believers" were in varying degrees of excitement (increased cardiac output). Some were relatively tranquil on occasion. If circulatory factors were important, there would have to be an enormous increase in cooling ability to protect what were often large areas of the involved skin from the direct local effects of the flames on epidermis, corium and subcutaneous tissues. Furthermore, these tissues should respond locally to the flames and in a great measure be independent of the circulatory of factors. Clinically, it should be noted that in several instances the fingers and toes, which are particularly vulnerable to serious burns, were unduly exposed to flames.

The hypothesis first put forward by Albertus Magnus—that the fire-handler's skin is protected locally from fire with a "recipe"—would not be relevant, because, as far as the author knows, there is no such preparation; and, in one instance, to forestall this criticism, a saint washed his hands before the ordeal, and the results were the same.

Since none of the "believers" took any drugs, the ingestion of drugs for protection cannot be considered possible. Humoral mechanisms are unlikely, because nothing has been isolated as yet which affords any significant protection against burns. If the procedure could be carried out without ruining the trance, it would, of course, be of interest to analyze, chemically and/or biologically, blood specimens obtained from Holiness people while in resting control states and while in states of religious exaltation, before and shortly after their fire ordeals—to see if any protection could be discovered for animals or humans undergoing experimental burns. Although the states of exaltation sometimes superficially resemble pathologic frenetic conditions, it should be pointed out that manic patients and agitated schizophrenics can develop bad burns, even though in some instances they appear to be, like Holiness people, subjectively free of pain. The suggested explanations of immunity from burns are, therefore, all inadequate, because in the literature, in histories given by the Holiness members, and in some instances that were confirmed by direct observations by the author, the apparent immunity to burning is even extended to other people watching the services and to clothing. "Brother [Smith] put hot coals in his shirt." In one reported case of 70 years ago, Crookes tested, in his laboratory, a fine cambric handkerchief that the medium D. D. Home had folded around a piece of red charcoal, then fanned to white heat with his breath without damaging the handkerchief. Crookes concluded that the handkerchief "had not undergone the slightest chemical preparation which could have rendered it fire-proof."

It was unfortunately impossible to measure in each instance the time of exposure and distances between the source of heat and bodily part in the examples reported from the Holiness sect. Nevertheless, in many of these phenomena, common sense and the reported experimental data (where lesser thermal stresses were imposed with resultant tissue injury) would indicate that the temperatures of the flames that were used (coal oil, acetylene, burning coal; and also the history of alleged contacts with red-hot and white-hot iron) were high enough so that the exposures witnessed should have sufficed to produce serious burns. The question—why these people are not burned on their bodies and their projected body images, when in their exalted states—remains a mystery for future probing.

Ordeal by Strychnine

Mark 16. 18 says " . . . and if they drink any deadly thing it shall in no wise hurt them." With this scriptural verse as a command, some of the saints undergo the ordeal by strychnine. This particular poison is most commonly consumed because of its ready availability, known toxicity, and widespread use as a rodenticide. However, it is also reported that "believers" have swallowed lye without any complications. The ordeal by poison is rare, and the ingestion of strychnine is believed to be the severest trial of faith. This event usually occurs at the acme of a service, and in the two observed instances it occurred in men 52 and 69 years of age. Their estimated weights, were respectively, 68 and 75 kilograms, and it was three hours since they had eaten. Immediately before the ordeal one of the saints alternately got up and sat down in his pew, trembled, cried and laughed. He discussed his one-and-one-half-inch-thick walnut coffin, funeral plans and experiences with "boogery" ("playing with the Devil") until he felt "the power of the Lord descend" upon him. While he was "hollering" and raving, the younger saint, who had just finished his ordeals with the flaming torch, copperhead, and blazing stone coal, paced the floor, puffed, whistled, and exhorted his brother minister to do what the Lord commanded. Suddenly, after the tumultuous "Resurrection Hymn" the older saint took out his pocket knife, pushed down the seal on a new bottle of strychnine sulfate, opened the cap and transferred an amount of the poison on the knife blade to a glass of water. He stirred it and within 12 seconds took two to three swallows and then passed the glass to his friend, who rapidly imbibed an apparently equal amount.* "In my stomach it feels like cold water, you can sprinkle it on my tongue and it tastes better than honey." Between them, the two saints drank slightly more than 80 ml. or a total of 34.4 mg. of strychnine sulfate.** Both ministers immediately returned to their preaching, jumping, handclapping and singing. Eight minutes later, the younger saint kindly permitted a blood specimen to be taken for analysis, and 26 minutes later he produced a urine specimen. However, to this date, conditions have not made it possible to analyze these specimens. At no time after drinking the strychnine were there any twitches, convulsions or other signs and symptoms.

Of all the Holiness people that were observed, only four gave histories of undergoing the strychnine ordeal. The saint who was alleged to have put his head into the red-hot iron stove, with live coals, claimed to have taken strychnine four to five times in his life, and "I feel the Lord—a cool feeling go down on my neck. I once took half a bottle of it."*** In no reported instances, were there ever any complications. In order to emphasize the danger of the strychnine ordeal, the preachers tell how ministers of other

---

*The total quantity taken by the two saints was estimated by measuring the column of strychnine sulfate solution in a slightly conical glass tumbler, then aspirating into a syringe an aliquot part which still remained in the glass.

**The qualitative and quantitative analyses of some of the portion remaining from the orally ingested aqueous solution, of suspected pure strychnine sulfate, were performed by William J. Lane, development chemist, analytical laboratory, Schering Corporation. "The total sample [of alleged strychnine sulfate] remaining in the vial was found to be 3.53 grams indicating that approximately 220 mg. had been removed if the label is assumed to be correct. A 1 mg. portion of the powder was ground thoroughly into 300 mg. of dried potassium bromide and a pellet was pressed from it and examined by infrared using a Beckman IR 5. A similar treatment was afforded a known standard sample of strychnine sulphate. The resulting spectra were identical in all respects. The submitted sample also gave positive tests for strychnine sulphate as outlined in N. F. X and the British Pharmacopoeia 1953. These tests indicate that the material in question is strychnine sulphate. Aqueous solutions of a standard strychnine sulphate were prepared containing 1, 2, 3, 4, and 5 mg. per 100 ml. respectively. These samples were examined on a Cary recording spectrophotometer from 200 to 400 mu. The resulting curves were all of the same shape and Beer's law was obeyed when optical density was plotted against concentration. This relationship is the basis of the quantitative analysis of the submitted aqueous solutions. Two aliquots were taken from the submitted solutions and were diluted to 100 ml. volume with water. The solutions were examined using a Cary recording spectrophotometer between 200 and 400 mu. The resulting curves were identical in shape to curves of similar concentration of standard strychnine sulphate solutions. Calculations showed that there were slight differences in the strengths of the examined solutions but that they were of the same general magnitude, being 0.46 mg./ml. and 0.41 mg./ml. respectively. The average of these results being the reported value of 0.435 mg./ml. The aqueous solutions gave positive tests for strychnine sulphate as outlined in N. F. X and the British Pharmacopoeia 1953. The shape of the above ultraviolet curves also substantiates these identities."

***Strychnine Sulphate, Merck, used by the Holiness saints is dispensed as 3.75 grams per bottle.

denominations have sprinkled some of the Holiness strychnine solution taken by the saints on meat for a dog who died while convulsing shortly after biting into it, or have told how a cat was similarly killed.

Discussion

The strychnine ordeal is an unusual feat, since strychnine is readily absorbed from the stomach and intestine. In amounts varying between 5 and 20 mg. it can produce convulsions in 15 to 45 minutes that could be fatal. The ordinarily fatal dose by the oral route varies between 60 and 90 mg. Furthermore, it is a characteristic of strychnine to make the subject who ingests it more responsive to various sensory stimuli (as lights, claps, pain, and so forth) which can precipitate convulsions. In sharp contrast to habituating drugs like the barbiturates, the repeated use of strychnine does not lead to tolerance, but on the contrary to an increase in nervous system susceptibility and effects.

It should be stated that the exact dose of strychnine sulfate that was orally taken by each saint was unknown. However, at best, if the total imbibed solution was evenly divided, then each should have had at least 17 mg. If it were not drunk in aliquot parts, one should have had a dose of more than 17 mg. and the other a lesser amount. However, whether each saint received approximately 17 mg. or one saint more, such an amount, by way of the method and times of administration might have been sufficient to produce convulsive, other toxic, and/or possibly, even lethal effects.

The data in an isolated and unique situation like this are too scant upon which to make generalizations. It should also be stated that the dosages employed, although presumably in toxic amounts, might have been insufficient to produce convulsive effects. The dangerous nature of this ordeal naturally precludes any thought of experimentation by using human beings. However, as in the ordeals by serpents and fire, these unusual reactions are facts; and they occur not infrequently. Therefore, it should be possible to study this ordeal further, and gather information which might elucidate the influence of the exaltation on the possibly changed absorption, detoxification, and/or metabolism of strychnine. It can be supposed that the apparent immunity to convulsions and other sequelae is related to these altered factors. Yet, like the ordeals by serpents and fire, the very nature of the strychnine trial makes it most difficult to study and obtain specimens without subjecting the participants to more serious hazards. It is noteworthy that the turbulent church services themselves provided a very intense and variegated form of sensory stimulation, which, in this respect, should have been an additional risk. As in the cases of failure to be bitten by the poisonous snakes or to suffer burns, perhaps the exaltation in this case was an important reason why no convulsions ensued. The only remotely similar situation the author could recall was where, in one instance at least, a blind faith in a scientific opinion (exaltation?) might have accounted for an extraordinary protection against serious effects, illness and possible death. That was at the turn of the last century when von Pettenkofer, in an attempt to disprove Koch's thesis that a cholera culture was highly poisonous, swallowed "virulent choleric culture from Gaffky's laboratory along with Emmerich, Stricker, Metchnikof, Ferran and other pupils." As in cases of suicides, homicides, and accidental deaths from strychnine, laboratory workers and others have become seriously ill and died as a result of the accidental ingestion of the comma bacillus. Perhaps then, exaltation—through its concomitant physiological changes—can act as a potent protective mechanism against the dangerous effects of strychnine, or, by analogy, some other poison.

Any minimal traces of data in this regard might throw some light on how the emotions can, in some instances, affect the thresholds of nervous-tissue irritability and discharge, and, for example, how convulsive-seizure thresholds can be influenced by prevailing affects. For instance, clinicians have long been aware of the fact that some seizures in epileptic patients can be precipitated by significant emotional experiences, whether happy, unhappy, conscious or unconscious. Some support for this opinion is provided by the observation of a seizure occurring in a 46-year-old catatonic woman during depth electrography and a structured interview. The patient (with her family members) was thoroughly studied via the collaborative technique and with concomitant scalp electro-encephalography and depth electrography. This observation was unique, because the patient had had no spontaneous convulsive seizures for more than 40 years before the structured interview.

In contrast to this catatonic woman, or to epileptic patients who can have convulsions when surprised or overwhelmed with anxiety, the worshippers in the strychnine ordeal are aware of their experience and, from their previous trials and faith, have some understanding about what they expect will happen. By the gradual build-up of exaltation, they have time for mastering their anxiety and for apparently (internally) bracing themselves against any untoward effects. They dissociate from the threat of certain death by involving the "power of the Lord" and then acting out the possible counterphobic defense of ingesting the strychnine. Other tangential support for this hypothesis might be provided by the common clinical observation that some patients, in different degrees of excitation, can show wide variations from time to time in the dosages of intravenously administered, short-acting barbiturates necessary to induce sleep.

Further support for this thesis may be provided by patients who, in undergoing pentylenetetrazol (metrazol) activation of an electro-encephalographic focal discharge, show variations from time to time in the amount of drug necessary to precipitate a focal convulsion. In both of these situations, then, the factors of previous experience and attitudes might be instrumental in mastering the anxiety and, secondarily, in affecting various neural thresholds. If the biochemical changes associated with the affective state responsible for the altered convulsive-seizure thresholds in the strychnine ordeal could be better defined or identified, there might be some clues here for the pathophysiology of convulsive disorders.

Summary

Some of the cultural and psychodynamic background factors in the members of the Free Pentacostal Holiness Church are described. Particular attention is devoted to the relationship between their states of exaltation that occur during the religious services and the more than 200 observed instances of successful manipulation of poisonous rattlesnakes and copperheads. Also the salient details are given of the many instances where several different worshippers, during ecstasy, handled "fuel oil" torches, acetylene flames, and flaming coal without having either thermal injury to their bodies or clothing. As a final psychosomatic phenomenon, the ordeal by poison, where two ministers, in exaltation, ingested presumed toxic doses of strychnine sulfate solution, without any harmful effects, is described. These observed data are related to additional material obtained in histories from Holiness people, reported similar data in the literature and some hypotheses toward the understanding of these phenomena. Some possible practical applications, from the study of these ordeals by serpents, fire and strychnine, to various fields of medicine are mentioned.

Acknowledgment

The author, who is of a nonsectarian Protestant background, hopes this report has been fair and factual, and he thanks the many ministers, brothers and sisters of the Holiness Church whose kindness, help and desire to show the medical world "the workings of the Lord" made these studies possible.

The author also wishes to note that, through the generosity and skill of Dr. Kenneth A. Hawkins, Mr. Wilbur S. Felker, and Mr. William J. Lane of Schering Corporation, Bloomfield, N.J., it was possible to obtain laboratory analyses of the specimens in the strychnine ordeal.

18

The Appalachian Log Cabin

Henry Glassie

While many aspects of Appalachian folklife have received little intensive study, until recently none was more slighted than mountain folk architecture. Detailed investigations of this subject date only from the 1960s, one of the pioneers being Henry Glassie (1941–   ). Unlike most previous writers on the topic who did most of their research in libraries, Glassie carried out a majority of his research in the field, studying traditional buildings firsthand. Beginning in 1961, Glassie spent much of five years conducting a field survey of folk architecture in the upland South, a region stretching from western Arkansas through eastern Pennsylvania. His papers, "The Appalachian Log Cabin" and "The Smaller Outbuildings of the Southern Mountains," are based on that research and are among the very first publications solely devoted to southern mountain folk architecture.

Glassie's two essays are among several others in which he refutes the contention first set forth by Henry C. Mercer in the 1920s, and followed by most subsequent scholars, that American log buildings were ultimately derived from Swedish settlers living in the New World during the early seventeenth century. The reasoning was that because log construction was Swedish, the form of log cabins and outbuildings must also be Swedish in origin. As Glassie demonstrates, the reasoning is faulty on several counts, not the least of which is that the English settlers had little contact with the Swedes. More reasonable, Glassie maintains, is the conclusion that the log cabin of southern Appalachia is basically Pennsylvania-German in origin with some Tidewater-English influence. To support his thesis, Glassie employs a modified version of the historic-geographic methodology that has generally been utilized in folktale studies. According to this approach it is possible to arrive at the probable archetypal form of an element of tradition by studying as many examples of the element arranged first in chronological and then in geographic order.

For more on Glassie's folk architecture thesis see "The Old Barns of Appalachia," *Mountain Life and Work* 41 (Summer 1965): 21–30; "The Pennsylvania Barn in the

Reprinted from *Mountain Life and Work* 39 (Winter 1963): 5–14.

South," *Pennsylvania Folklife* 15 (Winter 1965–66): 8–19; and "The Types of the Southern Mountain Cabin" in Jan Harold Brunvand, *The Study of American Folklore* (New York: W.W. Norton and Company, Inc., 1968), pp. 338–70. Also see Fred Kniffen, "Folk Housing: Key to Diffusion," *Annals of the Association of American Geographers* 55 (December 1965): 545–77. For views critical of some of Glassie's conclusions see C. A. Weslager, *The Log Cabin in America: From Pioneer Days to the Present* (New Brunswick, New Jersey: Rutgers University Press, 1969) and Terry G. Jordan, Matti Kaups, and Richard M. Lieffort, "New Evidence on the European Origin of Pennsylvanian Notching," *Pennsylvania Folklife* 36 (Autumn 1986): 20–31.

*   *   *

In the nineteenth century the log cabin was a symbol of America and, although it has been replaced in most of the nation by the suburban development and steel mill, it remains a symbol of Southern Appalachia. Recordings made for the mountain person moved to the northern city nostalgically remind him of "the little old log cabin in the mountains" and a log cabin is on the seal of the Southern Highland Handicraft Guild. As some aspects of Southern Appalachian culture have been studied in great detail since the days of Cecil Sharp, it is surprising that very little has been written about the architecture of the mountains, and surprising that the little bit that has been written is for the most part erroneous.[1] To clear up a great many misconceptions about the log cabin, to perhaps generate a bit of interest in the fading old structure, and to show that it is most certainly a fit symbol for the Southern Mountains, its development is here outlined.

Upon arriving in America, the English built rude huts in imitation of Indian dwellings which were in no way related to the log cabin. As soon as possible, they constructed half timber houses of the type they had known in England. The half timber house is one heavily framed with the spaces between the timbers filled with mud and sticks. It was found that American soil lacked the lime of the English soil and the filling between the timbers was unsatisfactory. The practice of covering the framed building with clapboarding, as was done in certain sections of England, thus became the rule throughout the English colonies.

In the mid-seventeenth century a group of Swedes settled on the Delaware River and built houses of horizontal log. When the English settled nearby in Pennsylvania, they had little intercourse with the Swedes and, although the Swedish log house was easier to build and sounder than a frame one, the English continued to split boards from logs and laboriously construct houses as they had done in England. Thus the Swedish form of log construction never spread beyond New Sweden.

Throughout the eighteenth century great numbers of Germans and

Scotch-Irish[2] arrived in Pennsylvania. They immediately moved west of the area settled by the English and began constructing the type of house each had known in Europe. The Scotch-Irish probably built the mud or stone cabins they had known in Scotland and Ulster. The Germans, like the English, brought the half timber tradition, but they also possessed the medieval tradition of horizontal log construction. Thus, unlike the English, they were able to abandon the half timber form in favor of the more economical log form.

The German log house was rectangular with a three room division of the first floor. It always had a central chimney and was often built on a hillside, producing a partially below-ground lower level like that of the great Pennsylvania barn. A few examples of this type of house remain in eastern Pennsylvania and the Valley of Virginia.

Upon arriving in America, the Germans and Scotch-Irish had similar histories of religious persecution, economic unrest and disastrous warfare; and, having similar religions, ideals, and hardships in the new world, they soon became politically and socially aligned against the English. Although great numbers of Germans remained in the rich farmlands of eastern Pennsylvania, many moved westward with the Scotch-Irish and by 1732 a mixed German and Scotch-Irish settlement had been established in the Valley of Virginia. Within thirty years the Valley, the Blue Ridge from Maryland to about Roanoke County, Virginia, and the lands just east of it were settled. Settlers from the Valley, directly from Pennsylvania, and Germans and Scots from eastern North Carolina soon had settled the North Carolina Piedmont. The battle of Alamance (1771) began the great movement from the Piedmont into the mountainous Watauga area of north western North Carolina and north eastern Tennessee. Before the Revolution the Watauga area had been settled and people had begun moving south down the mountains, and east into the valleys.

The hardships of Indian wars and agricultural settlement mutually endured by Germans and Scotch-Irish broke down any prejudice that existed between the two and there occurred a natural borrowing and meshing of cultural elements. The Germans almost fully adopted the British music and gave in return their musical instrument which was to become the Appalachian dulcimer. The similar German and British folktale traditions were combined, producing a stronger folktale tradition than that which had been known in Germany or Britain. In this way the German and Scotch-Irish cultures meshed, producing the basis of the Southern Appalachian culture which has been changed from the original by the early addition of English and Indian elements and the later addition of Negro and urban twentieth century elements.

The log cabin stands as a symbol of this meshing of German and Scotch-

Irish cultures. The Scotch-Irish, having inferior construction modes and few skilled artisans, quickly adopted German horizontal log construction which utilized skills similar to those of British military and half-timber construction. The Scotch-Irish did not fully adopt the German house form, but rather made certain changes in accordance with their architectural traditions which were reinforced by the arrival in the mountains of the English in about 1800. The house was constructed on a more square plan and had one large rather than three small rooms. The chimney was moved from the inside, as in German tradition, to the outside, as in British tradition, where it could be more quickly and easily built. The result was, therefore, a house built upon a British plan using German construction techniques which became the typical house of all settlers from Maryland to Alabama.

Not all cabins are log nor are all log houses cabins. "Cabin" is an Irish term applied to a small one room house, and large log houses, called "log castles" on the frontier, were often built in a fashionable form with numerous rooms. These grand log houses are rare in the mountains but many remain in the Valley of Virginia and the Tennessee Valley.

Wherever the Germans and Scotch-Irish moved after they had left eastern Pennsylvania the first house constructed was a temporary one which most people consider to be the authentic log cabin. It was low with a shallow pitched roof and was built of round logs, roughly notched, with overhanging ends. It had a dirt floor and a mud and stick or crude stone chimney. This dwelling could be raised in a day and served as a shelter until a better house could be built. Cabins of this type are still rarely built as hunting cabins and are called "pole shacks" to distinguish them from the much more neatly made log cabin. A few of these cabins remain in the Great Smoky areas settled in this century, but they are quite rare in the older sections as they were not built to last and a pole shack twenty years old is likely to be in worse repair than a log cabin two hundred years old.

The log cabin is a rectangular house averaging about sixteen by twenty feet, although there is great variation in size. In areas where the English influence is great the log cabin is often about sixteen feet square, which is the traditional medieval English single bay house size. It is almost always one and one-half stories high although it rarely attains a full two-story height. It was most usually built about a foot off the ground on a stone foundation and thus had a wooden floor. At the southern end of the Southern Mountains the cabin was often built up on stone or log piers rather than a solid foundation. The German practice of building on a hill side, although useful, was time consuming and was abandoned in house construction although retained in some smaller out buildings. The cabin usually had one large chimney of fitted field stone, although in some areas of eastern Tennessee where the clay was proper brick chimneys were built. Often next

Figure 18-1. A Double Log Cabin with Enclosed Dog-Trot
(*Southern Appalachian Archives, Berea College*)

to the large fireplace, which frequently had a fine mantelpiece, was a steep stair, very rarely a ladder, which led to the loft above. The stair may have been placed anywhere about the one large room but almost always has a small closet under it. The roof was generally lightly framed and covered with "shakes" which are long shingles split out of a short log.

The feature which most distinguished the log cabin from the pole shack was the log construction itself. In the pole shack the logs were round and the corners formed by simple saddle notching. In the log cabin the logs were much larger and were hewn square or split and hewn flat on two sides. The spaces between the logs which were often quite narrow were filled, "chinked," with clay or mud and often pieces of wood split off like shingles. The logs were joined neatly at the corners in variations on a dovetail pattern. The ends of the logs were cut off flush producing a square corner in which no rain water could collect and thus the corner could not rot out as so frequently happened with saddle notching.

In studying any cultural element some variable feature must be decided on by which one may learn about its development and geographical distribution. In architecture the form of the building is usually that feature but, as there is little difference in form from cabin to cabin, form is of little use in the study of the log cabin. The most distinguished variable feature is the method of corner timbering, the way the logs are joined at the corners. In eastern Pennsylvania, three forms of corner timbering may be found, all of which are traditional in Germany. One is the saddle notching of temporary buildings and barns. The two others, V and full dovetail, are the types found on all log houses in eastern Pennsylvania. V corner timbering was associated in early times with the Schwenkenfelders, although other German groups probably used it. V corner timbering was carried into the Valley of Virginia and virtually every log cabin in the mountains of Maryland and Virginia was constructed with this corner timbering. Full dovetail is not common outside of eastern Pennsylvania as it was early developed into half dovetail which could be more easily made and, as it had no inward-sloping surfaces to hold water, it was longer lasting. Half dovetail is virtually the only type found in the western North Carolina Piedmont from whence it was carried into the Watauga area and thence south and west. Many of the settlers of the Watauga area came directly from the Valley so that both V and half dovetail, with extremely rare instances of full dovetail, are found there whereas north of Watauga only V may be found and south generally half dovetail. There are, of course, exceptions owing to unconventional migrations. The reason for this division is unclear as the bulk of all the settlers came from eastern Pennsylvania. Perhaps the settlers of the Valley left before full dovetailing was introduced into Pennsylvania. Perhaps the influence of the Germans and Swiss from eastern North Carolina caused the division. It remains, however, a mystery.

In eastern American log construction there are two remaining corner timbering types. Diamond corner timbering is perhaps of Scandinavian origin. It is found from the Tidewater to the eastern North Carolina Piedmont, but no example has been found in the mountains. When the English encountered the horizontal squared log tradition they developed square corner timbering which was similar to the types of joining used in British half-timber and fort construction. This type is found in eastern Virginia and areas of the south settled by eastern Virginians. It is rarely found in the mountains and when encountered it is more usually found on newer buildings which have sawn rather than hewn logs as square corner timbering was easily made with a saw.

The log cabin, although sturdy, was not large and from the beginning of its development additions were made onto it. The most common form of addition, well within the British tradition, was a rear shed addition. Another British form, favored by the Pennsylvania Germans, was the ell addition. These additions, which were often kitchens, are rarely found of log, but are common in frame indicating that they were for the most part added after the introduction of milled lumber.

In medieval British house building tradition the one room, single bay, house was most usually enlarged by means of a one-room addition onto the end of the original house producing a two-room house with a chimney on each end. This form of house was popular in the early English colonies, but was rarely built of log. The existence of a few of log in south central Virginia reflects the attempts made by Englishmen to build familiar houses with unfamiliar but economical log construction techniques.

Frame additions were occasionally made onto the ends of log cabins. Unlike framed construction, when an addition of log is made to a log house the old and new logs can not be fitted into each other. Thus an end addition could not become an integral part of the old house but could only be built as close as possible, the area between the old and new sections usually being filled with vertical logs and chinking. One solution was to make the addition onto the chimney end as was often done in British tradition. The chimney thus joined the two rooms and supplied both with heat. This house is called a "saddlebag" and is found westward from the Watauga area and sporadically throughout the mountains where the addition is of frame as often as of log.

Another solution to the log end addition was the "dog trot" house. The second room, or "pen," was not built up to the end of the first but rather was built some feet away and the two were covered with a common roof.

The result was two log cabins, each with its own chimney, with an open covered passage between them. It bore a remarkable resemblance to the German double crib barn found throughout the mountains which may have been in some way an inspiration. Houses thus divided into three sections were common in northern Europe and Britain and so the form became quickly popular. This house seems to have sprung up west of the Blue Ridge and is very common from southeastern Tennessee through much of Mississippi and Alabama. The few examples found in the North Carolina Piedmont and the exceedingly few found along the Blue Ridge were probably brought from the West.

Thus the log cabin is a fit symbol of Southern Appalachia as in it were brought together the best of German and British architectural traditions. In this day of functional design it may be established as an architectural ideal in that it was molded by tradition and necessity into the perfect dwelling for our pioneers whose craft and hardiness it reflects.

Notes

1. I have read the few works on the subject but, to avoid the mistakes of their authors, I have spent more time studying the old houses first hand than I have in libraries.

2. The Germans referred to throughout this monograph are the Pennsylvania Germans, also called the Pennsylvania Dutch. The Pennsylvania Germans came primarily from the Rhenish Palatine and Switzerland, but also from Alsace, Wurtemburg, Hesse, Saxony, and Silesia. The Scotch-Irish were Lowland Scots who settled in Ulster before coming to America. The Scotch-Irish include small numbers of English, Irish and Highland Scots.

19

The Smaller Outbuildings
of the Southern Mountains

Henry Glassie

On every mountain farm there are one or more small outbuildings; there may be smoke or meat houses, tool sheds, spring houses, milk houses, pump houses, well houses, wash houses, root cellars, or apple houses. Their functions are many and changing and there is great variation in size; yet, there are only three basic forms, one derived from the tidewater areas of Maryland, Virginia, and North Carolina and two from eastern Pennsylvania.

Like the cabins and barns of the early settlers, the smaller outbuildings were, at first, made of log. Horizontal log construction was brought to eastern Pennsylvania by the Germans and thence down the Valley of Virginia and the Blue Ridge by the Pennsylvania Germans and Scotch-Irish. The logs were at least partially squared and neatly dovetailed at the corners, but outbuildings were built with somewhat less care than larger buildings and, as a result, did not last as long. With the introduction of milled lumber many older outbuildings were replaced by buildings, of the same types, of board over frame after the English fashion.

The Germans and particularly the Scotch-Irish excelled at dry stone masonry. This ability is reflected in the chimneys and foundations of houses and mills but in the mountains at that time houses were never built entirely of stone. In the mountains, as in Pennsylvania, outbuildings were, however, frequently built of stone. Spring or milk houses were built over springs or streams or had water piped through fitted log pipes into troughs in which dairy products were kept. Stone walls were more satisfactory than wood for maintaining the low temperature necessary for preservation of dairy products. Stone walls on a partially subterranean outbuilding were essential

Reprinted from *Mountain Life and Work* 40 (Spring 1964): 21–25.

for preservation of certain food, particularly root products. As wood is flammable, smoke houses were also often built of stone.

The Tidewater outbuilding type, which has a square floor plan, as is typical of English tradition, and a pyramidal roof, was brought to the mountains from the East by the English settlers. This outbuilding type is found rarely throughout the mountains but more usually on the eastern slopes of the Blue Ridge and southwestern Virginia and southeastern Kentucky where English influence is comparatively great.

The Pennsylvania one level type, which was brought into the mountains by Pennsylvania Germans and Scotch-Irish, is much more common than the Tidewater type. It has a rectangular floor plan, consistent with German and Scotch-Irish traditions, a regular double pitch roof, and a door in one gable end. Like many buildings in Germany, Switzerland, Ireland and Scotland, it was frequently built into a hillside and was thus partially underground. Although not always present its most distinguishing feature is a projecting roof, constructed on the cantilever principle typical of Pennsylvania German construction. The projecting roof was supported in log buildings by the forward extension of the top log in the wall and in masonry buildings by an extended beam set at the top of the wall.

In Pennsylvania the gable opening one level building frequently had a room added above it producing the Pennsylvania two-level type, which is the most common type of outbuilding throughout the Southern Mountains. The ground level was often but not always built into a hillside and constructed of stone for use as a spring house or root cellar. The upper level was used for a great variety of purposes and was constructed of log, although today more are found of board over frame.

These outbuildings were carried by diffusion and migration from the Southern Mountains to all parts of the South and are thus not only the mountain types but also the southeastern United States types. The buildings reflect the national and geographic origins of the pioneers of the old south, that is, primarily Scotch-Irish and German from Pennsylvania with strong English tidewater elements, and the adaptions made by the first settlers to the problems of pre-mechanical existence.

20

The Palen Fence:
An Example of Appalachian Folk Culture

E. Raymond Evans

While there have not been a large number of publications dealing with traditional fencing there has been a relatively steady supply of them since 1947 when H. F. Raup published "The Fence in the Cultural Landscape" in *Western Folklore*. Few of these works have treated Appalachian fencing; most of those that have are like Joe Clark's *Up the Hollow from Lynchburg* (1975) in that they consist of little more than photographs. Such sources are valuable but can hardly be called studies. Some of the possibilities for further research on one type of traditional fencing are suggested in the following brief essay by E. Raymond Evans. For example, it might be worthwhile to test Evans's conclusions about the demise of the palen fence. Similarly his assertions about the functions, methods of installation, and the lack of physical remains also need further testing. Also worthy of investigation is the role economics may have played in perpetuating this type of fencing. There is also a possibility that such fences are known by other names and, as Evans suggests, it may be possible to develop a regional typology based on structural differences.

*   *   *

When one thinks of fences in terms of material folk culture, the dry stone wall (cf. Glassie 1968: 99–101), or the split rail fence (cf. Buie 1964: 44–46; Via 1962: 33–40) immediately comes to mind. There is, however, a third type of fence, the "pale" or "palen" fence, which was introduced in North America by the first English colonists at Plymouth and Jamestown. Although usually neglected by researchers in the field, presumably because they were so commonplace, the palen fence nevertheless continued in popularity throughout the rural areas of the Appalachians until recent years.

Reprinted from *Tennessee Anthropologist* 3 (Spring 1978): 93–99.

Mr. Jack Buford, a life-long resident of northern Hamilton County, Tennessee, recalls: "Back when I was a boy, I remember we had old rail fences around some of the fields on the place, but around the garden spot an' around the house yard we always would have a palen fence." Mr. Buford made the following observations concerning the method of constructing a palen fence as it was done in northern Hamilton County about the period 1920–1930:

> When ye made a palen fence, back then, what ye would do was take an' put up your posts, jist like for a regular fence. Ye put the posts in the ground about eight feet apart. Then ye would nail on pieces of wood longways (*ie. horizontally*) one about a foot above the ground, an' one up close to the top, an' one in the middle. Ye nailed ye palens on to these strips of wood.

> The regular way to make palens was to split 'em out of oak er hickory, jist like ye split out the boards to go on the top of the house. Ye done it with a froe the same way. The palens was about this thick (*indicates approximately half an inch*) an' about this wide (*indicates approximately two inches*). They would be about five er six feet high. Ye nailed 'em right on to the cross-pieces.

> Before they nailed the palens up, most people would take an' sharpen them on the top with an axe. They was some people that was too lazy to split 'em out the right way, an' they would jist take a little old pole about the right size and nail it on. Ye had to watch the palens an' put up new ones ever so often when they started to rot close to the ground.

A "pale" is distinguished from a "rail," or a "post," by its size and placement. According to Shurtleff (1939: 42) "A rail must be a horizontally laid timber. If upright, it becomes a *pale* or, if *stout* enough, a post."

Regarding the primary function of the palen fence in the twentieth century, Ms. Ella Mae Horton of the Grandview community, Rhea County, Tennessee, provides additional information:

> The palens would go all the way down to the ground. This was because the reason that people made that kind of fences was to keep the chickens out of the yard. Everybody had chickens back then an they would let them run out to scratch around for food, and they could get under or over any other kind of fence that they could make. That was why they had to be so high and come all the way down to the ground. They was nailed close enough together that a chicken couldn't get through between them.

A review of the available documentary sources indicates that the earlier palen fences were designed to keep out more than chickens. This being the case, they were probably somewhat stronger than those described above.

The first English colonists in North America not only brought the "mental template" for palen fences, but also the necessary tools for their manufacture. In a list of necessary equipment for persons going to Virginia, dated 1621 (Lankford 1967: 154–55), we find, under the heading "Tooles for a family of sixe persons," the following:

Two broad Axes ...
Five felling Axes ...
Two Steele Hand-saws ...
Two two-hand-saws ...
Two Hammers ...
Two hatchets ...
Two froves to cleave pale ...

Similar provisions were made for those going to New England. A contemporary English writer (Wood 1634: 58) urges each family to be equipped with:

... All manner of Iron-wares, as all manner of nails for houses, and all manner of Spikes for building. ... Axes both broad and pitching axes. All manner of Augers, piercing bits, Whip-saws, Two-handed-saws, Froes, both for the riving of Pailes and Latches. ...

Soon after completing construction of their homes, Governor Bradford writes that the Plymouth Pilgrims "agreed to inclose their dwellings with a good strong pale ... with gates to shute." (Shurtleff 1939: 104). In 1611 the Governor of Virginia, Sir Thomas Dale, supervised the colonists at Jamestown in "providing pales, posts and railes, to im-pale his purposed new towne ..." (Shurtleff 1939: 143).

By 1640 the building of fences was in such demand that the General Court of New Haven, in the colony of Massachusetts Bay (now Connecticut), enacted the following wage rates for such work (Hoadly 1857: 36–38):

Fencing with pales, as house lotts now are for felling and cleaving posts and railes, crosscutting, hewing, mortising, digging holes, setting up and nailing on the pales, the work being in all the parts well wrought and finished, not above 2s (*two English shillings*) a rod, butt in this pales and carting of the stuff not included.

The above indicates that the first palen fences in North America were constructed with nails, in much the same manner as those described by informants from the twentieth century. However, when the settlers left the Atlantic seaboard, taking the "mental template" for palen fences with them, they had fewer tools. Nails, in particular, were extremely scarce west of the mountains. The ingenious solution to this problem is described (Byrd 1967:

94) in a narrative prepared by Colonel William Byrd II, which records a survey of the Virginia–North Carolina boundary undertaken in 1728. Colonel Byrd stated:

> They also set up their Pales without any Nails at all, and indeed more securely than those that are nail'd. There are 3 rails mortised into the Posts, the lowest of which serves as a Sill with a Groove in the Middle, big enough to receive the End of the Pales: the middle Part of the Pale rests against the inside of the Next Rail, and the Top of it is brought forward to the outside of the uppermost. Such Wreathing of the Pales in and out makes them stand firm, and much harder to unfix than when nail'd in the Ordinary way.

A photograph of a recent (ca. 1941) palen fence shows several of the individual pales to have been installed by means of a weaving technique similar to that described above by Byrd.

By the second half of the eighteenth century the Cherokee Indians, living in what is now Tennessee, were also constructing palen fences. In 1779 an American army, moving down the Tennessee River, mistakenly thought such a fence to be a military fortification. George Christian, the son of one of the officers present, gives the following account of the incident (Draper MSS, 14 DD 111):

> The army, on coming in view of the Town where they landed, seeing a newly pailed garden mistook it for a stockade Fort, and expecting to be repulsed when attempting to land orders were immediately given by the Commander to the officer in front (which on this day was Col. Roberson) to land his canoes. Campbell at this time was in the rear and father in the center. Roberson though seemed to sheer off from shore, making a contrary move from the Colonel's order, on which the Col. called out at the top of his voice, "Damn you, Col. Roberson, I say land your canoe!" Still the order was not obeyed, on which Shelby called to Father and ordered him to land his men which he did promptly.

Throughout the nineteenth century, and well into the twentieth, the palen fence continued to be the basic enclosure for small farm yards and vegetable gardens in the southern highlands. They served their intended function, just as their predecessors at Plymouth and Jamestown, and also, with their weathered wood and rustic charm, added much to the general beauty of the countryside. However, in the course of a recent cursory survey of Hamilton, Bradley and Rhea Counties, Tennessee, the author, while interviewing numerous individuals who vividly recalled the palen fence, failed to find a single example still in use.

Data supplied by the informants suggests that three factors have led to the demise of this once common form of material folk culture. First, the fact that the pales were so placed as to be in contact with the ground caused considerable absorption of moisture which led to rapid decay of the lower portions, thus necessitating constant maintenance and replacement of pales. Another factor has been the decline of chickens as an important economic consideration to individual rural families. The final factor has been the availability of modern wire fencing.

It is possible that additional research on this topic, despite the paucity of physical remains, could result in a development of regional typology based on structural differences, as well as a more accurate delineation of cultural relationships and diachronic stylistic change of the palen fence.

Acknowledgments

This brief study was made possible by the assistance of a number of individuals. Field informants who were particularly helpful were Ms. Ella Mae Horton (Rhea County), Mr. Jack Buford (Hamilton County) and the late G. E. McDonald (Rhea County). Help in obtaining obscure references was provided by the late Elsworth Brown of Chattanooga. The author also extends his sincere appreciation to Donald B. Ball and Charles H. Faulkner for their helpful advice and continued encouragement.

References Cited

Buie, T. S. 1964. Rail Fences. *American Forests* 70 (10): 44–66.

Byrd, William. 1967. *William Byrd's Histories of the Dividing Line betwixt Virginia and North Carolina* (with introduction and notes by William K. Boyd). Dover Publications, Inc., New York (originally published 1929, North Carolina Historical Commission).

Glassie, Henry. 1968. *Pattern in the Material Folk Culture of the Eastern United States.* University of Pennsylvania Press, Philadelphia.

Hoadley, C. J. 1967. *Records of the Colony and Plantation of New Haven, 1638–1649.* Private publication, Hartford.

Lankford, John. 1967. *Captain John Smith's America.* Harper and Row, New York.

Shurtleff, H. Robert. 1939. *The Log Cabin Myth.* Harvard University Press, Cambridge.

Via, Vera V. 1962. The Old Rail Fence. *Virginia Cavalcade* 19 (1): 33–40.

Wood, William. 1634. *New England Prospect.* Private publication, London.

Rethinking the House:
Interior Space and Social Change

Michael Ann Williams

Most studies of Appalachian folk housing have been largely occupied with determining matters of origin and diffusion of house types. Few give much attention to the ways in which the houses are used. In its consideration of how social change created changes in the way house space was used, "Rethinking the House" is an exception to the general trend. But, it is also valuable for another reason, namely its compelling evidence that it is difficult, if not impossible, to comprehend the varied functions a house serves without talking to the people who lived in them. Admittedly, for many forms of folk housing such testimony is unavailable for the simple reason that the buildings were constructed in a time period beyond the reach of human memory.

Dr. Williams is currently a member of the faculty at Western Kentucky University but for several years she lived in western North Carolina where she did intensive research on folk housing. The present article is based on material recorded during that fieldwork. For other studies demonstrating the value of folk architecture in historical studies see Henry H. Glassie, *Folk Housing in Middle Virginia: A Structural Analysis of Historic Artifacts* (Knoxville: University of Tennessee Press, 1975) and George W. McDaniel, *Hearth and Home: Preserving a People's Culture* (Philadelphia: Temple University Press, 1982). Neither of these books deals with Appalachia, and McDaniel covers housing as well as additional topics.

* * *

Of all the categories of historic artifacts, architecture is perhaps the richest, encompassing almost every aspect of human life.[1] Unfortunately, the majority of folkloric studies of architecture have dealt with buildings solely as artifacts, remote from living people. In western North Carolina, however,

Reprinted from *Appalachian Journal* 14 (Winter 1987): 174–82. © Appalachian State University. Used with permission. All rights reserved.

the human context is almost unavoidable in studying folk architecture. Pre–Civil War structures are scarce here, and the folk buildings that still exist were, to a large extent, built after 1890, a time period still in reach of human memory.

Some scholars argue that the study of folk architecture is most worthwhile in the absence of written or oral sources about a past people, but restricting the field to this type of pursuit separates the study of artifacts from the study of the human beings who created and used them. We need to reunite the study of artifacts with the study of human beings, and oral history provides one avenue to this reunion.[2]

Human testimony is particularly vital in understanding the symbolic and social aspects of spatial organization. Anthropologist Mary Douglas argues that although symbolic and social orders may be expressed in the use of domestic space, interpreting these orders from the physical remains alone is, at best, "hazardous."[3] For instance, the one- and two-room plans of the upland South give rise to discussions of generalized as opposed to specified room use, collective versus individual use of space, and relative notions of privacy. While these conclusions may not be far off the mark, we do seem to work toward them backwards, ending rather than starting with what these concepts mean in terms of human experience.

This study began when, after sixteen months of architectural survey, I began to realize that the information gleaned form oral testimony was substantially different from that derived from physical evidence.[4] Sometimes the information from these two categories of evidence could be neatly reconciled; at other times they seemed to negate each other. As a substantial degree of architectural survey had been accomplished in southwestern North Carolina,[5] I decided to concentrate for a time solely on oral testimony. The goal was to understand aspects of spatial organization not physically manifested in form and to understand how changes in this organization corresponded to what we know about physical changes in architecture during the same period.[6]

This study focuses on the oral testimony of people who grew up in small folk houses in rural southwestern North Carolina between the years 1890 and 1940. During this half-century, this region underwent vast social change, and the folk building traditions declined. The informants were generally not the builders of folk houses, but they grew up with a system of spatial patterns given them by their parents, who frequently were builders of folk houses.

Oral testimony reveals a far more conservative pattern of folk building than do surveys of surviving structures. A significant majority of the individuals interviewed reported that they had lived in a single-pen plan house sometime during their lives.[7] Often it was an early childhood home or the first house to which they "went to housekeeping" after they married. The majority of single-pen houses were built of log; frequently they were the product of community cooperative labor.

The single-pen plan is often described as a one-room house. A more accurate description, particularly as it pertains to log dwellings, is single unit. The single-pen house was often a story and a half in height, creating an upstairs room. The bottom floor of a rectangular single-pen house was sometimes partitioned. Therefore two or three rooms were possible within the log unit. By the late nineteenth and early twentieth centuries, cooking in the main room became less common as many individuals added separate kitchens. Whether it was a completely separate unit, at some distance from the house, or an attached ell or rear shed addition, oral testimony suggests that the kitchen was thought of more as an outbuilding than as an integrated part of the home.

Despite the possibility of two or three rooms within the plan, by modern standards single-pen houses were exceptionally small. Today it is often assumed that small log houses were built solely out of necessity, either by early pioneers who had no access to sawed lumber and skilled labor or by later mountaineers who were simply too isolated or poor to build anything else. This assumption needs to be reevaluated. While some early pioneers lived in log houses only until they could build a larger frame house, many western North Carolinians replaced small log "cabins" with slightly larger, more substantial, single-pen log houses. Of those who continued to build small log houses in the late nineteenth century, not all were poor or isolated. Many had both physical and financial access to milled lumber but opted instead for participation in the cooperative building system, which in turn reinforced the building of small log dwellings.[8]

Those who grew up in single-pen houses do not say "we could not afford a better house" but rather "it was all we knew." Of course, they were aware of the existence of larger houses, but they intimately "knew" the patterns of everyday life within the single-pen house. The survival of the single-pen house into the twentieth century is a testament, not to isolation and poverty, but to the continued acceptance of a radically different system of domestic spatial use.

Older people who speak of a single-pen house often refer to it as a "big house" or (more frequently) "big house and kitchen." Why would anyone call such a small house "big"? The term is not used in jest. While possible linguistic antecedents do exist,[9] those who use "big house" think it makes sense: "It was a large, large room, usually accommodated two or three beds, double beds, plus chairs."[10] It was conceptually big not only because it consisted of a large unbroken space, but because of the many functions unified within it. "We had three [beds] across the back of it. It was about, I

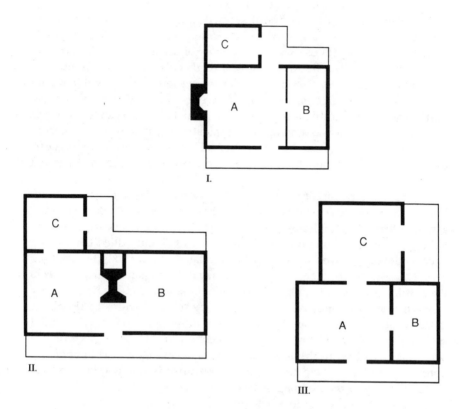

Figure 21-1. Typical House Plan of the Late Nineteenth and Early
Twentieth Century in Western North Carolina
I. Partitioned single-pen plan house with rear kitchen.
II. Central chimney double pen (saddle bag) plan with
kitchen. III. Front gable southern bungalow.
The use of space is very similar in all these plans. The
main difference between the two "folk" plans (I and II)
and the "popular" style bungalow, besides the
orientation of the gable, is the lack of a large hearth
around which family activity centers in the later
bungalow plan. A represents the fireplace room (I),
sitting room (II), or living room (III); B is a bedroom
(I or III) or a parlor (II), also used to sleep guests and
family members; and C is a kitchen.

don't know, I think it was twenty by, I don't remember. But there was plenty of room for three beds. And then all the front of it was then, we'd sit around the fire and there was a table and a stove."[11] It was a room for socializing and household chores, for sleeping and sitting, and for many it was also a room for cooking and eating.

Even those who had single-pen plan dwellings with several rooms tended to layer many functions within a single room. The kitchen was not part of the "big house." The "upstairs" or "other room" of the partitioned plan was thought of as a peripheral, sleeping room for older children. (As many individuals spoke of the big house as being both the main dwelling unit and the main living room within the unit, the "upstairs" and "other room" were both a part of, and separate from, the "big house.") The parents, infant children, and sometimes grandparents all slept in the main room. Despite its role as a sleeping room, the big house is primarily associated, however, with its function as the center of family and social activity: "That was the main living area, if, if you said the big house, then that was where we all gathered at any time, when, like what I was saying these parties or anything, we all went into the big house."[12]

One must use care in theorizing from plan alone about the implications of the single-pen house. Scholarly attention to the single-pen plan has tended to characterize it as representing extremes in generalized room use, collective use of space, and low valuation of privacy. Oral testimony suggests that patterns of use and attitudes tempered these extremes. Space was complexly divided with the big house, both physically (by use of blankets or arrangement of furniture) and conceptually (by conceiving of "rooms" within the single room) for social and symbolic purposes. While family members shared a single room, they strictly maintained individual spaces within the room. Privacy was difficult to achieve, but rather than devalue the concept, people did make attempts to achieve privacy, either through the arrangement of furniture or by strictly maintaining rules of personal interaction within the household:[13] "I think they really did [respect privacy], but they just went about it in different ways from the way you do now. Yes, you respected privacy."[14] Remarkably few people complained about the lack of room or privacy: "We didn't have room for nothing hardly, but we didn't get hot under the collar and worry and fret much about it because we were still just born and growed up that way. We just didn't need, or no use to want, for more room."[15]

The decline in acceptance of the spatial patterns represented by the single-pen house did take place during a period of economic change in southwestern North Carolina. It was not the case, however, that people could suddenly afford larger homes; for many rural people the change was not for the better. As farm life became less viable, male members of house-

Figure 21-2.   Single-pen Log House with Rear Plank Kitchen, Near
Hendersonville, North Carolina, circa 1890

holds were often drawn away from home for long periods of time in search of "public work" (paid employment away from home).[16] In fact, many families during the early twentieth century opted, not for more room in their houses but for more rooms. The large unbroken spaces in many old log homes were "cut down," partitioned into small rooms. Cooperative building continued in many communities, but people simply had less time to share, so many built quickly (and relatively cheaply) out of vertical plank. These new "boxed" houses, although they frequently followed traditional plans, tended to have more but smaller rooms.

While three or four room variants were possible in the single-pen plan during the nineteenth century, this number became the minimum in most small houses built during the third and fourth decade of the twentieth century. Formerly some effort had been made to segregate adults and older children in sleeping arrangements; it now also became important to separate children by sex and to provide separate bedrooms for adults of various generations. No longer was it acceptable for adults to sleep in the same room as their parents or in-laws. All generations began to retreat into the privacy of their own bedrooms, rather than sleep in the main living room. The single-pen plan house was partitioned or added to, and construction of the plan disappeared almost altogether.

As the acceptance of the single-pen plan declined, so did the use of the term "big house," which expressed a positive evaluation of the plan. People under the age of 70 tend not to know the meaning of the term, and older people are ambivalent about the plan. Most now prefer a house where everything is "cut to itself," but they understand and appreciate the patterns of life within the single-pen plan dwelling. Only through their memories can we now understand how these houses were big.

Not all rural folk houses in southwestern North Carolina had single-pen plans. Somewhat larger houses could be created by the arrangement of two (more-or-less) equal size units. The most common variant of the double-pen plan is the central chimney saddlebag plan, although double-pen houses with exterior end chimneys are found in western North Carolina. Double-pen houses could be built of log, frame, or boxed construction. In describing these houses, older western North Carolinians often say that they consist of two "houses." The saddlebag plan is further described as a house having a "double fireplace," "double chimney," or "stacked chimney": "Have two fireplaces in it, one room have one, you go into the other room and there'd be a room in there with a fireplace. Double chimney, double fireplace, you see. You could live on either end of the house, if you wanted to."[17]

The suggestion that you could live in either end is not apt, however, because the majority of everyday life still took place in one room. Despite the increased size of the house, the use of the main "living room" in the double-pen house was not significantly different from the use of the "big house." This room was the main gathering and activity area; it frequently served as a sleeping room, often for the head of household or "old folks."[18] It was also often used for dining and, in the absence of a separate kitchen, cooking. This room was variously referred to as the "main room," "the room we lived in," and "the house."

With most of living taking place in one room, what purpose did the other room serve? Some older people remembered the role of this room in its traditional manifestation as a parlor. Today it may be difficult to imagine that individuals living in mountain communities would reserve one of two main rooms in a small house for ostensibly formal purposes. Socializing, however, was an important part of life in rural western North Carolina. Family gathering and informal socializing took place in the living room; the parlor was used for entertaining special company (especially the preacher), for courting, and for holding family ceremonies such as funerals. The parlor was sometimes decorated a bit more than the living room, though both rooms had basically the same furnishings, including beds. Despite its formal purpose, the parlor was used for sleeping, especially for guests to stay the night. However, in many homes, family member also slept in parlor beds: "I'm trying to think of a separate parlor with nothing in it, no bed. I just can't think of a house in the community, to tell you the truth. 'Cause most people had reasonable big families. Their houses were small, they just didn't have that much room."[19] This private function, however, did not seem to detract from the parlor's formal role; people still insisted that the room was "special for company."

As with the single-pen house, the rear kitchen was often a part of the double-pen plan house by the late 19th century. While in western North Carolina, the addition of the separate kitchen may have been the first in a series of steps to "functionally purify" room use,[20] its correlation with the acquisition of a cook stove also suggests that it was essentially a compromise between modernity and traditional spatial use. By relegating the cook stove to the rear of the house, they preserved for a few decades the social and symbolic importance of the open hearth in the main living area. The kitchen, appended to the double-pen plans, was outside the complexity of the rest of the system of spatial use. While all the other rooms of the house could be, and often were, used for sleeping, the kitchen never was. This again suggests the idea that the kitchen was not thought of as being part of the house. This "apartness" was sometimes physically manifested by the rural carpenter who did not provide an interior doorway between the main part of the house and the rear ell kitchen.

The fact that every room except the kitchen was potentially a sleeping

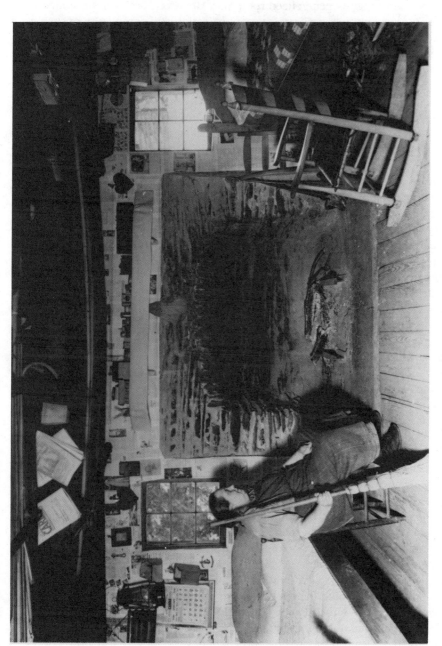

Figure 21-3. Interior of the Walker Sisters' House on the Tennessee Side of the Great Smoky Mountains National Park (Courtesy of the Great Smoky Mountains National Park)

room again suggests generalized room use. However, perhaps this concept does not give enough credit to the sophistication and complexity of such a system. Though nomenclature for the rooms is generally vague, and each room did have several actual purposes, it is clear that each room did have its function. Although lack of designated bedrooms would seem to devalue the concept of privacy, the multi-layered system of room use actually maximized privacy and at the same time maintained important distinctions between informal and formal space and public and private space.

The early twentieth century was a time of spatial change within the double-pen house and the parlor was clearly the most vulnerable to change. While a few people removed the beds from the parlor, eliminating its private functions,[21] the majority eliminated its formal role. Remembering the homes of his childhood. Monroe Ledford noted, "Usually the back room was the parlor, yeah, that's the way it was at our place; I guess that's the way it was all over the country. That is if it was built with a fireplace or something in it." The main difference between the parlor and back room was the presence of a fireplace in the parlor, which made it a nice place to entertain. However, while his childhood home had a parlor, the house in which he and his wife lived for forty years had only a front room and a back room, though the second house was identical in plan to his homeplace and also had a double fireplace.[22] "Back room" still does not emphasize the sleeping role of the room, but the transition from parlor to back room suggests the declining emphasis on its formal role. Formerly, "front room" had sometimes been associated with the parlor. The growing acceptance of the term in reference to the living room reflected the fact that this room was absorbing many of the formal functions of the parlor. Still the new front room was not "just for company." This room was still the family gathering place and, in many families, continued for a while to contain beds. It is probably that the vague front room/back room system, which reflected the formalizing of the living room and deformalizing of the parlor, provided a transition to the living room/bedroom distinction that now predominates in small rural homes.

As with change in building technology and house plan, the change in spatial organization came gradually, varying with community and family. Certainly change in plan corresponded to some degree with alterations in systems of use; however, they are not necessarily the same thing. Social change brought physical alteration and remodelling of houses, as well as the rebuilding of some communities. However, there can also be a restructuring of a house which is not physically manifested. People continued to live in unchanged old houses, houses in which the builder and original users had created a front room, parlor, and kitchen. Without physical alternation, the house now consists of a living room, bedroom, and kitchen. The change

Figure 21-4. Hiram Tallent House, Iotla Community, Macon County, North Carolina

Typical 1930s front gable bungalow in western North Carolina.

is not simply a matter of terminology. Nor is it necessarily a mater of furnishing; some people changed their furnishings little, and the main rooms may still contain beds. More than a change in actual use, it is predominantly a change in mental organization, a "rethinking" of the house.

On the other hand, systems of spatial organization are fluid enough to fit into different sizes and shapes. Elements of traditional spatial organization also made the leap to the popular style houses which were beginning to replace the rural folk houses of western North Carolina during the third and fourth decades of the twentieth century. The house eighty-four-year-old Ann Collett grew up in was a typical saddlebag plan house, but she saw little difference in the way this house was organized and the way her house was organized when she raised her children.[23] The latter house, in which she still lives, is not built according to traditional folk plan. One of the most prevalent popular style houses, which replaced folk houses in western North Carolina during the 1930s and 1940s, was a very simple stripped-down bungalow with a front facing gable. Although the exterior was different, the interior presents a familiar lay-out: two rooms side-by-side, with a rear kitchen—the same arrangement as the partitioned single-pen plan with kitchen and the double-pen plan with kitchen. The most important difference was the absence of the hearth as the central focus of the living room.

Obviously, oral testimony is not available for many of the folk houses we study. But to the extent that testimony is available, we need to begin to study and understand it, if only as cautionary measure against overestimating what we can understand from the physical shell of the idea of the house. Even with a full inventory or every item once contained within a dwelling and the names of all the rooms, we cannot understand the little house that was a "big house," nor can we understand ways in which privacy and individual space are asserted within plans which seem to devalue these concepts totally. And without human testimony, we cannot understand how, during periods of social transition, changes in competence for building a house are different from changes in living in or thinking about the house.

Notes

1. Henry Glassie argues, "It is no surprise that historically oriented folklorists have concentrated on architecture, which is tenacious, situated, and above all complex." "Folkloristic Study of the American Artifact," in *Handbook of American Folklore*, ed. Richard M. Dorson (Bloomington: Indiana University Press, 1983), p. 377.

2. The study of vernacular architecture using oral history sources has grown in recent years. Studies which incorporate oral history and architectural study include: Charles E. Martin, *Hollybush: Folk Building and Social Change in an Appalachian Community* (Knoxville: University of Tennessee Press, 1984); George W. McDaniel, *Hearth & Home:*

Preserving a People's Culture (Philadelphia: Temple University Press, 1983); and Henry Glassie, *Passing the Time in Ballymenone: Culture and History of an Ulster Community* (Philadelphia: University of Pennsylvania Press, 1982).

3. Mary Douglas, "Symbolic Orders in the Use of Domestic Space," in *Man, Settlement and Urbanism*, ed. Peter J. Ucko, Ruth Tringham, and G. W. Dimbleby (London: Duckworth, 1972), pp. 513–21.

4. I conducted two historic sites surveys, carried out under the auspices of the North Carolina Division of Archives and History. The Henderson County survey was undertaken from June 1980 through January 1981; the Cherokee County survey was carried out between June 1981 and January 1982.

5. Other surveys sponsored by the North Carolina Division of Archives and History in this area have been Douglas Swaim's survey of Buncombe County, Randy Cotton's survey of Haywood County, and Margaret Owen's reconnaissance survey of the ten westernmost counties.

6. This fieldwork was part of research for my doctoral disseration. See Michael Ann Williams, "Homeplace: The Social Use and Meaning of the Folk Dwelling in Southwestern North Carolina," Ph.D. dissertation, University of Pennsylvania, 1985.

7. Of fifty people interviewed, over two-thirds had lived in a single-pen house at some point.

8. An individual who desired a house which was significantly larger or different from the community norm would usually not benefit from unpaid cooperative labor.

9. "House" was sometimes used to refer to the living room in western North Carolina, a usage also found in post-medieval England and early New England. If the "house" was a large unbroken space, one of the only, or the only, room in the dwelling, it was a "big house." Another possibility is the old Scottish and northern English use of the word "big" as a verb meaning to live in or dwell. The "big house" was the dwelling house, as opposed to the various "houses" which were outbuildings.

10. Tape recorded interview with Oma Jenkins, Stecoah, Graham County, 23 May 1984.

11. Tape recorded interview with Essie Moore, Caney Fork, Jackson County, 5 September 1984.

12. Tape recorded interview with Mary Jane Queen, John's Creek, Jackson County, 24 August 1984.

13. For further analysis of spatial use of the "big house," see Michael Ann Williams, "The Little 'Big House': The Use and Meaning of the Single-Pen Dwelling," in *Perspectives in Vernacular Architecture, II,* ed. Camille Wells (Columbia: University of Missouri Press, 1986).

14. Tape recorded interview with Willia Mae Pressley, Bo Cove, Jackson County, 28 June 1984.

15. Tape recorded interview with Arvel Greene, Wilmont, Jackson County, 18 June 1984.

16. The timber industry provided the most work for rural western North Carolinians. As the timber boom declined, some individuals left their families temporarily to find work in the coal mines of Kentucky and West Virginia and the textile mills of Piedmont North Carolina.

17. Tape recorded interview with R. O. Wilson, Wilson Creek, Jackson County, 5 October 1983.

18. Tape recorded interview with Mike Rogers, Anderson Branch, Graham County, 27 January 1984.

19. Tape recorded interview with Monroe Ledford, Union, Macon County, 21 October 1983.

20. Glassie, *Ballymenone,* pp. 379–81.

21. Leo Gibson of the Cowee community, Macon County, noted that her family removed the beds from the parlor when the children "got to courting." From the same community, Eula Bryson noted that her family added a parlor when the girls got old enough to court. This suggests the adoption of mainstream, rather than traditional, concepts of the parlor. The elimination of the parlor was far more common in early twentieth-century western North Carolina. Tape recorded interviews with Leo Gibson and Eula Bryson, Cowee, Macon County, 12 October 1983.

22. Monroe Ledford interview.

23. Tape recorded interview with Anna Collett, Valleytown, Cherokee County, 13 October 1983.